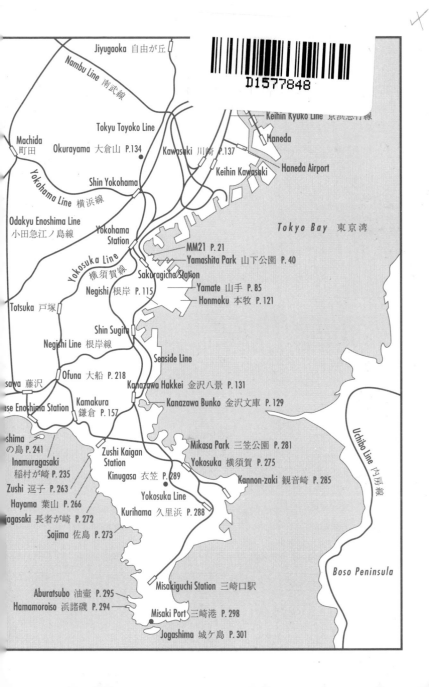

Jiyugaoka 自由が丘

Nambu Line 南武線

Keihin Kyuko Line 京浜急行線

Tokyu Toyoko Line

Haneda

Machida 町田

Okurayama 大倉山 P.134

Kawasaki 川崎 P.137

Keihin Kawasaki

Haneda Airport

Yokohama Line 横浜線

Shin Yokohama

Tokyo Bay 東京湾

Odakyu Enoshima Line
小田急江ノ島線

Yokohama Station

MM21 P.21

Yamashita Park 山下公園 P.40

Yokosuka Line 横須賀線

Sakuragicho Station

Negishi 根岸 P.115

Yamate 山手 P.85

Honmoku 本牧 P.121

Totsuka 戸塚

Shin Sugita

Negishi Line 根岸線

Seaside Line

...sawa 藤沢

Ofuna 大船 P.218

Kanazawa Hakkei 金沢八景 P.131

...ase Enoshima Station

Kamakura 鎌倉 P.157

Kanazawa Bunko 金沢文庫 P.129

...shima
の島 P.241

Zushi Kaigan Station

Mikasa Park 三笠公園 P.281

Uchibo Line 内房線

Inamuragasaki 稲村ヶ崎 P.235

Yokosuka 横須賀 P.275

Zushi 逗子 P.263

Kinugasa 衣笠 P.289

Kannon-zaki 観音崎 P.285

Hayama 葉山 P.266

Yokosuka Line

...agasaki 長者ヶ崎 P.272

Kurihama 久里浜 P.288

Sajima 佐島 P.273

Boso Peninsula

Misakiguchi Station 三崎口駅

Aburatsubo 油壺 P.295

Hamamoroiso 浜諸磯 P.294

Misaki Port 三崎港 P.298

Jogashima 城ケ島 P.301

TRAILS
OF
TWO
CITIES

TRAILS
OF
TWO
CITIES

A Walker's Guide to
Yokohama, Kamakura,
and Vicinity

John Carroll

KODANSHA INTERNATIONAL
Tokyo • New York • London

Note to the reader: Every attempt has been made to ensure that the information contained in this guide is correct. However, prices go up, restaurants disappear, to the extent that the publisher and author cannot be held liable for any changes which occur after the time of writing. The publisher welcomes updated information for future editions.

Jacket design: Nakajima Hideyuki
Maps: Ushio Works and Takanashi Satoru

Distributed in the United States by Kodansha International Inc., 114 Fifth Avenue, New York, N.Y. 1011, and in the United Kingdom and continental Europe by Kodansha Europe Ltd., 95 Aldwych, London WC2B 4JF. Published by Kodansha International Ltd., 17-14 Otowa 1-chome, Bunkyo-ku, Tokyo 112, and Kodansha America Inc.

First edition, 1994
94 95 96 97 98   10 9 8 7 6 5 4 3 2 1

ISBN 4-7700-1837-1

Library of Congress Cataloging-in-Publication Data
Carroll, John, 1949–
    Trails of two cities : a Walker's guide to Yokohama, Kamakura, and vicinity / John Carroll. — 1st ed.
          p.   cm.
    Includes index.
    ISBN 4-7700-1837-1
    1. Kanagawa-ken (Japan) — Guidebooks.   I. Title.
DS894.49.K342   1994
915.2'1360449—dc20   94-14590
                                                        CIP

Contents

Preface

In the dozen years I have lived in Japan I have learned one thing: as in other countries, the standard histories do not tell the whole story. Moreover what they leave out is often more enlightening, and certainly more entertaining than what goes in. There is usually a twist on things, too; even if the author will not admit so. History is a river whose color is different when viewed from different angles.

Living in Kamakura I have savored the twin joys of walking and discovering local history in the Yokohama and Kamakura area. The former is a friendly, modern port town with an intriguing past, the latter a relaxed repository of traditional culture in a beautiful natural setting.

Adventures on foot in the Yokohama/Kamakura area are facilitated by the ease of access and the highly developed transportation system in the area. Several lines link Yokohama to Tokyo including the JR Tokaido, Yokosuka, and Keihin Tohoku (Negishi) lines as well as the Keihin Kyuko Line from Shinagawa, and the Tokyu Toyoko Line from Shibuya. The JR Yokosuka Line from Tokyo Station runs directly to Kamakura (you can also transfer to it from the Tokaido Line at Ofuna Station) and on to Kurihama on the Miura Peninsula. The Keihin Kyuko Line skips Kamakura itself but goes deeper into Miura.

This book is a Janus-like creature. It is meant not only to be read, but also used. The idea is to let your feet walk even as you dream of the past and personally interpret the here and now. After all, Yokohama and Kamakura are not mere storehouses of historical lore; they are modern vibrant cities. You will be making your own history by meeting people, and seeing, hearing, and tasting new things. More than anything else, I hope that you will enjoy your forays into a delightful region of a fascinating country.

PART
1
YOKOHAMA

Yokohama: An Introduction

No one likes to be awoken from a deep sleep, especially when that slumber has lasted for nearly two and a half centuries.

On July 8, 1853, a fleet of four American warships commanded by fifty-eight-year-old Matthew Calbraith Perry appeared off Uraga with a letter from the president of the United States to the emperor of Japan. (At this time foreigners were unaware that the Tokugawa shogunate actually ran the country.)

A giant blue comet raged across the summer sky and the news plunged the shogun's capital of Edo into a panic, coming as it did in the wake of a series of fires, earthquakes, and epidemics. The black ships were regarded as "fire-breathing monsters," and Perry and his men were portrayed as *tengu*, roughly equivalent to werewolves, in drawings that immediately began circulating. Temple bells were rung and crowds ran aimlessly in the streets. This was truly the day old Edo died, although it was not realized at the time.

Since issuance of the seclusion edicts of 1636, the Japanese had refused to have anything to do with the "hairy barbarians," except for a few Dutchmen kept in the virtual penal colony of Dejima Island in Nagasaki Harbor.

Perry, of illustrious navy stock and the descendant of an early Quaker leader, was a battle-tested warrior who was prepared to land in force if his flag suffered any indignity—as had been the case in 1845 when a Japanese guard struck an earlier U.S. visitor to Japanese shores, Commodore James Biddle, and threw him back into his boat. With three thousand troops and 180 ships in the vicinity, the Japanese could have bloodied Perry badly, especially if they had launched a sneak attack. In a sense it was a miracle that Perry and his men were not massacred. However, the Japanese authorities were well aware of the humiliation that China had experienced during the 1842 Opium War, and feared that Edo might be bombarded. The timing was perfect for the opening of the country. The steamships in Edo Bay had made it crystal clear that Japan's Pacific neighbors were suddenly much closer than before. That reality could not be ignored.

Perry left only nine days after arriving, first handing over the letter and some presents at Kurihama and making it clear that he would be back the next year. However, afraid that a Russian admiral in the vicinity in search of warm-water ports would beat him to the punch, Perry wintered at Hong Kong.

Although his subordinates sometimes laughed at the odd habits of the Japanese such as the spiriting away of leftover food, even jam, in their kimono sleeves, and considered them distinctly inferior to the Chinese, Perry never used racial epithets about his unwilling hosts in his writings. All the American officers, however, recognized the Japanese mechanical genius and propensity for making sketches of any objects new to them.

Like his spiritual heir, General Douglas MacArthur, Perry was a master at public relations. When he finally landed at the little fishing village of Yokohama on March 8, 1854, Perry had two "stalwart six-foot Negros" carry his personal pennant in front of him. Twenty-six boats landed five hundred sailors preceded by a brass band—more for show than protection. The Japanese troops did not overly impress the Americans, but the eighty gargantuan sumo wrestlers who "tramped down the beach like so many elephants" in loincloths to grab a 150-pound bale of rice by each arm for loading on board ship certainly did.

First on the list for negotiation was a burial site for Private Robert Williams, who had fallen to his death on the deck of the *Mississippi*. After much haggling, the Japanese agreed to let the unfortunate be buried in a local graveyard. Perry won over his opponents by firm bargaining and judicious use of pressure tactics, such as inching his flotilla closer and closer to Edo. He only stopped when one of the chief shogunate officials threatened to commit *seppuku*.

Perry's many gifts astonished and pleased the Japanese officials, especially a telegraph set and a one-quarter scale miniature railroad

350 feet in circumference with accompanying Lilliputian locomotive, on which topknotted officials in flowing robes ludicrously whipped round and round. Among the presents Perry got in return were some *shunga* pornographic prints.

By the time the negotiations were concluded, both sides were on the best of terms. The Americans threw a big bash on one of their ships, to include entertainment by the Ethiopian Minstrel Band of the Powhatan. The Japanese had drunk the ship's cellar nearly dry when an enterprising officer came up with the idea of offering them a concoction of catsup and vinegar. They imbibed that with gusto, too. As they disembarked, one high shogunate official drunkenly embraced Perry, crushing his new epaulettes in the process, and gushed, "Nippon and America, all the same heart."

Thus, through an artful blend of persuasion and coercion, Perry finally got the shogunate officials to sign the Treaty of Kanagawa. The commodore's appraisal of the Japanese was that they were "very sagacious and deceitful." It would be up to the first U.S. consul, Townsend Harris, who arrived in Japan in 1856, to negotiate a full commercial treaty; it was finally signed two years later after many hassles.

Japan's feudal establishment was rigid and incapable of making the changes necessary to integrate the country into modern international society. The inflexible class system also acted as a brake on economic development, although Japan was already at a proto-industrial stage, ready for the big takeoff. The Western intrusion was a drop of nitroglycerin in a powder keg. When the smoke cleared not only had the traditional government system disappeared, but the fabric of society had been rent into many pieces.

One of the problems with the whole modernization process in Japan was that the Japanese had been forced by Perry to open up. If they had done so voluntarily, as they most likely would have very soon anyhow, the whole course of history might have been different.

The samurai rulers, who had become little more than brush-wielding, sword-flaunting bureaucrats, did everything they could to keep the Americans and the common people apart. A decade later the American merchant Francis Hall wrote: "The soldier is the idlest, most worthless man Nippon produces, but he has the privilege of caste and uses it to make all sorts of exactions upon those more humble than himself." For their part, the lower classes apparently showed a strong desire for fraternization. George Henry Preble, one of Perry's chief officers, who later went on to become a rear admiral, wrote about the second visit in his diary: "The inhabitants crowded the hill, and beckoned us on shore, and by the most unmistakable signs invited our intercourse with their women. One female went so far as to raise her drapery and expose her person to us. They are either a very lewd and lascivious people, or have catered before this, to the passions of sailors."

When Perry arrived there were only eighty households on the narrow, hook-shaped spit of sand and sediment known as Yokohama, meaning literally "Sideways Shore." They subsisted on fishing, farming, and the export of sea cucumbers to China. Although an Edo timber merchant, Yoshida Kambei, had launched the first of Yokohama's many land reclamation projects in 1654, resulting in the Yoshida Shinden rice paddies irrigated by the Ooka-gawa River, much of today's downtown Yokohama was under water as recently as the late Edo period.

The unequal treaties opened four treaty ports (including nearby Kanagawa on the heavily traveled Tokaido highway) for commerce, guaranteed freedom of religion, set very low tariffs, and provided for extraterritoriality. The last provision was most onerous to the Japanese, since a foreign malefactor could choose to be tried before the diplomatic representative of his own country—in effect Japanese law did not apply in certain parts of the country. Moreover, when the treaty ports were opened, there was no time limit placed on their existence. They were as good as eternal.

The Japanese went ahead and created a Potemkin village about two miles square on the spit at Yokohama, to which foreign merchants flocked when it was opened for business on July 1, 1859. Harris and the other ministers obstinately refused to budge from Kanagawa, however, fearing that the shogunate was simply trying to create a new Dejima, although its main concern seemed to be that there would be armed clashes between the foreigners and "expel-the-barbarians" fanatics. The first foreign traders appear to have been Dutchmen. Britain officially recognized the port in February 1860, dominating the trade for decades afterwards.

Four guarded bridges linked the settlement to the rest of the world, one armed with two brass cannons to discourage the approach of xenophobic terrorists. Japanese visitors were required to check in their swords and receive wooden tags to carry around at all times while in the settlement. All packages brought in or out of the settlement were carefully examined for contraband.

The first wave of settlers was mostly sent by established trading firms on the China coast, like Jardine Matheson. These "respectable merchants" (opium pushers that they generally were) were followed by many swindlers, runaway sailors, beachcombers, and other wastrels, whom the Japanese collectively referred to as *ketojin*, literally "hairy people from China." Many of these paragons of Western civilization thought nothing of using a revolver to bring a dispute with a "native" to a satisfactory conclusion. Japanese were even gunned down for having the temerity to ask for a bill to be paid. Dr. William Willis, who might be considered the father of modern Japanese medicine, summed it up succinctly: "We bully and beat the lower orders, and respect in no way the higher classes ... We may disguise it as we like, we are tyrants from the moment we set foot on Eastern soil."

However, relations between the Japanese and foreigners in Yokohama were never as testy as they were in the treaty ports on the China coast. For one thing, the transition from traditional society to a modern society was much more rapid than in China. For another, opium never developed into such a major problem as it had in the Qing Empire. Oddly enough, historians rarely point out that the treaties Japan negotiated with the foreign powers inevitably included a clause banning opium trade. Considering that this white poison was their major source of income, it is a wonder that the China traders went along so readily. Although opium was commonly possessed by Chinese in Yokohama, no trade really developed. There was never much demand for opium in Japan, apparently because traditional society had not disintegrated to the serious degree it had in China; the Japanese were far less demoralized than the Chinese. If the Japanese had taken to "chasing the dragon," Oshima Island to the south might well have become a major smugglers' den and the clash of civilizations could have become far worse than it did.

Yokohama's society was small, and because nearly everyone was making money, there was great camaraderie and optimism among the mostly male foreign population. When the false rumor went round that hundreds of bloodthirsty *ronin* (masterless samurai) were on their way to wipe out the despised foreigners around New Year 1861, residents of all nationalities closed ranks to meet the threat together. The danger was far from an illusion, however, since during the first year of its history alone, five foreigners were assassinated in the streets of Yokohama.

The murder of a British merchant in the Namamugi Incident in September 1862 (see page 93) resulted in a war between Britain and the Satsuma clan in the summer of 1863, that ironically led to them becoming close friends, paving the way for indirect support by the British for the Meiji Restoration. It also resulted in the stationing of thousands of British and French soldiers in Yokohama. These troops represented a sizable portion of the local population and gave local society an even more masculine tone. The large military presence did not, initially at least, solve the security situation, as was illustrated by the Kamakura Incident of 1864, in which two British officers were cut down by samurai assassins.

In any event, the early inhabitants of Yokohama were men who gloried in the pleasantly robust climate and outdoor life of horseback riding and hunting. Even young clerks could afford to live the life of squires, so word soon spread through letter and word of mouth that Yokohama was a paradise on earth, attracting even more adventurers.

The settlement also attracted many Japanese *ukiyo-e* artists, who were eager to introduce the queer foreign customs to their countrymen. Their prints, known as *Yokohama-e*, employed bold, dynamic colors and were wonderful examples of creative excess. Eighty percent of these prints came out in 1861 and 1862, although there were only thirty-four Western merchants there in the former year and perhaps 150 in the latter. It must have been a fishbowl existence for these pioneers.

Although they did not appear prominently in the art of the time, from the beginning the Chinese always represented the largest group of foreigners, while prior to World War II the British always formed the largest contingent of Westerners. On the other hand, the population of the native half of the town had by 1865 increased to about 19,000.

In its earlier days Yokohama was designed for the needs of trade, which meant it had many warehouses and customs houses, Chinese money changers, sprawling bungalows for the wealthiest merchants, a few churches, genteel hotels for proper visitors, and clapboard flophouses for the low life. The Wild West atmosphere of the age can well be imagined from the fact that, in 1861, the British consul ordered his compatriots to stop wearing firearms openly in the daytime. But as time wore on, the rough edges were generally smoothed off, especially after the opening of the Bluff to foreign residents the same year.

Yokohama continued to expand steadily, despite the temporary setback of the Pig-pen Fire of 1866, which destroyed much of the town. Brick and mortar replaced wood, and the community gained an aura of permanency and respectability. In *Glimpses of Unfamiliar Japan* Lafcadio Hearn wrote, "In these exotic streets the old and new mingle so well that one seems to offset the other." As was his melodramatic wont, Lafcadio seems to have overstated the case.

Others decried its makeshift "American look." The eccentric Victorian globetrotter Isabella Bird declared in 1878 that the town had "a dead-alive look" and "regularity without picturesqueness," and that "the gray sky, gray houses and gray roofs look harmoniously dull."

All in all, Yokohama probably bore by this time a likeness to Podunk, Iowa, with its own Barbary Coast slapped on in the form of Bloodtown. Perhaps due to the Albion influence, foreign society became quite class conscious, and "rowdies" were excluded from "select nights" at the Gaiety Theater.

The port quickly developed its own culture and distinctive pidgin. An expression commonly used today, at least in the circles I run with, was invented in the port. Drunken sailors out on the town were often advised to seek the safety of the main street, Honcho-dori. Once they reached there, everything would be simply marvelous, or hunky dory.

Gurubai was of course "good-bye," *hoisuke* was "whisky," and *jiggy-jiggy* meant quickly. The Dutch word *zondag* was also adopted as *dontaku* to refer to Sunday or other days off. Yokohamese involved more than simply vocabulary. It also developed a grammar of sorts, evolving into a language unintelligible anywhere but Yokohama. Here's a simple example: *Your a shee num wun curio high kin.* Translation: I would like to see some of your best little curios.

For decades after its opening Yokohama was Japan's premier gateway to the outside world, its chief laboratory for social and cultural change. Both elite and popular cultures from the West filtered in through Yokohama, which became the pacesetter for modernization throughout the entire country.

The mutual chicanery that has always seemed to characterize Japan's foreign trade was there from the start. The shogunate officials showed a predilection for managed trade, manipulated exchange rates, bribery, and insider trading that exasperated the foreigners. One early trader ranted in his journal that "a thousand difficulties were daily thrown in the way of trade by shogunate officials." On the other hand, foreign sharpies took merciless advantage of Japanese ignorance of international gold-silver exchange rates to drain Japan of its gold and make incredible windfall profits. The morality of foreign diplomats was also certainly no model for the Japanese. Consulate employees shamelessly indulged in land speculation, signing up for free land plots and then selling them to newcomers for outrageous prices.

From almost the earliest days, raw silk was established as the premier export, with Yokohama controlling the majority of the trade. In fact, it accounted for about 80 percent of the total trade through the treaty ports. The success of the early merchants very much depended on the fluctuations of the world silk market, and many fortunes were made or lost in the boom-bust cycles.

The demand for tea, silk, and other native products, as well as an inflow of cotton textiles and other cheap imports, and disastrous crop failures, resulted in hyperinflation throughout Japan, further eroding the already shaky foundations of the traditional system. This actually seems to have stimulated economic development, however, since the previous barriers impeding trade between independent fiefs began to collapse and a freer flow of goods and people resulted.

The Japanese detested the treaties and almost immediately tried to get them revised, while small foreign traders demanded access to Japan's "vast" interior. About the only people who were wholly satisfied with the status quo were big foreign trading houses like Jardine Matheson. It was Britain too that led the way in eliminating the treaty port system, with an 1894 agreement to abandon the setup five years later.

The Meiji government treated Yokohama and Kanagawa Prefecture, which was created in September 1868, with great care, naming a series of able governors, including Mutsu Munemitsu and Oe Taku. As part of their effort to promote "modern civilization and enlightenment," the Japanese banned many traditional customs, a move that proved easier said than done. In July 1873 alone there were 289 arrests for public nudity, 124 for fights, and 85 for urinating in public. The government also hired many foreign experts, the most conscientious of whom, like the rail engineer Edward Morel and the civil engineer Richard Henry Brunton, did much for Yokohama.

The development and reclamation projects they started were the first of many that continue to this day. When Yokohama became a city in 1889 it covered a mere 5.4 square kilometers, only a tad more than one percent of today's 430 square kilometers, and had a population of 120,000. However, inevitably Yokohama lagged in development behind Tokyo, a trend that was exacerbated when it became a center for the anti-government Popular Rights Movement.

Like any self-respecting town, Yokohama had its share of scandals. In 1870, many important Japanese officials, as well as foreign diplomats and merchants, were among the 150 passengers who went to a watery grave when negligence on the part of a foreign engineer caused the steamboat *City of Edo*, which plied regularly between Yokohama and Tokyo, to sink. Then there was the disgusting Normanton Incident of 1886, in which the British captain and foreigners on the ill-fated *Normanton* escaped by lifeboats while the Japanese were left to die. Although the Japanese government asked for the death penalty for the captain, the consular court only gave him three months in jail. Clearly a case of white-man's justice.

However, the scandal that evoked the lusty juices that still flowed behind the community's increasingly bourgeois facade was the Carew Trial of 1896, which took place at the staid British Consulate. Walter Carew, manager of the Yokohama United Club, was a heavy-drinking, would-be silk trader. His thirty-year-old wife, Edith, was an attractive young woman who, bored with the absences of her husband, took to running around openly with young men.

When Walter suddenly died after much vomiting, a doctor demanded an autopsy, and it was discovered that he had been poisoned. Thus followed the sensational trial that riveted the attention of the community. Complicating the proceedings was Edith's claim that Walter had been visited on his deathbed by a mysterious "woman in black." In the end, the jury took only twenty-five minutes to find Edith guilty. She was condemned to death, but her sentence was commuted by British Minister Ernest Satow. On Walter's impressive gravestone is a poem by Tennyson and the line, "In loving memory of my dear husband." It was erected by Edith.

Not until after the Russo-Japanese War were Japanese captains recognized by Lloyd's of London, and only with the founding of Mitsui in 1876 were the Japanese able to break the foreign trade monopoly. As late as 1877 foreign trading firms still controlled 96 percent of Japan's trade. Even by 1896 Japanese trading firms still handled only 25 percent of the exports going through Yokohama and 30 percent of the imports. However, after that foreigners were rapidly squeezed out.

The opening of the railroad to Tokyo in 1872, and later the Suez Canal and the Canadian Pacific Railroad, greatly aided the development of Yokohama, cutting travel time by nearly half and transport costs by 80 percent. By the early 1900s Yokohama was the largest and most modern port in East Asia, while its labor force was among the most radical. In fact the first May Day celebration in Japan took place in Yokohama Park in 1920, and anarchist and communist organizers were active in the shantytowns in the densely populated older quarters of the city. During the first two decades of this century, an intense rivalry also developed with Kobe, which was not opened until January 1868, with the Kansai port becoming tops in total trade in 1914 and in

1930 becoming the country's greatest export port.

Boom times during World War I, when European suppliers to Asia were cut off, were followed by depression—Yokohama was overdependent on the raw silk trade. The local economy was further depressed by the 1923 earthquake, the 1927 financial panic, and the Great Depression. All was not doom and gloom, however, since during these same decades the great Keihin industrial belt stretching from Shinagawa in Tokyo through Kawasaki to Yokohama was gradually coming into existence, to a large extent on land reclaimed from Tokyo Bay.

The Great Kanto Earthquake of 1923 took a terrible toll in Yokohama. Forty thousand people died and 95.5 percent of the city was leveled. In one yarn-spinning factory in Hodogaya 450 people were crushed to death when the roof careened down on them. A typhoon had been blowing before, and the still-strong winds fanned more than three hundred fires. Tens of thousands of people sought refuge from the inferno in mud-filled Yokohama Park. There was no escape, however, for the Koreans. Unfounded rumors that the Koreans were lighting fires and poisoning wells led to massacres of thousands of Koreans throughout the Kanto area, including Yokohama, by vigilante groups and military police.

The tremor did not discriminate according to wealth or nationality. The classic three-story French Consulate, built in 1897, disintegrated and two thousand of the five thousand residents of Chinatown were crushed in their homes. The one thousand passengers on board the *Empress of Australia*, just readying to sail for Vancouver, watched in horror as the earth writhed and the friends who had come to see them off tumbled into the ocean along with Osanbashi Pier. Otis Poole, a prominent businessman, later recalled, "The ground could scarcely be said to shake; it heaved, tossed and leaped under one."

The recovery process was slow. Despite the fact that Yokohama had suffered proportionately more heavily than Tokyo, the national government furnished the city only one-tenth as much aid. Many wealthy foreigners also left for good, moving to Shanghai and Kobe or returning to their homelands. More left as war approached, or were evacuated by the authorities during the conflict.

Trade expanded greatly during the late 1930s, but the boom was cut short by World War II. The opening of the Port of Tokyo in 1941 was another rabbit punch for Yokohama. Nearly all the newly reconstructed city was wiped out once again by the firebombings of the war. During the May 29 incendiary raid by 517 B29s, more than 1.5 times as many bombs were dropped as during the famous May 10 attack on Tokyo's downtown, or more than one bomb for every Yokohama resident. Nearly 50 percent of the city was burned to the ground and close to a half-million people were left homeless by the air raids.

One resident later recalled how she had joined a mob rushing from the center of the city toward the Bluff: "The crowd surged forward like a wave. No one spoke a word. We did not even seem like human beings any longer. No one who wasn't there could possibly understand what it was like. We couldn't tell if it was day or night. We never stopped running till we reached the fields of Yamate."

When General Douglas MacArthur and his convoy of thirty-five vehicles entered Yokohama on August 30, 1945, they saw a ghost town. Uncharacteristically, the general carried a sidearm. The air was electric with tension, with many of the Americans certain they would be ambushed or subjected to suicide attacks en route. Little could they know at that time that the Occupation would prove to be one of the great success stories of history.

Even before the signing of the formal surrender on the USS *Missouri* in Yokohama Harbor on September 2, the Allied Forces had begun requisitioning all the major buildings still standing in the center of the city. MacArthur himself operated out of the Hotel New Grand until he moved to Tokyo in mid-September. However, for all intents and purposes Yokohama was the real center of the Occupation. The port facilities were totally commandeered and overall about 27 percent of the city was occupied by the U.S. military. The huge American complex came to be referred to as the Kannai Bokujo ("Kannai Ranch"). Excluding Okinawa, 62 percent of the land held by the U.S. military was in the Yokohama area. Much of the area was not returned until well after the Occupation ended, leaving Yokohama well behind the rest of Japan when it came to recovery.

Once the GIs arrived, the black market and street girls as young as thirteen were not far behind. In the year and a half after the end of the war, prices for staple foods went up two hundred times over, and malnutrition and contagious diseases, including VD, were major concerns. So was crime. Occupation censorship prevented the reporting of the many rapes and robberies by U.S. servicemen. Tarts, tanks, and tangled barbed wire made Yokohama a symbol of shame for many Japanese elsewhere, who did not have to worry about such things.

However, the huge military presence also meant an estimated fifty thousand jobs at bases in the Yokohama area. Discharged soldiers and former settlers in Manchuria flocked to the city and from 1948 the Japanese economy began to recover, thanks largely to the Cold War and later the Korean War.

Occupation reforms totally changed Japanese society, leading to radicalization of labor, food riots, and eventually a backlash in the form of the "red purge." But soon there was another huge housing shortage, caused by prosperity, not war. The Keihin industrial zone became a center for Japan's manufacturing and export drives. Unwelcome by-products of the new prosperity included rampant water and air pollution—problems that continue to this day. But it was only in the 1970s, after most of the docks had finally reverted to Japanese control, that Yokohama regained the title of Japan's number one port.

The indiscriminate development and concentration of government in Tokyo after the war has led to the rapid suburbanization of Yokohama and other parts of Kanagawa Prefecture. Since the 1950s Kanagawa's population has tripled, and it continues to grow: in 1978 Yokohama passed Osaka to become Japan's second-largest city. As of 1994 there were 45,611 foreigners living in Yokohama, of whom 34 percent were Korean, 26 percent Chinese, 8 percent Brazilian, and 5 percent American.

The attractive living environment, cosmopolitanism, and relatively friendly, open attitude toward outsiders have made many people opt to move here—a Yokohama license plate is now considered a status symbol. It is estimated that by 2010 Yokohama's population will be 3.75 to 3.85 million. City planners also hope to add nearly two hundred jobs by the start of the twenty-first century.

1

Yokohama Old and New

⟳ Sakuragicho Station 桜木町駅 (JR Negishi and Tokyu Toyoko lines)—Minato Mirai 21 みなとみらい21—Silk Museum シルク博物館—Yamashita Park 山下公園

With its mild climate and broad, tree-lined boulevards, Yokohama is almost always a glorious town for walking. But when the skies are white-flecked blue and balmy breezes blow in from Tokyo Bay, it's an ambler's paradise. Such a day is perfect for this route, which covers the waterfront, taking in the city's oldest and newest neighborhoods, while letting you savor some of its most impressive vistas.

Yokohama is trying with all its might to break Tokyo's stranglehold in the fields of economics, finance, and media. Master plans envisage the city as a twenty-first-century internationalized port and industrial, high-tech, information, and fashion powerhouse, whose convention centers will rival Makuhari Messe in Chiba and similar projects in the waterfront district of Tokyo.

In the past Yokohama has been one of the prime victims of the overcentralization of population and power in Tokyo. But now the city seems prepared to take advantage of its location near to the capital. As the chairman of the Yokohama Chamber of Commerce and Industry puts it: "Being close to Tokyo has merits and demerits. Until recently we could think only of the demerits, but now we've come to see the merits as well. Precisely because we are so near, if we can develop facilities not available in Tokyo, people will come to live in Yokohama."

Come out of Sakuragicho Station and you'll see the centerpiece of this strategy for independence, the ambitious Minato Mirai 21

• MAP 22-23

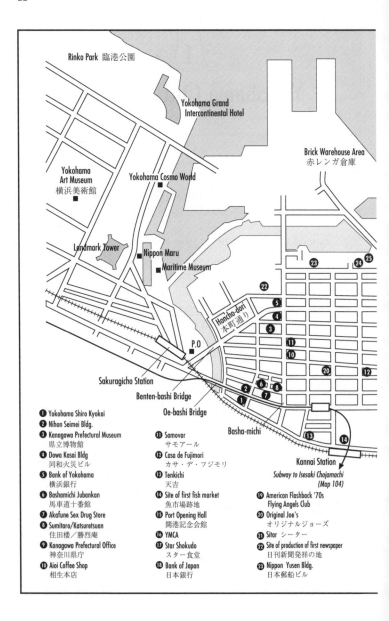

Rinko Park 臨港公園

Yokohama Grand
Intercontinental Hotel

Brick Warehouse Area
赤レンガ倉庫

Yokohama
Art Museum
横浜美術館

Yokohama Cosmo World

Landmark Tower

Nippon Maru

Maritime Museum

Honcho-dori
本町通り

P.O

Sakuragicho Station

Benten-bashi Bridge

Oe-bashi Bridge

Basha-michi

Kannai Station

Subway to Isesaki Chojamachi
(Map 104)

❶ Yokohama Shiro Kyokai
❷ Nihon Seimei Bldg.
❸ Kanagawa Prefectural Museum
   県立博物館
❹ Dowa Kasai Bldg
   同和火災ビル
❺ Bank of Yokohama
   横浜銀行
❻ Bashamichi Jubankan
   馬車道十番館
❼ Akafune Sex Drug Store
❽ Sumitaro/Katsuretsuan
   住田楼／勝烈庵
❾ Kanagawa Prefectural Office
   神奈川県庁
❿ Aioi Coffee Shop
   相生本店

⓫ Samovar
   サモアール
⓬ Casa de Fujimori
   カサ・デ・フジモリ
⓭ Tenkichi
   天吉
⓮ Site of first fish market
   魚市場跡地
⓯ Port Opening Hall
   開港記念会館
⓰ YMCA
⓱ Star Shokudo
   スター食堂
⓲ Bank of Japan
   日本銀行

⓳ American Flashback '70s
   Flying Angels Club
⓴ Original Joe's
   オリジナルジョーズ
㉑ Sitar シーター
㉒ Site of production of first newspaper
   日刊新聞発祥の地
㉓ Nippon Yusen Bldg.
   日本郵船ビル

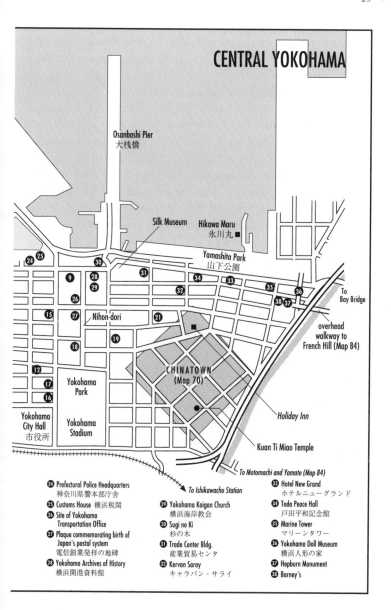

CENTRAL YOKOHAMA

Osanbashi Pier
大桟橋

Silk Museum

Hikawa Maru
氷川丸 ■

Yamashita Park
山下公園

To Bay Bridge

overhead walkway to French Hill (Map 84)

Nihon-dori

CHINATOWN (Map 70)

Yokohama Park

Yokohama Stadium

Yokohama City Hall
市役所

Holiday Inn

Kuan Ti Miao Temple

To Motomachi and Yamate (Map 84)

To Ishikawacho Station

㉔ Prefectural Police Headquarters
神奈川県警本部庁舎

㉕ Customs House 横浜税関

㉖ Site of Yokohama Transportation Office

㉗ Plaque commemorating birth of Japan's postal system
電信創業発祥の地碑

㉘ Yokohama Archives of History
横浜開港資料館

㉙ Yokohama Kaigan Church
横浜海岸教会

㉚ Sugi no Ki
杉の木

㉛ Trade Center Bldg.
産業貿易センタ

㉜ Kervan Saray
キャラバン・サライ

㉝ Hotel New Grand
ホテルニューグランド

㉞ Toda Peace Hall
戸田平和記念館

㉟ Marine Tower
マリーンタワー

㊱ Yokohama Doll Museum
横浜人形の家

㊲ Hepburn Monument

㊳ Barney's

(MM21) project near Sakuragi-cho in an area formerly made up of Mitsu-bishi dockyards, a railroad yard, and parts of several piers. Launched in 1989 in conjunction with the YES '89 expo, development of the 186-hectare zone, including 76 hectares reclaimed from the ocean, is expected to cost at least ¥3 trillion and be completed by the year 2000.

Every workday, approximately 600,000 residents of Yokohama commute to jobs outside the city, mainly in Tokyo, while only half that number come into town to work. If the MM21 plan comes off as visual-ized, by the turn of the century the daytime population of the planned community will be 190,000 and 10,000 people will live there in high-rise, mostly luxury apartments. The mini-metropolis will host an inter-national information center and be largely self-contained as far as utilities, waste disposal, and other essential services are concerned.

It seems almost sinful to start your Yokohama walking adventures with a ride on the glass-roofed 230-meter-long moving sidewalk con-necting Sakuragicho Station with MM21. If you are into guilt, feel free to force march along beside it.

Right in front of you, straight out of *Blade Runner*, looms the Land-mark Tower. The "long, thin one" is not only the symbol of MM21, at 296 meters it is also the tallest building in East Asia, costing a cool ¥270 billion (about $2.5 billion). It's definitely a perfect means to make arrogant Tokyoites look up to Yokohama—the 50-meter-shorter Tokyo City Hall had a very short reign as Japan's tallest building. With sev-enty stories above ground and three below, the super skyscraper boasts 392,300 square meters of floor space. The developers seemed gung-ho to go higher, but restrictions due to flight patterns at Haneda Airport set limits to their hubris.

Blow your nose and clear your ears before you hop on the world's fastest elevator to be whisked up at forty-five kilometers per hour to the top floor in forty seconds—truly a legal high. Be warned, however: there are only four elevators collectively capable of carrying only 12,000 people a day, so you may have to wait over an hour to enjoy your quickie. This uplifting experience will set you back ¥1,000 (¥500 for children) so make sure you choose a clear day. The Sky Lounge on the 70th floor, the scenic observatory on the 69th floor, and the Sky

• MAP 22-23

Restaurant on the 68th floor offer breathtaking panoramas encompassing eighty kilometers in all directions. This means that after paying the highway robbery toll you're free to ogle Tokyo Bay, Tokyo, and the Boso, Miura, and Izu peninsulas, and, of course, peerless Fuji-san.

Designed by American architect Hugh Stubbins, the building is to my untutored eye rather attractive, and the view down into the large central atrium from the fifth floor is spectacular in its own right. Clustered around it are about two hundred shops and restaurants. The acknowledged goal of the tower's owner, Mitsubishi Estate, is to have the Landmark Plaza offer a "unique" shopping and dining atmosphere. Unfortunately, most of the restaurants are not very exciting; many of them are branches of well-known family-restaurant and fast-food chains. Expecting twenty million visitors a year, the management may be in for a disappointment once the novelty wears off.

There are redeeming features, though. The Landmark Tower branch of Yurindo bookstores is excellent. There is also a large hall and a small hall on the fifth floor for cultural events. Most of the first forty-eight floors of the tower is office space; floors forty-nine to seventy belong to the Yokohama Royal Park Hotel. More restaurants are to be found fringing an old dry dock in front of the tower, where rock concerts and other events are held among the weathered, shell- and mold-encrusted stone.

Controlling the Long Thin One

The Landmark Tower was built with totally new technologies and materials developed in Japan. Because of its slim, towering shape, the top of the building is subject to considerable stomach-churning sway. Mitsubishi Estate integrated special wind-resistant and anti-earthquake technologies into the sturdy design. The key to them is the revolutionary computer-controlled compensation system, which, according to the engineer in charge, incorporates special techniques to control movement, including sensors and two 170-ton pendulum weights above the seventieth floor. The central computers order the motor mechanisms to compensate when high winds or a typhoon come howling around Big Slim's head. In effect the weights are moved in the opposite direction to which the winds are blowing. Sounds like a sophisticated application of the old spitting in the wind principle.

However, it will no doubt become the wave of the future since Japanese companies are already designing thousand-meter-high structures.

• MAP 22-23

Among the cultural amenities in MM21 is the Yokohama Art Museum. The architectural design by Tange Kenzo is most interesting, although the unkind might liken it to an atomic power plant or corn silo. Be that as it may, the building is very spacious and the layout tasteful, satisfying Yokohama's long-felt need for a really first-class art museum. The accent is definitely on the twentieth century in its five-thousand-work permanent collection. Among the joys are the children's room, a large photo collection, a gift shop, and a fountain outside that goes beserk under the lights at night.

In front of the Landmark Tower is another museum, the Maritime Museum. You can't miss it because docked right next to it is a splendid sailing ship, the *Nippon Maru*, the "Swan of the Pacific." Along with scale models of many famous nineteenth- and twentieth-century ships, the history of interaction between people and the sea is presented in innovative style. You can even captain a ship through the wonders of TV-game–type simulation.

From there go next door to explore the *Nippon Maru*, anchored in a former stone dockyard built in 1896. This beauty was once used as a training vessel for the Maritime Self-Defense Forces. Its corridors and cabins are amazingly narrow, although the captain's cabin is roomy and comfortable. A big ship in the age of sail was hardly a classless society. The giant sails of the *Nippon Maru* are unfurled about twice a month— call to check the dates.

All of the novel architecture at MM21 may have you thinking you are hallucinating, seeing windmills. But you are not. That 105-meter-high, 100-meter-diameter circle of steel in the sky is "Revolution," the world's largest Ferris wheel. It takes fifteen minutes to go around once. Revolution is part of Cosmo World, an amusement park built on part of the YES '89 site.

A line of zelkova trees marks the route between the Landmark Tower and the six-hundred-room Yokohama Grand Intercontinental Hotel and the adjoining National Convention Hall Pacifico Yokohama complex, which opened in the spring of 1994. A nautical motif is the rule in these parts; the hotel is supposed to represent sails, the exhibition hall waves, and the meeting hall shells. In front of the hotel is the

• MAP 22-23

quaint-looking restaurant Pier 21, featuring Mediterranean-style seafood dishes at hotel dining-room prices.

If you're into free entertainment, drop into the Minato Mirai 21 Yokohama-kan, a pavilion left over from YES '89, an event considered a failure by many, although it was visited by thirteen million people. Among other things, under what is purported to be the world's largest wooden dome, you'll find Yokohama Gulliver Land. There before your eyes is all of MM21 (after completion) and central Yokohama in the form of scale models of 3,500 buildings and 20,000 people. The lighting changes to reflect the seasons and time of day. I can't think of a better way for the serious walker to get accustomed to the lie of the land. You can also view more than a thousand selected NHK and private network programs dating back to the earliest days of Japanese TV at the Hoso (Broadcast) Library. In addition to dramas and documentaries, you can relive historic moments in Japan's cultural history, such as the day Hikaru Genji first sang their way across the screen on roller skates and Pink Lady's debut in front of the cameras. In the far back is the Rinkai (Seaside) Park, with grass, a lagoon, and a beautiful view of the harbor and Bay Bridge, especially at night when it's all lit up.

Parts of the project still under construction include COA CITY—a ¥400 billion complex of four high-rise buildings, the highest of which will be forty-two stories. At 498,600 square meters, it will be the largest single part of MM21. It will include yet another hotel, a state-of-the-art classical music hall, and more offices. Of note in this connection are the New Media Community Concept and the Teletopia Concept, backed by MITI and the Ministry of Posts and Telecommunications respectively, that envisage linking MM21, Tokyo, and overseas locations by satellite and other multimedia services. Other facilities will include a hospital, teleport, multimedia communications center, and an "industrial culture center," whose prime goal is to foster Yokohama as a global design and fashion center. The Minato Mirai Subway Line will link the zone to Yokohama Station from 1998.

All in all, MM21 is certain to change the face of Yokohama. The mini-city is also expected to serve as a stimulus to development in other parts of the city, including the Portside Zone, a residential and

• MAP 22-23

"art design" area with art galleries and auction halls on land formerly occupied by a warehouse and factories.

Double back to Sakuragicho Station, go out the opposite side and turn left. If you walk to the end of the block you'll see a monument marking the site of the original Yokohama Station. This was the terminus of Japan's first railway, opened in 1872, that ran to Shiodome in the Shimbashi district of Tokyo. The first section to Kanagawa actually opened in 1870. Most of the Meiji leaders had serious doubts about the huge investment involved, but Okuma Shigenobu and Ito Hirobumi pushed the plan through, arranging financing through British sources.

All the head engineers were British—Edmund Morel, aged twenty-eight, became the project head. He and two other British engineers working to build Japanese railroads died unusually young on the job, literally worked to death. The trip to Tokyo took only fifty-three minutes, compared to the previous four hours by coach. The train made nine round trips a day and was very expensive in terms of today's prices—the cheapest one-way ticket went for the equivalent of ¥3,000.

Go left under the bridge and head straight to the next corner, passing Sakuragi-cho Post Office on the left. Next head right over the bridge across the Ooka-gawa River. This is Benten-bashi, along with Yoshida-bashi one of the two most important bridges in Yokohama's history. We are now entering the Japanese section of the old settlement area, which later evolved into its shipping and banking hub. Keep to the left on this nearly half-mile-long road, Honcho-dori, which in the Meiji period was nicknamed "Curio Street" because of the many shops selling next-to-worthless knicknacks, as well as bronzes, ivory carvings, lacquerware, and porcelain, for often-outrageous prices. Many early visitors remarked on how avaricious and "sneaky" the merchants of the area were. As late as 1889 a resident foreigner remarked to Rudyard Kipling: "God knows I hate the Chinaman, but you can do business with him. The Jap's a little huckster who can't see beyond his nose."

The foreigners who barreled down this wide road on their Chinese ponies were not popular with the locals either. Wrote one early resident: "I have seen Englishmen and others of my acquaintance in different parts of Japan riding at rapid pace through the villages and suburbs

• MAP 22-23

of cities amid crowds of people, who had to scamper in hurried movements from side to side to avoid being knocked down, and who may doubtless be supposed to view with no kind feelings the presence of such equestrians."

On the third corner is the old headquarters of the Bank of Yokohama. The semicircular entrance balcony gives it the air of a Greek shrine. Turn left at this triangle-shaped corner. The regional government offices used to be the site of the Raw Silk Inspection Station. It was also where the first full-fledged Japanese-language daily newspaper, the *Yokohama Mainichi Shimbun*, was founded in 1870; a plaque (*Nikkan Shimbun hatsusho no chi* 日刊新聞初商の地) marks the spot.

The Roots of Japanese Journalism

The *Yokohama Mainichi Shimbun* was actually preceded by trade circulars like the *Japan Express* and the *Kaigai Shimbun* (Overseas news). Published by Joseph Heco, born Hamada Hikozo, a returnee castaway who had been educated in the United States, the *Kaigai Shimbun* was a summary of foreign news for Japanese readers and had a brief, sporadic existence in 1865 and 1866. The handwritten *Japan Express*, published by the American Jew "Old Schoyer," was a weekly appearing on Saturdays. In the early days Japanese still did not have a very good idea of what a newspaper was supposed to be: canvassers for subscribers would be told, "I've already got one newspaper, what do I need another one for?"

The *Mainichi* had the backing of the local governor and silk magnates, and soon became a forum for the debate of people's rights and other policy issues. The government, however, was not slow to react, and it got into a habit of censoring and banning newspapers that it did not break until the end of World War II. Being a newspaper editor was a vulnerable profession in those days, with nearly as much time spent in jail as at the desk. In 1879, the *Yokohama Mainichi Shimbun* moved to Tokyo, the political and social center of Japan, dropping "Yokohama" from its title in 1886.

Early Japanese newspapers were greatly influenced by English-language newspapers published in the settlement, and their articles even had some influence on domestic Japanese politics. Because of extraterritoriality, foreign journalists were free to report as they liked and editors attacked the Japanese government, and frequently each other, with savage glee. The most important of these, the *Japan Herald*, was founded in November 1862; it soon had several competitors, including the *Japan Times*, the *Japan Mail*, the *Japan Commercial News*, the *Japan Gazette*, and illustrator Charles Wirgman's highly satirical *Japan Punch*. When John Reddie Black, a former editor of the *Japan Herald*, dared to launch the Japanese-language *Nisshin Shinjishi* (The reliable daily news) in 1879, the Japanese government passed a law forbidding foreigners from owning Japanese-language papers. So much for freedom of the press.

• MAP 22-23

From the newspaper monument, take the fourth street on the right (Kaigan-dori) and get on the left-hand side of the road. The Nippon Yusen (shipping) Building, with its sixteen Corinthian columns, is an impressive monument to Yokohama's glory days. The building was constructed in 1936 and contains a small navigation museum and snack bar.

The tall, modern building with all the antennas on top is the prefectural police headquarters. Tiptoe past and you'll see before you a magnificent old light-brown brick building with a graceful green Moorish tower. This is the Yokohama Customs House, affectionately known as the "Queen" to generations of seaborne visitors. The sensitive blend of Spanish, Islamic, and Japanese influences certainly gives the building a feminine aura. On the second floor is a room with exhibits related to the building; if you apply at the information office (koho kanshitsu 広報官屋), they will be glad to show you around.

From here you can make a detour to the old red-brick warehouses that frequently appear in movies and on TV; occasionally they form the backdrop for rock concerts. Turn left and follow the road till you see them on the right. The docks of New Shinko Pier are still very much in use, so there are signs warning that no unauthorized personnel are allowed. But if you ignore them, the brawny stevedores will ignore you. It seems that there are always a few shutterbugs crawling around the edges of the graffiti-covered, decrepit warehouses that were built in 1910 and 1913. Note the lightning rods and gables, which add to the impressive effect. This area is scheduled to be developed into Red Brick (aka renga) Park, set to open in 1997 as part of a project that will have the largest international convention hall in eastern Japan. The original Yokohama port that was here was built by English engineer Henry Spencer Palmer in 1907 as part of general reconstruction in the harbor. Actually, as early as 1864 a dockyard was built at Yokohama, although no one seems quite sure where it was located.

Retrace your steps to the Customs House; across from it are two prefectural government buildings connected by an overhead walkway. The older one to the left is "King"—the Kanagawa Prefectural Building. When lit up at night, the angles of the intriguing geometric building float out of the shadows like Pythagorean specters.

• MAP 22-23

In the back of the prefectural offices is a plaque commemorating the site of the Yokohama Maritime Transportation Office, forerunner of the Customs House. It opened in 1859 along with the port and oversaw shipbuilding, outfitting, and other maritime business. Burned down in the 1866 fire, it was replaced the following year by the first two-story stone building in Japan, the town office (Yokohama Yakusho 横浜役所).

Across the street is a plaque marking the birth of Japan's modern postal system in 1872. Direct foreign service began in 1875 and in 1877 Japan joined the Universal Postal Union, whereupon Britain, the United States, and France closed down the postal services they had maintained because they didn't trust the Japanese. Today Japan's postal system is one of the most reliable in the world, although the same cannot be said for some Western countries. Incidentally, at first many people thought telegraphs were a form of Christian sorcery, but eventually they lost their fear and gathered around in the hopes of seeing the messages fly by.

Head back to the main road again. The former British Consulate, reconstructed in 1931, now serves as the Yokohama Archives of History. In eighteenth-century Georgian style, it has a graceful appearance. Exhibitions concerning the port of Yokohama, including a lot of original artifacts related to the Perry visits, are displayed on the first floor, and temporary exhibitions, such as one comparing the settlements in Yokohama and Shanghai, are held on the second floor. The library downstairs has copies of the oldest extant English-language newspapers, which you can browse through, and videotapes on Yokohama history.

The camphor tree in the center portico is said to have stood very near to where Commodore Perry negotiated with the shogunate representatives. It was burned down following the 1923 earthquake, but its roots sprouted into a new tree that miraculously survived the firebombings of the Pacific War.

To the side of the Archives is the Yokohama Port Opening Square, the site where Commodore Perry and the shogunate officials signed the 1854 treaty. It faces the entrance to Osanbashi Pier, the main gateway for foreign ship passengers. With its fountain, wave-like designs in

• MAP 22-23

stone, brick manhole covers, leafy trees, and steel columns that reflect the water beautifully, it is an urban oasis, as the winos who often hold parties in the park have evidently discovered. Perry and his men also did a lot of partying on their second visit, including at the home of the village headman, Ishikawa Tokueimon. By all accounts the Americans got along a lot better with the common people than with the stodgy two-sworded bureaucrats.

Next to the park is the Kaigan Kyokai, the oldest Protestant church in Japan, established by American missionaries in 1871. The driving force was James Ballagh, spiritual father of the Yokohama Band of early Japanese converts. Along with flocks in Kumamoto and Sapporo, the Yokohama Band became one of the cornerstones of Japanese Protestantism. By the end of the 1870s there were hundreds of thousands of Japanese Christians, and the various sects vied with each other to lead the elect down their own chosen path to salvation.

Dr. James Curtis Hepburn

One of the most extraordinary early residents of Yokohama was Dr. James Curtis Hepburn (1815–1911). He and his wife arrived in Kanagawa in 1859 as missionaries for the American Board of Foreign Missions of the Presbyterian Church. They had already served in China from 1841 to 1845. In Japan he became best known for his medical work and for his studies of the Japanese language that culminated in the first reasonably thorough Japanese-English dictionary, which was finally published in 1867 after eight years of strenuous effort. He also had a key role in the first translation of the Bible into Japanese along with Nathan Brown. The romanization system Hepburn invented is, with modifications, still in wide use today.

Hepburn had a lot more humanity than your typical nineteenth-century Presbyterian is given credit for. For one thing, he operated a free clinic out of his home—many of the early missionaries were medical men and made up the bulk of the early doctors. Hepburn provided free treatment for tuberculosis, smallpox, and eye diseases, and won renown when he amputated the gangrenous leg of well-known kabuki *onnagata* Sawamura Tanosuke and fitted him with a peg leg. Together with his wife he founded a school that developed into Meiji Gakuin, where several future government leaders and journalists studied. Even the Meiji leaders, who in the early days of the new regime vigorously persecuted both Christianity and Buddhism, openly expressed their admiration for Dr. Hepburn. In 1892 the Hepburns finally returned to America because of illness.

A monument to the memory of Hepburn is to be found around the corner from the Yokohama Doll Museum in front of a Yokohama government office.

• MAP 22-23

The original church was destroyed in the 1923 earthquake, but it was rebuilt in 1933, although the church bell was forged in 1876. The building is a study in white simplicity.

Holland was the first country to relocate its consulate from Kanagawa to Yokohama, in July 1860. At first the settlement was only 0.3 square kilometers, so it had to be quickly expanded. The persnickety French also wanted to have their own settlement, as in Shanghai, although they soon abandoned the demand and settled for their own wharf, the French *hatoba*. Foreigners were not allowed to own land; instead they rented plots at ridiculously cheap prices. Rights to land in the foreign quarter could also be transferred and no Japanese could legally occupy land or buildings there.

Efforts at self-government soon foundered, primarily for financial reasons, and the Japanese were allowed to handle problems like security and other public services. For this reason a situation such as in China, where the local inhabitants were treated like strangers in their own land, never really developed. All in all the relationship between the Japanese and the foreigners was remarkably relaxed from the beginning, considering that the port had been opened by force. In fact, interaction between foreigners and Japanese in Yokohama gave birth to a new culture whose synergistic energy changed the face of Japan.

The shogunate spent a small fortune constructing a boomtown almost overnight on the sands and dirt of Yokohama. The customs house was located in the center near the 110-meter-long stone pier, with the foreign community stretching to the right in the direction of the Bluff, while Japanese merchants of all kinds, who had been promised tax-exempt status, set up shop on the other side in the direction of what is today Sakuragi-cho. The shogunate had given orders for merchants it had close ties with to start doing business at Yokohama, but all, including even the mighty House of Mitsui, were reluctant to get involved for fear of xenophobic fanatics and doubts about profits. Those that did take the plunge quickly closed shop, fearing "Heaven's wrath," only to be replaced by nobodies from the countryside, some of whom ended up the top business leaders of the Meiji and Taisho periods—silk kings among them.

• MAP 22-23

At first these native merchants had no idea what the foreigners wanted to buy. Many showed up with seaweed or dried radishes. Soon it became clear that silk was the product that would make a fortune— by May 1860, of the two hundred Japanese businesses operating in Yokohama, eighty-nine were raw silk merchants. The global silk market was highly volatile and merchants of all nationalities operating in Japan celebrated when France or Italy had poor silk harvests. But many were broken by a slump and even resorted to burning thousands of their silkworm egg cards to keep export prices propped up.

Across from the Port Opening Square is the Silk Museum, which tells the whole story of silk in fascinating, easy-to-understand fashion. Although not as high-tech as more recently constructed museums, it still is worth at least an hour or two. The exhibits show everything involved in the process that transforms the exudations of grubby silkworms into the most gorgeous kimono imaginable. Take the elevator up to the fourth floor and through a glass window you can observe silk exchange members actually trading silk futures. There is also a prefectural tourist information center on the ground floor.

The first foreign firm to establish a presence in Yokohama was Jardine Matheson, the China traders who had built their fortune on selling opium to the less-than-happy Celestials. Their office, built in 1859 and the earliest Western-style building in town, became known as Ei-ichibankan (English Building No. 1). They were soon followed by compatriots from Dent and Co. and the Americans Walsh and Hall at Ame-ichibankan (American Building No. 1).

Jardine's, which always remained the "king" of the foreign trading companies, or hongs, employed many Japanese and Chinese. In the 1860s, Jardine's alone accounted for an estimated 20 percent of total Yokohama trade. Opium constituted by far the most important product in its China trade, but in Japan the firm became a model of respectability and establishment consciousness, early establishing close ties with future Meiji leaders. The company was, for example, responsible for sending a group of students to Britain that included Ito Hirobumi and Inoue Kaoru. A plaque marking the site of the Ei-ichibankan is in front of the Silk Museum.

• MAP 22-23

Life in Yokohama was wild and wooly at the beginning. The makeshift community was frequently compared to a California gold-rush outpost. One observer referred to its inhabitants as "greedy vultures" and the "most unscrupulous specimens of all nations." The majority of the earliest traders had come from the China coast and included a mixture of legitimate traders, in terms of the prevailing morality in those days, and rank adventurers. At the start most slept with their rifles or six-guns in clapboard single-room houses that served as office, warehouse, kitchen, and bedroom.

Things quickly improved, however, and after the first rough years, the hongs all developed impressive compounds. Most of the Western traders' houses became low-slung wooden bungalows with verandas. Some had a second floor, but brick had not come into use yet. The warehouses were in the back with their entrances on the Bund, or Water Street, as the main street along the waterfront became known.

Buildings in the foreign quarter were routinely referred to by number rather than name. The Grand Hotel, for example, was No. 20. The Japanese part of town, however, used names that indicated the part of Japan the inhabitants hailed from: Odawara-cho, Kaga-cho, etc. This was quite different from the practice in Edo, where the neighborhood names indicated the occupations of the residents.

An Italian diplomat who visited Yokohama in 1866 wrote, "The town looks just like a port in Europe. The only thing different is that some of the buildings are in Japanese style and there are Japanese craftsmen and laborers to be seen."

At first there were many crooks among the Japanese silk merchants. Since the price of a batch of raw silk was determined by weight, they took to mixing wet thread or paper with the silk to make it heavier. There are tales of such sharpers being stripped naked and kicked around by irate foreign merchants. Finally, the Silk Inspection Center was established in 1873 to ensure the quality of silk exported by the brokers, who had become necessary middlemen.

Because they had the transport and knowledge of the world silk market, the foreigners could call the shots. With the dramatic rise of the domestic silk industry in the 1880s, Japanese businessmen began

• MAP 22-23

demanding that the country regain control over its exports. They were at the mercy of world silk prices and dissatisfied with foreign business practices that appeared to put them at a disadvantage.

The direct export movement was the ultimate result. In the early 1880s the government encouraged direct exports through loans. Taking advantage of their better financial position, the brokers tried to eliminate foreign middlemen and export directly. By forming the Federated Raw Silk Warehouse they sought to establish a cartel with control of the supply of raw silk. The foreigners refused to buy, however, and the Japanese silk merchants' effort at exerting independence ended in defeat.

Next door to the Silk Museum is the Trade Center Building, which contains the Kanagawa International Association Library—a nice place for a break with its good collection of English books and newspapers—and tourist information offices. Next to that is the glass-faced Kenmin Hall where concerts, plays, and other cultural events are held.

A couple of interesting restaurants run by "children of the Silk Road" are in the area. Sitar is owned by a third-generation Indian resident of Japan; the food is northern Indian, the food of the Moghuls.

The Yokohama Indian Community

Kumar Mahtani, the personable young owner of Sitar, moved from his hometown of Kobe in 1986 to start the restaurant on land his grandfather had bought after arriving in Japan back in the 1930s from Sind Province in India, an area that is now part of Pakistan. The neighborhood where Sitar is located used to be the heart of the Indian community, but many left after the earthquake. Now there are reportedly only about a hundred Indian residents in Yokohama, compared to a thousand or so in Kobe.

"The majority of Indians here are from Sind," Mahtani says. "Indians tend to stick together with people from their own area and go where they have connections and can land jobs." There is even an Indian merchant association clubhouse where Hindu prayer services are held, although there is no formal language training for young Indians. "When I was small, I wasn't interested in the Indian language and culture, but now I am and wish I had preserved more of my heritage," he says.

On the life of a foreigner born in Japan, Mahtani admits, "The Japanese make you feel like a foreigner, no matter what you do, although I'm married to a Japanese and my lifestyle is pretty much like that of a Japanese, speaking Japanese at home and eating Japanese food."

"But as soon as you go outside, you're a foreigner," he adds philosophically.

• MAP 22-23

Then there's Kervan Saray, located two streets behind the Kenmin Hall (turn right at the next corner past the easy-to-spot Roma Station Italian restaurant, which is in the former home of an Indian family). It offers Turkish delights whipped up by its owner, who goes to Turkey nearly every year and claims Turkish food is one of the world's three greatest cuisines. You can even get cold lamb's brain and Turkish beer or anise-flavored wine to whet your romanticism as you feast your eyes on the artifacts gathered from the plains of Anatolia, including a Turkish dragoon's giant pistol. There are also a number of restaurants across from the Port Opening Square, including Sugi no Ki with good pizza and paella, chianti bottles hanging from the roof, and Mediterranean ambience. In the same building there's Scandia with, you guessed it, Scandinavian cuisine, and Mediterranean, run by a Greek man named Jimmy.

Continue past the Kenmin Hall and the Yokohama Hotel. Soon you will see the only commercial building that survived the earthquake intact, the two-story reinforced-concrete office of Butterfield and Swire trading company, British Building No. 7, that had just been completed the year before. One-third of the original structure remains today as the Toda Peace Memorial Hall, maintained by the Soka Gakkai religious organization. Our next stop is the queen of Yokohama's hostelries, the Hotel New Grand, an old Renaissance-style building that opened its doors in 1927. In its day, Yokohama's most famous hotel had many famous foreign visitors, including Charlie Chaplin, Babe Ruth, Douglas Fairbanks, Mary Pickford, Ronald Coleman, and General MacArthur. Osaragi Jiro wrote some of his most famous novels here in Room 318, which has a big glass window with a view of the harbor. For a touch of the old days, take a stroll down the carpeted central staircase in the classic old wing.

General MacArthur stayed here a few days before moving his headquarters, but the New Grand remained an Allied officer billet till July 5, 1952, the very end of the Occupation. Its truly international background is reflected in a slogan it used before the war: "The best of the West in the fascinating East." It was from here that Mac and his staff departed on the morning of September 2, 1945, for the *Missouri*

• MAP 22-23

to sign the armistice that finally brought the war to a close.

The new eighteen-story tower opened in July 1991, since the old building's sixty rooms clearly had to be supplemented. The president of the hotel is Hara Noriyuki, the adopted son of legendary artist and businessman Hara Tomitaro, who in turn was the adopted son of Meiji-period silk magnate Hara Zenzaburo.

Although it is often said that the Hotel New Grand is the lineal "descendant" of the Grand Hotel, this is simply not true, as the New Grand was established brand new by the city and wealthy private citizens as part of the Earthquake Recovery Project. In fact, no one is quite sure where the first hotel in Japan was. By 1866 a large number of small hotels, tent hotels, and grog shops, that no doubt slept a few, were already in operation in Yokohama. The first real hotel might have been the Club House Hotel, run by W. H. Smith, although it actually seems to have been something of a dormitory.

"Public-Spirited Smith," as he was generally known, was an ex-Royal Marine who played quite a part in the life of the little foreign community of Yokohama. He had much to do with the establishment of the Yokohama United Club, of which he was manager for many years, and the Grand Hotel, of which he was managing director. He introduced brickmaking and several other industries to Japan. He is also given credit for the introduction of market gardening.

In any event, at the time of the 1923 earthquake there were reportedly fourteen full-fledged hotels in the waterfront area, of which the Grand, built in 1873, was the largest. Since less than a half-dozen businesses had earthquake insurance, most, including the Grand Hotel, became insolvent after the disaster. Only then did earthquake-resistant buildings come into their own.

Returning to the early days, there is an account of how one occupant of a hotel for foreigners was nearly scared to death when a band of *ronin* entered but then quickly withdrew. Not only intruders caused alarm, but also much of the clientele. Margaretha Weppner, a German visitor to Yokohama, wrote that it was her misfortune "to see Man in the lowest state of depravity and degradation." She was referring to her fellow guests in the Grand Hotel.

• MAP 22-23

In her opinion, the foreign men who frequented Yokohama's hotels were nothing but violent, drunken, gambling, whoring louts who had a uniform "kind of idiotic state" acquired from total concern with "only what directly attracts the stomach and senses." It should be added that the fastidious Fräulein also believed that all of them had designs on her person.

As an aside, it's interesting to note that in the early *ukiyo-e* prints of Yokohama it is not unusual to find blacks represented. Local legend has it that the bartender at the Yokohama Hotel in the 1860s was black. That watering hole was noted for the clock above the door that was used for target practice by the customers. Nineteenth-century gentility. There was also a French-run hotel, since many French visitors refused to stay at the British-operated inns.

In the early days of the port, Britannia ruled the seas, and the British constituted by far the largest community of Westerners in Yokohama. It must have been a glorious sight from the Bluff watching a tea clipper like the *Cutty Sark* or a man-of-war parading through the waves into the harbor against a colorful backdrop of fishing nets, straw-thatched homes, forests, buckweat fields, and the godowns and hotels on the Bund. One English captain was moved to declare the sight "unsurpassed anywhere in the world." Incidentally, Bund was a word of Persian origin that in China and Japan came to refer to a shoreline embankment or quay. During the American Civil War, the British presence became even more predominant, although Dutch, Prussian, and other European ships were also usually to be seen in port.

The 1869 opening of the Suez Canal and the advent of more powerful steamships doomed the graceful ships of sail. The P&O Steamship Line established its Hong Kong–Yokohama route in 1864 and soon was serving Europe as well. The 155-day passage from London to Yokohama was admittedly very expensive, but it included all the beer and wine the passengers could handle. And from all indications they handled quite a bit. In any event, in the early 1860s regular steamship service to Shanghai was established, and a few years later regular cross-Pacific service was added.

Around the turn of the century ocean liners were two to three

• MAP 22-23

thousand tons in weight and more than a hundred meters long; they could not dock at the piers of Yokohama. Instead they anchored out at sea, and smaller ships carried the cargo and passengers to shore. It was only when the Shinko Futo (New Port Pier) was completed that large passenger and merchant vessels could dock easily.

Osanbashi Pier to the left was built between 1889 and 1894 and was called the British *hatoba*, or "elephant's trunk," because of its elongated, irregular shape. Small boats unloaded on the inside, while bigger ships anchored on the outside. The French *hatoba* was a bit farther down across from where the Marine Tower is today.

Japanese and foreigners alike tend to forget how poor Japan was just a few short decades ago and how millions of Japanese emigrated overseas in search of a better life. Yokohama was also the major port of embarkation for emigrants crossing the Pacific to North and South America. The first Japanese emigrant boat left for Guam on May 2, 1868, with forty-two Japanese emigrants abroad. At the height, tens of thousands of people, mostly poor, left here annually in search of a new life abroad. The last emigrant boat left in 1973, when 190 Japanese went to South America. I wonder how those crammed into the emigration ships in the 1920s must have felt gazing at the luxury ships berthed next to them. First-class fare to San Francisco on one of these floating palaces could have built a home in Japan.

The Shinko Pier was completed in 1916 and a mere seven years later was totally destroyed in the great earthquake. Crowds that had gathered on Osanbashi Pier to bid farewell to loved ones were thrown into the water when the wharf collapsed, and many were drowned. Imagine the feelings of those who witnessed this from shipboard.

The sensuous romance of one-kilometer-long Yamashita Park opposite the Hotel New Grand is something not soon to be forgotten, especially once you've seen summer fireworks reflected in the offing. Yamashita Park and Kaigan-dori, or Water Street, was the main entranceway to Japan. What a joy it must have been to first set foot onto Japanese soil in a park. Even Yokohama oldtimers constantly feel drawn back to Yamashita Park, and if one spot has to be named the spiritual heart of Yokohama, this is it. At the far left in the direction of

• MAP 22-23

Osanbashi Pier is a Moghul-style water tower monument in memory of Indians who died in the 1923 earthquake. Check out the beautiful mosaic ceiling with its Islamic design.

Right near it is the humorous *zangiri* statue in honor of Japan's first Western-style barbers, who naturally did their snipping in Yokohama. *Zangiri* refers to a uniform short cut. During the Meiji period there was a famous saying: "Knock a cropped head and you will hear the sound of civilization." Civilization must have resounded through the streets of early Yokohama. The first Western-style barbershop seems to have been the Hair Dressing and Shaving Salon that opened in the Yokohama Hotel in March 1864, although, as is the case with many "firsts," there are several rivals to the title.

And then there is the statue of the girl in red shoes, immortalized in a children's lullaby:

> Oh, little girl in red shoes,
> The foreigner has taken you away,
> You left from Yokohama harbor,
> The foreigner has taken you away.

The sad face on the statue that stares wistfully out to sea is definitely that of a Japanese youngster. Who then was Little Red Shoes, and who was the dastardly foreigner?

The park itself is a legacy of the great earthquake, designed as a dumping ground for the huge amount of rubble clogging the city. What a practical idea: build a grassy park to celebrate life on the desolate site of death and destruction! The gingko trees across from the Hotel New Grand, planted after the earthquake, have become a symbol of Yokohama, and the big sign of the hotel that lights up at night a Yokohama landmark.

Standing guard at the right of the waterfront is the 11621-ton, 163-meter-long *Hikawa Maru*, which was built in 1930 for the Seattle run, and became a naval hospital during the war. It was the only Japanese passenger ship to survive the war, and it returned to the Seattle route in 1953. It also carried food and coal from Hokkaido in the immediate postwar period and was therefore referred to as a *yamibune*, or black-market boat.

• MAP 22-23

Another of the services it performed over the years was the repatriation of many soldiers stranded abroad after Japan's defeat. Having crossed the Pacific 246 times, the *Hikawa Maru* is now permanently docked at Yamashita Park, where it serves as a museum. You can visit the state-room that Charlie Chaplin and foreign royalty used on their cruises to Japan. There is also a classy restaurant inside; if you are coming to eat you do not have to pay the admission fee. Beyond the *Hikawa Maru* is a pier from where you can catch a boat to cruise the bay in style.

In the immediate postwar period thousands of stevedores labored in Yokohama. Their lives were controlled by *oyabun*, or bosses, who were often affiliated with *yakuza* groups. These organized crime groups ruled the docks and decided who would work and when. Half-starved day laborers gathered at about 6:30 to sign up with the *oyabun*. The lucky ones engaged in backbreaking work all day for pocket change. Within twenty years everything had become highly mechanized. Little was left from the earlier days except the now-unemployed workers.

Just about the same time the *Hikawa Maru* was retired, the Port of Yokohama began shifting toward containerization. A ship that took a week to be unloaded before could now be dealt with in a single day.

Yokohama Bay Bridge

Yokohama's horrendous traffic congestion has been greatly relieved since the opening of the Bay Bridge, one of the largest bridges of its type in the world. At 860 meters long and 55 meters high, it is designed to let even the largest luxury liners go under. For those so inclined, the Bay Bridge may be crossed part way on foot via the Sky Walk—join the courting couples in summer when it's open until nine. As with nearly all novelties in Japan, you will have to pay for the privilege, however. A see-through elevator carries you up to the observation deck, where you begin your death-defying feat, inching down the 320 meters of the Sky Walk, that hangs like a papoose under the bridge, to the Sky Lounge.

Unfortunately, no bungee jumping is allowed, but you do get a spectacular view of Fuji-san, the Tanzawa Range and, of course, the boats put-putting down below that all seem so small. Sip a cup of coffee in the Sky Lounge, and enjoy the 360-degree view without exerting yourself. Buses run from Sakuragi-cho Station bound for Sky Walk スカイウォーク; get off at Sky Walk Mae, the last stop; the trip takes about thirty minutes. Blue Line buses from Yokohama Station also stop here (see page 44).

Bay Bridge Sky Walk

☎ 045-506-0500

🕐 9:00–21:00 April to October; 10:00–18:00 the other months; closed third Monday each month. ¥600

• MAP 22-23

More traffic caused more problems, however. So bad in fact that Honcho-dori came to be known as Container-kaido ("Container Highway") and in the late 1960s it took about forty minutes just to cover a couple of kilometers near Sakuragi-cho. Yokohama still has the worst road system of any of Japan's major cities, and more and more residents are demanding their own international airport, although it is hard to imagine where they would put it.

The 106-meter-tall Marine Tower across the road opened in 1961. For many years it was the only choice in town for a bird's-eye view of Yokohama, but it has a lot of competition now.

Port Square next door specializes in overpriced trinkets and food that will go down easy with suburban palates. On the fourth floor of the tower is the Kikai Jikake no Omocha-kan, which holds a unique collection of mechanical toys. On the first floor of the tower and also on the sixth floor of Takashimaya Department Store near Yokohama Station are Yokohama Goods Shops offering many kinds of goods with Yokohama historical motifs, including bandannas and tableware, which make perfect souvenirs.

If you enjoy having a unifomed doorman open the door for you when you are out shopping for socks and jockey shorts, you might want to drop in at Barneys New York, on the left-hand side of the street after you turn right at the corner just past the Marine Tower. The large numbers of visitors is proof positive that, despite the alleged economic hard times, the Japanese are as status conscious as ever. Depending on what your game is you might want to visit the special golf or lingerie corners.

At the Yokohama Doll Museum, across the bridge from Yamashita Park on the former site of the Grand Hotel, close to four hundred dolls from 120 countries live together in true international harmony. Most are dressed in traditional costumes. There is also a quaint doll theater. Many of the dolls were collected by Ono Hideko, a former guide for Mikimoto Pearls. In the gift shop are dolls and coasters made by volunteers depicting swaggering sailors, red-coated British soldiers, pigtailed Chinese, and Indians in loincloths.

If you retrace your steps to the main road in front of Yamashita Park, you can catch a bus to go back to Sakuragicho Station.

• MAP 22-23

Minato Mirai 21 Yokohama-kan (みなと
みらい21横浜館) ☎ 045-221-0511
Ⓗ 10:00–17:00; July 21–Aug. 31
10:00–18:00; closed Mon. Free

Yokohama Art Museum (Yokohama
Bijutsukan 横浜美術館) ☎ 045-221-0300
Ⓗ 10:00–18:00; closed Thurs., yearend.
¥900

Yokohama Maritime Museum 横浜マリタ
イムミュージアム ☎ 045-221-0280
Nippon Maru 日本丸
☎ 045-319-8888 Ⓗ 10:00–17:00 March–June;
July–Aug. 10:00–18:30; Sept.–Oct. 10:00–17:00;
Nov. to Feb. 10:00–16:30. ¥600 (museum
and ship included)

Cosmo World よこはまコスモワールド
☎ 045-221-0232 Ⓗ Tues.–Fri. 13:00–21:00;
weekends 11:00–22:00; summer and Christmas open every day and all night; Feb.–mid-
March closed Mon.; exceptions so call to
make sure. Pay by attraction

Broadcast Library 放送ライブラリー
☎ 045-223-2111 Ⓗ 10:00–17:00; summer
10:00–18:00; closed Mon.

Yokohama Archives of History (Kaiko
Shiryo-kan 横浜開港資料館) ☎ 045-201-
2100 Ⓗ 9:30–17:00; closed Mon. ¥200

Silk Museum (Shiruku Hakubutsukan シルク
博物館) ☎ 045-641-0841 Ⓗ 9:00–16:30;
closed Mon., New Year. ¥300

Kanagawa International Association Library
☎ 045-671-7070 Ⓗ 10:00–18:00; Sat.
10:00–17:00; closed Sun.

Hikawa Maru 氷川丸 ☎ 045-641-4361
Ⓗ 9:30–20:00; on weekends 9:30–21:00;
open all year. ¥700

Marine Tower マリンタワー
☎ 045-641-7838 Ⓗ 10:00–20:00; in summer 10:00–21:00; in winter 10:00–18:00;
open all year. ¥700 (to observatory)

Kikai Jikake no Omocha-kan 機械じかけ
のおもちゃ館 ☎ 045-641-7838
Ⓗ 10:00–21:00; varies somewhat by season; closed seven days a year. ¥200

Yokohama Doll Museum (Yokohama
Ningyo no Ie 横浜人形の家) ☎ 045-671-

9361 Ⓗ 10:00–17:00; July and Aug.
10:00–19:00; closed Mon., yearend. ¥300

Cruise Information
☎ 045-671-7719 (Port Service)
Marine Shuttle—3 courses: 40 minutes (bay
area) ¥750; 60 minutes (bay and Bay
Bridge) ¥1,200; 90 minutes (bay, MM21,
open sea) ¥2,000. Cafe-bar; dinner reservations can be made.
Marine Rouge—90-minute lunch cruises
and 120-minute cruises from ¥2,500; dinner extra.

Blue Line Bus Information
☎ 045-671-3195
Blue Line buses leave every 40 minutes
between 9:35 and 17:30 (on weekends
and hols. every 30 mins.) from the east
exit of Yokohama Station, stopping at
Yokohama Art Museum, Sakuragicho Station, Kencho-mae (prefectural offices), Chinatown, Motomachi, Harbor View Park,
and Bay Bridge. An alternative route also
takes in Honmoku, Yokohama Doll
Museum, Yamashita Park, Osanbashi
Pier, Basha-michi, and Isezaki-cho.

One ride is ¥270 (¥250 if you don't go
to the Bay Bridge); buy a ¥600 ticket and
you can get on and off as often as you like.

Sitar シタール ☎ 045-641-1496
Ⓗ 11:30–14:00, 17:00–21:30; Sun.
12:00–21:00; open all year

Kervan Saray キャラバンサライ
☎ 045-664-4387 Ⓗ 11:30–21:00; closed
Mon.

Roma Station ローマステーション
☎ 045-681-1818 Ⓗ 11:30–22:30; Sun.
12:00–21:30; open all year

Scandia スカンディヤ
☎ 045-201-2262 Ⓗ 11:00–24:00; Sun.
17:00–24:00; open all year

Sugi no Ki 杉の木 ☎ 045-212-4143
Ⓗ 11:45–22:00; open all year

Mediterranean ☎ 045-212-5954
Ⓗ 11:30–14:00, 5:00–02:00; Sat., Sun.
17:00–02:00; very occasionally closed

• MAP 22-23

2

The Heart of Hama

○ Sakuragicho Station 桜木町駅 (JR Negishi and Tokyu Toyoko lines)—Basha-michi 馬車道—Port Opening Hall 開港記念館—Yokohama Park 横浜公園—Kannai 関内

Sakuragicho Station is the start for this walk that explores the heart of the old foreign settlement area, where numerous Western inventions were first introduced to Japan and which remains to this day the commercial center of Yokohama.

The station has seen a lot of history in its own right. In 1951 a train caught on fire while stopped at Sakuragicho Station. People struggled in vain to get out of the windows, but before they could be rescued 106 burned to death. Somehow tragedies like this seem to be scarier and closer to home than the mass destruction wrought by war or a mammoth natural disaster.

Come out the exit away from MM21, turn left, and go past the railway monument. Go under the bridge and then cross the Ooka-gawa River over the Oe-bashi Bridge. You're now entering what was the Japanese portion of the settlement. The area is not that large, so the best strategy is to walk up and down each north-south street within the parameters set by this street and Honcho-dori, making sure to check out the side streets, where there are a lot of delightful little surprises.

Our first destination is the Yokohama Shiro Kyokai, named after Shiloh of biblical fame. Dr. Hepburn preached at the forerunner of this present building, which was built in 1926 in an early French baroque style influenced by Notre Dame Cathedral. Cross the street and turn

• MAP 22-23

left after the Nihon Seimei Building. On weekdays these streets are bustling with office workers, but on the weekends they're half-deserted.

After walking about eight blocks, you'll see a huge, stone building in classic Baroque style in front of you on the right. This is the Kanagawa Prefectural Museum, completed in 1904 after five years of construction as the headquarters for the Yokohama Specie Bank. This institution was closely associated with the government and helped finance Japanese expansion on the Asian continent. After the war, it was privatized at Occupation order and transformed into the Bank of Tokyo. It is as solid-looking as the bankers of the Gilded Age. Note the ornate decorations on the outside. Part of the massive dome was burned away following the 1923 earthquake, but otherwise it was miraculously unscathed. In 1967 the building was made into a museum with 160,000 items on display, including impressive collections of Buddhist statuary and local history and folklore.

Visitors can also learn about the *makuzuyaki* style of porcelain that was introduced to Yokohama by the Kyoto potter Miyakawa Gozan, who opened a kiln in the hills south of the city center. His innovative style, which incorporated motifs showing daily life in the port, made a big hit at exhibitions around the world. The tradition has all but died out, however. Also, have a look at the works of Goseda Yoshimatsu, a Yokohama-based Meiji-period Western-style painter who reportedly was the first Japanese painter to be welcomed into the Paris salons, and paintings by the famed cartoonist Charles Wirgman. Both capture the atmosphere of early Yokohama.

The building, an Important Cultural Property, has been undergoing major refurbishing and is scheduled to reopen in March 1995.

Next to the museum is the three-story Dowa Kasai Building (the former Yokohama Branch of Kawasaki Bank), built in 1922 and beautifully restored in 1989 when upper modern stories were added like icing to a vintage birthday cake. This excellent example of the German Renaissance style was designed by Matakichi Yabe, a Yokohama native who studied in Germany as well as under Tsumaki Yorinaka, the architect of the Prefectural Museum. Also, check out the quirky architecture of the Yokohama Bankers Club (Yokohama Ginko Kyokai 横浜銀行協会)

• MAP 22-23

on Honcho-dori. This was Main Street when Yokohama was young, and most of the major foreign firms and banks were concentrated here. Benten-dori, which linked up with Honcho-dori, was where the big Japanese silk merchants had their offices and souvenir shops sought to entice foreigners.

Head back toward the Negishi Line along the street that reaches a dead end in front of the museum. About five blocks down on the right is Bashamichi Jubankan, a classic wood-paneled restaurant that serves French food. It has a bakery and coffee shop on the first floor, a bar on the second floor, and an elegant dining-room on the third floor.

The Red Boat

On the left near Bashamichi Jubankan, you'll find the Akafune Sex Drug Store. You can't miss it. Look for the sleek, black-glass front and a sign that reads, "Instruments, advice, medicine, and sex problem." Akafune (Red Boat) was Japan's first pharmacy devoted solely to the treatment of sexual disorders. Significantly, it opened in 1929, the year of the Big Crash. Besides selling various medicines, prophylactics, and pick-me-up tonics (try the *aka mamushi* snake drink), it is also a bit of a mini-museum with displays in exotic wooden cabinets of various paraphernalia, including antique French letters, Kama Sutra statues, and other fascinating tools of the trade. Note the suggestively shaped shellfish in formaldehyde solution—unfortunately not much of a morale booster since they're badly deteriorated. However, the explanatory signs are classic and are to be savored.

The founder, who made the displays and signs, died in 1993 at the ripe old age of eighty-seven, but his family is carrying on the tradition and the lore he passed on to them. According to his grandson, one day in late 1945 when the founder was in his shop, which had miraculously survived the war, he was astonished to see several jeeps stop in front of the door and giant MPs line up on both sides of it. Then lo and behold, the white shogun himself, General MacArthur, came strutting in. (The grandson was not sure whether he had been puffing on his famous corncob pipe or not.) As the grandfather liked to tell it, the general seemed flabbergasted that the Japanese could be peddling sex drugs amidst the ruins of the war. Mac lingered inside the tiny shop for about thirty minutes, scrutinizing the displays and merchandise. He did not utter a word until he was ready to leave, when he said "Carry on" to the store's owner.

In any event, the shop never had any trouble with the military police. MacArthur might have been a bit of a stickler, but he apparently was no prude. The rate of venereal disease among his troops might have had something to do with it. Akafune's clientele in the early postwar days consisted almost entirely of GIs, with an occasional merchant seaman. "Even then, just after the war, Japanese rubber had an excellent reputation," reports the third-generation purveyor of aphrodisiacs with obvious pride. These days, however, the customers are almost all Japanese.

• MAP 22-23

Note the old-time phone booth in front of Bashamichi Jubankan; makes you want to call your granny. The water trough next to it was erected by Japan's first animal protection society as a rest spot for horses and cattle. From here go one block over to the right to Basha-michi (Horse Carriage Road), which ran from Yoshida-bashi Bridge, the main entrance to the settlement, to Honcho-dori. This eighteen-meter-wide thoroughfare opened in March 1867 and was the modern showpiece of the Japanese quarter, lined with brick buildings and always bustling with horse and carriage traffic and the odd palanquin. There were no rubber wheels in those days, only wooden and steel rims, so the noise must have been nerve-shattering. A carriage service operated by entrepreneurs from Australia ran twice a day between Yoshida-bashi and Nihon-bashi in Edo, the trip taking about four hours.

The *jinrikisha* came into common use in the 1870s, although no one seems quite sure of its origins and there are several, probably apoc-ryphal, stories. Tourists came to adore the rickshaw boys, who, in addi-tion to guiding them, attended to their smallest needs, even cooking for them.

Everything possible is being done in Yokohama to recreate the feel of the early days. The colorful tiles in the sidewalk represent scenes and objects from the port opening days and antique phones and gas lamps (you can see an original one in front of Kannai Hall) add to the retro effect. One thing that is missing from those days is the primitive public toilets. In 1871, in response to constant requests from the for-eign residents, officials erected public privies on eighty-three corners. Nevertheless, the first modern sewer system had to wait until 1887.

Sumitaro on Basha-michi is the oldest traditional Japanese sweet shop in Yokohoma. The founder was an Edo confectionery maker on his way to Kansai to try his luck there when he heard about the port opening. Well known for its mammoth chestnut treats, Sumitaro also has a coffee shop attached in case you want to try on the spot.

There are many interesting businesses in this area. The Toho Geki-jo in Basha-michi, affectionately known as Yokoho, opened in 1935. It was only one of the dozens of movie theaters in those days. Sho Boys (the character for Sho is *warau* or laugh) puts on an all-boys show from

• MAP 22-23

around 2:00 A.M. or whenever the clientele is judged worked up enough for one. Shinanoya, a tailor and purveyor of men's fancy goods and ladies' wear, first threw open its doors in 1866. On a side street is Samovar, which has a hundred kinds of blended teas; it is located around the corner from the photography memorial that is shaped like a vintage camera.

No one is quite sure who was the first commercial photographer to begin operations in Yokohama. Circumstantial evidence suggests it might have been the sundries merchant Raphael Schoyer, who turned part of his shop into a photo studio. W. Saunders apparently operated the first photography studio, while the first Japanese professional photographer appears to have been Shimooka Renjo. After serving his apprenticeship under foreigners, Shimooka opened his own shop, which was cheaper than those of foreigners. He converted to Christianity and seems to have had numerous foreign contacts.

But probably the most influential photographer of the early days was Felix Beato, a British citizen born in Venice, Italy, who had covered the Crimean War, the Sepoy Revolt in India, and the Arrow Incident in China, before arriving in Japan in 1863. His photos of Bakamatsu Japan, including some of the heads of executed criminals on display next to major roads, are some of the most evocative taken of the country in the twilight of feudalism.

Aisukirin

Toward the harbor on the right side of Basha-michi, you'll find the Taiyo no Boshizo, or "mother-and-child in the sun" statue, which marks the site of the first ice cream parlor begun by Richard Risley in 1865 with imported ice. One serving of *aisukirin* cost the equivalent of ¥8,000 in today's prices, or roughly half a month's salary for the common man, even though its consistency and taste were more like sherbet than ice cream as we know it today.

At first the Japanese gathered to gawk at the Westerners eating the strange concoction. Some braver souls gave it a try, but on more than one occasion when a customer discovered that the cool treat was made from cow discharge, he or she rushed outside and vomited violently. In 1869 Machida Fusazo opened the first Japanese ice cream parlor. A local company has reproduced a close replica of these early ice creams based on original recipes. Bashamichi Aisu, as it is known, is available in four flavors at Aioi Coffee Shop as well as at Sogo Department Store and the shop at the Marine Tower.

Aioi Coffee Shop 相生本店 ☎ 045-681-1661 ⊕ 9:00–21:00; closed 3rd Mon.

• MAP 22-23

Spanish food, including garlic soup, can be enjoyed in a rural Iberian atmosphere to the accompaniment of a flamenco guitarist at Casa de Fujimori. Across the street is a Spanish-style pub, Bar Espanol, that offers tapas and other snacks. For traditional Yokohama food try Tenkichi in front of Kannai Station, a restaurant founded in 1873 and now operated by fifth-generation owners, that offers high-quality *tempura* and other fried dishes. Some recipes date from post-earthquake days when the owners had to make do with whatever they could get; the frying oil used combines six parts sesame oil with four parts peanut oil.

A plaque marking the founding of Yokohama's first fish market can be seen near City Hall outside Kannai Station, across from the public restrooms. At first both Japanese and foreigners were fascinated by each other's "barbaric" dietary habits. The first Western restaurant, the Suehirocho Kaiyotei, opened in 1869 to cater to Western tastes. Initially, the government had to make strenuous efforts to convince the Japanese public that they should be eating blood-dripping beef (Buddha forbid!) and drinking milk for the sake of enlightenment and civilization. Early Western diarists invariably noted that there were a lot of monkeys around and that they showed up in the local food markets. The meat-gorging foreigners were disgusted by the uncanny likeness to human beings these primates had. No doubt the Western hunters who were devastating the wildlife of Kanagawa also found the methods of the trappers unsporting—Japanese hunters were wont to leave a platter of saké in the wild for the simians to get drunk on and pass out.

Where Minato O-dori meets Honcho-dori you will find perhaps the most beautiful building in Yokohama, the Port Opening Hall, or simply "Jack," as it has been known to generations of sailors and sailors' friends. Bands of white granite across the red-brick exterior of the Neo-Renaissance building create a soothing atmosphere, and its clock tower, with a clock on each face, has become a symbol of Yokohama. The designers were Yamada Shichiro and Sato Shiro, disciples of Tatsuno Kingo, who in turn was a disciple of the English architect Josiah Conder, a prolific designer who had an enormous impact on Meiji architecture in Japan. Jack went up only six years prior to the great earthquake, during which the outside held up well, although the

• MAP 22-23

interior was demolished. It was used as a dormitory for female personnel by the U.S. military during the Occupation; today it is a public hall. Ask at the public affairs office to see the beautiful stained-glass windows on the second floor and the theater. Note that the building is closed on Mondays.

To the left of the stairway at the front entrance of the building is a monument marking the site of the Yokohama Chokai-jo, which served as Yokohama's first administrative office from the beginning of the Meiji period in 1868 to 1889, when Yokohama became a municipality. Across from here is a bronze relief indicating the birthplace of Okakura Tenshin (1862–1913), who played an enormous role in popularizing Japanese philosophy and art abroad through influential books such as *The Book of Tea*. Tenshin's father was a retainer of the Fukui clan, managing Ishikawa-ya here from 1859 to 1868, a major silk dealership for the clan. Friendships with the American art lover Ernest Fenellosa and several of modern Japan's most important artists sparked Okakura's interest in East Asian classical arts and aesthetics. He went on to found the Tokyo Fine Arts School and hold top positions with both the Tokyo Imperial Museum and the Boston Museum.

As a rule the buildings in Yokohama were designed by Western architects and built by Japanese contractors. There was one area where Japanese officials took the initiative, however—the Miyozaki brothel district that stood in the area where Yokohama Stadium and Yokohama Park are today. This was originally a swamp, whose only claim to fame was the Kompira Shrine. In this uninviting environment the shogunate built a wonderland of enjoyment and sin on an artificial island that was surrounded by a moat and linked to the mainland by one guarded causeway with a drawbridge. Miyozaki-cho opened for business in November 1859. The obvious intention was to recreate Edo's famous Yoshiwara, which had been established under similar conditions.

Prominent brothel-keepers were brought in from Edo and Kyoto to run things. The big cheese among the whoremongers was Hatagoya (Sato) Sakichi, who ran the Gankiya in the Shinagawa district of Edo. In Miyozaki-cho he built the opulent Gankiro, known to the British as the Crystal Palace and to the Americans as the Grand Cairo. The incomparable

• MAP 22-23

Gankiro was equipped with crystal chandeliers, ponds stocked with carp, and gushing fountains. There was a three-story, Western-style building for Western customers and a two-story, Japanese-style house for the Japanese. The girls were assigned to one or the other, the better-looking ones ending up in the Japanese house, it would seem, if the complaints of foreigners are anything to go by.

The tariffs at the Gankiro were several times those in Edo. The easy money and easy morals of early Yokohama ensured that the overwhelmingly male population would be knocking at the doors no matter what the prices. At its height, Miyozaki-cho, also known as Kozaki-cho, or simply Yoshiwara, had eighteen high-class brothels, about eighty-five more plebeian ones, and as many as 1,400 women who lived the lives of slaves, forbidden to leave the quarter except under the most exceptional circumstances. In addition to the elegant brothels, the quarter also contained tea houses, geisha houses, and other amenities.

Several hundred prostitutes were soon offering their services on everything from an hourly to a monthly basis. Freelancers, known as *jigoku* (literally hell) or *teppo* (guns), lurked in the shadows outside the quarter, seeking to avoid the police and make a living. Their customers often got more than they bargained for, and even stodgy diplomatic representatives were soon grousing that their staff was riddled with pox. A doctor who regularly inspected British troops wrote, "It is a perfect nuisance to have such an amount of disgusting disease to treat, but it is only just to the men to say that they treat it as the most natural thing in the world, and neither see the shame nor disgust of it."

Sakichi apparently was very hip to the business promotion techniques of the day. For one thing, he distributed publicity hand-towels that read, "This place is designed for the pleasure of foreigners." Crowds of curiosity-seekers from all over the Kanto area flocked to the Gankiro, also known as the Ryugu-jo, or Dragon Palace Castle, even in the daytime and paid to see the premises and take home some of its famous sweets as a souvenir. Among these tourists were *ukiyo-e* artists who later portrayed the foreigners eating, drinking, or playing strip poker with the girls. Perhaps this open lewdness is what provoked Edward de Fonblanque to write, "The Japanese are depraved, sensual,

• MAP 22-23

and obscene in every sense. The men of all classes from the first *daimyo* in the land to the meanest of his retainers delight in contemplating human nature in its most animal form."

Especially shocking to Western sensibilities was the display of the lower-class harlots in cages. These were the barred fronts to the houses, where the girls sat and occasionally called out to customers, while maintaining a hopeless calm or immovable and strenuous indifference. Then there was the heartbreaking sight of the little ones brought up from birth in the profession. The Swiss diplomat Aimé Humbert could not hide his outrage: "The greatest curiosity of the Gankiro is its children's theater ... operettas, little fairy pieces, and costume ballets are executed by these children with infinite grace and dexterity... The sight only supplies an additional protest against these horrible institutions."

Some of the inmates simply could not take it and escaped the *kukai* or world of pain by drowning themselves in the moat. At O-bon time (All Soul's Day) Buddhist priests held services in boats and made offerings of fruit, wine, and money to the souls of these unfortunates.

The Tragedy of Kiyu

The most famous story about Miyozaki-cho concerns a beautiful prostitute at the Gankiro called Kiyu, who catered to Japanese clientele. She caught the attention of a French arms merchant who went by the American-style pseudonym Abbot, reportedly because Americans were more popular among the girls. Abbot had a voracious appetite for flesh, but was dissatisfied with the slim pickings offered foreigners and became enamored with Kiyu. He insisted to Japanese officials that she become his, thundering that he should be accorded special treatment because he was such an important go-between working with the shogunate and the French government.

The brothel-keeper approached Kiyu, but she flatly refused to have anything to do with the hirsute foreigner. Complicat-

ing the situation was the fact that her physician father was of the "Expel the Barbarians" persuasion—because of his involvement in a murderous attack on the British Legation in Edo he had been forced to give up his profession. In fact, this had been the reason why his only daughter had been forced to sell herself into a life of shame. Kiyu continued to refuse and when she was finally ordered by the magistrates to submit, she committed *seppuku* like a samurai, with the brothel-keeper administering the *coup de grace* with a short sword to the throat.

The tragic story of Kiyu and her escape from a fate worse than death became popular with *ukiyo-e* artists and playwrights. Kiyu was frequently depicted in woodblock prints along with the *rashamen*, the paid mistresses of foreigners.

• MAP 22-23

The overthrow of the Tokugawa system in 1868 plunged many former shogunal retainers into abject poverty, and some of their daughters became *oiran*, or high-class prostitutes. They did not find their way to Miyozaki-cho, however, because the area was completely destroyed by the great fire of November 26, 1866. Since this conflagration started at the Tetsugoro-ya butcher shop near the quarter, it came to be known as the Pig-pen Fire. The holocaust lasted from eight in the morning till ten at night, leveling two-thirds of Kannai and most of the foreign merchant establishments along the waterfront.

Miyozaki-cho was the hardest-hit neighborhood, however, since the obstacles set up to prevent the prostitutes from running away from their owners also prevented them from escaping. As a result, over four hundred of these flesh slaves burned to death, some leaping from the towers of the brothels with their silk kimono alight, as foreigners and Japanese alike strove vainly to get to them in time and a fascinated crowd watched the fugitives, customers, and courtesans alike trying to rush en masse across the single ramshackle bridge that sagged under their weight.

Ernest Satow later wrote, "I saw a few poor wretches plunge into the water in order to escape, but they failed to reach the nearer bank. It was a fearful sight to see flames darting among the roofs of the houses on the causeway and sending forth jets here and there where the fire had not yet attained full mastery, when suddenly one half of the street nearest blazed up with a tremendous flash and a volume of black smoke arose which obscured the sky."

There was a volunteer fire corps but fire equipment was practically useless and the fire had to burn itself out. In fact they were hampered in their efforts by British troops landed from the ships in the harbor. Some of the redcoats behaved disgracefully, Satow complained. They had managed to get hold of liquor and stood by drinking and jeering, while civilians did the work they had been brought down to perform.

In the end one-quarter of the foreign settlement and one-third of the Japanese town burned to the ground. However, the phoenix that emerged from the ashes was not another boomtown of clapboard houses and narrow streets, but rather one of the most beautiful port cities in the world, with wide boulevards and handsome brick and

• MAP 22-23

stone buildings in Italian Neo-Renaissance and other styles. New fire regulations also required that structures in the Japanese quarter be built with brick and limestone and have tiled roofs.

After the fire the brothels and inns were moved farther afield, and in 1877 the municipal government turned the area into a park at the request of foreign consuls. It was dubbed Higa Koen ("Theirs and Ours Park"), since it was open to both foreigners and Japanese. Later it became simply Yokohama Park, making history in several ways. Although it was not Japan's first Western-style park (contrary to the plaque in it, that honor belongs to Yamate Park), it sported the nation's first cricket field, and in 1896 it became the site of the first international baseball game, won by the Japanese. Babe Ruth and Lou Gehrig played here in 1934, and it was called Lou Gehrig Stadium during the Occupation. This was also where Japan's first May Day demonstration took place in 1920—rice riots in 1918 had already set the mood.

Tradition has it that all who managed to make their way to the park during the 1923 earthquake survived. Although the area was a sea of mud due to the rupture of water pipes, it proved to be a sea of life. Today Yokohama Park is an urban oasis only a few minutes' walk from Kannai Station, boasting many trees, although they are dwarfed by Yokohama Stadium, which occupies over 80 percent of the park.

As part of an agreement made between the foreign representatives and the magistrates after the 1866 fire, there were to be three major thoroughfares each sixty feet wide (approximately eighteen meters), namely Basha-michi, Kaigan-dori (the Bund), and a street stretching from Yoshida-bashi to Nishino-hashi, as well as a central avenue 120 feet wide to separate the Japanese and foreign communities and serve as a fire break. Although the last, Nihon-dori, did not end up that wide, it is still the city's most sprawling boulevard and along or near it are located several interesting buildings: parts of the original Yokohama headquarters of Mitsui, built in 1911 and the city's first ferroconcrete building, and the Roa Bank Building on Honcho-dori, built about 1921, now an annex of Keiyu Hospital. Other interesting buildings are the City Bank, built in 1929, and the Showa Shell Sekiyu Building across the street, designed by the Czech architects A. Raymond and B. Feuerstein.

• MAP 22-23

An interesting find is the friendly Mission to Seamen's Flying Angels Club across the road from Yokohama Park on the third floor. For years it has been a haven for merchant seamen stopping over in Yokohama. However, landlubbers are more than welcome. Have a game of darts or pool or lounge in comfortable armchairs with a long drink. This is a good spot to rest your legs and plot your strategy for the rest of the walk. For truly sick individuals there is American Flashback '70s, a pub featuring music from the seventies near the Mission. And you thought you'd heard the last of the Bee-Gees, Abba, and the loathsome Osmond clan.

There are plenty of dining possibilities in this area: Original Joe's is an Italian joint near Casa de Fujimori, Katsuretsuan serves *tonkatsu* (fried cutlets) and other fried dishes with a secret sauce made with over twenty vegetables, near Bashamichi Jubankan. To get a feel for Yokohama in the days of the Occupation, hang out at the retro diner, Star Shokudo, opposite the YMCA near Yokohama Stadium, which is decked out with lots of nostalgic goods from America and Japan in the fifties.

From here it's a short hop over to Chinatown (page 57) or to the Yamashita Park area (page 40). Otherwise, head back to Kannai Station.

Kanagawa Prefectural Museum
(Kanagawa Kenritsu Hakubutsukan 神奈川県立博物館) ☎ 045-201-0926. Due to reopen at end of March 1995.

Bashamichi Jubankan 馬車道十番館
☎ 045-651-2621 ⏰ 11:00–22:00; open all year

Sumitaro 住田楼
☎ 045-681-3101 ⏰ 9:00–18:00; Sun., hols. 10:00–17:00; no fixed hols.

Sho Boys ☎ 045-201-4633
⏰ 22:00–06:00; closed Sun.

Samovar サモアール ☎ 045-201-7175
⏰ 11:00–22:00; open all year

Casa de Fujimori カサ デ フジモリ
☎ 045-662-9474 ⏰ 11:00–23:00; Sun., hols. 12:00–21:30; open all year

Bar Espanol バール エスパニョール
☎ 045-651-1074 ⏰ 11:30–14:00, 17:00–22:00; closed Sun.

Tenkichi 天吉
☎ 045-681-2220 ⏰ 11:00–14:30, 17:00–21:00; Sat. 11:00–21:00; Sun, hols. 11:00–20:00; closed 2nd and 4th Fri.

Flying Angels Club ☎ 045-662-1871
⏰ 11:00–23:00; open all year

American Flashback '70s
☎ 045-651-9051 ⏰ 17:30–04:00; Sun. 17:30–02:00; open all year

Original Joe's ☎ 045-651-2315 ⏰ 11:30–24:00; Sun. 5:00–22:00; closed 3rd Mon.

Katsuretsuan 勝烈庵 ☎ 045-681-4411
⏰ 11:00–21:00; open all year

Star Shokudo スター食堂
☎ 045-661-0188 ⏰ 11:30–14:00, 17:00–22:00; Sat., hols. 17:00–22:00; Sun. 15:30–21:00; open all year

• MAP 22-23

3

Way Down in Chinatown

◐ Ishikawacho Station 石川町駅 (JR Negishi Line)

No people (except the Japanese, of course) has played a more prominent part in the development of Yokohama than the Chinese, although in standard accounts they are usually only mentioned in passing. Commodore Perry, for example, had a Chinese scribe named Luo Sen in his 1854 expedition and Chinese compradors and technical experts arrived from Canton and Shanghai along with the first European merchants. They were indispensable, first of all, because of the language barrier, which, with the exception of bureaucratic obstructionism, was the biggest obstacle to commerce. Chinese could communicate with the Japanese by writing things down in Chinese characters.

However, since the Qing Empire and Japan did not sign a treaty until 1871, they had no legal basis for residence at first and were under the joint control of the Japanese magistrates and foreign diplomatic corps. A racket naturally developed in which Westerners were paid to sponsor illegal Chinese immigrants as their servants. Chinese were in fact preferred as cooks or menials, in part because of the reputation of the Japanese as being notoriously dishonest. This reputation may not have been entirely unwarranted. Not only did many Japanese bitterly resent the foreigners being around to begin with, native criminals also gravitated to Yokohama, teaming up with the Chinese to run contraband and operate illicit gambling dens in Chinatown. Gradually, however, Japanese began to fill these positions, partly because the Chinese were eager to start their own businesses.

• MAP 70

All the major Western trading houses had Chinese compradors, who were the treasurers of the firms they worked for. It was they who established the exchange rates and commodity prices and controlled the essential day-to-day money-changing and brokerage activities. They were the oil that made the Japan trade function smoothly. An 1864 *Illustrated London News* drawing by Charles Wirgman proves the point in his depiction of Chinese clerks zealously counting the loot handed to the British by shogunate officials as reparations for the Richardson affair. Jardine's comprador, Ho Kon, was for half a century from 1869 the most important person in that hong after the British taipan himself. He and most of his large extended family were wiped out by the earthquake.

The compradors, known locally as *kampu* or *kanpeita,* squeezed their masters out of principle but the Japanese for pleasure. As early as 1700, the Dutch visitor, Christopher Fryke, observed the interaction between the Chinese and Japanese at Nagasaki, writing, "There is a certain antipathy between them and the Chinese, they cannot bear one another." Incidentally, it is often inaccurately stated that Japan was isolated for nearly two and a half centuries during the Tokugawa period, with the exception of the Dutch trading post at Nagasaki. Actually, a Chinese trading post continued to operate at Nagasaki as well and Yi Korea sent periodic diplomatic missions to Edo that also engaged in trade.

The effects of the cataclysmic Taiping Rebellion, estimated by some historians to have cost up to forty million lives, and extreme poverty caused many Cantonese to emigrate to Japan in search of a better life. Chinese tradesmen specialized in services for the Westerners, working as tailors, barbers, shoemakers, suppliers of furniture, and so on. It was only decades later, around 1900, that they got into the restaurant business, the field for which they are best known today.

In the 1880s many Chinese started exporting seafood and other Japanese products to China and importing herbal medicines from China and sugar from Taiwan. It was only four days by sea to the China coast and soon an extensive Chinese trade network had developed, closely linking the treaty ports in Japan with ports in China and Southeast Asia. This was reflected by the fact that in 1898 alone

• MAP 70

twenty businesses went bankrupt in Yokohama Chinatown because of violent price fluctuations on the Hong Kong rice market.

The area that became Chinatown, first called Tojin-gai, then in the Taisho period Nankin-gai, and finally in the postwar period Chuka-gai, was one of the last in the central area to be reclaimed. It opened in 1863 and by 1871 the Chinese had their own temple, the Kuan Ti Miao, and soon after a theater for performance of Chinese opera and other dramatic arts. By 1872 there were reportedly nearly one thousand Chinese in Yokohama living in 130 houses there, around 60 percent of all Chinese in Japan. In 1880 they accounted for perhaps two-thirds of the three-thousand-strong resident foreigner population in the city.

The *Maria Luz* Incident

The celebrated *Maria Luz* Incident of 1872 did much to improve ties between the Chinese and Japanese communities. On the evening of July 9 the 350-ton Peruvian *Maria Luz* entered Yokohama's harbor carrying a cargo of 229 indentured Chinese laborers from Macao to South America. It had a broken mast that required repair. On the fifth night after arrival a Chinese swam to a nearby British warship and told its officers that he and his comrades were being treated as virtual slaves. He added that he would rather die than be returned to the ship. The British turned the man over to the Kanagawa magistrates, who turned him over to the captain of the *Maria Luz*.

All might have been swept under the rug like this except that two weeks later another Chinese escaped and claimed that the first fugitive had been beaten within an inch of his life. British and U.S. diplomats requested that the Japanese take action, but the authorities were in a quandary because they had no diplomatic relations with Peru. Slavery had been outlawed by Western countries, but most foreigners in Yokohama opposed letting the Japanese interfere with their business.

A special court was convened at the urging of Oe Taku, a progressive official, who ordered the ship to be impounded. A sensational trial followed in which the court ordered the laborers to be freed. They sailed home shortly after. The government of Peru protested, but arbitration by the Russian Czar ultimately supported the Japanese decision.

There was a good deal of good theater during the trial. At one point the British defense attorney for the ship's captain provoked an uproar when he alleged that slavery existed in Japan since girls were sold to geisha houses. Oe penned a decree declaring white-slavery contracts illegal in Kanagawa and that all the girls should be freed without having to pay compensation. It had no real impact since social norms usually are stronger than law, but the Solomon-like reasoning is worth quoting: "Prostitutes and singing girls have lost the rights as human beings. They may be likened to cattle. There is no sense for human beings to endeavor to exact repayment from cattle! Therefore no repayment shall be demanded from prostitutes or singing girls for any money lent or debts due."

• MAP 70

Although at first a majority of the small businesses in Yokohama were run by foreigners, small Japanese merchants soon began supplanting them and by the 1880s not even the large Western firms could just sit back and reap windfall profits. The Chinese, however, generally managed to hold their own. As Lafcadio Hearn put it, "The Japanese have been learning wonderfully well, nearly as well as the Chinese."

The indomitable Victorian traveler Isabella Bird leaves a vivid impression of the Chinese she saw at Yokohama: "If they were suddenly removed, business would come to an abrupt halt. Here, as everywhere, the Chinese immigrant is making himself indispensable ... His face is very yellow, his long dark eyes and eyebrows slope upwards towards his temples, he has not the vestige of a beard, and his skin is shiny. He looks thoroughly well-to-do. He is not unpleasant-looking, but you feel that as a Celestial he looks down upon you."

There was a great deal of movement back and forth between Yokohama and the continent. When the Sino-Japanese War broke out in 1894, the Chinese population dropped by about half, to 1,800; likewise after the 1911 Revolution it dropped from 6,200 to 4,200. Chinatown also became a hotbed for Asian radicals. Among them were Chinese reformers Kang Youwei and Liang Qichao and revolutionaries Sun Yat-sen and Chiang Kai-shek. Phan Boi Chau from Vietnam and Dr. Jose Rizal of the Philippines also sought refuge from oppressive governments here and arms to carry on their revolution. They received support from Japanese radicals like Miyazaki Toten. The Japanese government was at first wary of them and later became downright antagonistic once it had committed itself to the path of imperialism.

Sun had a firm belief in the tenet, "The *Huaqiao* (Overseas Chinese community) is the mother of revolution." The father of the Chinese Revolution came to Japan eleven times in all after 1895. The first time he landed secretly on the coast south of Yokohama and was smuggled into Chinatown incognito. Yokohama quickly became one of his bases for plotting and fundraising among Overseas Chinese. At first he lived with the family of a printer near where the Keiyu Hospital stands today behind the Trade Center (Sangyo Boeki Center).

The Qing had put a 1,000 yuan price on Sun's head, Chinese and

• MAP 70

Japanese government agents kept him under constant surveillance, and professional assassins were reportedly on his trail. The Qing wanted him so badly that they no doubt would have given him a 1,001 cuts treatment rather than the usual 1,000 slices. In 1896 they did get their hands on Sun in London, imprisoning him in their consulate there. He was just waiting for shipment back to China and the knife man when the news leaked out to the newspapers and public opinion forced his release.

Sun had adventures in Japan as well, with professional assassins reportedly on his trail, although he and Chiang Kai-shek liked to go out drinking and singing in Yokohama. On many occasions he was protected by a motley group of Japanese friends, including future prime minister Inukai Tsuyoshi, liberals like Miyazaki, and Toyama Mitsuru, godfather of Japanese ultranationalists and head of the Dark Ocean Society and Amur River Society ("Black Dragon Society").

The blue-and-white flag with the cartwheel design that became the emblem of the Kuomintang (Nationalists) and eventually the Republic of China was designed in Yokohama and used at the time of the unsuccessful 1900 uprising. Sun never wavered despite repeated failures like this. He often said that the first requirement of an exile is endurance. "You have to learn to wait patiently when the wind is blowing against you and not get all flustered," he counseled his followers.

However, the majority of the *Huaqiao* probably found the revolutionaries too radical for their tastes. They preferred constitutionalists like Kang and Liang, who had fled abroad after the failure of the Reform Movement of 1895. The constitutionalists at first worked with the revolutionaries, but after the Qing government began to enact reforms in the wake of the 1900 Boxer Rebellion, a bruising fight for influence among the Triad secret societies and residents of Yokohama broke out between the two sides. Newspapers published locally in Chinese expressed their respective views.

The tide of history was on the side of the revolutionaries, however, and after 1902 they shifted their attention to Tokyo where thousands of Chinese students were studying. The first thirteen Chinese students had come to Japan in 1896 and by 1906 their number peaked at about ten

• MAP 70

thousand. In prewar days students who had money went to England or the United States, and those who did not went to Japan or France. Examples of the latter category are Chiang Kai-shek, Zhou Enlai, and Deng Xiaoping. Interestingly, many of Sun's early supporters were women.

The numerous abortive uprisings organized by Sun served to gain him more supporters and donations. As Jonathan D. Spence notes in *The Search for Modern China*, "Sun Yat-sen's bold call for revolutionary activism was steadily becoming more compelling than Kang Youwei's more cautious call for constitutional monarchy and protection of the emperor Guangxu. This despite the fact that the Japanese government was increasingly backing the constitutionalists."

Japan's defeat of Czarist Russia and a wave of Pan-Asian spirit that swept Japan, but largely disappeared in later years, except in the perverted form of the East Asian Coprosperity Sphere, helped fuel revolutionary movements in several Asian countries. Phan Boi Chau and other prominent Vietnamese nationalists operated out of Chinatown for a time and were introduced to powerful Japanese by Liang Chichao and also met with Sun. Eventually, however, they were forced to leave by the French and Japanese governments.

Incidentally, later Indian independence leader Chandra Bose also operated out of this area—a secret hideout near Gokuraku-ji Temple in Kamakura that had been put at his disposal by Toyama.

When extraterritoriality finally ended in 1899, many Westerners moved to Tokyo, Kobe, or even the countryside. But many Japanese vehemently opposed granting the Chinese freedom of movement, since they feared they would work for less money than they did. The 1923 earthquake killed around one thousand Chinese and left Chinatown in a shambles and its prewar population of twelve thousand plummeted, as many former residents moved to Kobe or returned to China. It did not reach three thousand again until a decade later.

In the years leading up to the war the military police and civilian thought-police made life miserable for residents of Chinatown, but they certainly did not have things as bad as the Chinese who were brought from the mainland to work as slave laborers in Japanese mines. The area was especially hard hit during the air raids in the closing days

• MAP 70

of World War II. Food warehouses along the waterfront went up in flames, and, despite police warnings, Chinese squatters moved into those buildings that still stood or camped in the ruins.

The Chinese and Koreans living in Japan were technically considered as citizens of Allied powers by the Occupation and were therefore not subject to its control, as were the Japanese. This was a two-edged sword. On the one hand, these minorities got priority when it came to the distribution of food and other relief supplies, which naturally meant that the black market flourished in Chinatown and many Chinese grew rich, to the envy of the Japanese. They also had a place to live since their homes and property were not subject to confiscation. But after the early honeymoon, Chinese and Koreans alike started being treated harshly by both the Japanese government and the U.S. military. This was when the highly unpopular Alien Registration Card system came into being.

Many Chinese businesses went bankrupt in the economic bust that resulted from the Occupation's deflationary economic policies or were driven out by competitors with black-market connections. The Communist takeover of mainland China resulted in an influx of émigrés, some illegals, and a bitter political rift in the local community between the supporters of the Nationalists and the Communists. During the Cultural Revolution this internecine warfare became quite nasty, with neighbors reportedly refusing to talk to each other. Each side started its own school: the pro-Taiwan one is in the middle of Chinatown, while the pro-PRC one is on the Bluff near the foreigners' cemetery.

In recent years the two sides have become overtly friendly, cooperating on such projects as restoration of the Kuan Ti Miao Temple (*Kanteibyo* 関帝廟), dedicated to the *Tale of the Three Kingdoms* hero Kuan Yu who has become deified as guardian deity of the *Huaqiao*. The community also plan the construction of eight traditional Chinese-style gates, each of which will be unique, and are developing ambitious plans for a Chinese cultural center where Chinese opera and other traditional arts can be performed. It is at Kuan Ti Miao that the local Chinese pray for prosperity and the welfare of their families, and it is from here or the park marking the site where the Qing consulate stood that parades usually originate.

• MAP 70

No real plan is needed for walking Chinatown, but do make sure you visit Kuan Ti Miao, which has been the spiritual heart of the area since it was originally built in 1887. During the Song Dynasty Kuan Yu was officially recognized as the god of war by the government, and although he has not been able to protect the temple from burning down three times, he has helped heal the ideological rift in the community. A 1987 fire completely destroyed the structure that had been built after the war. The pro-Taiwan elements in the community tried to push through a quick rebuilding plan but were blocked by Beijing supporters. Eventually a neutral group was able to broker a compromise solution that consciously eschewed all traces of ideology. Strangely enough the three statues inside survived the holocaust. Also take note of the stone dragon carvings at the entrance.

Although it measures only five hundred meters from east to west and three hundred meters north to south, Yokohama's Chinatown, which claims to have passed San Francisco's Chinatown to become the world's most popular, draws more than eighteen million visitors a year. A quarter million show up for the three-day Chinese New Year festivities alone. The opening of the Bay Bridge, the gourmet and ethnic food booms, establishment of relations between Japan and China in 1972, trendiness among the younger crowd, proximity to the baseball stadium in Yokohama Park, and other factors have all combined to make Chinatown a bigger tourist attraction than Tokyo Disneyland. Altogether there are around 520 shops and restaurants, of which sixty percent are Chinese owned. Several shops reportedly have an annual income of close to ¥4 billion. Before the recession, sales were increasing at a pace of 20 percent a year, and the area is one of Yokohama's biggest shopping zones.

In Chinatown you can find around 160 restaurants serving all the major styles of Chinese cuisine (compared to ninety-three just ten years ago), as well as herbalists, Chinese foodstuff merchants, import shops offering products from China and other Asian countries, and even outlets for Chinese books and music. Of course, there are all kinds of take-out shops selling *char sui* pork and other standards and also confectionery shops, such as Komen offering moon cakes and

• MAP 70

other scrumptious Chinese sweets. You can get lychee ice cream; some shops even have coconuts outside and they'll crack one open for you if you left your machete at home. Also you'll see people walking around eating *nikuman* (meat-filled buns) and other treats. One Chinatown restaurant owner confided that it is a reflection of the hard times—people don't want to pay restaurant prices. In any event, a different etiquette for eating in public applies here than in most other places in Japan, so do your own thing. You'll be rubbing shoulders not only with Japanese, but also with tourists from abroad and no doubt some of the many illegal workers who are seeking to evade immigration officials.

I love tea, Japanese tea, oolong tea, Earl Grey, Darjeeling, just about any kind you can name. There are many shops selling tea in Chinatown, but probably the best specialty shop is Tenjin Meicha. This tea emporium offers seventy different kinds of Chinese tea, including some pure, high-grown teas from Taiwan that have won a following in Japan. The owner will show you how to select and prepare Chinese tea properly. This company has fifty-five shops in Taiwan and eleven overseas, including seven in North America and two in Japan.

Strolling through Chinatown you can stumble across all kinds of strange things, like restaurants that look like hotels, baths, or bordellos. With the exception of Heichinro, Anrakutei, and a few other oldtimers, all Chinatown restaurants were built in the postwar period and more spring up all the time, even though land prices here are reportedly equivalent to those on the Ginza. You'll see a lot of jewelry shops—the Chinese love their gold, especially with the Hong Kong reversion·fast approaching. Unlike the Japanese, Chinese customers place more emphasis on weight than design. The instability of modern China has convinced many of its people to keep their assets close to them. Not a few Chinese refugees have drowned under the weight of the gold they were carrying.

Until recently Japanese banks were far from eager to lend to Chinese, so they developed self-help financial pools that helped them overcome their lack of credit. Everyone who contributed could draw from the pool and pay back at moderate interest rates. There was no legal basis for collecting these debts, but there were few welchers since total

• MAP 70

ostracism within the Chinese community would be the inevitable result.

Funky import shops selling clothes from Indonesia or Vietnam, a store offering Southeast Asian Buddhist images—the Silk Road connection is frequently stressed. Turkumen has gone even further afield, importing antiques and musical instruments from Africa and India. Incidentally, during the early days of the port brass bands would march through this area and on national days the flags of various countries would fly. This was the tradition of public celebration known as *dontaku*, a word borrowed from the Dutch. The *ukiyo-e* artist Sadahide made several prints of *dontaku* parades, which are still staged every fourth Sunday, along with lion and dragon dances.

It is only in the last few years that the residents of Chinatown have begun to change the area's image as dark and dirty. There is no denying that in the old days things could get a little rough, especially in the bars for sailors. One infamous area on Honmura-dori on the edge of Chinatown was referred to, affectionately by some, as Bloodtown, because of the bloody brawls that occurred there in the cheap, lurid saloons bearing names like Blood Street Joe, selling Jack-rabbit whisky and discount girls. Late spring and summer were especially dangerous times to be frequenting these haunts, because the fearsome seal poachers who operated during the winters in northern Russian waters were then in town. These ruffians, used to indiscriminate killing on sea or land, became the subject of Kipling's poem "The Rhyme of the Three Sealers."

> He'll have no more of the crawling sea that made him suffer so,
> But he'll lie down on the killing-grounds where holluschickie go.
> And west you'll sail and south again, beyond the sea-fog's rim,
> And tell the Yoshiwara girls to burn a stick for him.

No doubt the rollicking Vietnam-era R&R bars could seem just as intimidating. However, after the return of the Honmoku wharves in 1971, the number of GIs visiting Chinatown bars dropped drastically. There are still many drinking holes in Chinatown, but most are quite staid. The American owner of the Windjammer bar is a Chinatown longtimer who offers a cosmopolitan mix of Western, Japanese, and Chinese food and a choice of over four thousand different cocktails.

• MAP 70

The Windjammer is really as much a restaurant as a drinking spot; a good percentage of the clientele is foreign. Live jazz bounces off the polished wooden walls from 19:00 every evening. The favorite drink at American House is Sex on the Beach for ¥900. Bottoms up! Jazzmen Club also presents live music. The Tavern has stout on tap and for a nightcap of ouzo try Athens, which is open till 6:00 A.M. Better change that to Woozo! Then there are the Scandinavian bars, including New Norge and Eric's Last Stand—real sailor haunts. Maybe you'll be Shanghaied from Yokohama.

Despite the general air of prosperity in Chinatown, residents are not without their problems. There is a glut of restaurants, although few seem to be losing money. Some owners are trying to diversify. The Holiday Inn is run by a local Chinese restaurateur, for example.

The gentrification of Chinese families resulting from the gourmet boom is ironically threatening the survival of restaurant businesses. There in fact have been cases in which prosperous restaurants closed their doors because there were no sons to manage them. Unlike the Japanese, the Chinese normally do not adopt heirs. As with Chinatowns in the United States, prosperity has meant that many former residents have moved out of Chinatown to areas with better environments; now only about 2,500 of Yamashita-cho's 6,300 residents are "sons of the Yellow Emperor."

📖

Tenjin Meicha 天仁茗茶
☎ 045-641-0818
🕐 9:30–20:00; Sat. and Sun. 10:00–21:00

Komen 紅棉
☎ 045-651-2210
🕐 10:00–20:00; open all year

Turkumen トルクメン
☎ 045-651-7950 🕐 11:00–21:00

🍴

Windjammer ウインドジャマー
☎ 045-662-3966 🕐 17:30–00:30; Fri., Sat. 18:00–02:00; Sun. 17:30–24:00

American House アメリカンハウス
☎ 045-681-6780 🕐 17:00–05:00; Sat. 15:00–05:00; Sun. 13:00–03:00

Jazzmen Club ジャズメンクラブ
☎ 045-662-6699 🕐 17:00–24:00; closed Sun.

The Tavern ☎ 045-641-3950
🕐 Mon.–Fri. 18:00–02:00; Sat. 18:00–04:00; Sun. 18:00–06:00; open all year

Athens ☎ 045-641-6614
🕐 18:00–06:00; also sells Greek-style meat outdoors 11:00–24:00; open all year

New Norge ニューノルゲ
☎ 045-662-2309 🕐 17:00–05:00; open all year

Eric's Last Stand ☎ 045-681-2528
🕐 18:00–03:00; closed Mon.

• MAP 70

China Dining

The big question of course is where to eat. Cantonese food still predominates, but you can also get Peking, Shanghai, Sichuan, and Hunan fare. Top cooks are scouted from Hong Kong and Taiwan, but they soon adjust their cooking to Japanese tastes. The level of the restaurants is pretty much the same, but prices vary widely.

Tastes differ according to individuals: one man's meat is another man's thousand-year-old egg. However, mention must be made of Shatenki, which specializes in Chinese-style rice porridge, a healthy and delicious meal in itself. The porridge, or *okayu*, comes in several varieties, including scallop eyes (*kaibashira*) and mixed meat (*gomoku niku*). A must with your porridge is *youtiao*, a long, deep-fried bread roll that tastes a little like a donut. The long-established Manchinro also has a specialty medicinal rice-porridge shop (045-651-4004) where smoking is banned.

To know the best restaurants go on a weekday and note which ones are packed. Those are where the locals go. For best eating, avoid weekends at all costs and book two or three days in advance for as many people as you can get together. If you're alone or without reservations, early evening is a good time; the cooks and waiters have overcome their midday torpor but have not yet been overwhelmed by the evening rush. Also, many restaurants offer cheap lunches.

Just as in revolutionary politics, the search for that perfect Chinese restaurant requires patience. If you get anxious, just remember: Experts agree it takes at least ten years to train a really good chef of Chinese food. Below is a list of some of the more popular restaurants in Chinatown, according to style of cuisine:

BEIJING ─────────────────

Peking Court cooking is really a mixture of regional cuisines, influenced by Mongol and Manchu cooking. It features a lot of meat, especially beef and lamb, and, of course, Peking duck (which originated in Nanjing but was refined in Beijing after the capital

was moved there). There's also shark's fin soup, and hot pots with lamb and beef innards. Before the war Northern Cuisine was reportedly the most popular in Japan.

Shatenki 謝甜記—bargain basement prices—☎ 045-641-0779

Kaseiro 華正樓—elegant and prices to match—☎ 045-681-2918

Eiko 栄興—reasonable; don't miss the prawn balls—☎ 045-681-2715

Toen 東園—cheap—☎ 045-681-5513

Keikaro 慶華樓—plot a coup in this basement hideout; reasonable—☎ 045-681-2365

Peking Hanten 北京飯店—¥15,000 for a duck: bring your friends—☎ 045-681-3535

Yokohama Daihanten 横浜大飯店—homemade noodles—☎ 045-641-0001

CANTONESE ─────────────────

Cantonese is the regional cuisine best known to Westerners: a lot of seafood, vegetables, sweet and sour, non-spicy. Some of these restaurants serve *kampo* herb dishes. Most offer dim sum snack service at lunch, so you can try all kinds of different things in small portions, selected from a cart or photo menus.

Heichinro 聘珍楼—the granddaddy of Chinatown; 7 floors to choose from: try the dim sum on the 1st—☎ 045-681-3001

Manchinro 萬珍樓—slightly expensive—☎ 045-681-4004

Rokuhokyo 六鳳居—great atmosphere and pigeon, too—☎ 045-681-0664

Shuko Hanten 珠江飯店—also branch Saiko 菜香, reasonable—☎ 045-681-4150

Dohatsu Hanten 同発飯店—Meiji-style interior, reasonable—☎ 045-681-7273

Tokki 徳記—famous for its noodles—☎ 045-681-3936

Suihan Bireiji 翠亨邨茶寮—Dim sum, take-out—☎ 045-681-2052

Anki 安記—authentic atmosphere and very reasonable, too—☎ 045-641-3150

Daichinro Shinkan 大珍樓—slightly expensive—☎ 045-663-5477

• MAP 70

SHANGHAI SEAFOOD

Seafood and more seafood, especially luscious crabs in fall flown in direct from China every day. One restaurant orders two tons a year! Soups and plump *gyoza* dumplings are also Shanghai specialties.

Daishanghai 大上海—great retro interior, wide variety—☎ 045-651-0612

Jogenro 状元楼—slightly expensive—☎ 045-641-8888

Korin 香森—modern atmosphere; reasonable—☎ 045-641-4981

Toko Hanten 東光飯店—very reasonable—☎ 045-681-4617

Kokuhin Saikan 國賓菜館—friendly; great *gyoza*—☎ 045-662-9300

SICHUAN

Spicy, garlicky, and heavenly. Surrounded by mountains, Sichuan Province is almost an independent country: a fertile plain rich in just about everything except seafood, so Sichuan cooks are nothing if not eclectic. Although very spicy, Sichuan cuisine actually has a subtle blend of various flavors; it's often toned down for Japanese tastes.

Jukei Hanten 重慶飯店—over forty years of history—☎ 045-641-8288

Shiei Shiei 謝謝—cheap lunch—☎ 045-681-5554

Kao Hanten 華王飯店—reasonable—☎ 045-882-0200

SEAFOOD RESTAURANTS

Chinese-style seafood is popular with Japanese. Crossing regional culinary lines, it features abundant use of shellfish, including abalone and some sashimi.

Riman Saikan 鯉鰻菜館—cheap lunch menu—☎ 045-651-5101

Haiwan 海王—renowned for fish (and glitter interior)—☎ 045-681-8101

Suiro Bekkan 酔樓別館—great gaudy interior; reasonable—☎ 045-662-4464

Kaiseno 海鮮王—great backstreet atmosphere; reasonable—☎ 045-641-7090

Suuro Saikan 四五六菜館—luscious prawns at reasonable prices; next to Suuro Saikan—☎ 045-681-3456

TAIWANESE

Unique regional fare influenced by Chinese and Japanese traditions and Taiwanese ingredients. Lots of seafood, not that spicy.

Aoba 青葉—cheap lunch—☎ 045-663-3770

Keiko 慶興—homey—☎ 045-662-9193

SOUTH CHINA

Yangtze Valley cooking that mixes and blends ingredients and styles from various neighboring areas. Fish dishes are especially well known.

Akai Hoseki 紅い宝石—reasonable—☎ 045-662-6647

HUNAN

This is the food that made Mao Zedong what he was. (Watch out girls and capitalist roaders!) Very spicy with lots of stamina. Influenced by both Sichuan and Shanghai cooking.

Minyan 明揚—reasonable, unusual—☎ 045-681-0231

NANJING/SUZHOU

Food of the rich, highly cultured region near the mouth of the Yangtze River. Heavily influenced by techniques of Peking Court cooking as well as seafood and sauce traditions of Shanghai.

Kashoro 華勝楼—unusual food; reasonable to slightly expensive and decor totally over the top—☎ 045-681-6781

INTERNATIONAL CHINESE

Adventurous souls have begun mixing Chinese cuisine with other traditions such as Italian food.

Kosho 興昌—truly international with *romaji* menu—☎ 045-681-1293

China Garden—superb view of temple from roof-top garden—☎ 045-651-0366

• MAP 70

70

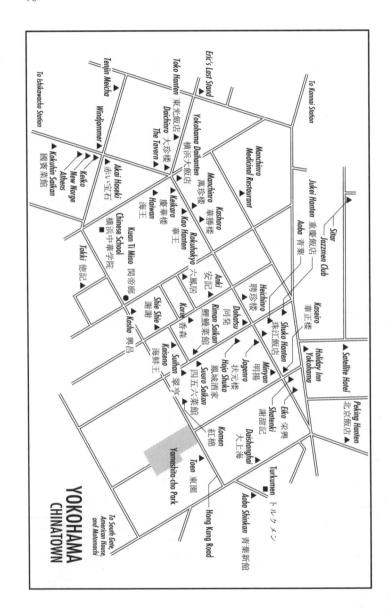

Back in Time

◑ Yokohama Station 横浜駅—Deco Wall 桜木町駅ガード下—Gaslight Memorial ガス事業発祥旧跡—Miyako-bashi Arcade 都橋商店街—Nogeyama Zoo 野毛山動物園—Nogeyama Park 野毛山公園

If you glory in the sight of crowds cascading out of ticket gates, the sounds of bodies ricocheting off bodies like muffled billiard balls that occasionally emit gasps, or the nearly palpable feel of unbridled public rudeness—in other words, if you get your kicks out of visiting Shinjuku or Umeda stations at rush hour—then you'll love Yokohama Station.

Yokohama Station is a hub for seven rail lines: the JR Tokaido, Yokosuka, and Negishi lines, the Tokyu-Toyoko Line, the Keihin Kyuko Line, the Sotetsu Line, and the Yokohama Municipal Subway. Every day 1.7 million people scramble or stroll through its halls, as many as transit Tokyo's main subcenters, such as Ikebukuro and Shibuya.

Here the two faces of Yokohama are clearly juxtaposed. The fashionable shops and trendy-looking restaurants reflect the image of Yokohama held by many outsiders: a romantic, cosmopolitan, progressive port as portrayed in numerous songs, movies, and stories. The resident has a different perspective, however. For him or her, Hama is most likely a bedtown. The advantage of its nearness to the office in Tokyo is offset by the fact that in terms of urban amenities, such as parks per capita, the city ranks at or near the bottom of the standings for Japan's major cities. Because of its symbiotic and in many ways subservient relationship with Tokyo, to some extent Yokohama remains a half-city.

The present site of the station was chosen only in 1928. The very

• MAP 72

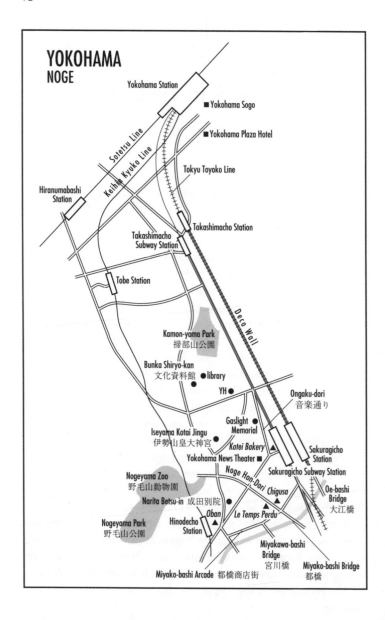

YOKOHAMA
NOGE

Yokohama Station

■ Yokohama Sogo

■ Yokohama Plaza Hotel

Sotetsu Line

Keihin Kyuko Line

Tokyu Toyoko Line

Hiranumabashi
Station

Takashimacho Station

Takashimacho
Subway Station

Tobe Station

Deco Wall

Kamon-yama Park
掃部山公園

Bunka Shiryo-kan
文化資料館   ● library

YH ●

Ongaku-dori
音楽通り

Gaslight
Memorial ●

Iseyama Kotai Jingu
伊勢山皇大神宮

▲ Kotei Bakery

Sakuragicho
Station

Yokohama News Theater ■

Sakuragicho Subway Station

Nogeyama Zoo
野毛山動物園

Noge Hon-Dori

Chigusa ▲

Oe-bashi
Bridge
大江橋

Narita Betsu-in 成田別院

▲ Oban   Le Temps Perdu ▲

Nogeyama Park
野毛山公園

Hinodecho
Station

Miyakawa-bashi
Bridge
宮川橋

Miyako-bashi Bridge
都橋

Miyako-bashi Arcade 都橋商店街

first Yokohama Station, of course, was today's Sakuragicho Station. Once the Tokaido Line was extended to Kobe, the military demanded that a direct route be opened from Hodogaya to destinations south. Yokohama citizens protested loudly, but ultimately to no avail. In 1889 Yokohama was left high and dry off the main east-west train route. In 1915 a new station, in architecture similar to that of today's Tokyo Station, was opened in Takashima-cho on the new route. This building served as Yokohama Station until 1928, when an imposing new building in German Art Deco style went up on today's location.

That building survived World War II, but in the immediate postwar period it resembled Dante's inferno in a Wagnerian setting. U.S. military police swarmed throughout checking for black-market goods and the homeless and derelicts could be seen sleeping everywhere. Out on the west side was nothing but a mountain of sand punctuated with fetid pools of oily water. One oldtimer described the station area in the immediate postwar period: "The east exit brought to mind a cow town in Texas, while the west side was a terrifying dark continent." Few, even brawny men, ventured the way of the wild west late at night.

In 1956 a mall was built on the east side and big stores and department stores started sprouting up. In the mid-sixties there was a reversal of fortune, and even as the east side began to become a bit ragged at the edges, the formerly forlorn west side started prospering mightily. The reason why the station area started developing so quickly was that from the mid-fifties Yokohama's night population outnumbered its daytime population. In other words, the jobs were in Tokyo. This shift was greatly intensified by the construction of huge housing complexes in rural parts of the city, which had previously been referred to with something other than religious awe as Yokohama's Tibet.

To be brutally honest, there is really not all that much to see around Yokohama Station, but you can certainly shop till you drop. The Joinus Shopping Arcade, the west side's big claim to fame, has an outdoor garden with artificial pigeons—Brave New World Revisited. The neighborhood west of the station lacks personality, to put it mildly. Things liven up slightly in the evenings at the row of sixteen or so *yatai*, or outdoor food stalls. The bluff above offers a spectacular view of the city.

• MAP 72

History buffs may, however, want to visit the plaque commemorating Japan's own silk road that is near the west exit. Everyone knows the famous Silk Road that in the days of the Tang Empire in China stretched ten thousand kilometers from Alexandria in Egypt to the Tang capital of Chang-an, today's Xian. However, few people realize that a different silk road had a major impact on Yokohama's development. Go out the west exit and turn left; keep going straight till you get to the bridge. The memorial marker is on the right side where the road meets National Highway 1. This spot in Sengen-cho is where the special road to Hachioji established by the Bakufu met the Tokaido. Raw silk supplies from what are today the prefectures of Yamanashi, Nagano, and Gunma came down it in huge volumes. Mulberry trees were planted along the route and the Yokohama Line was also opened by the government between Yokohama and Hachioji. Prior to that rail shipments of raw silk had been routed through Tokyo, which caused considerable trouble.

Ramen City–Shin Yokohama

Japan is well known as the venue for some of the world's more bizarre museums. A mere five-minute walk from Shin Yokohama Station (reached by subway from Yokohama Station) is one of the wackiest yet—a museum dedicated to the study of *ramen* Chinese noodles. Poke your way through the collection of implements and objets culled from ramen joints all over the country. Check out the state of ramen in your neighborhood on the data base. Finally, treat yourself to a bowl of steaming noodles from one of the shops lining the street re-created in sixties style complete with grimy alleyways and grubby shop curtains. The choice could be difficult, however. How about Tonkotsu from Kyushu, where the thick broth is made from pork bones. Or perhaps the Chinese-style Nagasaki Chanpon, or maybe the clear soy sauce-based noodle soup from Sapporo in Hokkaido? At any rate, the museum offers a good opportunity to appreciate the different regional styles of *ramen* noodles.

Shin Yokohama Station was built in the Olympic year of 1964 as Yokohama's stop on the then new Shinkansen Tokaido Line. Subsequently it languished for many years because of its somewhat isolated location before enjoying something of a boomlet recently, with many new hotels, including the 1,002-room Shin Yokohama Prince Hotel, and office buildings popping up here and there. It even has Yokohama Arena, a spectacular venue for sports events and concerts three times the size of Tokyo's Budokan. Nearby, a super *danchi* residential area, Kohoku New Town, will be home to 300,000 souls when completed. It will have 87 parks within its 2,530 hectares. Simply awesome.

Ramen Museum (Ramen Hakubutsu-kan ラーメン博物館)
☎ 045-471-0943
🕓 11:00–23:00 (gates close at 22:00); closed Tues. ¥300

The opening of the port of Yokohama could not have come at a more propitious time. Japan's domestic economy was already highly developed and foreign merchants were very interested in porcelain, kimono, tea, lacquerware, and other native products. The area where the merchants really looked to make their fortunes, however, was silk. China was in turmoil because of the Taiping Rebellion and other massive uprisings and a silk blight in Europe. Moreover, Japanese silk was in demand worldwide because of its superior quality. Jardine Matheson and the other big China traders quickly realized the potential of the Japanese market.

Those with time and a deep interest in World War II might care to take a look around Hiranumabashi Station, one stop from Yokohama on the Sotetsu Line. This whole area was severely bombed during World War II, but while in most parts of Japan there is absolutely no evidence suggesting such a cataclysm ever took place, here if you look carefully at the concrete buttresses under the rails you can see spots that were blown out by ordnance.

Now, for the walk. Go out the east exit of Yokohama Station, either on the ground floor or on the first underground floor via the Porta shopping complex, and follow the signs to the Sogo Department Store. Completed in 1984, the Sogo is Japan's largest in terms of floorspace, with 156,000 square meters. If you're having trouble finding clothes in your size, this is a good place for shopping. From the terminal nearby cruise boats leave to Yamashita Park and other destinations (see page 313). All day long Blue Line buses that hit the main sights in town depart from the east side of Yokohama Station (see page 44).

The Yokohama department store war has been a favorite topic among business writers for some years now. It should be heating up even more since Isetan is building a branch on the east side in the Portside Zone near the site of the Mitsubishi warehouses. Despite the economic downturn development continues at a torrid pace in the station area.

Return to the main east exit. Cross over the big road at Asayama-bashi. You want to be walking parallel to the Negishi Line (blue cars), on the side away from the harbor. You will soon reach Takashimacho Station. Stay to the left side of the road and you'll come to a wall several

• MAP 72

hundred meters long covered with spray paintings and messages of all kinds. Some of the drawings are incredibly artistic, while others are simply junk graffiti that would make New York aficionados of the art cringe. Kids show up at night to do their work, sometimes staying for hours and painting over the works of those who went before. A pity really, since some of them should be preserved for posterity or reproduced in a museum of contemporary culture. Whoever said the Japanese are unopinionated and psychologically incapable of expressing themselves? The messages range from the romantic (Happy Birthday Kumiko) to the philosophical, theological, and overtly political (Uprising Now!). If you can't get it off your chest here, go over to the military supply store on the next large street toward the hills, which runs parallel to this road, and check out the air guns and model military equipment.

This is the road you want to be on anyway when you have had your fill of pop culture. About halfway down the length of the wall is the cutoff to the road that leads over a red bridge to the right. Turn left just on the other side and head straight ahead. On the right-hand side in front of Honmachi Elementary School is an old-style gas lamp marking the site of the first gas works in Japan, established by Takashima Kaemon. In 1870 a German company received authorization to start a gas service, but a rival Japanese group raised capital to oppose it. With the aid of considerable hanky-panky and backing from the Yokohama municipal government and the Ministry of Finance, Takashima won the duel and brought in the French engineer Henri A. Pelegrin to erect three hundred gas lamps in the Japanese quarter in 1871, two years before Tokyo's Ginza got lit up. This same Takashima had years earlier been thrown into a debtor's prison in Edo, where he undertook an exhaustive study of Chinese-style fortune-telling based on the *I Ching* (The Book of Changes) and *yin-yang* principles. Later, he founded his own school of the science that survives to this day.

On October 31, 1873, Basha-michi and other main streets of Japanese town were for the first time bathed in the warm glow of gaslight. The newspapers went wild and residents of the Foreign Settlement seethed because they had been beaten to the punch. But the gas charges were extremely high and there were frequent problems with service. In

• MAP 72

addition, it was discovered that Takashima had lined the pockets of politicians with kickbacks in order to win the contract. (Seems like old traditions die hard.) Outraged citizens brought the gas company to court. The knock-down, drag-out fight led to increased political consciousness among the public and some reform. In fact Kanagawa Prefecture, especially around Hachioji, became one of the centers of the People's Rights Movement, which sought democracy and a constitution. This was one reason why Hachioji was snipped off by the central government and absorbed into Tokyo. As for Takashima, he is now treated as one of the great city fathers, and no mention is made of the scandal.

Keep going straight on this street and you will hit a big road, the main artery of the Noge district, one of the key areas of Yokohama's *shitamachi* or downtown. On the left is Kotei Bakery, a remnant from the dark ages with home-made cookies and the bizarre "Siberia Pan," a sponge-cake with various fillings. Turn right at the corner and on your right hand side you will soon see the Yokohama News Theater, which has all-night programs every night except Monday, usually B-grade *yakuza* and trucker flicks or comedies from a couple of decades ago. This is a must for nostalgia buffs, or those who have missed the last train. Go straight ahead and you will reach the off-track betting center. You can't miss it on a weekend: just follow the crowds of guys with punch perms coming from the direction of Sakuragicho Station. Many will have their eyes glued on copies of the Japanese version of the racing form.

A *chonmage* topknot, not a perm, was of course the accepted style for men during the Bakamatsu period. Japanese who learned to wield scissors and a straight razor on board ships stopping in the harbor soon started opening their own shops. Ogura Torakichi, who is generally credited as Japan's first professional barber, had his shop in Noge. After the Meiji government issued an order banning the *chonmage*, would-be barbers descended on Yokohama, eager to learn how to snip and lather.

Turn left at the crossroads onto Noge Hon-dori for the center of Noge, long a blue-collar paradise. Come on a Saturday when a race is on and you'll find most of the drinking establishments filled with customers staring blankly at their ponies flying across the TV screen, beer in hand.

Most of the drinking holes in Noge cater to a clientele who have

• MAP 72

little more than a workingman's Ph.D., but you can run into some interesting types, such as authors who specialize in SM stories or radical leftists of the sixties whom Hegel and history have left behind. Le Temps Perdu reportedly has some thirty different kinds of Belgian beer. One real find for cool cats like myself is Chigusa, a coffee shop which boasts a collection of 65,000 jazz records—everything from New Orleans Swing to Bird and Coltrane. The owner says, "You got a question about jazz, just ask me." There are signed autographs on the wall by some of Japan's top jazz performers, including Watanabe Sadao and Akiyoshi Tomiko.

A good majority of the middle-aged, respectable-looking individuals you see walking the streets of Tokyo, Yokohama, and other major cities of Japan are criminals who never served a day in jail. Actually, it's not quite as bad as it sounds: In the immediate postwar period, when there was a dire shortage of food, medicine, and other necessities, most Japanese faced a stark choice—use the black market or die. A famous Tokyo judge deliberately starved to death rather than break the law. During those first horrible months, an average of three people a day died of malnutrition. And even after food imports reached a grand scale, most Japanese remained dirt poor; it was only with the boom induced by the Korean War that the country really got back on its feet.

In those days, Noge was preeminent among the several black market areas in the city. "Go to Noge, and if you show the color of your money, you can buy anything," the saying went. Whereas in other parts of central Yokohama signs reading, "No sales to Japanese" were to be seen everywhere, in Noge they usually read, "Off limits to Allied personnel." Here the smells of whale fat frying and cheap hooch hung heavy in air that trembled with the vibrancy of life on the edge of the abyss. Curbside roulette wheels whirled and clicked like the spinning wheels of weaving maidens in happier times. Mixed-blood children, many the products of hasty liaisons with GIs, vied with other street urchins for survival through shoe shining or picking pockets. Some orphans ten or younger made a fortune from theft; others simply gave up for good and headed for the pier.

At the height of the black market there were 445 stalls on the main road alone, each of which had to pay a fee to the local *oyabun*, Higo

• MAP 72

Morizo. They offered black-market food that had made its way there from Occupation warehouses and trash cans. Koreans and Chinese, who had their own sources of food and the power that stemmed from it, sometimes threw their weight around, although gang warfare such as developed in Kobe between Korean and Japanese *yakuza* never really became a problem in Yokohama, perhaps because it was the center of the Occupation and there were too many MPs around. That does not mean Noge could not get rough at times. Kujira Yoko-cho (Whale Alley) near Sakuragi-cho was a killing grounds reminiscent of Bloodtown and other rough quarters of Yokohama's wild early days. MPs came here every morning to check for dead bodies. Higo himself was knifed to death in 1954, just after the Occupation had come to an end.

But Noge was also the place where the Japanese came to enjoy an *après guerre* culture characterized by pornography, violence, and a desire to get by without regrets. Here a young singer named Kato Kazue made her debut at eight and soon was wowing standing-room-only audiences at Noge's Yokohama Kokusai Gekijo and big clubs in Isezaki-cho. By the age of twelve she had become nationally famous under the name Misora Hibari. Japan's answer to Edith Piaf later built a huge mansion with swimming pool in Isogo, the area where she grew up.

Turn right a few blocks after Le Temps Perdu for Miyako Shotengai, a fifties-style dilapidated arcade of shops with bars on the second floor reached by a rabbit warren of terraces and staircases, a sight increasingly rare in Japan. Keep on straight; turn right and on the other side of the big T-junction is a fish bar, Oban, decorated with—fish. Dozens of them. Dried up, blown up like balloons, and strung along the bar. On the left is Hinodecho Station on the Keihin Kyuko Line.

From Oban turn left and you'll soon come to Nogeyama Park, which offers generous greenery, wonderful vistas of the city and port, and enough cuddly animals to make a child's heart purr with delight.

At the highest point in the park is a statue of Sakuma Shozan, erected to mark the centennial of the port opening. Sakuma was an early advocate of opening up the country and modernization. He studied *yogaku*, or Western studies, under the progressive shogunate official Katsu Kaishu. Since he argued that Yokohama would make an ideal

• MAP 72

place for a foreign trade port, he may be considered the father of modern Yokohama. Yoshida planned to sneak out of the country when Perry returned but was arrested and executed by the government. Sakuma was cut down in Kyoto in 1864 by a swordsman while riding a horse in Western clothes. Katsu arranged for the last shogun to step down and for the peaceful surrender of Edo Castle to Saigo Takamori before becoming a top official in the new Meiji government. Such are the vagaries in the way the Fates reward the efforts of men.

Past the gardens is Nogeyama Zoo, home to around 1,500 animals of three hundred different species. On a recent visit, I communed with a swamp wallaby and saw a sleek black jaguar jump on a log, scaring the bejeezus out of a bunch of kids who had been knocking on his cage. Across the road at the top of the hill is an open expanse that includes a petting zoo for the wee ones and a swimming pool that is open in summer. There is also a monument marking the development of Yokohama's water and sewage systems. Richard Brunton originally came from England to build lighthouses, but he ended doing much more, including creating a sewer system with clay pipes. Up to that time the area had been periodically ravaged by cholera, dysentery, typhus, and other communicable diseases. Another example of his handiwork was the Yoshida-bashi Bridge. This monument marks the place where Japan's modern sewer system got its start. There is a superb view from here of Yokohama in the direction of Negishi.

Where mansions once used to stand are now gardens of three varieties: Japanese, Western, and crossbred. This whole area was where the silk magnates like Hara Zenzaburo and Mogi Sobe had their mansions, which all came undone in the earthquake. During the mid-Meiji period, in terms of wealth these silk kings were on a par with the *zaibatsu* families like Mitsui, Mitsubishi, and Sumitomo. However, after the end of extraterritoriality, the power of the Japanese traders declined precipitously, along with that of the foreign trading houses.

Go back to the main road and continue down the road; notice on the right the entrance to Naritasan Betsu-in, a temple with a weird assortment of Buddhist statues from all over Asia. At the big crossroads turn right. You are entering the area where the government offices

• MAP 72

were concentrated in the early days of the port. This location on a high hill to the northwest of the port gave them an unobstructed view of the entire harbor. Incidentally, the Kanagawa Magistrates' Office was established here because the magistrates preferred to live as far away from the foreigners as possible, so as to keep them from ascertaining the workings of the Japanese government. They also wanted a secure position that could serve as a stronghold should military hostilities break out.

Down the hill to the left you'll see a complex of government buildings including a concert hall, the Kanagawa Youth Hostel, a women's center, and the Kanagawa Prefectural Library, which boasts a large collection of English books, which reportedly are being transferred to the new city library near Hinodecho Station. The youth center is built on the former site of the Kanagawa Magistrates' Office, established in 1859.

Public Executions in Noge

Terror of course has always been a favorite tactic of despotic governments for enforcing control. In the past, public executions were common. Francis Hall described in gory detail the execution of an arsonist at the stake: "The flames leaped over the dry rushes as if they had been powder, and quick as a headman's ax, quicker than the hangman's rope, the victim within must have been stifled. In two or three moments the rushes were burned away exposing the blackened, scorched body still fast to its pillar, yet faster in death. Torches of lighted straw were placed to the mouth and nostrils to make assurance double sure ... water was thrown on the smoking embers, and the body was left to stand for three days a public spectacle..."

Undoubtedly the most famous executions that took place in the Noge area were those of Shimizu Seiji and Mamiya Hajime, the men responsible for the murders of Major Baldwin and Lieutenant Bird at Kamakura in 1864. The executions were performed expressly for the delectation of the foreign community, and first the men were paraded around town.

Shimizu, the mastermind, was a young *ronin* consumed with hatred and envy of the hairy barbarians, whom he blamed for his failure to make it in life. Even the men of Bird and Baldwin's regiment were impressed by the stoicism with which Shimizu died. According to an account written by Swiss consul Robert Lindau, just before the executioner's sword swung down on his neck, Shimizu burst into the following chant in a resounding voice: "Now dies Shimizu Seiji, a homeless man. He dies without fear and without regret, for to have killed a barbarian redounds to the honor of a Japanese patriot."

His accomplice, the nineteen-year-old Mamiya, was arrested a few months later. According to Lindau, he was thrown on the ground and, like a helpless animal dragged to the slaughterhouse, he fell beneath the executioner's sword.

Shimizu and Mamiya are buried at a nearby temple.

• MAP 72

Yokohama's first real hospital was also built in this area in 1868 to treat those wounded in the Boshin War that overthrew the shogunate. It was run by William Willis, a young British doctor at the British Legation. He took care of wounded combatants from both sides free of charge and performed the first major surgery in Japan. His Tobe Military Hospital was the forerunner of Tokyo University Hospital.

Behind the library and youth center is Kamonyama Park, which contains a statue of Ii Naosuke, one of the losers in the Restoration period who, as Great Elder or shogunal premier, sought to reenergize the shogunate by opening up the country while crushing internal opposition. He accepted the warning from Townsend Harris that England and France had imperialistic designs on Japan and that it was in his country's interest to sign a commercial treaty with America as soon as possible. The creation of the port of Yokohama was of course the most important result of the 1858 Treaty of Amity and Commerce.

Because of his agreement to the treaty and his high-handed domestic policies, including the execution of the pro-emperor theoretician Yoshida Shoin, Ii earned the enmity of pro-emperor xenophobes. In March 1860 he was beheaded in the spectacular Sakuradamongai Incident in front of Edo palace by a band of disguised anti-Western loyalists. His successors had none of his determination and political savvy, and the shogunate's days were numbered after his elimination.

Undoubtedly the man who did most to make a smooth port opening was Iwase Tadanari, the shogunate official who negotiated with Harris. Iwase had visionary plans for Yokohama as an important international port long before hardly anyone else was even aware of the fishing village's existence. In an 1857 report to his superiors he advocated the opening of Yokohama rather than Osaka since it would benefit Edo's economy. There is a statue of Iwase in Nogeyama Park.

The statue of Ii has something of a history to it. It was originally built in 1909 by a former samurai from Ii's home fief of Hikone, near Lake Biwa. The morning after its dedication, the statue was found beheaded. Perhaps it was no coincidence that the then governor of Kanagawa was from former Choshu, the home fief of Yoshida Soin, where Ii had been considered a mortal enemy. In 1914 the city of

• MAP 72

Yokohama received the statue and the garden as a gift from the Ii family. The statue was melted down to make armaments during World War II; the present bronze statue was built in 1954.

On the right is the entrance to the Iseyama Kotai Jingu. Although it only dates from after the Meiji Restoration, its interesting layout on the hillside and the fact that it is Yokohama's premier Shinto shrine make it worth a visit. Prior to the Restoration, Yokohama's principal shrine had been the Shukan Benten Shrine located in a grove on a long, narrow promontory in the Sakuragi-cho area. The Meiji government ordered it out in 1869, so it could build a state shrine that would encourage emperor worship. That shrine was moved here in 1900, in order to make way for a land reclamation project and a direct road running through the Sakuragi-cho area, and it was renamed the Iseyama Kotai Jingu. Notice the sacred water and sacred fowl, as well as the Japanese garden behind the Kaiyotei Wedding Hall.

Keep walking down the hill and you'll soon come back to the cut-off for Ongaku-dori. From here it's a short walk along the tracks to Sakuragicho Station.

All in all, Noge has seen better days, but it's still worth a visit. Local shopkeepers are trying to revive its fortunes by holding street festivals every Saturday in April and October, 12:00–16:00. Step right up and see the jugglers, clowns, fire eaters, and other artistes, including many foreigners. There are also flea markets and open-air art galleries.

Nogeyama Zoo (Nogeyama Dobutsu-en 野毛山動物園)
☎ 045-231-1307
🕐 9:30–16:30; closed Mon.

Yokohama News Theater
☎ 045-231-2769
All-night shows every day but Mon.

Kotei Bakery コテイ ベイカリー
☎ 045-231-2944 🕐 8:00–21:00; closed Sun.

Chigusa ちぐさ ☎ 045-241-7301
🕐 12:00–22:00; closed Tues.

Le Temps Perdu ル タン ペルデュ
☎ 045-242-9777 🕐 17:00–23:00; closed Sun.

Oban 大番 ☎ 045-231-3481
🕐 17:00–23:00; closed Sun.

• MAP 72

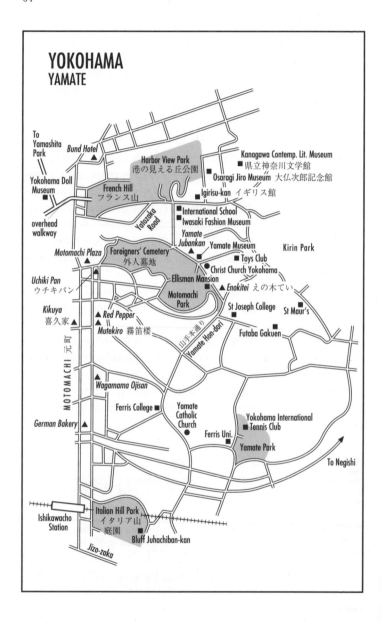

YOKOHAMA
YAMATE

To Yamashita Park

Bund Hotel

Yokohama Doll Museum

overhead walkway

Harbor View Park
港の見える丘公園

French Hill
フランス山

Yatazaka Road

Kanagawa Contemp. Lit. Museum
県立神奈川文学館

Osaragi Jiro Museum 大仏次郎記念館

Igirisu-kan イギリス館

International School

Iwasaki Fashion Museum

Yamate Jubankan

Yamate Museum

Kirin Park

Toys Club

Christ Church Yokohama

Motomachi Plaza

Foreigners' Cemetery
外人墓地

Ellisman Mansion

Enokitei えの木てい

Motomachi Park

St Joseph College

St Maur's

Uchiki Pan
ウチキパン

Kikuya
喜久家

Red Pepper

Mutekiro 霧笛楼

山手本通り Yamate Hon-dori

Futaba Gakuen

MOTOMACHI 元町

Wagamama Ojisan

Ferris College

Yamate Catholic Church

Yokohama International Tennis Club

German Bakery

Ferris Uni.

Yamate Park

To Negishi

Ishikawacho Station

Italian Hill Park
イタリア山 庭園

Bluff Juhachiban-kan

Jizo-zaka

5

Above it All

◐ Ishikawacho Station 石川町駅 (JR Negishi Line)—Motomachi 元町—French Hill フランス山—Foreigners' Cemetery 外人墓地—Yamate 山手—Italian Hill イタリア山

This jaunt through Yokohama's best neighborhoods, the Motomachi shopping district and the famous Bluff, begins at Ishikawacho Station on the JR Negishi Line. Go out the rear side, turn left, and keep going straight. You will soon be walking on the city's Golden Half-Mile.

When Yokohama was chosen by the shogunate as the site for the foreign settlement, the original inhabitants were forcibly relocated to the area at the foot of the Bluff. Originally named Honmura, it later came to be known as Motomachi, the "town of the original ones." Most of these ninety families had been eking out an existence partly by farming and partly by fishing. Now along with outside merchants they sought to provide specialized services to the resident foreigners. Some succeeded or made a fortune by hanging onto their property till it inflated greatly in value, but most soon lost all they had and once again moved on.

Incidentally, there were some trades that were absolutely essential in those days that no longer exist today. Blacksmithing and carriage-making, of course, but also water selling. Getting decent water was vital in the early days—for supplying ships in the harbor, putting out fires, and because diseases like cholera and typhus were rife due to contaminated water. Drilling took place on Daikan-zaka, one of several slopes that link Motomachi to the Yamate bluff, and in several other locations. The cholera epidemic of 1879 claimed many victims, but it was only in 1882 that Dr. A. J. C. Geerts, a Dutch sanitation engineer, was able to

• MAP 84

take the first steps towards creating a proper drainage system.

In the early days over 70 percent of the customers for the Motomachi stores were foreigners, and shop owners used to pick up people arriving on ships and take them directly here. However, from about the time of the 1960 Olympics, the majority of the shoppers became Japanese. The five-hundred-meter-long promenade is now one of the smartest shopping districts in Japan, with around 250 shops offering merchandise that is unique, fashionable, and *très* expensive.

The famous writer Tanizaki Jun'ichiro lived in Yokohama a few years prior to the earthquake. He marveled at the many elegant shops catering to the needs of foreigners and how Western couples swarmed down from the Bluff on their daily walks. Of the air of Motomachi, Tanizaki wrote, "The smell of tobacco, the smell of chocolate, the smell of plants, the smell of perfume—amongst these the smell of tobacco was strongest, which together with the smell of boiled-down cocoa or coffee surreptitiously permeated the air of the streets."

Motomachi's Bakeries

For me the glory of Motomachi is its bakeries. Going up the main road from Ishikawacho Station, you first encounter the German Bakery on the right side of the road just past the main crossing. It sells all kinds of scrumptious cakes and cookies and has a coffee shop that serves light meals. On the left is the Kikuya pastry shop, founded in 1938. Wagamama Ojisan no Mise ("Selfish Uncle's Shop"), which specializes in mouthwatering cheesecake, is off to the right on a smaller street toward the hills. The owner steadfastly refuses to make more than five hundred cakes a day, so there is usually a long line outside.

First chronologically and also in the hearts of many local residents, is Uchiki Pan on the right side of the street leading past the Motomachi Plaza toward the Bluff. Founded around 1888, it is at least a century old and, like its forerunner, the Yokohama Bakery, founded in 1862, it uses fresh yeast and hops in its English-style white bread. Uchiki Hikotaro took over the business after its founder, Robert Clarke, returned home to Britain. Alternative stories have him learning the bread-making techniques that his descendants still use today from other British or French settlers. An Uchiki Pan advert from 1906 reads, "Purveyors to British, American, German and French in the City every Morning. 12,000 lbs. of Bread Turned Out Per Diem."

German Bakery ☎ 045-681-8546
⏱ 9:30–20:00; closed Mon.

Kikuya 喜久家
☎ 045-641-0545
⏱ 10:30–19:30; closed Mon.

Uchiki Pan ウチキパン
☎ 045-641-1161 ⏱ 9:00–18:30; closed Mon.

Wagamama Ojisan no Mise わがままおじさんの店 ☎ 045-661-2306
⏱ 11:00–19:00; closed Mon.

• MAP 84

Motomachi has also been the setting for several famous stories, including Mishima Yukio's *Gogo no Eiko* (The Sailor Who Fell From Grace with the Sea), whose ill-fated heroine ran a fashionable dress shop.

The eating spots around here range from classy French cafes frequented by the well-heeled Bluff crowd to the usual fast-food suspects. The California-style cuisine at the Red Pepper is reasonable and it boasts of a salad bar. Mutekiro ("Foghorn"), named after one of Osaragi Jiro's most famous novels, offers French food in the re-created decor of a high-class bordello from the wicked port-opening days. With its tatami, *Yokohama-e* paintings, chandeliers, and stained glass windows you can imagine yourself in the old Gankiro as you sip your wine. Naturally, the waitresses wear kimono and there is a rickshaw by the door. On the first floor is an English-style bar. Garlic Jo's (near Uchiki Pan) believes in generous use of the pungent bulb and hot peppers and guarantees you a root-tooting good time. Incidentally, distinctive Yokohama furniture in Belle Epoque style is sold in some of the shops.

Check out the awesome award-winning public restrooms on the left at the end of Motomachi. Go straight past the entrance to French Hill on the right; when you hit the big intersection, on the right you'll see the Bund Hotel and the truly riotous Punta Del Este nightclub next door, which holds frequent reggae and salsa nights.

Head back to the entrance to French Hill. On the left you'll see a plaque marking the former site of the palatial French Legation—the fall of the beautiful building during the earthquake was even faster than that of Napoleon a century before. For years the area was overgrown with vegetation, but the French government eventually sold it to the city. Today the park is covered with chinquapin, dogwood, oaks, and other trees, and in May lilacs. This part of the Bluff that overlooks Yokohama's harbor became the site of British and French permanent military garrisons as a result of the Namamugi Incident (see page 93). The French garrison of 250 men was next to the British Hospital, while the British docks were directly below. As elsewhere, the British and the French delighted in games of one-upmanship. The French, for example, built their flagpole higher than that of the British, while the British made sure they had more troops than the French.

• MAP 84

The French also cultivated shogunate officials, especially the highly capable Oguri Tadamasa, who, along with Kurimoto Kon, welcomed their help in constructing a naval shipyard at Yokosuka. The French also established a language school and a small iron and steel plant near Ishikawa-cho. All this reflected the desire of Paris to build up its influence as part of its global competition with the British. The French minister, Léon Roches, who had served as a translator for the French army for several years in North Africa before joining the foreign service, vastly overrated the shogunate's chances. But his liberal support for the government no doubt encouraged Harry Parkes, the British minister, to cultivate contacts with the pro-Emperor party. Eventually, Roches lost the trust of the French government, which ordered him home in the middle of 1868.

The foot soldiers could not have enjoyed all this tit-for-tat tomfoolery very much, since the conditions under which they were forced to live on Camp Hill were hardly idyllic. At first the British simply erected tents on fields covered with nightsoil that stank to high heaven, while a damp fog clung to the heights in the morning. Many soldiers died of smallpox. When drunk, which by all accounts was a frequent occurrence, the English *akatai* ("red troops") were referred to as *akatombo*, or "red dragonflies." Similarly, the French were known as the "blue troops."

Foreign residents were allowed to lease land on the Bluff from 1867. Nevertheless, the foreign residents were clearly happy to have the troopers nearby. Writing in 1866, A. B. Mitford, then Second Secretary to the British Legation, admitted that "for nearly four years I never wrote a note without having a revolver on the table and never went to bed without a Spencer rifle and bayonet at my hand." The foreign troops were not withdrawn till 1875.

On the small street branching off from Yatozaka Road near the side entrance to the park is a monument marking the spot where the modern cleaning industry began in Japan—the soldiers obviously needed to have someone help them get their uniforms clean after nights of carousing and wandering around in the putrid paddies.

The park on French Hill closes at nightfall, but the neighboring Harbor View Park offers a spectacular nocturnal panorama. You are

• MAP 84

almost tempted to reach out and touch the Bay Bridge. (Better bring a parachute if so inclined.) Past the lookout is a rose garden and on the other side is the British House (Igirisu-kan イギリス館), a big, white, colonial-style building erected in 1937 as the official mansion for the British consulate general. In 1969 it was bought by the city, and is now rented out to groups that want to stage special events.

Across the road from it is the Osaragi Jiro Memorial Museum, which opened in 1977. The dandyism of the writer is mirrored in the architecture of this museum. Note the design on the front of the building that is meant to suggest the Tricolor. Osaragi (a pen name whose alternate reading is "Daibutsu," or Big Buddha) was well known as a best-selling author and confirmed Francophile who wrote novels about the French Revolution, the Dreyfus case, and many stories about Yokohama. The best-known Yokohama story is *Muteki* (Foghorn), the story of a Japanese servant working for a sinister foreign businessman during the 1870s. Osaragi's knowledge of foreigners came from his predilection for writing at the Hotel New Grand where, prior to the 1950s, foreigners made up the bulk of the clientele. He could imbibe some cosmopolitan atmosphere along with his whisky in the hotel bar.

Actually, Osaragi (1897–1973) had had an international upbringing from the beginning. His father worked for Nippon Yusen, the steamship line, so he was exposed to Western culture from his youth. By all accounts Osaragi successfully managed to capture the port atmosphere for his Japanese readers. Inside the museum you can see many of Osaragi's books, a model of his study, and a small library that includes his Paris Commune collection containing 2,600 political cartoons by over fifty artists. Osaragi's wife designed the salon, which contains his favorite sofas. Take note of the statue of a cat at the entrance. Osaragi seems to have had something of a love-hate relationship with felines. The author didn't allow anybody into his study in Kamakura except his cats. Here you can see several hilarious sketches, paintings, sculptures, and other representations of cats from his collection. On the other hand, he once threatened to walk out on his wife if she took in another stray cat, since they already had fifteen. One day when he went out to the kitchen, he found sixteen felines lined up sipping milk from dishes. The maid was

• MAP 84

quick-witted, however, and explained, "He's only a guest. He'll be going home just as soon as he eats." There is also a coffee shop here.

One aspect of the quasi-colonial relationship between the Westerners and the Japanese in the early days that is often passed over in silence, more often than not accidentally on purpose, is sex.

Dr. William Willis estimated that as of 1867 there were over a thousand prostitutes in Yokohama of whom two to three hundred were contractural mistresses for foreigners. Known as *rashamen*, these ladies delighted in flaunting their finery in front of fellow Japanese when they rode in carriages through the town. They were frequently greeted by insults and occasionally stones. Most of the *rashamen* do not seem to have had any education, except in the mercenary sense. The shogunate was more than happy with the arrangements since it was able to recruit the mistresses and servants in the homes of the foreign merchants to report on all their movements.

Rudyard Kipling sojourned briefly in Yokohama twice, in 1889 and 1892. On one occasion a local resident explained to him that Yokohama, like other ports in the East, was full of Eurasian children and that it was accepted practice for foreigners to take Japanese "wives" even if they already had families. When the time came to go home, the men simply left. The more conscientious provided financially for their partners and the offspring from their unions, if there were any. Even many top diplomats had mistresses and not a few had mixed-blood children. Kipling's confidant further claimed that the chances of the women finding marriage partners were in no way hurt by these temporary marriages with foreigners. Kipling himself noted that he saw numerous mixed-race children in the Foreign Settlement, some of whom were "exceedingly good-looking." Hardly any references to these Eurasian children, or those born during the Occupation, are to be found in Japanese sources. Their very existence seems to be something that the Japanese would rather forget.

Besides Osaragi and Tanizaki, other writers closely associated with Yokohama include novelists Yoshikawa Eiji, the author of *Musashi*; Naoki Sanjugo, after whom the Naoki Literary Prize is named; Arishima Takeo, whose father was the official in charge of the Customs House;

• MAP 84

Yamamoto Shugoro, well known for his stories of common people; Hasegawa Shin, famed for his works portraying gamblers and gangsters; playwright Shimamura Hogetsu; and poets Kitamura Tokoku and Sato Haruo. Shimazaki Toson, the famous proponent of the naturalist style, worked at a general store in Isezaki-cho for several years. You can learn more about these authors at the Kanagawa Contemporary Literature Museum nearby. Not far from here is a house where Dr. James Hepburn lived during some of his thirty years in Yokohama.

From the Osaragi Museum, turn left and go straight out to the main road, cross to the opposite side of the street, and turn right. You will pass the International School, and when you get to the corner turn left. The red-brick building in front of you on the same side of the street is the Iwasaki Fashion Museum. This building was remodeled in 1992. On the second and third floors are dozens of examples of women's fashions from ancient Egypt to the present. You'll be interested to know, for example, that in ancient times Celtic women apparently wore topless dresses. There are also displays of art and Art Nouveau glassware and a corner with materials related to the Gaiety Theater during the Meiji and Taisho periods. On the first floor you can have your picture taken in a traditional costume; the cost is ¥1,000 to ¥4,000, depending on costume and arrangements. Opera, classical, and jazz concerts are held in the concert hall on the bottom floor.

The Gaiety is a famous name in Yokohama's history. In the 1830s amateur dramatic clubs sprang up in eastern ports such as Singapore and Shanghai. The Chinese community had the first theater in Yokohama, which was sometimes rented by Western groups. A permanent theater was finally established in December 1870 on Honcho-dori near the present studios of TV Kanagawa by Dutchman M. J. B. Noordhoek Hegt (1821–94), a dedicated firefighter and one of the many people who made an unsuccessful attempt to brew beer commercially.

In April 1885 the Gaiety Theater was relocated to the Bluff and housed in a spacious two-story brick building with a Greek-style facade. It could accommodate almost four hundred spectators, and in addition to dramatic performances was used for musical performances, vaudeville, political speeches, and even boxing matches. For more than fifty years

• MAP 84

this was the center for Thespian activities in Yokohama. Regrettably, however, it was never rebuilt after the 1923 earthquake.

Akutagawa Ryunosuke wrote about a performance of Oscar Wilde's *Salome* staged here in 1912. Most of Japan's famous playwrights and writers of the day seemed to make their way to the Gaiety at one time or other. Some, like Tsubouchi Shoyo, the father of modern Japanese drama, were regulars. Since they could not return to Tokyo the same day, student theatergoers would bring blankets and camp out in Yamate Park or the station.

The famous Gaijin Bochi, or Foreigners' Cemetery, is on the right. The first foreigner to be buried in Yokohama was Robert Williams, a member of the crew of the *Mississippi* on Commodore Perry's second expedition, who died at the age of twenty-four after falling from a mast. He was buried at Sotoku-in Temple, which stood below the present cemetery, but his remains were relocated to Shimoda three months later.

The 1.9 hectares for the cemetery were provided free by the shogunate. In 1869 management passed to the hands of the Committee of the Yokohama Foreign General Cemetery, dominated by the British, where it has remained ever since. It used to be made up primarily of diplomatic representatives but is now composed mainly of businessmen and other residents. It is now building a museum that is set to open in 1994. The dedication on the front gate was written in 1968:

> Many who lie here lived among you and gave much to their foster land. Others found only a place of last repose. Revere their memory and honour this place.
>
> > "And all that beauty, all that wealth e'er gave
> > Awaits alike the inevitable hour
> > The paths of glory lead but to the grave."
> > Thomas Gray (1716–1777)

To the right of the entrance is a monument to the unknown dead. Out of the 4,500 inhabitants from 49 countries, there are approximately 1,500 English, 1,000 Americans, 300 Germans, 190 French, 120 Russians, and 120 Japanese including the wives of foreigners and a few Japanese men who received special permission to be buried here. There is also great

• MAP 84

variety in the tombs, with some of the older ones in particular being very unusual or ornate in style. There is even one in late Han Dynasty Chinese style. The small tombstones of the children are heartbreaking. An estimated 80 percent of the deceased no longer have relatives to tend their tombs. Even so, the atmosphere is much brighter than at most Japanese cemeteries, and some twenty to thirty burials still take place here every year.

The cemetery is open to the deceased of all faiths, although the Jews and Chinese are clustered in their own sections. The first permanent occupants of the cemetery were two Russian sailors, Roman Mophet and Ivan Sokoloff, who were cut down in the streets of Yokohama by unknown assailants, presumably xenophobes. The earliest years were a reign of terror for the foreigners. From July 1859 to October 1864 nine foreigners were assassinated in or around Yokohama, including a Chinese employed by the French Consulate. Two Dutch captains who are buried here were literally chopped into pieces.

The Namamugi Incident

Perhaps the most famous guest at the Foreigners' Cemetery who died a violent death is Charles Richardson, the victim of the famous Namamugi Incident. He was slashed to death in September 1862 by the bodyguard of Lord Shimazu Hisamitsu of Satsuma for not paying proper deference to the *daimyo*. In a sense his murder was the result of a cultural misunderstanding and insensitivity on the part of Westerners. Richardson had lived in China for fourteen years where, according to some accounts, he treated locals with contempt. Other contemporaries claim he was a friendly, easygoing type. Be that as it may, he did not move to the side of the road when his companions, who were familiar with Japan, told him to. However, sketches show that at this point the Tokaido was a narrow, tree-lined road, and it is clear that there was not much room to maneuver.

In another sense the affair can only be regarded as cold-blooded murder, since the outraged samurai could easily have driven off the offenders without injuring anyone. After all, there were a thousand of them and the four Europeans on horseback, one a woman, posed absolutely no threat.

This incident, incidentally, is an interesting illustration of samurai honor. Witnesses were in accord that the first member of Shimazu's entourage to attack was a prominent member of the group. However, when the British demanded his murderer be turned over for punishment, the Japanese blamed it all on an *ashigaru*, the lowest-ranking samurai. Just like with companies that get involved in scandals today, a scapegoat had to be found so that the power and perks of the real malefactors would not be jeopardized.

• MAP 84

The Japanese were not immune from violence either, especially if they were perceived as quislings by the pro-Emperor *ronin*. That was amply illustrated by the murder of British minister Rutherford B. Alcock's right-hand man, "Dan Ketch," in 1860. Danny started out as a ship-wrecked sailor named Iwakichi who was taken to San Francisco where he learned English and took to calling himself Dan Kichi. He made his way to the China coast, went back to Japan with Perry, and eventually was hired by the British, becoming a British subject. Dan Ketch was invaluable to the British as an interpreter, but even they were put off by the airs he put on and his superciliousness toward other Japanese. His death may have been occasioned by an affair with a teahouse girl whose family could not stand him, rather than for political reasons.

Edmund Morel, the father of Japanese railways, and several other foreign railroad men are also to be found here. Although some of the highly paid foreign experts hired by the Meiji government played the white sahib role to the hilt, this wasn't true of Morel and nineteen other foreign railroad engineers who came to Yokohama in the 1870s. While on the construction sites they survived on ships' biscuits and kippers in temples near the tracks, greatly impressing the Japanese with their dedication. Four died of illness and three went home for the same reason. Morel was the best example of selfless dedication. He had worked in New Zealand and Australia, and came from Ceylon to Japan, where he continued to work in spite of being sick with tuberculosis.

Many Meiji leaders initially had grave doubts about the wisdom of making a huge investment in railroads, but they were championed by Okuma Shigenobu and Ito Hirobumi. Okuma wanted Morel to concentrate on his work so he introduced him to his future wife, Kino, who may have been a domestic in the Okuma household.

Morel died on September 24, 1871, just before he was to go to India to recuperate. A few hours later Kino died in mysterious circumstances. Some claimed she was "following her lord unto death," while the less unkind claimed she died out of shame for having been forced to marry a "hairy barbarian." The official version was more mundane—she died from exhaustion brought on by attending him constantly during his last days. If we are to leave the decision to the court of

• MAP 84

tradition, the first would be correct, since the plum tree planted by their graves supposedly yields both red and white blossoms, expressing their mutual affection even though they had no common language. Morel's tomb, which is shaped like a railway ticket, was built in 1934 by a native of Motomachi who was the grandson of a money changer.

Among the other experts who lie here are some of the French involved in the building of a shogunate steel foundry at Yokohama and the big dockyards at Yokosuka, the father of Japanese pharmacology, A. J. C. Geerts (1843–83), and K. Von Seebach (1859–91), father of the Japanese penal system. Others, although less famous, also died in the line of duty. There was the German, Conrad Bremerman, who joined the local police force that had been set up under a British head. As we know, Yokohama's streets were mean in those days, with many rough types packing firearms or knives who got particularly unruly when they had some rum in them. On November 1, 1882, Bremerman was shot in what is now part of Chinatown near the Holiday Inn while trying to break up a fight between a Frenchman and a Filipino. Kanagawa Prefecture police place flowers on the grave on that day each year.

Young Japan author and newspaper editor John Reddie Black is here along with his wife, his oldest son, Henry, and his oldest daughter.

The Blue-Eyed Raconteur

Henry James Black (Kairakutei Black, 1859–1923) became the blue-eyed *rakugo* or comic raconteur rage of the Meiji and Taisho periods. As a young boy, Henry helped his father, John Black, edit his newspaper and seemed destined to be a journalist. His father's disillusionment with his treatment by the Japanese government may have influenced Henry's decision to go into the theater.

Henry, whose command of Japanese reportedly was as good as his English, started out by telling historical stories, or *kodan,* in vaudeville theaters, describing the executions of Charles I and Joan of Arc. He was ridiculed by fellow foreigners as a disgrace to his family, while his anti-government speeches got him into trouble with the authorities. Henry responded by shifting his base of activities to Kansai, where he specialized in telling tales of crosscultural *faux pas* and retelling in his own words famous Western novels like *Oliver Twist* or true crime stories. The novelty of his stories, his appearance, and innovations of his own, like musical skits and hypnotism, won him fame. However, as the tastes of the audience changed, his popularity waned. He attempted suicide with arsenic in a theater in Kobe, but was stopped in time. He died of a stroke at the age of sixty-four.

• MAP 84

Several of the leading lights of the early English-language media are buried here. One of the most famous of the early journalists was the brilliant cartoonist Charles Wirgman (1832–91), whose tomb in the Jewish corner bears a quote from Shakespeare: "A man of infinite jest." Wirgman loved Japan but detested arrogant bureaucrats and self-serving politicians. He doubted whether Japan was gaining more than it was losing in its rush to modernize and he savagely satirized political and social trends, while seeking the heart of Japanese culture.

Wirgman, a native of London, began his career as a military officer. Although a self-taught artist, he arrived in China in 1860 as an illustrator for the *Illustrated London News* and became its correspondent in Japan the following year. His drawings portray the major events of the day as well as scenes from daily Japanese life. Wirgman had the uncanny knack of being or not being in the right place at the right time. He was in the British Legation in Edo when it was attacked by reactionary samurai and barely escaped with his life by hiding beneath the floorboards. He was supposed to have gone to visit the Big Buddha on the very day that Bird and Baldwin were cut down. One biographer has even suggested that Wirgman's acumen in ferreting out information was due to the fact that he was a professional spy. If that was so, Wirgman became a highly domesticated spy, since he married a Japanese woman, Ozawa Kane, and settled down in Yokohama, gaining his greatest fame as founder-editor of the first European-language humorous periodical in Japan, *Japan Punch*, which was modeled on the English magazine, *Punch*. Unlike his extremely realistic and detailed newspaper illustrations, Wirgman's *Punch* cartoons were drawn with broad strokes, accentuating their satirical effect. The magazine appeared from 1862 until 1887, and in the early days traditional woodblock printing was used. Even though only about three hundred issues were printed at its peak of popularity, the magazine was so influential that *ponchi* became the Japanese word for cartoon for a time.

Every February 8, the cemetery is the site of the Punch Flower Matsuri, which is actually a big memorial ceremony for Wirgman. Many people lay wreaths on his grave, and across the street at the Yamate Museum a lecture is held on Wirgman and his lasting influence.

• MAP 84

Among the more unusual, more contemporary inhabitants of the cemetery are sixty-one German navy personnel who were aboard a cruiser that exploded and burned in the harbor on November 30, 1941. Thirty-six Chinese and five Japanese also died in the incident. They were buried in a mass grave.

Many of the people interred in the cemetery consciously chose it as their last resting place because of their love for their adopted country. None was more of a Japanophile than C. K. Marshall Martin (1862–1949), the British merchant who arranged for the purchase of land leases from foreigners to make possible the creation of Yamashita Park. Marshall, who loved classical Japanese literature, kabuki, and *ukiyo-e*, interpreted for the Yokohama courts on a gratis basis. He was also the organizer of the local society for the prevention of cruelty to animals and operated the *Japan Gazette* for ten years until 1907. Marshall was nothing less than "public citizen number one" and is referred to by name in Tanizaki's reminiscences of Yokohama, *Minato no Hitobito* (Port people).

This is not the only foreigners' cemetery in Yokohama. Another was established at Negishi at the end of the last century and there are three thousand graves there now, many for people who died in the earthquake. Then there is the Commonwealth Cemetery at Hodogaya, with more than two thousand occupants including some POWs who died during the war.

Across the street in the Victorian-looking building is the Yamate Jubankan. On the first floor is a coffee shop and on the second floor a restaurant serving French food, which is not too expensive for lunch.

Next door to the Yamate Jubankan is the Yamate Beer Garden (Bluff Garden). This was where once stood the home-cum-beer-garden of William Copeland, the man who founded Japan's first beer company. The beer garden, like Copeland's beer company, fell flat.

The upper-crust foreigners guzzled brandy or wine; the common folk favored gin. Everybody liked beer, but neither stratum seems to have liked the foul-tasting stuff arriving on ships that was sold under that name. Several local foreigners made unsuccessful attempts at brewing beer locally—the Japan Yokohama Brewery on the Bluff may

• MAP 84

have been the first—and as early as May 1865 a beer hall opened downtown serving imported beer, mainly Bass. William Copeland, the man generally credited with starting the beer industry in Japan, was a Norwegian-American whose Spring Valley Brewery on the Bluff used hydraulic power, manpower, and horsepower to produce its suds. However, Copeland was not the best manager and he soon lost control of the enterprise. Incidentally, Copeland was one of the first Westerners to marry a Japanese, Umeko, the daughter of a Hakone inn owner. After his failure at running the beer garden, he ended up going to Hawaii to try marketing Japanese goods. He returned to Yokohama shortly before his death in 1902 at the age of seventy-six.

Japan's largest beer company, Kirin, started as the Japan Brewery Company Limited, an outgrowth of Spring Valley Brewery. The distinctive griffin-like Kirin trademark was introduced in 1897. Serious amateur historians might be interested in paying a visit to the monument that marks the site of the first brewery in Japan. Turn left at the next corner and follow the road until you reach a small park near Kitagata Primary School, appropriately enough dubbed Kirin Park. The well from which the water for the brew came is nearby.

The Brewery Trip

Those with a real thirst for knowledge should consider a trip to the Kirin Brewery at Namamugi. The factory is a seven-minute walk from Namamugi Station on the Keihin Kyuko Line, a twelve-minute trip from Yokohama Station. To get there, go out the east exit and head south in the direction of Yokohama. (The site where Charles Richardson met the Grim Reaper is near the station.) Kirin moved here after the 1923 earthquake and in 1991 the huge facility became the first fully automated beer factory in the world. Wandering among the stainless steel pipes and cauldrons is like being in a scene from the classic Fritz Lang film *Metropolis*. Robots are busy twenty-four hours a day producing soma for the masses.

You can enjoy a free tour of the plant and a sample nip compliments of the management; juice for the kids and teetotalers. Two-fisted guzzlers should repair to the red-brick outbuilding that is a recreation of the original Yamate brewery. Here, and here alone, you can enjoy Spring Valley Beer along with tasty treats like charbroiled seafood. At night the whole complex is lit up, as are many of the visitors, I should imagine.

Kirin Yokohama Beer Village キリン横浜ビアビレッジ

☎ 045-503-8250 (for reservations for brewery tour)

☎ 045-506-3013 (restaurant)

🕐 11:30–21:30; closed Mon.

The Yamate Museum (next to Yamate Jubankan) is housed within a structure originally built in 1909 for a wealthy Japanese family, the Sonodas, and is the oldest wooden building in Yokohama. Designed and built by Japanese, it was actually part of a larger mansion that stood in Tobe. Check out the lion-faced fire hydrant in front that was part of Japan's first pumped public water supply. Inside is a scale model of the Foreigners' Cemetery that shows where each grave is located and photos of some of the occupants, a collection of *Yokohama-e*, *Japan Punch* cartoons by Wirgman, a boundary marker from the old settlement, the oldest organ built in Japan, which dates back to 1884, and many other valuable historical relics, such as real Venetian blinds! You'll also be interested to know that the official chop, or seal found in all Japanese companies, originated in Yokohama in 1882.

At the corner turn left, go down toward the end of the street and on the right is a toy museum and shop, Toys Club, a private collection of tin toys dating from the 1890s to the 1960s. There are 16,000 different items, including 399 wooden toys, plastic dolls, and other associated toys. For better or worse, this place will bring back a flood of memories to anyone over forty. You'll be wallowing in nostalgia even before you turn the corner and see the poster for the cult film classic *Creature from the Black Lagoon*. Next door is Christmas Toys, run by the same management, where Christmas cards and other items related to St. Nick are on sale every day of the year and Christmas music fills the air. Imagine working here and having to listen to "Little Drummer Boy" 365 days of the year! Notice the politically incorrect posters on the door advertising Aunt Jemima Pancake Flour and Banjo Tobacco.

Go back to the main road now. This main route through Yamate still retains the flavor of elegant old Yokohama. Prior to the earthquake, resident foreigners lived in colonial style and had little use for Japanese culture or things Japanese, except for those that amused or brought pleasure. At first mammon and mayhem were their passions, but gradually the town became a staid, settled community in need of churches, schools, and recreational facilities. Statistics tell the story: By 1888 two-thirds of the houses in Yamate were occupied by families. Drinking and whoring gave way to yachting and golfing, and rank materialism began

• MAP 84

to be balanced by at least the external trappings of religion.

Here at the corner is Christ Church Yokohama. The original building, designed by Josiah Conder, opened its doors on October 18, 1863, but was destroyed in the quake. This was actually an Anglican riposte to the establishment of a Roman Catholic cathedral, known to the Japanese as Tenju-do, or "Jesus Temple," near Chinatown in January 1862 by L'Abbe Girard of the French Legation. The insecurity of the age was symbolized by the fact that the French officer who consecrated the bell, Lieutenant Henri Camus, had it toll for him at his funeral only a few days later. He was massacred by xenophobes in the Idogaya Incident. That bell and a statue of the Virgin Mary that survived the quake are today to be found in the Sacred Heart Cathedral, a hundred meters or so further down the road. It was built in 1933.

Turn left onto the main road. Next to the cemetery is Motomachi Park, with a *kyudo* archery range, and at the bottom of the hill a swimming pool where Frenchman Alfred Gerard's brick and tile factory used to stand. At the corner is the Ellisman Mansion, built in 1926 for a Swiss trader. It was designed by Czech architect Antonin Raymond, who assisted Frank Lloyd Wright in designing the Imperial Hotel and had incalculable influence on modern Japanese architects. Note the white clapboard walls, green roof, chimney, and pull windows. And don't forget to check out the antique phone at the entrance—it would make Alexander Graham Bell proud. Old photos on the walls, some in color, show what ambiance Yamate-style was like before the great shake. You quickly realize that what remains today represents only a very small part, a pale shadow of what once was. Take a break at nearby Enokitei: the homemade cheesecake with cherry sauce is scrumptious.

Ever observant, Kipling noted how Japanese children were coddled, and wrote, "The grown-ups exist on sufferance." One thing the foreigner and Japanese could see eye to eye on was the importance of education, and you will find many famous schools in Yamate, including Ferris Academy, whose forerunner, the Ferris School for Women, was cofounded in 1875 by Mary E. Kidder, an instructor at Dr. Hepburn's academy, as the first school in Japan for young women. It received vital

• MAP 84

encouragement from Kanagawa Governor Oe Taku. There's also Kyoritsu Girls' School, which opened its doors in 1871 as the American Mission School and is where the Bible was translated into Japanese, Saint Joseph's College, founded in 1901, Futaba Girls' School, St. Maur's, and Yokohama Girls' Commercial School.

Behind the Catholic cathedral is Yamate Park, a facility that came about in 1870 largely as a result of the efforts of W. H. Smith, or "Public-Spirited Smith" as he was often called, the long-time manager of the United Club. This human dynamo was the driving force behind many civic projects. Smith introduced many vegetables and other plants from Europe, such as cauliflower, and planned the earliest walking and bridle paths on the Bluff. Others followed his example, and soon lettuce and other exotic roughage started to appear on Japanese dinner tables.

Peripatetic Smith was also responsible for the establishment of cricket and tennis clubs in Yamate. The Yokohama International Tennis Club near the entrance to Yamate Park is celebrated as the birthplace of lawn tennis in Japan in 1878 and is the oldest tennis club in Japan. Membership was only opened to Japanese nationals in 1964 at the request of the city of Yokohama.

The decades immediately before the earthquake were the golden age for Yamate. During the 1920s Japanese began to move into Yamate in large numbers. Tanizaki was one. He came to Yokohama to write for Japan's fledgling movie industry, living first in Honmoku and then in Yamate, where he stayed a year and wrote four scripts. At this stage in his career Tanizaki was fascinated with anything from the West, and he hired a maid to serve him kidney pies, roast mutton, turkey, and other good old Anglo-Saxon fare. As an avowed Clara Bow and Greta Garbo fan, he was entranced with fair skin and blonde hair and took English lessons so he could appreciate Western women more deeply.

At that time many White Russians, stateless fugitives from Lenin's revolution, temporary wayfarers on a course to oblivion, lived in Yamate. In fact they had their own apartment houses, a restaurant at the foot of Daikan-zaka, and their own movie studio here. Naturally, the sensual, ever-curious Tanizaki was soon in touch with them, and

• MAP 84

White Russians figure in his classic novel *Sasameyuki* (translated into English as *The Makioka Sisters*). Theirs was a special world of sweet Easter cookies, samovars, balalaika music, and a benefit dance once a year at the Bund Hotel. Russian credit tailors with their materials wrapped in *furoshiki* were a common sight on the trains, and former aristocrats subsisted in extreme poverty as tutors. By 1938 there were 124 Russians, yet in 1947 only 93 remained, concentrated near the small Yokohama Foresters' Orthodox Church off Jizo-zaka. However, the community and its place of worship have now disappeared without a trace.

By the early 1920s the sun was beginning to set on foreign trade as foreign businesses were losing out to the *zaibatsu*—World War I had been the turning point that allowed Japanese to establish a preeminence in Far East commerce that they never relinquished. The old world of Yokohama was already fast fading before that Saturday in 1923 when the earth below struck the final blow.

The Big One

Jennie M. Kuyper had returned to the Isaac Ferris Seminary from the summer resort at Karuizawa only the day before. The children were due to return in a couple of days for the new school year, her second as principal. She had just seen an alumnus off to the gate and was returning to her office when the quake struck. She was buried alive under a huge pile of bricks and was unable to move. A janitor and another school employee rushed to help extricate her but by this time the building had been engulfed by a sea of fire rushing up from Motomachi. Turning to her would-be rescuers, the fifty-year-old educator said clearly, "You can't do anything for me if you stay." Then she ordered them to leave.

By this time Yamate was in ruins. The police station had collapsed and a five-story apartment house with over forty White Russians in it tumbled down a slope, killing nearly all. At St. Maur's dozens of nuns were crushed to death with dozens of their students and stained glass windows and religious statues were smashed. At the Foreigners' Cemetery over 80 percent of the tombstones fell over or were damaged. Motomachi was aflame and the British Naval Hospital built in 1871 was crackling in the wind. Two hundred people who had fled to its garden burned to death.

Tanizaki was lucky enough to be away in Hakone, but Ho Kong, Jardine's ultra comprador for over half a century, was in his Yamate mansion. He and twelve of the fifteen members in his family perished, his youngest son while desperately trying to make his way back home from his office. Only one son survived. Thus luck finally ran out for Yokohama's luckiest man.

• MAP 84

After the earthquake only a few foreign families returned to Yamate. However, across the road above the rail tunnels in Italian Hill Park is Bluff Juhachiban-kan, a pleasant white-walled building with an attractive French tiled roof. Built after the earthquake for a foreigner, it was recently turned into a small museum with furniture and other remnants from the good old days. On a clear day you can see as far as the Tanzawa Mountains from the house.

Nearly every foreign shipping, trade, and silk company relocated to Tokyo, from where they moved to Kobe, Shanghai, or the home country. The glory days for Yamate were over.

To go back downtown, catch a bus on the main road or keep going straight on this road for Negishi. Ishikawacho Station is very close; walk down Jizo-zaka and turn right at the main road before the river.

British House (Igirisu-kan イギリス館)
☎ 045-623-7812 ⏰ 9:00–17:00; no regular holidays

Osaragi Jiro Museum (Osaragi Jiro Kinen-kan 大佛次郎記念館)
☎ 045-622-5002 ⏰ 10:00–17:30; October to March 10:00–17:00; closed Mon. ¥200

Kanagawa Contemporary Literature Museum (Kenritsu Kanagawa Kindai Bungaku-kan 県立神奈川近代文学館)
☎ 045-622-6666 ⏰ 9:30–17:00; closed Mon.

Iwasaki Fashion Museum 岩崎ミュージアム
☎ 045-623-2111 ⏰ 9:40–18:00; closed Mon. ¥300

Foreigners' Cemetery (Gaijin Bochi 外人墓地) ☎ 045-622-1314
⏰ Officially open on Fri., Sat., Sun., and holidays, from late March to Nov. 30 and on Feb. 8, Charles Wirgman's birthday when the Ponchi Hana Festival is held; but entrance is usually possible through the side gate. Call to make sure.

Ellisman Mansion エリスマン邸
☎ 045-211-1101 ⏰ 9:30–17:00; closed Mon. Free

Yamate Museum (Yamate Shiryo-kan 山手資料館) ☎ 045-622-1188
⏰ 11:00–16:00; summer 11:00–17:00. ¥200

Toys Club (Buriki no Omocha Hakubutsu-kan ブリキのおもちゃ博物館) ☎ 045-621-8710 ⏰ 10:00–20:00; open all year. ¥200

Bluff Juhachiban-kan ブラフ18番館
☎ 045-662-6318 ⏰ 9:30–17:00; closed Mon. Free

Mutekiro 霧笛楼 ☎ 045-681-2926
⏰ 12:00–15:00, 17:00–22:00; open all year

Red Pepper レッド ペッパー ☎ 045-664-0723 ⏰ 11:00–23:00; closed Mon.

Garlic Jo's ☎ 045-662-4660 ⏰ 18:00–05:00; Sun. 18:00–03:00; closed Mon.

Punta Del Este ☎ 045-621-6771
⏰ 18:00–02:00; Sat. Sun. 18:00–04:00; closed Mon. and Tues.

Yamate Jubankan 山手十番館
☎ 045-621-4466 ⏰ 11:00–21:00; summer 10:00–21:00; open all year

Enokitei えの木てい ☎ 045-623-2288
⏰ 11:00–20:00; closed Mon.

• MAP 84

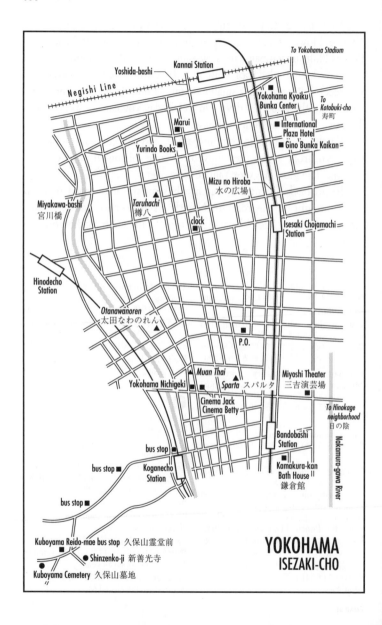

6

A Walk on the Wild Side

○ Kannai Station 関内駅 (JR Negishi Line)—Isezaki-cho 伊勢佐木町—Kuboyama Cemetery 久保山墓地—Miyoshi Vaudeville Theater 三吉演芸場—Kangai 関外—Hi no Kage 日の陰—Kotobuki-cho 寿町

You can leave your diamonds and furs home for this saunter. We're going to the other side of the tracks for a look at how the other half lives, with a stop in a giant graveyard to lift our spirits. This is important if you want to know Yokohama's soul; throughout its history Yokohama has been more than just a place where wealthy foreign merchants and Japanese silk kings could hang their top hats—more than anything else it has been a worker's town.

We start at the southwest exit of Kannai Station. As you face straight ahead to the left you will see a narrow mall stretching off into the distance. This is Odori Park. Its nearly mile-long length is dotted with numerous sculptures, including some by Henry Moore, as well as fountains and outdoor stages, and it is broken up into a number of thematic subsections, such as Ishi no Hiroba (Stone Plaza), Mizu no Hiroba (Water Plaza), and so on.

At the corner on the far side of the park is the Education Culture Center and in the next block the International Plaza Hotel. In the block past that is the Gino Bunka Kaikan (Vocational Training Hall). Inside is a small museum, the Takumi Plaza (Artisans' Plaza), which offers an interesting look at traditional craftsmanship. If you are an enthusiastic do-it-yourselfer, you can come here to drool at the hundreds of different tools that Japanese carpenters use. There is also a diorama showing how things were in the port's early days, examples of

• MAP 104

Yokohama's own unique style of Shibayama lacquerware using Meiji-period motifs, early photographic equipment, and videos with simple Japanese commentary describing the creative process in traditional crafts such as wig making.

Double back to Kannai Station via the park. On the left of the station is Yoshida-bashi Bridge. Notice the colorful illustrated tiles that cover it. This is actually the fifth bridge that has gone by that name. The original wooden one, 180 meters in length, was built in 1859 to link the foreign settlement with Yoshida Shinden, which was rapidly being filled in to provide a living place for Japanese workers.

In 1869 it was replaced by an impressive 24-meter-long, 5.8-meter-wide steel bridge designed and built by British engineer Richard Brunton. It was dubbed the Kane-no-hashi because it was supposed to be the first steel bridge in Japan. It was not, however, since a small one had already gone up two years earlier in Nagasaki. Local wags said it earned its name because it was the first toll bridge in modern Japan—*kane* can mean either metal or money. In any event, Yoshida-bashi became the main entrance into the city, the spot where the Silk Road terminated. The site of the steel bridge around where the bus stop stands today is marked by a commemorative plaque.

If you don't want to travel on an empty stomach, for a truly historic feed you might try the *gyunabe* at Otanawanoren, which is not exactly a fly by night establishment, considering that it was founded in 1868. It is the granddaddy of the beef hot-pot restaurants in Japan and uses only the finest Matsuzaka beef sliced extra thin. The restaurant also offers steak and *sukiyaki*. It is small, a bit pricey, and utterly unique.

On the other hand, if reading about Commodore Perry's visit has got you counting sumo wrestlers in your sleep like sugarplum fairies, why not chow down with the big boys at a *chanko nabe* restaurant only three minutes from Kannai Station. Run by a former sumo wrestler, Taruhachi is as funky as any sumo stable you can imagine.

Across from the Yoshida-bashi marker is the entrance to Isezaki-cho, which was prewar Yokohama's premier shopping district. During the 1920s modernism was the name of the game and the *Ise-bura* (Isezaki-cho stroll) became Yokohama's answer to the famous *Ginza-bura*

• MAP 104

among the *mobo* and *moga* ("modern boys" and "modern girls"), and the dandies and their frails, who sought to emulate Rudolph Valentino and Clara Bow.

Today the 1.5-kilometer-long street, thoroughly renovated in 1978, has over 500 shops. As in the Meiji and Taisho periods, Isezaki-cho is a mecca for serious shoppers and families content with window shopping and streetside snacking. I personally prefer it to the other two major shopping areas, Motomachi and Yokohama Station, and it is certainly more fun than the soulless MM21. Isezaki-cho's stores are great: Browse through the CDs at the Virgin Megastore on the third floor of the Marui 2 Building or pick up a bestseller at Yurindo Bookstore.

In the middle of the mall in front of the shoe store is the beloved mechanical clock, with nine little mechanical musicians who play for your pleasure every thirty minutes between 9:00 and 21:00 (They either belong to the musicians' union or they're terribly considerate of their neighbors at night.) Walk past the end of the arcade and you'll find the Higi area, home to Higi Shrine, the spiritual heart of Isezaki-cho, and several cheap seafood markets and Japanese doll shops.

Isezaki-cho, affectionately referred to as Zaki by locals, started out as an entertainment area around 1878 with many kabuki, *shimpa* drama, and vaudeville theaters, which frequently became venues for People's Rights Movement oratory. Zaki culture was a blend of port sophistication and *shitamachi* earthiness.

The earliest entertainment area had been down near the docks, where *misemono* tents abounded: here you could eyeball freaks of every conceivable hew and hue, as well as puppeteers, circus performers, sumo wrestlers, and other assorted strongmen. The Pig-pen Fire ruined all this fun and the motley herd was moved to the vegetable patches of Isezaki-cho. The advent of the moving picture led to the gentrification of even old Zaki. The Odeon, the most famous Yokohama movie palace, opened its doors on Christmas Day 1911 and soon won a reputation throughout Japan for first-run Western imports. Many foreign movies premiered here, and fans flocked to the cinemas from Tokyo. Several large department stores also went up as part of the post-earthquake reconstruction effort. The arcade is a postwar addition.

• MAP 104

All of this reflected Japan's helter-skelter urbanization and cultural homogenization during the 1920s and 1930s, direct outgrowths of the burgeoning mass media and standardized education system.

Not all the entertainment was so cerebral. Prewar Yokohama had at least three major red-light districts and the dance halls, cafes, and coffee bars were packed with willing waitresses. The period of cultural liberation was short-lived however. As the war clouds spread, hot jazz and "frivolous" movies were not to the liking of Japan's military masters. During the Occupation, Zaki was taken over lock, stock, and barrel by the U.S. military. They set up offices in the bombed-out department stores, turned the theaters into canteens, and posted off-limits signs and rifle-toting guards at the doors. They even established a mini-airport for Cessnas next to the Quonset huts. Next came the gum-chewing shoeshine boys and chocolate-popping, scarlet-lipped *pan pan* girls, spouting a mish-mash lingo, a stew of English and Japanese, the newest form of that ever-evolving *lingua franca*, Yokohamese. The Negishiya was a huge bar in Isezaki-cho that flourished during Occupation days. Open twenty-four hours, it was frequented by foreign sailors and Japanese alike. The cabaret scene toward the end of Kurosawa Akira's movie *Tengoku to Jigoku* (Heaven and hell) took place here.

One of the few places you can get a whiff of the old days in today's city are its several Greek bars frequented by Greek seamen from the freighters. While in most Japanese bars or restaurants, it is normal to pay while heading out the door, here you have to cough up for each drink or appetizer as it is served. At Sparta, located on Hamako-dori only a couple of minutes from Isezaki-cho Mall, you can savor moussaka, Greek salad, and fried sardines, and also boil your brains on ouzo.

A good time to make an excursion to Zaki is May 3, when the International Masquerade Parade is held to the delight of more than three hundred thousand spectators. Kids from many schools step high down the arcade, and young bucks from the neighborhood carry *omikoshi* portable shrines through the streets.

Yes, prewar Yokohama was to a large extent a worker's town. Just as the area "inside the gate" was known as Kannai, the area outside bore the name Kangai, *gai* meaning outside. Here in Kangai were

• MAP 104

cheap tenements for dock workers and young women who worked in the tea-processing factories. In 1903 there were an estimated six to seven thousand such unfortunates living in Miyoshi-cho alone, most of whom hailed from northern Japan. There were a hundred men for every eighty-three women and only one in twenty of the men had a family. Still, one foreign observer, in crossing Hanazono-bashi near Yokohama Park, noted "many children with black eyes and runny noses." Many were put to work at such trades as chimney cleaning when only seven or eight. There was little except the theaters to brighten the lives of these workers. So many seamstresses attended the plays that they came to be known as *hankachi shibai* after the handkerchiefs the girls carried to dab their eyes with.

During the mid-Meiji period, scarf factories and other sweatshops sprang up like mushrooms after rain, offering employment to young women from the countryside. However, the working conditions were not nearly as horrific as those found in the stifling tea-firing sheds. On visiting a large shed in which three or four hundred people labored round the clock amid nerve-shattering din and sweltering temperatures, a European noted: "The large high building lighted by flares of some kind, the burning charcoal, the misty dust or steam from the leaves, the perspiring men and women, the former almost quite naked, the latter naked to the waist—it was an inferno!"

Even among the poverty of Kangai, the particularly hard lot of the Koreans was noticeable. There used to be a Korean ghetto near Miyakawa-bashi Bridge between Noge and Isezaki-cho. The shacks here were roofed with metal sheets held down by stones; chili peppers and garlic inevitably hung from the rafters. The children were ill-clothed and ill-fed and Japanese parents discouraged their own children from playing with them. One elderly Hama resident remembered in his memoirs a ditty he and his friends sang as a child:

> *Chosenjin ga kawaiso,*　　Those Koreans are pitiful,
> *Naze ka to ieba,*　　Why you ask,
> *Jishin no tame ni*　　Well, the earthquake came,
> *Ouchi ga pecchanko.*　　And their homes just went *kaputt*.

• MAP 104

Many people were so poor that they lived on flatboats on the Ooka-gawa River and other waterways. The interiors of the low-roofed vessels were dark even at midday. At least the residents did not have to worry about inheritance taxes or big development companies taking their land away for a pittance. Some of these boat people were Japanese fishermen who chose this style of living not purely out of economic necessity.

After Miyozaki-cho was burned down during the 1866 Pig-pen Fire, the red-light districts were moved farther away from the city center. One of these was Eiraku-cho, whose brothels used to leave fancy name cards in the sitting-rooms of hotels. One of those cat houses, old Number Nine, whose mouthwatering qualities also led it to be known simply as "The Nectarine," was immortalized by Rudyard Kipling in his 1894 epic poem of regret, "McAndrew's Hymn," which reads in part:

> Blot out the wastrel hours of mine in sin when I abode—
> Jane Harrigan's an' Number Nine, The Reddick and Grant Road!

Eiraku-cho is still there, on the opposite side of Odori Park from Isezaki-cho. I can't testify to Number Nine's continued existence, but the surfeit of love hotels would indicate that the area has not been turned into a Calvinist summer camp.

On the opposite side of Isezaki-cho across the river, is Koganecho Station on the Keihin Kyuko Line. Under the tracks is a warren of dozens of little bars, staffed by girls in diaphanous dresses and other flimsy attire, who obviously reached the wilds of Yokohama via Bangkok and Manila. Ever since the Occupation this area has been a center for prostitution and drug dealing. In the 1950s it was stimulants, today it appears to be cocaine and crack. One resident told me the area is known locally as "outlaw town."

Back across the river, you'll find a strip theater and a fascinating little area that is a mix between Southeast Asia and downtown Japan. Here you'll find Muan Thai Restaurant, whose customers are mainly Thais living in the vicinity. You can watch Thai videos, including kick-boxing matches, on four monitors while you eat. The food itself is luscious and truly authentic. The most astounding thing about Muan Thai, though, is that it is open twenty-four hours a day, every day of

• MAP 104

the year. Have a fiery dish on your way to work. There are also Thai food stores and another Thai restaurant down the road. Also, check out Jack and Betty Yokohama and Yokohama Nichigeki—great theaters offering first-run and vintage Western and Japanese movies at about one-third less than the going rate, and an international market that stocks products from just about everywhere between Riyadh and Seoul.

Fittingly, perhaps, a kilometer or so from Koganecho Station, is Kuboyama Cemetery, Yokohama's oldest and the final resting place of many early city fathers and 3,300 of the victims of the Kanto earthquake, including Koreans massacred in its wake. The easiest way to get there is by bus from Koganecho Station; get off at Kuboyama Reidomae. On the way there, in the hills near Kogane-cho, is Shinzenko-ji Temple, where you'll find the Akaboshi Sanraku statue, established in honor of Saito Kojiro (Sanraku), an early-Meiji philanthropist and ex-barber who built a poorhouse for beggars and the unemployed. Saito put many of the indigent to work in disctinctive gear as garbage collectors and consciously sought to instil in them a work ethic and a sense of pride. According to tradition, at least, beggars all but disappeared from Yokohama streets thanks to his efforts. He also built a small hermitage in Kuboyama where impoverished patients were cared for free and given medicine. Saito personally treated them like a father and developed into something of a Johnny Appleseed–type eccentric who went around in red coat and cap giving candy to children.

Three hundred meters after the temple is the cemetery, where among the graves of samurai and early silk traders are also the bones of Tojo Hideki and six other Class A war criminals who were executed at Sugamo Prison in Tokyo, 1948. Because of fears that they would be considered martyrs, the Occupation adamantly refused to turn the bodies over to their families or friends. Instead they were shipped here in the dead of night and cremated. Nevertheless, Japanese got hold of the ashes and buried them without knowledge of the Allies on the outskirts of Nagoya. Later a monument was erected here to honor them.

Retrace your steps back to the area where the theaters are and then go straight across the main road and Odori Park to the entrance to the Nippon Shotengai shopping arcade, which is filled with small shops of

• MAP 104

all kinds. You'll soon come to another large street. Cross it and go straight until you're in front of Nakamura-gawa River. Don't go across—look to the left and you'll see one of Yokohama's plebeian treats, the Miyoshi Engei-jo vaudeville theater, which received a culture award back in 1989. The perfect finale for a visit to the theater is a trip to a bath-house. Try Ganso Kusatsu Onsen next door or the nearby Kamakura-kan, an ancient tub in a superb wooden building with cathedral-like ceilings. Apart from a sauna and small outdoor bath, no attempt has been made to yuppify the place—you can still buy pre-war hairnets and gaze at a huge, gaudy seascape as you scrub down. Highly recommended.

Miyoshi Vaudeville Theater

Each day at 17:00 the big drum on the roof booms out its message: The theater is opening. Beginning promptly at 17:30 the show lasts till 21:00. All this for ¥1,500 and the price drops as the evening goes on. Typically there are two short plays, one tragedy and one comedy, and then song and dance performances by the various members of whatever troupe is performing. Each troupe knows hundreds of plays by heart. The photos outside announce which troupe is performing; they rotate regularly and never repeat the same play during an engagement. Like traditional kabuki, most of the plots have to do with the conflict between duty and passion and are enacted with much bravado and Edo hero-style posturing.

Most of the dialogue is in standard Japanese, although the honorifics can be formidable. Not only are the plays a good chance to improve your Japanese, they also give insights into what kabuki must have been like in earlier days before middle-class matrons got control of the theaters—this is about as close as you could want to get to Japanese pop culture. It can be a bit disconcerting, however, to have a samurai duel take place to the strains of rock music.

At least as interesting as what is going on on stage is the audience. This is far from the blue-stocking crowd. No *bento* in fancy lacquered boxes to be accompanied by saké from an elaborate decanter. Here snacks are washed down with canned beer. People wander in from the public bath (Ganso Kusatsu Onsen) next door, which is run by the same management. Middle-aged women in somewhat blowsy fashions predominate, but you get a smattering of workers in boots, *yakuza* types, and even youngsters on dates. Tattoos, not tutus, are in style here. If a handsome young actor performs an especially fine pose, you might see an enthusiastic female fan rush up and stuff a couple of thousand yen inside his sash. At the very least, there should be some shouts of approval from the audience.

The present owner took over in 1973. She says: "I enjoy this kind of business, so that's why I'm hanging in here. When a good show draws customers, it really makes me happy."

Miyoshi Vaudeville Theater (Miyoshi Engei-jo 三吉演芸場)

☎ 045-231-7633 ⊙ 17:30 show; Sat., Sun. also 12:30 show; closed first and third Mon. Last day of Jan., Mar., May, and Oct. *rakugo* performance is held.

• MAP 104

Across the river from the Miyoshi is Hinokage, a working-class neighborhood that started out in the postwar years as a home to squatters and is now starting to go upscale.

Okinawa and Yokohama were the two major victims of the Occupation. Outside of Okinawa, Yokohama represented 62 percent of Japanese land requisitioned by the Allies. Much of this was not returned to the Japanese until years after requisitioned land in Tokyo and other areas had reverted to its owners. By 1955 two-thirds of the occupied land and one-half of the buildings had been returned, but large areas of the docks and hillsides were still in military hands. The delay left Yokohama several years behind when it came to economic recovery and even now the gap has not been completely closed.

Laborers poured into Yokohama to work for the U.S. Army. Since the Allied forces had occupied nearly all of the central part of the city, shacks were thrown up to house them and the thousands who had been left homeless by the air raids. Barges on the Ooka-gawa were converted into "water hotels." Conditions were so bad that they became spawning grounds for typhus and other diseases. Some also became so crowded they became death traps of a different sort when they turned turtle.

Hinokage, which literally means "shadow of the sun," refers to the area below the heights of Yamate and Negishi, including parts of Yamamoto-cho, Nakamura-cho, and Ishikawa-cho. Here you can still find corrugated metal homes like those built in the immediate postwar period, although they are gradually getting crowded out by modern apartment houses. You can imagine how things were in the dark starvation days following the war when thousands struggled to survive here, while all the while they could see utopia on the other side of the barbed-wire fences: Green lawns and golf courses, comfortable buildings with central heating, well-stocked commissaries. Local resentment against the military presence continued long after the Occupation ended. During the Vietnam War there were several major protests in Yokohama, including one against opening a field hospital at Negishi.

Walk toward Ishikawacho Station and you can get a feel for life in Hinokage. It is still rather poor, but the neighbors all know each other, and you don't find that uncaring coldness common in large cities.

• MAP 104

Before reaching the station, swing back over to the other side of the river for the last stop on this route, namely Kotobuki-cho, a most unapt name for Yokohama's skid row, since *kotobuki* means "long life."

Early Western settlers in Yokohama noted the large number of Japanese beggars, many obviously professional. Some of them, including religious beggars, could be very intimidating. There were also many inebriated Japanese wandering the streets. Francis Hall summed it up in a pithy journal entry: "Intemperance in drink and intemperance in lust are the national sins of Japan."

The beggars are largely gone, but the public drunks still abound. You'll find them in Kotobuki-cho, Yokohama's shame, just a ten-minute walk from the glitz of Chinatown and Motomachi.

After the war, the U.S. military turned Kotobuki-cho and neighboring Matsukage-cho into a giant dump, so vegetation grew wild and it came to be known as Kannai Pasture. In 1955, when the area was returned, it acted like a magnet for more than six thousand day laborers who worked at the city's harbor and construction sites. Since that time, lonely, often unemployed men have lived in small, filthy rooms that do not even merit the name tenement. They have come to be known as *doya*, or flophouse, and the general area is often called Doya Town. Take a look at the multistoried Prefectural Labor Center in the center of Kotobuki-cho, which looks a highrise in the seventh circle of hell.

The slump of the early nineties has hit Kotobuki-cho hard. You can see it in the curbside soup-kitchens, in the hard laughter from the cheap bars that are open all day, and in the haunted eyes of the men who wander its streets. More and more of those men come from Southeast Asia.

Takumi Plaza (Gino Bunka Kaikan 技能文化会館) ☎ 045-681-6551 ⏲ 9:00–17:00; closed Mon.

Jack and Betty Cinemas ☎ 0120 198009

Yokohama Nichigeki ☎ 045-242-8750

Kamakura-kan 鎌倉館 ☎ 045-251-0211 ⏲ 15:30–23:30; closed Mon. ¥340

Ganso Kusatsu 元祖草津 ☎ 045-251-0211 ⏲ 15:30–23:30; closed Mon. ¥340

Otanawanoren 太田なわのれん ☎ 045-261-0636 ⏲ 16:00–22:00; Sun. 12:00–20:00; closed Mon.

Taruhachi 樽八 ☎ 045-261-3410 ⏲ 17:00–02:00; Sun., hols. 17:00–24:00; open all year

Sparta スパルタ ☎ 045-261-3491 ⏲ 17:00–01:00; Sun. 17:00–24:00; open all year

Muan Thai ☎ 045-262-4827 ⏲ Open 24 hours a day, every day

• MAP 104

7

Horsing Around

○ Yamate Station 山手駅 (JR Negishi Line) or bus from Sakuragicho Station—Nankin Bochi 南京墓地—Negishi 根岸—Sankei-en 三溪園—Honmoku 本牧

One of the primal joys for the early foreign residents of Yokohama was equestrian in nature. In other words, they adored riding over the fertile fields and gently undulating hills that surrounded the little settlement. The breeze from the nearby ocean was exhilarating and, especially on cold winter mornings, the view of snow-topped Fuji-san to the southwest was dazzling. Tall blue cranes standing stock-still observed these curiously clothed, curiously complexioned horse folk as they dashed from one hamlet of thatched cottages to the next.

Of course, if these rough riders ran across dinner on the way, that was all for the better. At first the area abounded with wildlife, including wild pigeon, pheasant, woodcock, and snipe. But within a few short years Western hunters and their packs of hounds imported from Shanghai had all but exterminated the birds and beasts around Yokohama.

The Japanese authorities attempted to stop the slaughter, but lacking the power to arrest the culprits, their efforts were futile. This was highlighted by the celebrated Moss case of 1863. Michael Moss, a British merchant, was unfortunate enough to be caught by Japanese officials with a wild goose. He was hardly the first foreigner to have been apprehended while committing this vile crime. However, while resisting arrest he shot a Japanese samurai, whose shoulder was so badly shattered that he could no longer wield a sword. The Japanese warned that unless they received justice from the British, they would exact it themselves in blood.

• MAP 116

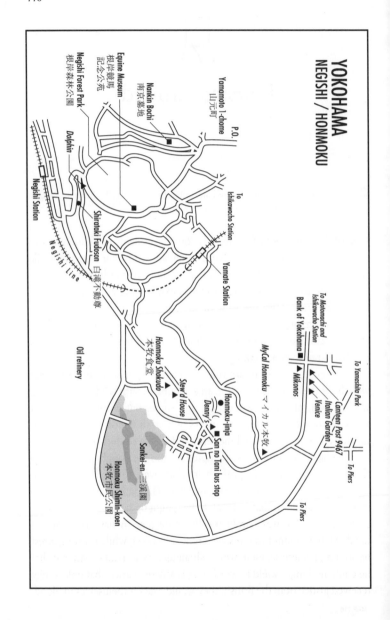

The Consular Court found Moss guilty and sentenced him to a stiff fine and deportation. But the consul, Rutherford B. Alcock, saw fit to top that with a six-month jail sentence to be served in Hong Kong. The foreign population was outraged and Alcock became *persona non grata* in all the local clubs. Moss was released from the slammer after only a few days, but when he got back to England, he filed charges against Alcock and tried to get the draconian diplomat dismissed from the foreign service. This vendetta did not run its course for several years.

To begin this trail, take a bus for Negishi from Sakuragicho Station and get off at Yamamoto-cho 1-chome. At the second intersection turn right and walk for five minutes. On the left is a Chinese-style gate with the sign Jizo Obyo (地蔵王廟). This is the Chinese cemetery, commonly known as Nankin Bochi, attached to the Ti Ts'ang Wang Miao Temple.

In the beginning the Chinese were buried along with other foreigners in the Gaijin Bochi, albeit segregated in their own corner. Overcrowding and differences in burial customs eventually led to the prefectural government granting in 1871 the request from the Chinese community for their own cemetery. The first was in Yamashita-cho, and this site in Negishi was set aside in March 1873. Craftsmen were brought especially from Guangdong Province in 1892 to construct the red brick building which survived the earthquake.

In the early days most Chinese intended for their bodies to be shipped back to their hometowns in China. They would spend a good portion of their hard-earned wages to purchase expensive camphor plank coffins lined with coal to keep the worms away and retard decomposition. In these they could rest in comfort after death until they could make the final journey back to China aboard the "coffin ship" that came to Yokohama every few years.

This custom disappeared after the earthquake—when the practice of cremation began taking hold—and the war, although about fifty coffins are still stored here in special rooms. Some have been waiting for more than three-quarters of a century for the boats that never came. With time some of the names have even disappeared with the weathering of the wood, so that no one knows whose remains are inside.

In the main hall (currently undergoing renovation), there is a *jizo*

• MAP 116

statue on the altar in the center, with a memorial tablet for female ancestors on the left and males to the right. The gold-gilded *jizo* was brought from China. Note the Indian-style Buddhist robes and Chinese cap.

The Reian-do, a six-sided yellow, white, and blue building where bones are stored, is often referred to as the "Yellow Crane Tower" because it supposedly resembles a crane in flight. Perhaps it's a comforting symbol for those who believe in rebirth, as the crane represents longevity in Japan and China. Within the building are hundreds of lockers in which boxes containing the bones of the dead are stored. Written on them are the names of the deceased, and photographs are attached, too. Sometimes the place of birth in China is also given.

In the past there were many knoll-type, traditional Chinese-style graves, but now most are hardly distinguishable from those of the Japanese. Many Chinese come here on April 5 for the Ch'ing Ming "Sweeping of the Tombs" Festival and July 15 for the Chinese version of the O-bon (All Souls) Festival. Reportedly there are about six hundred graves, at least a quarter of which contain unknowns. The ongoing project for restoring and improving the cemetery includes a monument to the unknown and religious services for them. At the back of the graveyard is a memorial to victims of the earthquake, where you can often see fresh flowers.

Double back to the main road, turn right, and continue in the original direction. Our next stop is the split-level Equine Museum of Japan, next to where the Negishi Racetrack used to be. You will see it on the right-hand side in front of a huge, grassy depression—the old track.

This unique museum traces the interrelation between human beings and horses since prehistoric times. It is spacious and the displays are tastefully done. Natural history, art, history, and folklore are all explored in the exhibits and videos (some in English), and special exhibitions are held on a regular basis. Make sure to catch some of the videos showing the racing life in the early days of the port, rare footage of past sweepstakes, and introductions to festivals around the country that are in some way related to horses. There are also royal coaches, saddles, and all kinds of samurai equestrian equipment. Just about everything you could want to know about horses in Japan. At the Pony Center next

• MAP 116

door, children can ride free on the third Sunday each month.

Racing in Yokohama began in 1861, along the Ooka-gawa River in what is today Sakuragi-cho. Later a course was built in Yamashita-cho near Chinatown with some of the reparations from the Namamugi Incident. The first Yokohama Derby was staged there on August 1, 1862, but the race track was abandoned the following year in favor of one near the British camp on the Bluff. Next, it was suggested that a permanent track be set up in what became the Isezaki-cho area. But because of security considerations, and perhaps because the "Dirty Village" had already developed something of a sporting tradition in the area, Negishi was chosen instead. The 1,900-meter-long, 32-meter-wide oval Negishi track was established in 1866 by the Yokohama Race Club in an area of sweet-potato fields and dairy pasture.

In its heyday the Negishi Racetrack was the social epicenter of the community during the spring and autumn racing seasons. Silk gowns and silk top hats were as common as the silks on the backs of the jockeys. The first Japanese member admitted to the club was Saigo Takamori's younger brother, who joined in 1876. (Foreigners seem to have had an especially soft spot in their heart for the romantic, reactionary Saigo.) Aristocrats and elite businessmen, as well as Chinese compradors, held court, and the first Japan Derby was run here in November 1902. The Emperor's Cup race also had its first running here and Emperor Meiji attended the races at least a dozen times.

The track was badly damaged in the earthquake—the present stands date from 1929—and in 1943 a stop was put to racing when the Imperial Navy, which was interested in improving its horseflesh for the utilitarian purpose of mayhem abroad, occupied the track.

After the war the U.S. military seized the entire area, turning the track into a golf course. A sizable base still remains to this day; you can see the Stars and Stripes flying here and there in the neighborhood. However, from 1969 the U.S. government began returning the track area itself and during the 1970s it was transformed into Negishi Forest Park with twenty thousand trees, including many cherry and plum.

This huge, grassy expanse just may be the best spot in Yokohama for picnicking and serious tomfoolery. Bring a football and you can do

• MAP 116

your Joe Montana imitation. When you enter the park, off in the distance you can see the enormous black ferroconcrete stands looming forebodingly in the distance like the ruins of Niniveh. Walk over to get a close-up view of the decrepit structure and dream what it must have been like crowded with the well-heeled during its heyday.

Trivia buffs and straight shooters might be interested to know that Negishi was also home to the Swiss Rifle Club. Another knowledge nugget of no significance was alluded to by Osaragi Jiro in his novel *Kikkyo* (The homecoming), namely that all slopes in the area have animal names, such as Buta-zaka ("Pig Slope"), Ushi-zaka ("Cow Slope"), Saru-zaka ("Monkey Slope"), and Tanuki-zaka ("Raccoon Slope"). Yoshikawa Eiji, the king of Japanese popular literature, was born near here.

When you're through looking around the park, go down the road to Negishi Station, which begins directly across from the U.S. military fire station. Pass the Dolphin restaurant, made famous by Yumin's monster pop hit "Umi Mite Ite Gogo" (An afternoon looking at the sea), and turn left at the intersection about five minutes along. Go straight for another seven minutes and on the right you'll see the rear entrance to Shirataki Fudoson, a little wooden shrine known to locals as Ofudo-san. The Fudo Myoo image inside is said to have appeared from a well on the premises. Paralleling the hundred steps leading down the hillside is Shirataki Falls, once twenty meters high and five meters wide, but which is now little more than a trickle. Still, it is the only waterfall in Yokohama. In front of you is Negishi Bay, known in settlement days as Mississippi Bay.

There used to be great scenery and swimming all along this coast from Honmoku to Kanazawa Hakkei. They have been replaced by one of the nation's largest petrochemical and industrial districts, the 610-hectare Negishi Bay Seaside Industrial Zone. The reclamation work was started in 1959 and completed in 1964, the same year that a train link was opened between Sakuragicho and Ofuna. Among the companies with plants here are Nippon Petroleum, Tokyo Electric, Tokyo Gas, and Nisshin Oil Mills. Either out of a desire to compensate the local people for what they had lost or out of a diabolical sense of humor, the metropolitan government built in place of the beaches a giant pool complex at Isogo that can accommodate twenty-five thousand people a day.

• MAP 116

Yokohama has, of course, always been looked down upon by residents of Tokyo and it was undoubtedly one of them who first said, "*Sankei-en wa Yokohama niwa sugita mono da,*" which roughly translates as "Sankei-en is too good for Yokohama."

Honmoku certainly seems a rather strange site for one of Japan's most beautiful gardens. But when its founder, Hara Tomitaro, built it at the end of the last century, he had no idea that it would one day be ringed with smokestacks belching their dark, tainted expirations into the air.

When you reach the bottom of the staircase leading down from Shirataki Falls, go straight till you reach the main road and then turn left. A couple of hundred meters to the right is Negishi Station on the Negishi Line. However, turn left and keep on going straight, staying along the coast and not turning off at the main cutoff; in about twenty minutes you will reach Seaside Park and the entrance to Sankei-en Garden. Unless you are enamored with looking at factories through the fence you may prefer hopping on a bus (numbers 54, 58, 99, 101, and 108 from Negishi Station). Get off at Honmoku Shimin Koen-mae bus stop.

First stop is the octagonal, ferroconcrete Chinese-style Hasseiden (Hall of the Eight Sages), intended by its creator to be a replica of the Yumedono Hall at Horyu-ji in Nara. It was built in 1933 by Adachi Kenzo (1864–1948), former home minister and avowed ultranationalist, for "spiritual training." On the second floor are life-size statues of the "Eight Sages of the World"—Jesus Christ, Socrates, Confucius, Gautama, Prince Shotoku, Kobo Daishi, Shinran, and Nichiren. The large mirror in the center of the statues is supposed to symbolize the universe. There are also interesting displays of artifacts related to the daily lives of farmers and fishermen. Nearby is a mammoth swimming pool that'll hold seven thousand. To get to the entrance to the Sankei-en, you have to go five hundred meters back to the east through the park. On the way be sure to stop in at the Shanghai-Yokohama Friendship Park, a Chinese-style garden with a permanent pleasure barge that would have pleased even China's First Emperor.

Usually when a nouveau-riche art fancier decides to do it big, what results is a bizarre monstrosity like William Randolph Hearst's San Simeon Castle on the California coast. Sankei-en is something entirely

• MAP 116

different. Normally if you heard that someone had bought up several priceless architectural specimens of great antiquity and transplanted them to his private garden, you would be tempted to think that he was a crazed megalomaniac. That was exactly what Hara Tomitaro (1868–1939) did, but he was one of the most cultured men of modern Japan, a good friend of novelist Natsume Soseki, the Indian philosopher Tagore, and patron of countless artists, including Yokoyama Taikan.

Tomitaro, born the son of a village head, was adopted as the son and heir of silk king, Hara Zenzaburo, after studying classic Chinese literature and civilization at Waseda University. He became a noted calligrapher, artist, and poet in his own right, under the pseudonym Sankei, meaning "three glens." At the same time he was a highly successful and innovative businessman who modernized and globalized the silk empire he received from Zenzaburo and also served as first president of the Yokohama Koshin Bank, the forerunner of the Bank of Yokohama.

Hara had Sankei-en, which has been described as a "product of perfect harmony between nature and man-made structures," built on a swampy site. He landscaped the seventeen hectares himself around Honmoku Hill and brought expert gardeners from Kyoto and Nara to attend to the details. The spectacular garden was opened to the public in 1906, although the Hara family has continued to live in a mansion on the premises. Cherry and plum trees, irises, azaleas, wisteria, chrysanthemums, water lilies, and lotuses bloom in their respective seasons. But the real attractions at Sankei-en are the many priceless historic buildings gathered from Kyoto, Kamakura, and elsewhere that have been registered as Important Cultural Properties.

Perhaps the most important is the twenty-five-meter-high three-story pagoda on the top of a hill that towers over everything. It is reputed to be more than five hundred years old and was brought from Tomyo-ji Temple in Kyoto. The Rinshunkaku, built in 1649, was a villa of the Kii branch of the Tokugawa clan. It is the only intact example of villa architecture of feudal lords. The Choshukaku tea ceremony hermitage, the handiwork of the third Tokugawa shogun, Iemitsu (1604–51), once stood within the grounds of Nijo Castle in Kyoto. It is typical of the style for such structures popular during the transition

• MAP 116

from the Momoyama to the Edo periods. The feudal hegemon Toyotomi Hideyoshi originally erected the tomb-like Tensuiji Juto Sayado in 1592 within the grounds of Daitoku-ji Temple in Kyoto to celebrate the longevity of his aged mother. (Hideyoshi was one of the greatest mama's boys in a national history replete with mama's boys.) It was moved here in 1960. Other outstanding buildings are the Gekkaden and Shunsoro teahouses, and the Tenju-in.

The Yanohara Residence, a gigantic three-story farmhouse brought from Shogawa Village, Gifu Prefecture, is also worth mentioning. It was originally built in 1763 and relocated here in 1960 when it was due to be submerged by an artificial lake created by the construction of a dam. Look as hard as you might, you won't find a single nail in the massive thatched building. It serves as a reminder of the age, not too many years ago, when Japanese farm families, especially the richer ones, were huge and "skinmanship" was necessary for survival and not just a business skill. Be warned that the Sankei-en is divided into an inner and outer garden and that you have to pay separately to get into each. Another fee is charged for entrance into the Yanohara Residence. But, considering the cost of upkeep for the gardens, the fees are not excessive.

Although normally such things as videos on the life of an entrepreneur whose descendants are charging you to see his legacy might be considered offensively promotional or even hero worship, that is not true in the case of Hara Tomitaro. The fact that he was a remarkable individual is evident from the displays of his calligraphy and brush painting in the small museum inside the entrance to the inner garden. Life was not all smooth sailing for Hara, either. Despite the fact that the silk industry collapsed in the post–World War I depression and his bank was in trouble, he led the post-earthquake reconstruction effort in the city. Many of his friends and some relatives in the business community, who like him had been identified as internationalists, were assassinated by rightists during the 1920s and 1930s. Perhaps it is best that he did not live to see the severe damage that his beloved Sankei-en suffered during the war. Of course, it has been repaired since then.

The garden and its buildings are not only important culturally but also represent a style of culture that cannot be found anywhere else in

• MAP 116

the Kanto region, remaining as a concrete legacy of the Yokohama silk industry, which has all but disappeared. If not for Hara Tomitaro and the Sankei-en, Yokohama's age of silk would have been like a fleeting dream that disappeared with the morning mist. The irony is that a place of beauty created with profits from industry has to an extent become one of many victims of industrial pollution and it is a disconcerting sight to see factory smoke rising skyward in the distance.

Go out the front entrance of Sankei-en past the large pond. Follow the main road that veers to the right about ten minutes to Honmoku-dori. Turn left at the police box and then get on the other side of the road. At Denny's on the corner, turn right onto Ouma-dori, and walk toward the new shrine at the foot of the hills. Although the buildings and the imposing *torii* were only erected in late 1993, the Honmoku Shrine has an eight-century history. It used to overlook Tokyo Bay, and the gods enshrined here were responsible for safety in the bay. However, the shrine was moved out when the U.S. military took the area over after World War II. Then for many years it was to be found at the other side of Honmoku, before being relocated to these present pastures. This *jinja* preserves a very unusual sea–horse festival tradition. The Honmoku Oumanagashi or Wara Uma (Straw Horse) Festival, which takes place on the first or second Sunday in August, originated way back in 1566, when the shrine was still at the water's edge.

Every year the men of the Hattori family make six straw horses, forty-five centimeters in length. Each takes a week to complete and represents an offering from one of the six original villages at Honmoku. Actually the necks and heads of the totems resemble horses, while the bodies are shaped like turtles. White Shinto paper offerings are attached to the heads. The ponies are taken to the shrine the day before the festival, where ears of rice are placed in their mouths and they are feted on soybean and wheat-flour cakes and sacred rice wine.

Their entry into the shrine is rather special. They are placed on one-meter-long wooden planks and passed from head to head by the participants, all men, who move forward in measured steps. At the shrine the horses undergo ritual purification. Then they're ready for the big day.

The ultimate purpose of these images is to serve as "scapehorse-turtles,"

• MAP 116

that will take ill fortune with them out to sea, where they'll request the gods to protect the locals from disasters. The festival appears to be rooted in ancient beliefs and is actually a combination of two traditions: in one horses take away the bad luck, in the other it is sent out to sea.

On festival day the images are again carried out in stately fashion on their custom-made planks. The six mounts of fate are taken down to D Pier near the Umizuri Pier bus stop by truck. There they are loaded onto a fishing boat and carried at least four kilometers out to sea to be set adrift. If they do not return to land, it is believed that the local fishermen will enjoy a good catch and avoid diseases and other disasters.

But if they return? Reportedly in August 1923, the horses returned to shore. Less than a month later the Great Kanto Earthquake struck.

Go back to Honmoku-dori. If you turn right you'll find several restaurants including Stew'd House and Honmoku Shokudo, an Art Deco cafe. Many foreigners associated with shipping companies live out in Honmoku—in fact Honmoku has always been a haven for foreigners.

The Japanese and Meat

Honmoku was the first center of Japan's meat industry. Meat did not figure prominently in the traditional Japanese diet, because of the Buddhist prohibition on taking life. However, by the 1870s the Japanese were being exhorted by their rulers to "eat meat for enlightenment." The government created a special area on the coast at Honmoku for slaughterhouses. Licences were issued for one butcher per nationality, which seems not entirely kosher considering the number of British and American residents. At least two foreign butchers had been active in Yokohama by 1861, but they caused such a stink by dumping the offal into local canals that residents asked the authorities to banish them to more distant areas.

That demand fitted in nicely to existing Japanese cultural prejudices. Jobs related to butchering, tanning, and so forth had been relegated to the outcast class. These pariahs were treated as subhuman and forced to live as outcasts on the outskirts of towns, living their entire lives in a kind of twilight zone.

There is a disconcerting *Yokohama-e* woodblock print by Hashimoto Sadahide, the foremost artist of that style, that shows a couple of foreign butchers. The bloody hands, bulging eyes, and the depraved looks on their faces no doubt reflected the traditional image of this trade. In a record of strange customs among the foreigners in Yokohama, Sadahide relates how crowds of curious Japanese gathered to watch the gruesome butchering process. They grew so noisy that, in the end, a foreign carcass carver set a pack of dogs on them.

For a taste of Honmoku meat, try the stew cooked up at Stew'd House on Honmoku-dori.

Stew'd House ☎ 045-623-3001
🕙 10:00–21:00; closed Tues.

• MAP 116

However, turn left at Denny's and go straight for about ten minutes. As you proceed down Honmoku-dori you will soon find yourself in the midst of an out-of-body experience. You better toss away your Japanese-English conversation dictionary into a nearby trash can and reach instead for your Frank Zappa primer on Valley Girl talk. For you are now entering the MyCal Honmoku zone.

In case you haven't guessed it already, let me make things perfectly clear. MyCal Honmoku is a huge California-style shopping mall (no doubt that's where the Cal comes from) that seems primarily designed as a date center for trendy young adults. The complex of nine Spanish colonial-style buildings that started going up in 1989 claims to be the biggest shopping center in Japan. Before that for four decades the area was occupied by a U.S. military housing complex taking up eighty-eight hectares, a Little America surrounded by barbed wire.

The complex is supposed to have an "urban resort" flavor to it; Orange County in the Orient is more like it. Altogether there are about 240 shops, eateries, live houses, and cinemas. At the Fisherman's Wharf in Building 1 you can choose what you want to take home for dinner from a tank. Another section features environmental photos to soothe the heart of the urban beast.

After exploring MyCal, keep going straight on Honmoku-dori. About ten minutes along you'll come to an area with several interesting businesses reminiscent of the GI days. On the right is the canteen for Post 9467 of the Veterans of Foreign Wars (VFW). Drop in to swap old war stories with the ex-troopers, Elvis impersonators, and other "friendlies" (as opposed to "hostiles") that hang out here. Non-members are welcome although it's cheaper if you're a VFW member. Next door is a bar, the Italian Garden, and Venice restaurant, which has fine pizza.

On the other side of the road is Mikonos, a Greek restaurant. The Japanese chef started out with Italian and Spanish cuisine before moving on to Greek. He served as head cook at a hotel in Rhodes before creating his succulent seafood menu featuring over forty dishes. From here you can catch a bus to Sakuragi-cho Station. Get off at Motomachi bus stop and you're only five minutes from Ishikawacho Station.

The waterfront of Yokohama has been the setting for much fiction,

• MAP 116

the wild youth stories of Ishihara Shintaro when he was starting out as a novelist, and more recently hard-boiled detective novels. And Honmoku remains one of the most important dock areas to this day. According to customs officials, the types of drugs and other contraband flowing through the port have changed with the times. In the immediate postwar period it was food, including sugar from Taiwan. Handguns were confiscated in the early 1950s, then heroin and other opiates became the focus of attention in the early sixties, along with Rolexes and other luxury items. For a time gold was the in-thing, especially for sailors, who secreted it in orifices not normally inspected. Recently stimulants handled by the mob have become the biggest headache for customs officials.

To get a feel for the docks and a clear view of Tokyo Bay and Fuji-san, hoof it out to Pier D, where you'll find the chalk-white forty-eight-meter-high Yokohama Port Symbol Tower fronted by a huge stainless steel sculpture of a giant scallop—bring your own lemon juice. Besides serving as an observatory, the tower is also used to send signals to ships entering and leaving Yokohama Port. The tower is set in the midst of the large Honmoku Fishing Park, where you can fish to your heart's content. Buses leave from this area for Sakuragicho Station via Yamashita Park. If you're coming from Sakuragicho Station, take bus #26.

Equine Museum of Japan (Uma no Hakubutsukan 馬の博物館 in Negishi Keiba Kinen Koen 根岸競馬記念公苑) ☎ 045-662-7581 ◷ 10:00–16:00; closed Mon. and hols. ¥100

Sankei-en 三溪園 ☎ 045-621-0634 ◷ outside *gaien* 外園 9:00–17:00; inside *naien* 内園 9:00–16:30. Fee according to section.

Yokohama Port Symbol Tower 横浜港シンボルタワー ☎ 045-622-9600 ◷ 10:00–17:00; Nov.–March 10:00–16:00; Sat., Sun., July 10:00–18:00; summer 10:00–21:00; closed Tues.

Honmoku Fishing Park (Honmoku Umi-zuri Shisetsu 本牧海づり施設) ☎ 045-623-6030 ◷ Nov.–March 7:00–17:00; Apr.–Jun. 6:00–19:00; Jul.–Oct. 6:00–21:00; closed Tues. ¥1,000; free in summer

Dolphin ドルフィン ☎ 045-681-5796 ◷ 11:00–23:00; bar lounge 17:00–23:00

Honmoku Shokudo 本牧食堂 ☎ 045-621-0092 ◷ 17:00–22:00; Sat, Sun. 12:00–22:00; closed Tues.

Post 9467 Canteen ☎ 045-622-7661 ◷ 18:30–02:00; open all year

Italian Garden イタリアンガーデン ☎ 045-622-0654 ◷ 18:00–3:00; closed Weds.

Venice ☎ 045-621-3056 ◷ 17:00–01:00; Sun. 17:00–24:00; closed Tues.

Mikonos ミコノス ☎ 045-623-9465 ◷ 17:00–02:00; closed Weds.

• MAP 116

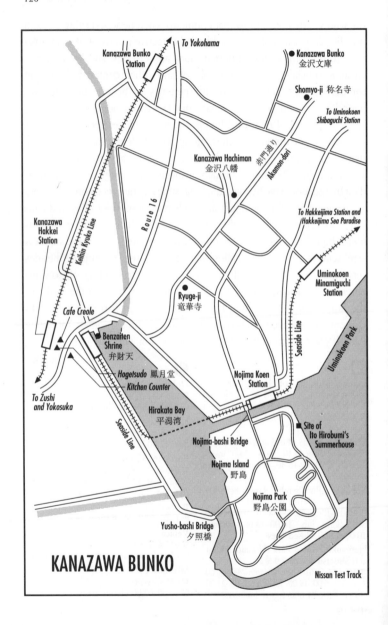

KANAZAWA BUNKO

8

Scrolls and Gills

◐ Kanazawa Bunko Station 金沢文庫駅 (Keihin Kyuko Line)—Kanazawa Bunko 金沢文庫—Shomyo-ji 称名寺—Kanazawa Hakkei 金沢八景—Nojima 野島—Hakkei-jima 八景島

This walk is recommended for a sunny summer day. If you bring a bathing suit along, you can even take a dip in the ocean after visiting one of the most famous traditional culture centers of the Kanto region.

Come out of Kanazawa Bunko Station, cross the street, and go straight ahead. When you get to the big street, take the road next to the bus stop. You'll notice a church on the left. About ten minutes or five hundred meters along on the left, you will see a red gate, the Akamon.

This is the entrance to the spacious, beautifully landscaped precincts of Shomyo-ji, which include a trail around the surrounding hills. It starts in back of the Kanazawa Bunko, which was founded in 1275 by the Hojo, making it the oldest library in Japan. It has well over twenty thousand volumes and seven thousand documents in the fields of Japanese and Chinese literature, classics, and books related to Buddhism and Confucianism. Some are national treasures, or extremely rare—such as a copy of the *Issaikyo* (a complete collection of the Buddhist scriptures) published in Song China. Exhibitions in the second-floor museum are held regularly on themes such as "Women in Medieval Japan."

After the fall of Kamakura to imperial forces in 1333, the collection was split up, becoming the property of various prominent families, including the Ashikaga and Tokugawa. Scholars believe that the famous *Azuma Kagami* history of the early days of the Kamakura shogunate was compiled here. The library is on the west side of the large

• MAP 128

pond. You'll notice strange-looking, long, narrow rocks in the pond, protruding sharply seventy to eighty centimeters out of the water. According to a story about the lagoon, which in the past was supposed to be much more extensive, a princess was once walking along with her wet nurse after a storm, when she fell into the water. The nurse jumped in to save her, but both were turned into stones. It is referred to as the A-Un Pond, in reference to the alpha and omega of all things as explained in Sanskrit. Waterfowl abound and beautiful woods all around add to the tranquility. The garden is supposed to be in the form of a Jodo mandala.

Another spot somewhat unsettling is the Shingu or "Temple of Dolls," just inside the main gate to the left. Here you'll find dozens of dolls brought by mothers who have miscarried or otherwise lost children.

Shomyo-ji itself was founded around 1267 by Hojo Sanetoki as a household shrine attached to his villa. It contains several important items. The main hall, for example, houses a 1.9-meter-high wooden statue of the Miroku-Bosatsu (Maitreya), future Buddha, made in 1276, and one of the most famous bells dating from the Kamakura period. Like the Kamakura culture, the temple is eclectic in style, combining architectural effects from several sects. It started out as a Jodo temple, then officially became Shingon, because of Sanetoki's friendship with the famous monk Eison whom he invited from Todai-ji in Nara. However, like everything the Hojo constructed, it also has the smell of Zen, as well as blood, to it. The reclusive priest Kenko, who wrote the famous rambling essay *Tsurezuregusa*, apparently studied here as well.

When you come out of the Shomyo-ji Temple complex, look for the Coffee Gallery near the front gate. You can sip or sup amongst paintings, sculptures, and pottery, or maybe even chat up an artist. If you turn left at the end of the various stalls and go straight, you will eventually come out in front of Uminokoen Shibaguchi Station and the Uminokoen seaside park, which has the best swimming in Yokohama.

But for this walk we want to avoid confusion when you come out by going straight along Akamon-dori, directly away from Shomyo-ji to Kanazawa Hachiman Shrine. There are still some thatched-roof homes along the route. Our next stop is Ryuge-ji, a temple that is supposed to date back to the twelfth century; its bell dates from the mid-sixteenth

• MAP 128

century, although it is in Kamakura-period style. Keep bearing to the right on the main road. Cross the bridge and stay on the large road till it splits off on the side of Hirakata Bay past the small island and Biwashima Benzaiten Shrine dedicated to the patron goddess of commercial success and seafarers. It supposedly was patronized by Hojo Masako, Yoritomo's wife. A festival takes place here on May 15. If you're feeling peckish, there are two excellent cafes, Cafe Creole, which also has an interesting collection of antique typewriters and record players, and the Kitchen Counter, a delicatessen with a small dining area, along with an old-fashioned Japanese cake shop, Hogetsudo. All fired up, continue your walk by going back to the turn-off; turn right and skirt the bay till you get to Yusho-bashi Bridge. Cross the bridge to Nojima Island and Nojima Park. The view from the hill in the center is quite interesting. Among other things you have a bird's-eye view of a Nissan Motor test track on Natsushima, which also used to be an island.

The Eight Views

The Kanazawa Hakkei ("Eight Views") area was famous throughout Japan for its scenery, especially during the Edo period, when it was on a regular tourist route from Edo that took in Seto Shrine on the main road to Kamakura, an object of popular worship. Pilgrims generally made a grand tour through here on the way to Kamakura and Enoshima.

No one seems sure exactly when the name became applied to the region. As late as 1633, the famous Zen priest Takuan wrote that Kanazawa Bunko was nothing but ruins, with fishermen living in the buildings and the temple grounds a vegetable patch. In 1684 the visiting Chinese priest Xin Yue composed a poem comparing its scenery to the eight famous views in the West Lake district of his homeland. Traditionally, the *hakkei* (eight views) were as follows: sunlight dispersing the mists at Susaki; the autumn moon over Seto; Koizumi on a rainy evening; sailing boats returning to Ottomo Shore; Shomyo-ji at the hour of the twilight bell; wild geese descending at Hirakata; the sunset at Nojima; and Uchikawa on a snowy evening.

Hiroshige drew the Hakkei area on several occasions. Hamlets dotted the landscape to the west in the direction of snow-capped Hakone and Fuji-san; hilly ridges carpeted with cedars peeked down on the shiny belt of the Uraga Channel; and to the southeast whitecaps danced in sunlight from the white-flecked sky.

Since the days when Hiroshige portrayed the Kanazawa Hakkei so eloquently the area has changed tremendously, particularly in recent years with the reclamation of some 660 hectares of land from the sea. In fact, over a quarter of the land in Kanazawa Ward is now reclaimed earth. Prefectural officials envision the Kanazawa Hakkei area as becoming a center for high-tech and biotechnology research.

• MAP 128

The park has extensive barbecue areas, gardens, and a memorial to the writing of the Meiji Constitution. Large numbers of shell mounds (*kaizuka*) dating from the mid-Jomon period five thousand years ago have been discovered along the bluffs facing the sea and down below at the shoreline. The oldest shell mounds on Nojima date back to around 5000 B.C. while some on Natsushima are nearly ten thousand years old. Other similarly old archaeological sites have been found on the Miura Peninsula, and pit dwellings from the late Jomon period have been discovered all over the Yokohama area.

There is another historical tradition of interest connected with Nojima. During the Gempei War that brought Yoritomo to power as head of the first shogunate, the Ise Taira clan was more or less eliminated by the Seiwa Genji (Minamoto). However, some members of the family were said to have escaped to isolated areas, including Okinawa, Tohoku, and Nojima.

The story behind the constitution monument is an interesting one. In the summer of 1887 the most powerful Meiji government leader, Ito Hirobumi, came to this area with a select group of young aides to write the Imperial Constitution. Ito had a summer house on Nojima where they worked. Inoue Kaoru did most of the draft writing, while Ito made numerous revisions. The whole business was extremely hush-hush, since the men did not want members of the People's Rights Movement to get wind of the contents of the crucial document.

Although he is now respected as one of the principal founders of modern Japan, at that time those opposed to the autocratic tendencies of the Meiji government thought of Ito as the devil incarnate. For one thing he was known as a confirmed lecher who frequently consorted with geisha and was on one occasion accused by the opposition press of having tried to rape a fourteen-year-old girl inside the famous Rokumeikan social hall in Tokyo.

While all this was happening, the briefcase in which the working draft was being transported was stolen. It was discovered the next morning in a nearby soybean field and there are doubts about whether the theft was politically motivated. Be that as it may, some of the contents got leaked to the press in one way or another, and the drafting

• MAP 128

process became even more secret than before. In fact the final document was adopted even before the public had been informed of its contents. Foreign observers marveled at the tremendous celebrations in the streets over a totally incognito constitution. Closed-door politics is nothing new in Japan, it would seem.

After exploring Nojima Park, catch one of the spruce-as-a-goose trains on the Seaside Line for the short trip to Hakkei-jima, two stops away. The Hakkei-jima Sea Paradise amusement complex opened in 1993. The entrance fees are worth it for the Aqua Museum, but avoid the rides in the amusement park, unless your wallet is inordinately thick. The Aqua Museum was the first aquarium in Japan where you can glide up through an Aquatube on an escalator, observing the inhabitants of a huge tank. Wouldn't like to be caught inside when a major earthquake hits. Some of those sharks look like they would enjoy a little morsel on the side.

Computer-controlled graphics and state-of-the-art sound equipment in the ultramodern pyramid-shaped building add to the educational experience. If you have kids, the seal and dolphin show is a must.

For dinner, try the Coca Restaurant, which specializes in "Thai Sukiyaki"—whatever that is—or Yondon, which offers Korean court cuisine. There's also a yacht harbor nearby and a guest house for those too fagged out to sail their yachts home for the night. Exciting alternative transportation includes a one-hour shuttle cruise to Minato Mirai 21. The Seaside Line links up to the JR Negishi Line at Shin Sugita. It is an eighteen-minute trip. Alternatively, you can head back to Kanazawa Hakkei Station and transfer onto the Keihin Kyuko Line.

Kanagawa Kenritsu Kanazawa Bunko
(神奈川県立金沢文庫) ☎ 045-701-9069
🕒 9:00–16:30; closed Mon. ¥200

Hakkei-jima Sea Paradise (八景島シーパ
ラダイス) ☎ 045-788-8888
🕒 10:00–17:30 Dec. 1–Mar. 18; 10:00–21:00
Mar. 19–Nov. 30; 9:00–21:00 on Sun. and
hols; closed Thurs. from March 19–Nov.
30. ¥2,400 adults; ¥1,400 children; ¥700
small children.

Coffee Gallery ☎ 045-783-4088
🕒 11:00–23:00; closed Mon.

Cafe Creole ☎ 045-784-7427
🕒 10:30–22:00; closed Sun.

Kitchen Counter Bon Appetit
☎ 045-783-7007
🕒 10:00–20:30; closed Sat. and Sun.

Hogetsudo 鳳月堂 ☎ 045-701-9922
🕒 9:00–20:00; closed Weds.

• MAP 128

Time Out: Picnic and Bath

This walk is a picnic. That is to say the *raison d'être* for the walk is to enjoy a picnic in beautiful Okurayama Park. So choose a good day; preferably when the cherry or plum blossoms or azalea bushes are blooming. The walk itself can easily be handled in two to three hours.

Take the Tokyu Toyoko Line from Shibuya. If you take a *kyuko* limited express train, transfer at Tsunashima. When you come out of Okurayama Station you will be facing a shopping street that runs for about a kilometer. Go to the right and you'll find Elm Street, Athens of Kanagawa Prefecture. "Elm" is actually the name of a famous street in Athens—OΔOΣ to be exact. There is a story behind the name, to be sure.

In the last couple of decades this area has changed tremendously, as Tokyo's bed-town tentacles have spread into the Kanagawa countryside. More and more Tokyo office workers as well as old-time residents have become accustomed to doing their shopping in Shibuya, Yokohama, or other major shopping districts.

This trend has not necessarily been to the advantage of local shopkeepers. In fact, back in 1988 Okurayama merchants woke up to the fact that this main shopping street had become decidedly ragged at the edges. As with many other such shopping arcades, they decided that a facelift was in order. But in Okurayama they went wild and engaged in massive plastic surgery. The local shopkeepers' association decided that perhaps, just perhaps, the Greek gods would bear them gifts (in the form of ringing cash registers and clacking abacuses.)

So in a very brave and expensive move they remodeled this whole street, providing its establishments with marble Hellenistic facades, columns and all. The effect is very striking, although it strikes me more as Modesto, California, than Athens, Greece. Any way you look at it, Elm Street is rather attractive.

Actually, Okurayama is characterized by a distinctively eclectic blend of East

and West. For example there is an "Indonesian hand-woven Ikat art" craft shop in front of the station. Farther down the street there is a "cycle boutique" and a large Dickensian head sculpture hanging above a real-estate office. As if that weren't enough, on a side street I stumbled upon a huge concrete cow parked in front of a *yakinikuya*-cum-Chinese restaurant. By this time my head was spinning. Be that as it may, many nice traditional Japanese houses still remain on the quiet back streets at the foot of the hills.

On the street next to the train station, you will notice a marble replica of the famous "Wings of Victory" statue. Follow this road up for three hundred meters and you will reach Okurayama Park. The view from up here is quite nice, and you can watch the Odakyu Line express trains speeding by below like half-pint Shinkansen trains. The centerpiece of the park is the Okurayama Memorial Hall (Okurayama Kinenkan). This pre-Hellenic style marble building is supposed to resemble the Parthenon, but it looks more like an administration building on an American college campus. This unusual structure, designed by Nagano Heiji, was built in 1932 by paper magnate Okura Kunihiko (1882–1971), ostensibly as a center for philosophical interchange between East and West.

However, Okura got a little carried away by his attempts to blend the Eastern traditions of Shinto, Buddhism, Taoism, and so on with Western philosophy. In fact he became a little crazed from "pan-Asiatic fever," using the center during the war as a training ground for spiritual warriors who were to labor for Japan's imperialistic mission (no doubt with proper philosophical detachment). When the Allied troops showed up, Okura was arrested for his over-zealousness but was released without being prosecuted.

Later the building was bought by the City of Yokohama and refurbished. It was opened to the public in 1975 and is used for various kinds of classes and meetings.

The library is open to public use (open 9:30–16:30, closed Mondays). You can borrow books even if you are not a Yokohama resident. Most of the volumes in the 100,000 collection have to do with religion, philosophy, culture, or history.

There is a picnic area off to the left and several more are spread over the hills to the right along the trail to a grove where there are one thousand plum trees. Open the picnic basket and party down.

When the stomach is full and the spirit refreshed, press on along the concrete road. To the right you will see a four-hundred-year-old Zen temple called Ryusho-in, which has a delightful carp-filled garden pond. In some ways these little Zen temples tend to be more impressive than the big complexes. Enshrined here is Monju Daibosatsu, the patron deity of academic success. There are also a couple of interesting Shinto shrines around here.

The road continues on through a small valley; eventually you will come out on a heavily traveled road. Turn right and keep going straight for about twenty minutes and you will reach two bridges over the Tsurumi-gawa River—one for the Keihin Kyuko trains and the other for vehicular and foot traffic. If you can, try to get down to the embankment of the river and follow it, since the road is narrow, hot, and smelly from the exhaust smoke of too many trucks.

After you cross the river you will be in Tsunashima, which I like to call the "phantom spa." This area is filled with alkaline springs with waters of fourteen to seventeen degrees centigrade. A mere decade or so ago it was a major resort with around sixty Japanese-style restaurant-hotels. However, beds for Tokyo's worker bees took precedence over miracle waters to soothe the body and soul. Every last one was knocked down to make way for shops and condominiums.

But if you are determined to have your bath, it can be done. One public bath still remains open, the venerable Tsunashima Tokyo-en, which has been operating for some six decades. You'll find it on the main road on the side of the station where the Daiichi Kangyo Bank is. It's a white concrete building across from a pharmacy and Mini Stop market that from the outside looks like a school gymnasium. There is no sign to identify the building. When I visited in April I asked the proprietress why not. (I was very much in a philosophical mood by this time.)

"It got blown down by a typhoon," she said. "When was that?" I asked. "Last autumn," she replied somewhat sheepishly.

Most of the clientele at the baths tends to be slightly elderly. Patrons hold all kinds of meetings and activities here, so the entry fee system is a little bit complicated. Everyone pays ¥800 upon entry. But if you are only popping in for a bath and finish within an hour, you pay just ¥360 and get the balance back. I hasten to add: Tokyo-en is especially well known for its radium baths.

How civilized—a picnic stroll followed by a mineral bath. In the tub you can sing that old rock favorite "Radioactive Love," or maybe hum the theme "Zorba the Greek."

Okurayama Memorial Hall (Okurayama Kinen-kan 大倉山記念館) ☎ 045-544-1881 ◷ 9:00–21:00, all rooms open 1st and 3rd Sun.; closed Mon.

Tokyo-en 東京園 ☎ 045-531-0003 ◷ 10:00–20:30; on 10:00–17:00

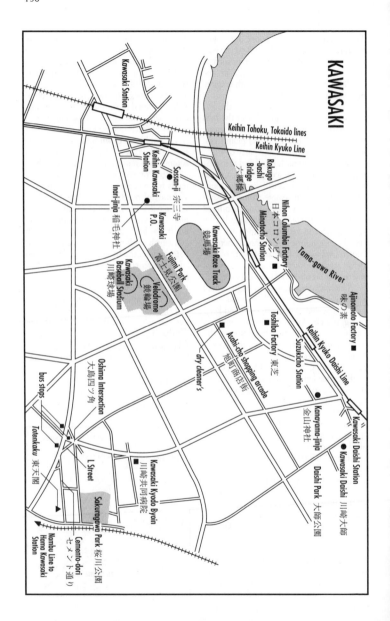

KAWASAKI

Kawasaki Station

Keihin Tohoku, Tokaido lines
Keihin Kyuko Line

Rokugo-bashi Bridge 六郷橋

Keihin Kawasaki Station

Sosan-ji 宗三寺

Inari-jinja 稲毛神社

Kawasaki P.O.

Nihon Columbia Factory 日本コロンビア

Minatocho Station

Kawasaki Race Track 競馬場

Fujimi Park 富士見公園

Kawasaki Baseball Stadium 川崎球場

Velodrome 競輪場

Tama-gawa River

Ajinomoto Factory 味の素

Toshiba Factory 東芝

Suzukicho Station

Asahi-cho shopping arcade 旭町商店街

dry cleaner's

Keihin Kyuko Daishi Line

Kanayama-jinja 金山神社

Kawasaki Daishi Station

Kawasaki Daishi 川崎大師

Daishi Park 大師公園

Oshima Intersection 大島四ツ角

bus stops

Totenkaku 東天閣

L Street

Kawasaki Kyodo Byoin 川崎共同病院

Sakuragawa Park 桜川公園

Cemento-dori セメント通り

Nambu Line to Hama Kawasaki Station

9

Smokestack Passion

⊙ Kawasaki Station 川崎駅 (JR Tokaido, Keihin Kyuko, Nambu lines)—Kawasaki Daishi 川崎大師—Kanayama Shrine 金山神社—Cemento-dori セメント通

This walk goes through the center of Kawasaki, a city of factories and factory workers, race tracks, and other popular pleasures. But things have been changing in recent years and the name Kawasaki is no longer synonymous with pollution, labor unrest, poverty, and despair. You'll find no slums on this line of march, but some fascinating glimpses of working-class Japan.

Kawasaki has really gotten its act together: the roads are clean and several striking public buildings invite a second look. But ragged people still float half unseen through the streets like life-smudged specters. You'll stumble upon them washing up in the parks or scrounging through garbage cans. Now seen, then gone. That's you. They remain behind.

We begin the walk at Kawasaki Station, which is spicky-spanky new and, like Yokohama Station, encased by a spider's web of underground shopping arcades. Kawasaki was one of the fifty-three post stations on the Edo-period Tokaido highway. As a matter of fact, it was the last to be established—in 1623, twenty-two years after the road opened. At that time there were only 120 households here.

Kawasaki's fortunes were greatly affected by the great Tama-gawa River. "Great" may seem a bit of an exaggeration to describe what, these days at best can be characterized as a placid meandering. But you have to remember that before flood control was instigated, Japan's short but fast rivers could cause tremendous destruction when they

• MAP 136

flooded, as happened repeatedly at Kawasaki. As recently as the Occupation period, farmers demonstrated for relief at the prefectural headquarters.

Wayfarers also had to take a *wataribune* ferry boat across the Tamagawa here. At Rokkyo-bashi Bridge you can see black metal replicas of the *wataribune*. One heavyweight who came through Kawasaki was Basho, "the god of *haiku*." When he left Edo for the last time in May 1694, several disciples accompanied him this far. He left them a *haiku*, one of his last, since he died in Osaka the same October:

Mugi no hoo o	Ears of barley
tayori ni tsukamu	Trusting in them,
wakerekana	we part.

All the recognized Tokaido post stations had inns for the needs of travelers. In those days sex was one of the physical needs that men expected to have satisfied as a matter of course. Each inn had a number of indentured female servants, known as *meshimori*, who in addition to handling the washing, meals, and other domestic duties were also expected to warm the guests' *futon*. These poor women had generally been sold by their families, but many died of overwork or disease before they could work off their contracts. Their shells were then summarily dumped into mass graves.

At Sosso-ji near Keihin Kawasaki Station a local merchant association has erected a monument to assuage the tortured souls of the *meshimori*. Say a prayer as you walk through this neighborhood, the location of Kawasaki-juku, the old post station. The legacy of the *meshimori* is very much in evidence in the many soaplands and bars. At Ichigyo-ji nearby you'll see a large plastic chest filled with plastic toys, offered for the souls of lost fetuses and babies.

Inage-jinja is the guardian shrine for Kawasaki-juku. The main shrine building is attractive, although all you can see inside is a large mirror. Make sure to catch the *junishi meguri* (zodiacal wheel of fortune) monument. There are twelve metal heads of the hoary animals; you start at the animal representing the year of your birth and then make a circuit while praying for good fortune. There is a big festival here in August.

At the major intersection, cross over the attractive concrete bridge

• MAP 136

to the big post office on the corner and head down this main road. This is a neighborhood of the sporting life. To the left is the Kawasaki horse-race track, while on the right is a velodrome and the baseball stadium. On race days there are a number of outdoor food stands set up on this road, so you might stop for a snack of *yakitori* or *oden*.

A bit farther you'll see a sign pointing to the Asahi-cho Shopping Arcade. Turn left, and then right at the dry cleaner's on the corner, and you'll be in for an old-time experience. Old-fashioned Japanese popular songs come lilting out of the loudspeakers. But times are changing, and you'll notice a Sichuan noodle shop and Filipino shoppers.

If you really want to know what Kawasaki is all about, walk along the big road toward the river. For miles and miles there's nothing but a solid phalanx of factories and warehouses. The spark for industrialization in the area was the construction of the Keihin Kyuko line in 1899, the first electrical railway in Eastern Japan. People flocked here from far and wide with their lunch boxes, simply to observe the marvel.

The factories soon followed. The first big factory was built in 1909 by the forerunner of Toshiba. Japan's first vacuum tubes, Braun picture tubes, and fluorescent tubes rolled off assembly lines here. Other big factories like confectionery giant Meiji Seika soon followed. After Ajinomoto opened a factory in 1914, a terrible stench began to fill the area and the trees started to die. This was only a sign of things to come.

The Smokestack Man

In 1930 a twenty-eight-year-old by the name of Tanabe became an instant celebrity, as the "smokestack man" (*entotsu otoko*). On November 1 a strike began at the Fuji Gasu spinning factory over pay cuts and wholesale dismissals . On November 16 Tanabe climbed to the top of a belching company smokestack and began waving a red flag. Simultaneously workers sabotaged company property. Before the police could react with water cannons and other tactics, a crowd had gathered and newspapers had published stories about the smokestack man and photos of him on his perch.

Complicating the matter was the fact that the emperor was due to pass down the Tokaido on the way to military maneuvers in western Japan. After 130 hours, the company finally capitulated under police pressure and Tanabe came down to the cheers of fifty thousand spectators. He was arrested on charges of trespassing and other minor violations but never convicted. However, in 1933 the smokestack man was found drowned in a drainage ditch. The authorities claimed it was suicide.

• MAP 136

From 1931 the Keihin zone became a center for armaments production. Kawasaki suffered during World War II, but postwar reconstruction was rapid. However, along with unbridled economic development came the horrendous pollution that made Kawasaki infamous. Things have improved recently, but many people still complain of ailments caused by industrial waste, such as asthma among children.

The Asahi-cho Shopping Arcade imperceptibly merges into the Ise-cho Shopping Arcade. Watch out for the John Bull figure with a barrel of whisky under one arm climbing a ladder. At the big crossroads, turn left. You'll pass an eyeglass shop with an old Model T type car in its window. Look for the arrow pointing right to Kawasaki Daishi Temple, about five minutes away.

We are going in the back entrance to the big temple complex, entering near a Thai-looking building, where drivers buy amulets to ensure safety. There is a vast parking area where vehicles are parked while their drivers pay ¥3,000 to purchase a little protection. A ceremony is held every thirty minutes from 9:00 to 16:00. Fleets of taxis and other vehicles zoom in and then zoom out. Since this arrangement began in 1963, hundreds of millions of yen are said to have been raised.

This Shingon temple is among the biggest drawers at New Year's and during the February bean-throwing festival. The origins of the temple are unknown. According to one legend, in 1127 a fisherman, Hirama Kanenori, was asked in a dream by the famous ninth-century prelate Kobo Daishi to go to the shore and retrieve a statue that he himself had carved while in China. He promised that it would ward off evil and bring Hirama good fortune. Hirama found the image and put up a building to house it, thus giving birth to the temple. Another version has it that this fisherman in question was really a samurai who had been unfairly expelled from his home fief for a crime he had not committed. After the man properly honored the statue, his lord took him back.

During the Edo period a statue of the hag who decides at the Sanzu River whether the blind will have to be tried before Enma, the king of the dead, or not was popular with people suffering from eye diseases. Secret rituals are regularly held here to wipe out spiritual danger, ensure success in business, recovery from disease, or fulfillment of

• MAP 136

other desires. What amounted to a Daishi cult spread down from the samurai to the common people during the later part of the Edo period, and the opening of the railroad at the turn of the century gave it a big boost.

During the 21st of every month and the night before the 21st a festival is held, when the temple grounds are very lively. However, things really get going in March, the month of Kobo Daishi's death.

In the main hall is a rich altar service, including huge brass candelabra in the shape of a divine lotus and a sparkling canopy of bells. Although some of the newer parts of the complex have a haphazard look to them, the old gates and main buildings are magnificent. Several of the shops on Nakamise-dori specialize in a sweet cake known as *kuzumochi*. Very tasty. Go down to the corner, turn left, and then left again at the next corner and you'll find yourself on the main approach to the temple from Kawasaki Daishi Station. During the Edo period this approach used to be famous for its "green tunnel" of trees and its peach orchards, but they were killed off by pollution. The price of progress.

Pass Kawasaki Daishi Station and turn left on the road that goes diagonally away from it like the spoke on a wheel. On the right is Kanayama-jinja, the most famous fertility shrine in the Kanto area and the scene of the annual Kanamara Festival April 9–10 that draws thousands.

The Phallus Festival

Kanayama-jinja Shrine is dedicated to the sacred couple Kanamarahiko and Kanamarahime, patrons of sex-related activities and blacksmiths. Strike while the iron is hot! During the November 8 Fuigo Festival, factory owners and metal workers of various kinds gather here for a special ceremony. But the famous Kanamara Festival is what really draws the crowds. Sweating festival-goers drag giant phalluses through the streets and masked participants advertise the benefits of reproduction. The costumes sometimes stretch the limits of the imagination. Better leave your Moral Majority friends at home.

However, it should be emphasized that this is an authentic festival. It is not something artificial dreamed up by promoters for its titillation value. Kanayama-jinja has been a center of popular worship since time immemorial, and during the Edo period prostitutes from Kawasaki-juku would come to participate in the festival. In one of the small shrine buildings you can see a fascinating collection of phalluses.

You will also see a picture of five monkeys in various poses, with the legend: "See no evil, Speak no evil, Hear no evil, Transmit no evil, Receive no evil." The last two seem especially appropriate these days, and in recent years the Kanamara Festival has also become internationally known for its prayers for protection from AIDS.

• MAP 136

If you're tired, you might want to call it a day and go to Kawasaki Daishi Station. But if you're up for another fifteen minutes or so of walking, check out Cemento-dori (Cement Street), alias Yakinikuya-dori, where you can get authentic Korean food. It is a favorite among gourmets, some of whom come all the way from Tokyo just for a meal.

Koreans first started arriving in Japan in large numbers after 1910, when the Korean monarchy was abolished and the country was absorbed into the Japanese empire. Countless poor peasants were swindled out of their land by Japanese landlords who had suddenly materialized on the scene. A rootless peasantry made a perfect pool from which to recruit workers for Japan's rapidly expanding factories.

By the early 1920s there were hundreds of thousands of mostly illiterate Koreans in Japan. The Japanese looked down upon them as filthy, dishonest bums out to steal their jobs. Labor strife and severe unemployment in the aftermath of World War I served to dry the tinder. The spark that set off the conflagration came with the 1923 earthquake.

Martial law was declared almost immediately and false rumors were purposely spread by government agents to the effect that the Koreans were running wild, committing arson, and poisoning wells. Vigilante groups led by sword-toting military veterans roamed the streets on their mission of *Chosenjin-gari* ("Korean hunting"). Hideous incidents of death and torture of Koreans of all ages took place at Hodogaya and other areas. Scores were also settled with socialist and anarchist "troublemakers." Since suspects were routinely given a pronunciation test to make sure they were Japanese, Chinese, Okinawans, and Japanese with speech impediments inevitably took their place on the pyres.

Atrocity was not universal, however. Amidst this mindless panic and deluge of blood lust, acts of incredible courage stood out for their very gratuity. In nearby Tsurumi, for example, a lynch mob surrounded the police station where 301 local Koreans were being held in protective custody and demanded that they be turned over. The local station chief ordered that water from the "poisoned wells" be brought to him so that he could drink it in front of them. No Pontius Pilate here. The crowd dispersed. After the war the Koreans built a monument to this honest cop at a local temple.

• MAP 136

The hundreds of thousands of Koreans who freely migrated to Japan or were brought here as conscript laborers were mostly low-paid coolies who worked on railroads or other infrastructure projects, in factories or in sweat shops. Five families lived in each fifteen-tatami barrack. Many prewar factories had signs outside reading, "Koreans or Okinawans Need Not Apply," and innumerable Korean women were also forced by circumstances to become prostitutes, even though they earned only about one-third what a Japanese would. Said one Korean who was repatriated to Korea after the war, "The Japanese treated us like dogs or pigs, even though they got most of their culture from Korea."

In the years since, most resident Koreans, the majority of whom are now third or fourth generation, have sought, at least to some extent, to "pass" in Japanese society. According to a recent survey by Kanagawa Prefecture, 91 percent of resident Koreans had adopted Japanese names, compared to only 17 percent of the local Chinese. However, the Korean community still remains ideologically divided between pro-Pyongyang and pro-Seoul partisans.

From the Kanayama Shrine area, keep walking straight past two major intersections. About four blocks past the Kawasaki Kyodo Hospital you will reach the Oshima intersection. There are about ten thousand Koreans living in Kawasaki, and approximately one-third of them live in this area around Sakuramoto-cho and Hama-cho.

Turn left at the intersection. Soon on the left you will see a shop specializing in Korean food items. To the right is a small street. This is "L Road." Follow it to the second corner. On this street are a couple of Korean barbecue restaurants and pubs. But it is on the next street that you will find about a dozen Korean restaurants. Some are simple affairs, but others, like Totenkaku, are veritable meat-roasting palaces.

Of course, they offer the regular types of *yakiniku, kimchi,* and mixed vinegared vegetables. But you can also find many treats that are not available in typical *yakiniku* restaurants, such as Korean seafood, *dojo* (loach) soup, and *sangetan*. The latter is very popular in Korea, but has only become known to Japanese gourmets in recent years. This hot pot consists of a specially raised chicken stuffed with chestnuts, *mochi* rice, and ginseng. Try it—it's a thoroughly unique experience.

• MAP 136

The reason why this street is known as Cemento-dori is that prior to the war Korean workers who slaved in a nearby cement factory lived in tenements here. For years, there has been talk of turning the neighborhood into a Korean version of Yokohama's Chinatown, with shops of all kinds, a Korean-style garden, and even a theater for performances of Korean plays and performing arts. In fact, a local merchant started the ball rolling in that direction in the early 1990s, but he died unexpectedly in 1992. Ideological divisions, the recession, and formidable access problems must be overcome if his dream is to be fulfilled.

I asked one *yakiniku-ya* owner about the prospects for a true "Koreatown. "It won't come about anytime soon, even within five years," he replied. And then, patting the head of his young son, he added, "But, maybe by the time this little tyke has grown up, it'll come about."

Go back to the main road you came from Kawasaki Daishi on. You can catch a bus directly to Kawasaki Station from the bus stop across from the gigantic Kotobuki pachinko parlor.

If you feel like working off all that meat and garlic, washing off the pollution, or are just wild at heart, take the #29 bus from the east exit of Kawasaki Station and get off at Heian Koko-mae (Heian School) bus stop. Nearby is the aquapalace Wild Blue Yokohama.

The colossal main pool "Big Bay" is 93 meters long and 55 meters wide. It takes a minute to come down the spiral chute or fly through the air on the overhead pulley before you plop into the heated water. Lounge on the artificial beach and sniff the real flowers as you enjoy the laser show or watch the two-meter-high rollers come in. Check out the "beachside amenities" such as the tropical drinks. Forget that such things as crowded commuter trains exist. All this escapism does not come cheap, however. All day admission for an adult at peak season is about ¥3,500.

Wild Blue Yokohama ワイルドブルー横浜 ☎ 045-511-2323 ◷ 10:00–21:00; Fri., Sat., hols. 10:00–22:00; closed Tues. 15-minute bus ride from bus stop 2 at Kawasaki Station east exit, or bus stop 5 at Tsurumi Station east exit; get off at Heian Koko-mae

Totenkaku 東天閣 ☎ 044-355-1234 ◷ 11:00–23:00; closed 2nd and 3rd Weds. each month

• MAP 136

Time Out: Nihon Minka-en

This short walk in northern Kawasaki is highly recommended, since it includes a visit to Nihon Minka-en, the Japan Traditional House Museum Park, a unique outdoor museum that like a time machine will allow you to conjur up images of what life was like in Japan in days of yore.

Take the Odakyu Line to Mukogaoka Yuen Station. Come out the south exit to the left and then follow the main road that parallels the monorail that goes to the Mukogaoka Yuen amusement park, which also has a mammoth swimming pool. The big Daiei store will be on your left.

At the main intersection, keep going straight on the road that crosses the river and curves to the right. There will be hills on both sides. This Tama-gawa River Basin and Tama Highland area is historically very important. Many archaeological remains from the Jomon, Yayoi, and Tumulus periods have been excavated in the two hundred small rice paddy and grove studded valleys of the area, and countless battles have been fought on the level areas. However, in recent decades industrial and residential developments have eaten away white oak forests and fields and completely changed the complexion of the land.

The museum is located in a large public park, the Ikuta Ryokuchi, which also includes the Kawasaki Youth Science Center, an iris garden, and fountains and ponds. To the right of the entrance is a map showing the layout of Minka-en and its two dozen buildings and a bulletin board listing special lectures on folk life, such as how to make straw sandals.

Since 1965, the Minka-en has been gathering folk houses, hamlet protection stones, traditional agricultural tools, folk arts, and everyday utensils from various parts of Japan. The garden itself is, to a certain extent, organized on a regional basis: Tohoku, Kanto, Shin'etsu (Nagano), Kanagawa Prefecture, and so on. Several of the buildings have been designated Important Cultural Assets by the national or prefectural governments.

You can go in and out of many of the buildings freely and some of them are furnished just as if people were living there. And we are not talking about little out-houses; these buildings are big, big, big. The Japanese did not always live in rabbit hutches, it would seem. Of course, these buildings belonged to rich farmers, merchants, or samurai. Anyone who has read Tanizaki Jun'ichiro's magnificent essay "In Praise of Shadows" will appreciate the subdued shades of the wood and subtle interplay between darkness and light.

Among the more impressive structures are a kabuki theater from a small fishing village in the Ise area, a water mill, an inn for horse traders from the Oshu-kaido in Tohoku, a boatman's hut, and a Polynesian-looking storage house for rice raised on stilts from Okinoerabu Island, near Okinawa. Some of these buildings date back to the early Edo period. The mind boggles at the amount of work involved in dismantling, transporting, and re-erecting these priceless buildings.

There are also two museums: one just inside the entrance, and the other halfway through the course on the second floor of the Shirakawa House that has over one thousand items related to life in the countryside in the old days. The latter also contains a noodle restaurant selling *sansai* (mountain vegetable) noodles, and *yamakake* (sliced fish with grated yam) and other noodle dishes.

What makes all of this so nice is that thanks to careful landscaping with the use of streams, stone pathways on the face of the green hillside, bamboo groves, silkworm shrines, *dojin* protective stones, and other authentic touches, all of the buildings, although of diverse origins, blend brilliantly into a single picture of pastoral beauty. Add to that the fact that, except for the intrusive soft-drink machines, there is hardly an outside distraction. (I couldn't even find a public telephone.)

• MAP 146

You can easily spend an enjoyable two or three hours here. The park makes you feel like an Urashima Taro caught in a wonderful time warp. Don't beam me up Scotty!

When you leave the park, turn to the right and climb the long series of wooden staircases up the side of the mountain. Toward the top you will come to the Mingei-kan folkcrafts center, where free demonstrations are given on topics such as traditional natural methods of dyeing cloth using peat and indigo. There are also items for sale. The view from the top of the hill is quite impressive. To the right is a golf course and to the left Kanagawa Prefecture spread out below your feet. You can go down through the gardens of Senshu University, past the amphitheater and then down through part of the university and a street with student-oriented restaurants and shops back toward the station.

But we are going to take a different route down to the station. Go back down through Ikuta Ryokuchi to the entrance of the park near the entrance to Nihon Minka-en and turn in to the left. Soon you will reach Masugatayama Park. This was the site of Masugata Castle, established in the late Heian period by Inage Saburo Shigenari, who married Hojo Masako's younger sister. In 1205, ten years after her death, Shigenari was done in by the Hojos, like so many others. Later the area was contested for by several famous warlords, including Hojo Soun and Takeda Shingen.

There is an excellent view from the top of the mountain and the red and yellow benches lend the park a cheery air. This is a wonderful place for a picnic.

Go down the path on the other side of the park till you reach Togashi Fudodo. This long, narrow temple contains the Shojuichimen Kannon Bosatsu statue. On the eighth of every month special prayer ceremonies for healing are held here that include a holy fire invocation rite.

Go down the slope to the right and then up the narrow lane and you will soon reach the entrance to Kofuku-ji, said to have been established by Jikaku Taishi in 837. In its precincts you will find a tall bo tree, and around its periphery wild cherry trees. The main hall dates from 1789 and the gate and Kannondo hall from 1716. The wooden Kannon and *jizo* statues have been denoted Prefectural Important Cultural Treasures.

Go down to the next corner, and turn left, and follow the path till you reach Kitano Shrine. Then go straight down to the road paralleling the railroad line until you come to Mukogaoka Yuen Station.

Mukogaoka Yuen Amusement Park 向ヶ丘遊園
☎ 044-911-4281 ⏰ 9:00–17:00; Dec.–March closed Fri.; April–Nov. open every day. ¥300

Ikuta Ryokuchi Park 生田緑地公園
☎ 044-933-2511

Kawasaki Youth Science Center (Seishonen Kagaku-kan 青少年科学館)
☎ 044-933-2511; closed Mon.

Japan Traditional House Museum Park (Nihon Minka-en 日本民家園)
☎ 044-922-2181 ⏰ 9:30–4:00; closed Mon. ¥300

PART
2
KAMAKURA

Kamakura: An Introduction

Perhaps the ideal way to get a feel for what things were like during the early days of the Kamakura shogunate would be to view the *Godfather* trilogy. Having done so you would be prepared for an appalling history of boundless brutality, greed, and deceit. Sad to say, but even though "once upon a time" stories of when "knighthood was in flower" or retainers were invariably faithful to their lords may be more appealing than unvarnished facts, the actions of the samurai, at least during this period in history, were more akin to Chicago gang wars or the purges of Bolshevik Russia than to romantic tales of derring-do.

Minamoto Yoritomo was not the first shogun (that title dated back to the late eighth century), but he was the first individual to institutionalize the office as a hereditary position with control over most of the nation's samurai. He was lucky to have even been alive to do so. After the Heiji Insurrection of 1159–60, his father and most of the Genji (Minamoto) clan were massacred by Taira no Kiyomori, with the notable exception of himself and his half-brothers Yoshitsune and Noriyori. Yoritomo was exiled to the Izu Peninsula by Kiyomori, a fatal mistake on the part of the head of the Ise Heike clan.

Two decades later, in 1180, one of Yoritomo's two wardens was given orders to execute him, but he delayed. The other was Hojo Tokimasa, who was only a minor power even in the Izu area. Yoritomo used the two months of hesitation to escape with Tokimasa's daughter Masako, win Tokimasa's forgiveness and support, and kill the procrastinator, whom Tokimasa had considered marrying Masako to. These goings-on started the revolt that eventually made Yoritomo shogun. It might be more accurate to say that Tokimasa launched the rebellion, taking a calculated chance on Yoritomo. Other uprisings had already taken place, and it was obvious that the dictatorial Taira were losing control. There was a great deal of latent pro-Minamoto feeling in eastern Japan, especially in Sagami (present day Kanagawa Prefecture) and Musashi (Tokyo). Many local samurai had participated in Minamoto expeditions to Tohoku led by Yoritomo's ancestors during the eleventh century.

However, after initial success, Yoritomo's forces were smashed at the battle of Ishibashiyama, near present-day Odawara. Remnants made it to the Boso Peninsula, where they received huge reinforcements and counterattacked. The tide never reversed again. Yoritomo dispatched Yoshitsune and Noriyori to deal with the Taira and other claimants to power in the west, while he remained in Kamakura and laid the foundation for a permanent system of military rule, the Bakufu, or "tent government." In March 1185 the last of the Taira forces were annihilated in the decisive naval battle of Dannoura, near the straits separating Honshu from Kyushu.

Among the many ironies involved in Yoritomo's rise to power was the fact that his most important supporters, the Hojo, Kajiwara, Miura, and Wada clans, and some of the families in the motley "Kamakura Band" were all of Taira lineage. Many of the highly independent warrior families chafed under Taira rule, and many considered Yoritomo as simply first among equals. Other Kanto clans stalwartly stood with the Taira, and families were torn apart. On one occasion, Yoritomo ordered a follower to execute his captured brother, which he did.

Yoritomo also completed the revolution that Kiyomori had begun, a permanent shift from an aristocratic to a feudal society. The vast majority of the eastern warriors had no formal education, so Yoritomo recruited highly educated lower-ranking officials from the imperial court in Kyoto, like Oe Hiromoto and Miyoshi Yasunobu, to establish legal codes and rules to bind his *gokenin*, or "honorable house-men."

In 1192 Yoritomo established his shogunate at Kamakura and it thereafter remained the de facto capital of Japan for 141 years, and long after that continued to be a local power center. Although it is only forty square kilometers, Kamakura has had an enormous impact on Japanese history. The area is a natural fortress, surrounded by mountains on three sides and Sagami Bay on the other, into which entry was in Yoritomo's day possible only through seven defiles (the *nanakuchi*, or "Seven Mouths") that were later heavily fortified.

Although guidebooks frequently claim there was nothing but a tiny village before Yoritomo's arrival, recent archeological evidence suggests differently. The original Tokaido highway opened in the Nara period passed through Kamakura and the Miura Peninsula to near the modern city of Yokosuka. Travelers then passed by ship over to the Boso Peninsula and on to Hitachi (present-day Ibaraki Prefecture). So Kamakura was already a trading center long before Yoritomo's arrival. Furthermore, a fortress seems to have been built here in the early twelfth century, and Yoritomo's father clearly had a mansion here.

Kamakura is mentioned in the *Kojiki* (Record of Ancient Matters), but no one is quite sure of the origin of the name. According to one theory, the perhaps mythical first emperor, Jimmu Tenno, conquered this area. So many of his enemies were slain during the invasion that the corpses were piled as high as mountains, thus the name Kabanekura, or "storehouse of corpses." The most commonly accepted story is that the seventh-century general Fujiwara no Kamatari buried a *kama*, or large knife, on a hill behind where Tsurugaoka Hachiman-gu now stands, making it the "storehouse of the knife." On the other hand Kamakura's name might simply have been derived from a description of local topography as pronounced in ancient times.

Another mystery relates to the term *yagura* used in the Kamakura area for mountainside caves that in the past were often used as sepulchers. One theory has it that the first character in the two-character compound was the same as that meaning "great filth." Shinto's emphasis on ritual purity caused the dead to be considered as impure. The use of *yagura* as tombs might also have been encouraged by intercourse with China and the Ryukyu Islands, where the custom was prevalent. In any event Kamakura is the only place in Japan (outside of Okinawa) where cave tombs are common.

No one knows for sure how Yoritomo died, but considering the constant bloodletting that occurred in his family, it is not surprising that there are conspiracy theories. It is generally said that he was thrown from his horse while returning from the dedication of a bridge over the Sagami-gawa River and that he died soon after. But a legend has it that while on his way back to Kamakura Yoritomo was set upon by the vengeful shades of his many victims, including little Emperor Antoku, who drowned with the Taira forces at Dannoura.

Yoritomo could be extremely cold and suspicious, especially when it came to those he considered threats to his personal power, but he could be very generous to those who stood by him in times of need, men like Kajiwara Kagetoki and Wada Yoshimori.

From the start the shogunate was torn apart by disharmony and bitter rivalries among the most important retainers. Some of these predated the appearance of Yoritomo, and the Hojo skillfully took advantage of them to eliminate one rival after the next. Almost before the shogun's body was cold the slaughter among his closest allies began.

The first to get it was Kajiwara, his closest confidant, who was almost universally detested as a lying schemer. Then came Wada, head of the *samurai-dokoro* (Board of Retainers), and all his clan and their allies. In rapid succession the Hiki, Miura, and Adachi clans were extinguished, which left a Hojo hegemony. In some of these incidents hundreds, perhaps thousands, died. By the time it was all over, most of the great families of Sagami had disappeared forever.

Yoritomo's direct descendants did not escape the holocaust either. Yoritomo had had his two half-brothers Yoshitsune and Noriyori mercilessly hunted down, even though it is doubtful whether he could ever have won power had it not been for their military exploits. His oldest son and second shogun, Yoriie, was eliminated by the Hojo in 1205. Few tears were shed, however, since he had been a violent libertine who even raped the mistress of one of his top lieutenants. He had been replaced as shogun while still alive by his brother, Sanetomo, a noted poet. However, Sanetomo was kept on a short leash by the Hojo, even though he tried to link up with the Miura and other powerful clans to develop independent power. He was eventually assassinated by his own nephew in 1219.

Judging from his poetry, Sanetomo had both hot and cold sides to his character. It is certain that he led a lonely childhood and after being disfigured by smallpox as a teenager lived as a semi-recluse. Portraits show him as having a rather puffy, weak face more suitable to an aristocrat than a warrior. One of Sanetomo's more bizarre actions was to have a ship built that would take him to Song China. Although huge sums were spent on it, it proved a total disaster as it was unseaworthy. It was most likely a case of sabotage on the part of the Hojo or others.

Sanetomo's murder ended Yoritomo's direct line, and the now powerless shoguns were selected from members of the imperial family or the ancient Fujiwara clan. But it was always a regent from the Hojo family that held the real power.

The Kamakura period was a time of religious as well as political ferment. In any event, the leaders of all the major new sects founded at this time, with the exception of Shinran, originator of the True Pure Land sect, gravitated to Kamakura. The Hojo viewed Zen as an important tool to help them in their goal of developing a distinctive *bushi* (warrior) culture in contrast to the effeminate aristocratic culture of Kyoto, and they gave lavish support to major Zen establishments.

No doubt to their disgust, both Yoriie and Sanetomo had been addicted to *kemari*, a form of football played by Kyoto aristocrats, and Sanetomo had been in constant communication with court poets, including the famous Fujiwara Teika. Ironically, in the centuries to follow Zen had incalculable influence on what is considered traditional Japanese high culture, in such things as the tea ceremony, Noh theater, and *sumi-e* ink painting.

The priest Eisai is said to have introduced the Rinzai school of Zen to Japan from China in 1191. Seven years later he arrived in Kamakura to dedicate Jufuku-ji, established earlier by Yoritomo, as a Zen establishment. Dogen, the populizer of the Soto school of Zen, which stressed *zazen* meditation, also visited the city. In their desire to break away from Kyoto's influence, the Hojo invited famous Zen prelates from China to head the major new Zen centers like Kencho-ji and Engaku-ji, some of which had up to two thousand residents. These Chinese holy men often could not, or would not, speak Japanese, believing themselves to be the guardians of the Song cultural heritage.

As the Hojo became more cultured, especially after the construction of the Kanazawa Bunko library in 1275, they fostered a sophisticated synthesis of Kyoto and Chinese cultural elements. Trade with China flourished through the nearby port at Mutsuura and Chinese fashions, Chinese architecture, Chinese furniture, and Chinese utensils for religious services were widely adopted. The last eventually evolved into the original woodcraft of Kamakura-bori (see page 160).

The object of meditation or wrestling with seemingly illogical, unsolvable *koan* riddles is to break through the clouds of spiritual static engendered by the "real world" so that we can hear the voice of the ultimate. In other words, daily life acts as an intrusive screen that prevents us from seeing what is right in front of us, like daylight prevents us from seeing the cosmos. Zen seeks to eliminate the screen, at least temporarily.

The official support for Zen did not mean that the shogunate neglected older mainstream sects such as Tendai and Shingon. Some of the most important temples belonged to them and they were frequently commissioned to perform official prayer ceremonies. But economic and political instability, endemic warfare, famine, and pestilence had caused many people of all classes to adopt a millenarian belief that the degenerate days of Mappo, "the latter period of the Law," had arrived, in which traditional Buddhism would be incomprehensible and of no avail.

People therefore looked to new religious movements for radical solutions to the problem of salvation, of which Zen was only one, albeit perhaps the most exotic. Others, which held that salvation could only be achieved through reliance on the strength of another (*tariki*), clearly had native roots.

The most popular of the new sects were those of the Amida, or Pure Land, persuasion. The Jodo ("Pure Land") sect was founded in 1175 by Honen Shonin, who taught that salvation through rebirth into the Western Paradise could be achieved by placing total trust in Amida Buddha (Amitabha) and by repeating the *nembutsu* formula *namu amida butsu*—"I take my refuge in Amida Buddha." This egalitarian doctrine was further simplified by Shinran, Ippen Shonin, and others, who rejected aristocratic Heian Buddhism and promised followers rebirth into paradise no matter how dissipated and violent their lives had been. This belief naturally attracted many adherents.

The shogunate gave the Amida believers the cold shoulder, although it did not actively persecute them, either. That is, except for a little bit of forced striptease ordered by Yoriie. He proclaimed that all itinerant priests trying to enter the city in black robes should have their garments stripped from them and burned. (The priests at the officially sanctioned temples wore white.) He also forbade the chanting of the *nembutsu*.

Nichiren (1222–82) was a fiery street-corner preacher, a thundering prophet of the Old Testament mold and the first apostle of sectarian strife in Japan. He was also an egalitarian radical who scorned distinctions of sex, age, or status. All who honored the Lotus Sutra were eligible for salvation as well as wealth and success in this life. The Nichiren or Hokke (Lotus) sect was a very practical religion that appealed to merchants and uneducated folk. However, Nichiren also gained followers among samurai and had a major influence on life in Kamakura.

Nichiren and his followers delighted in acerbically attacking their opponents. Several disciples died while trying to protect their master from the consequences of this verbal offensive. Nichiren's intolerance was summed up in his famous denunciation of rival sects: "Jodo is the path to hell, Zen is the teaching of devils, Shingon is the ruin of the country."

Nichiren was born in an area along the southeast coast of the Boso Peninsula. Although he personally claimed to be the offspring of a fisherman or a diving woman, many historians believe him to have actually been the son of an estate manager. He entered the priesthood at the age of fifteen and thereafter studied at some of the most important temples in the country, including the great Tendai center at Mt. Hiei. Nichiren reached the point where he could not fathom why there were so many diverse sects when the Buddha had left only one true teaching. When he was thirty-one he had a profound religious experience while watching the sun rise near his birthplace and uttered the formula *namu myoho rengekyo* ("All glory to the Lotus Sutra of the Wonderful Law"), which his followers believe is the key to salvation.

Shortly afterwards, in 1253, Nichiren came to Kamakura for the first time, where he lived in the Matsugayatsu Valley and preached at crossroads to anybody who cared to listen. He ended up operating in Kamakura for about seventeen years, and it was there he wrote his famous tract *Rissho Ankokuron* (Establish the righteous law and save the country).

In 1260 a mob bent on his blood drove Nichiren from his hermitage. On his return he was exiled to the Izu Peninsula as a troublemaker. As soon as he was released, he was back in Kamakura. In 1271 he was sentenced to death, and only escaped at the last moment in what his followers claimed was a miracle. He was exiled to Sado Island instead. Three years later he again returned to Kamakura and met with shogunate officials. However, by this time even Nichiren had become discouraged by the cool reception he was getting and he left almost immediately, never to return to the city. He spent most of his last years in a retreat on Mt. Minobu near Fuji-san.

What perhaps contributed most to Nichiren's success was the first invasion by the Mongols, which he had seemed to have predicted eight years earlier. During the first Mongol invasion of Kyushu in 1274, the samurai were certainly getting the worst of it because of the Mongol explosives, strong bows, poison arrows, and long lances. The timely arrival of a typhoon, however, saved the situation. The Japanese were much better prepared when a second Mongol invasion force landed in 1281 and held their own during two months of hard fighting before another devastating storm arrived.

The establishment of the military capital at Kamakura caused a huge influx of prostitutes, entertainers, and ne'er-do-wells. Public intoxication and resulting altercations became so serious that the shogunate had to limit the number of saké jugs per household. Crime also seems to have been a big problem, since in 1240 special magistrates were appointed to deal with brigands, gamblers, vagabonds, rapists, arsonists, overly persistent door-to-door salesmen, and other troublemakers collectively referred to as *akuto*, and to regulate the restricted areas where merchants were allowed to operate.

At the height of the Hojo regency Kamakura's population might have been as large as 150,000, an astonishing figure considering the shortage of fresh water in the area. The different classes mixed freely, unlike in later castle towns where samurai, artisans, and merchants were segregated. However, because of the prevalence of communicable diseases and the fact that cremation had not yet become common, the shogunate restricted burials to high-ranking civil or religious officials.

Commoners buried their dead on the beaches or in out-of-the-way places. Although slavery had been formally outlawed centuries earlier, people were still more or less openly bought and sold.

Finally, in 1333, the time had arrived for the Hojo to die. Emperor Go Daigo raised the banner of rebellion, and forces led by Nitta Yoshisada stormed into Kamakura in fighting that killed thousands.

According to the *Taiheiki* chronicle, the ninth and last Hojo regent, Tadatoki, was so obsessed with dogfighting that he dressed his thousands of mutts in brocades and silk, housed them in gold and silver cages, had them carried around in palanquins, and fed them tasty morsels.

In most guidebooks the story of Kamakura ends with the destruction of the Hojo. Some even declare that thereafter it was nothing more than a sleepy country and temple town. This is a gross distortion.

During the Nambokucho civil war period, Kamakura was traded back and forth by the imperial and shogunate armies on several occasions. Once the Ashikaga shogunate was firmly established, Kamakura became the military government's headquarters for eastern Japan. The rivalries and betrayals of the following centuries were truly Byzantine and need not be gone into here. Suffice it to say that it was only after the mid-1400s that Kamakura, no longer a power center, became a real backwater. From the mid-Edo period it revived as a major destination for religious pilgrims and plain tourists, as commoners gained more disposable income and the new Tokaido became heavily traveled.

There were reportedly close to two thousand temples in Sagami Province in the late Edo period, with Zen the most popular with about twenty percent of the total. However, the Meiji Restoration hit many Kamakura temples hard because the government dispossessed much of their land.

Finally, during the late Meiji period Kamakura and surrounding communities became home to wealthy businessmen, politicians, artists, and writers. More recently the community of 180,000 has become a true bedtown for Tokyo and generally tops the polls when Tokyoites are asked where they would most like to live.

1

The Salt Route

⬤ Kamakura Station 鎌倉駅 (JR Yokosuka Line)—Nichiren Preaching Site 日蓮聖人辻説法跡——Kamakura-bori Museum 鎌倉彫資料館—Myoryu-ji 妙隆寺—Harakiri Yagura Cave 腹切やぐら—Sugimoto-dera 杉本寺—Jomyo-ji 浄妙寺—Hokoku-ji 報国寺—Myoo-in 明王院—Kosoku-ji 光触寺—Asahina Hiking Course 朝比奈ハイキングコース

What kind of image does the city of Kamakura conjure up?

Almost without fail to a Tokyoite it is an upper-crust bedtown, an extreme tentacle of the megalopolis octopus, or a weekend resort—Buddhas and beaches. It is what tourism promoters like to call a "little Kyoto." And all a mere hour's train ride from the capital.

But ask long-time Kamakura residents and the story is different. To them, Kamakura is *inaka*—country. The soul of this ancient city is not to be found in the trendy shops that cater to the one-day sightseer. Seek it instead in the brooding hills and tranquil valleys where the toll of the temple bells is but an echo of distant centuries.

One thing you should bear in mind is that the temples and other historical sites bear little resemblance to how they were in Kamakura's heyday, when Yoritomo's seat of power boasted a population of perhaps 120,000. Time after time the city has been razed by fire or other natural disasters and what remains is only a shadow of its former self.

When you come out of the east exit of Kamakura Station turn around and look back. The station has a faintly Victorian look to it. If it's a weekend or during one of the peak seasons when flowers of various kinds are in bloom (which is just about any time) or the summer sun is blazing, the churning crowds might spoil the laid-back mood.

• MAP 158

158

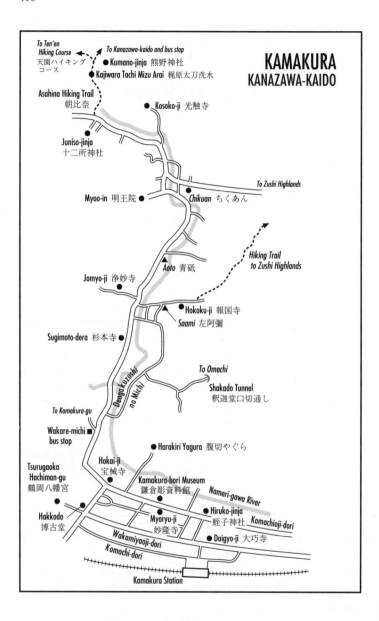

Kamakura is a stroller's paradise, but the roads are mostly narrow so try to go on a weekday or before 10:00 A.M.

Go straight from the wickets (Komachi-dori shopping street will be to your left); the main street you exit onto is Wakamiyaoji-dori. This broad, mile-long road was the main thoroughfare during the days of the Kamakura shogunate. The "Young Prince Road" was supposedly built for the presentation of Yoriie at the shrine after his birth. According to another story, it was built by Yoritomo to apologize to Masako for his extracurricular activities, giving rise to the nickname the "Road of Love." The southern end of the avenue is marked by a big stone *torii* erected in 1618. In olden times, this main road was 9.1 meters wide at the first *torii* and 2.7 meters wide at the third *torii*—the northern end. It is said the principle of perspective was used to make the avenue appear longer than it actually was. Midway the avenue is flanked by cherry trees and azaleas.

The Tsurugaoka Hachiman-gu Shrine is to the left, Yuigahama Beach and Suruga Bay to the right. Kamakura has an estimated three hundred temples and shrines, but it also has many Christian churches, several of them on Wakamiyaoji-dori. Although the number of Christians in Japan is infinitesimal in relation to the general population, many of them are intellectuals or professionals. Kamakura is home to many writers, educators, and other such individuals, so it is not at all surprising that there should be so many churches. Strum the heartstrings of Kamakura and you are likely to hear a prayer, be it sutra or psalm.

Cross over to the other side of Wakamiyaoji-dori. To the right of a bookstore you will see a phallic-shaped purplish red rock about four feet in height. This is the entrance to Daigyo-ji, a Nichiren temple that was founded by Saint Nicho in 1274. Its principal image is Onme-sama, a nickname for the goddess of birth. Expectant parents come here to pray for an easy delivery. They can also supposedly find out if their child is to be a boy or a girl through fortune telling. If a helmet comes up, it'll be a boy; if a crane, it'll be a girl. Look inside the temple and you will see sunflowers decorating the altar and multicolored *origami* decorations that resemble leis hanging from the rafters.

Exit from the back gate of Daigyo-ji; you come out in front of a saké shop. To its right is the entrance to Hiruko-jinja, a rustic wooden

• MAP 158

shrine somewhat like a typical mountain shrine. Behind it flows Kamakura's most important river, the Nameri-gawa. The vermilion bridge to the left provides an elegant touch to the scenery.

Go back to the road, turn right, and walk on about 150 meters. On the right you'll see a marker commemorating the spot where Nichiren, whom Alan Booth aptly referred to as "the Reverend Ian Paisley of Japan," first began to preach in public in Kamakura. The location he chose for his in-your-face proselytizing was intentional—it was right on the borderline between the district where the offices of the Bakufu were located and the quarters of the merchants and ordinary townspeople. The fire-and-brimstone–spewing fisherman's son obviously took great pleasure in tweaking the high-strung noses of his social betters.

A little bit farther on to the right is the Kamakura-bori Museum which has an extensive collection of exquisite Kamakura-bori.

Kamakura-bori 鎌倉彫

Kamakura-bori refers to a distinctive type of lacquerware intricately carved with floral and geometric designs developed in Kamakura in the thirteenth century. The main distinguishing feature is that the wooden base is carved and not the lacquer itself, which is more usually the case. According to tradition the artist Koun, grandson of the sculptor Unkei, is said to have introduced the technique which was first produced in China. Kamakura-bori was primarily a temple art and many of the objects made, such as incense containers, are related to the practice of Zen. Although the technique was originally used to imitate carved lacquer, it eventually became highly sought after in its own right, particularly during the nineteenth and twentieth centuries and in recent years this ancient art form has started incorporating very innovative styles.

At present there are approximately 400 professional Kamakura-bori carvers, mostly men. It takes four to five years to learn the essentials; true pros can carve with their eyes closed. One master carver is Goto Shuntaro, a twenty-eighth generation descendant of Unkei, who began carving at the tender age of seven. To the right of the entrance to Tsurugaoka Hachiman-gu is Shuntaro's shop, Hakkodo, where you can view intricate red and black lacquerware. Shuntaro's daughter, Keiko, a prizewinning Kamakura-bori artist in her own right, says, "Kamakura-bori articles are meant to be used not just looked at. In fact, daily use enriches their luster and hues. That's a point we like to emphasize."

To learn more about the various stages involved in making Kamakura-bori, check out the Kamakura-bori Museum and the English video there.

Kamakura-bori Museum (Kamakura-bori Shiryo-kan 鎌倉彫資料館)
☎ 0467-25-1502
⏰ 10:00–16:00; closed Mon. ¥200
Hakkodo 博古堂
☎ 0467-22-2429 ⏰ 9:00–17:30; closed 2nd Sun. each month

• MAP 158

Across the street from the museum is Myoryu-ji, another Nichiren temple founded in 1385. Here Nisshin, one of Nichiren's immediate disciples, underwent cold water ablutions for one hundred consecutive days. In a fit of irony, perhaps, shogun Ashikaga Yoshiie tortured him by putting a hot cauldron on his head after cutting off the tip of his tongue. Nisshin had had the temerity to criticize Yoshie's rule, or misrule. By all accounts Nisshin was quite into sadomasochism, spending much of his time either being tortured or torturing himself. In perhaps one of the first urban myths he is said to have pulled out one fingernail a day for ten days.

Go around to the right and you will see a small graveyard that includes a monument to Maruyama Sadao, one of the guiding lights of the *shingeki* modern drama movement, and a lover of wine, women, and song. He was performing in the Hiroshima area on August 6, 1945, when the A-bomb was dropped. After ten days of horrible suffering he died incognito in the storehouse of a local temple. Only years later were his mortal remains discovered by friends. The poignant carving on the tomb shows him perfoming a scene from Molière.

A bit farther down the road from the museum, turn right at the hardware store and you'll find the Harakiri Yagura cave, the site where the last Hojo regent Takatoki reportedly committed suicide with more than eight hundred retainers in May 1333 after their defenses were overwhelmed by the imperial forces led by Nitta Yoshisada. You will find it right next to a Catholic retreat. All this area was once part of the mammoth Tosho-ji Temple. The *Taiheiki*, or *Chronicle of Great Peace*—never was the name of a literary work more malapropos—tells of the tragic last days of the Hojo clan. On the evening of May 22 a final party was held for 283 Hojo retainers. They then proceeded to commit suicide and were followed by the lower-ranking samurai who had been guarding the festivities. Takatoki's retainers feared that the pleasure-loving Takatoki would not be up to committing *seppuku*, but when he observed a fifteen-year-old boy calmly cut his abdomen open, the "dog regent" took heart and went to his ancestors with dignity.

Harakiri Cave is only about eight feet deep, reminding me of the caves at Mabuni in the southernmost corner of Okinawa Island where tens of thousands of Japanese died in the waning days of World War II.

• MAP 158

On one recent visit to the Harakiri Cave some of the offerings placed for the souls of the Hojo included a rotting tomato, an orange, and a cup of rancid sake that had obviously been there for weeks. In Japan there is frequently little honor for the historical losers. But no doubt the soul of the passionate prelate Nichiren must have gloated with thoughts of sweet revenge at what happened that bloody spring. A statue of Jesus Christ, "the man of sorrows," stares compassionately from the grounds of the retreat directly toward the entrance to the cave. It is hard to get away from religion in Kamakura. Because of the large number of Hojo ghosts said to haunt this area, drastic exorcism steps had to be taken in subsequent years. One wonders whether all the ghosts are really gone.

Let's not worry about it. Instead pick up some of the famous cookies made by the brothers here. They come in nine varieties.

Back on the main road, continue three hundred meters in the same direction. On the right you'll see Hokai-ji—a Tendai temple erected in 1335 by Emperor Go-Daigo, who apparently was being tormented by the vengeful ghost of Takatoki, as a place where prayers for the souls of the Hojo could be recited. Its nickname is the Hagi Temple, because of the lovely white flowers of the bush clover that cloak its precincts every September. Some believe them to be the transmigrated souls of the Hojo. This was the only temple whose gate faced Wakamiyaoji-dori, because it enjoyed the sponsorship of the emperor.

Backtrack to the narrow road to the right of Hokai-ji (it curves to the left) and follow it for 180 meters; on the right you'll find the Momijiyama Yagura, a cave where the remains of some of the Hojo regents were discovered. In fact, the whole Kamakura area is honey-combed with thousands of cave tombs dug out from the volcanic soil, dating from the Kamakura and Ashikaga periods and even earlier.

Go back to Hokai-ji and continue on, veering to the right. You'll now be on the ancient Kanazawa-kaido Highway, which during the Kamakura era was one of the key supply arteries for the city. Salt and other important goods were brought in from Mutsuura near Kanazawa Hakkei, giving rise to its nickname, the "Salt Highway." Stay on the right after the road splits at Wakare-michi. The road to the left goes to Kamakura-gu and several important temples covered in the next chapter.

• MAP 158

The sidewalks along the edges of the highway are extremely narrow and crowded with pedestrian and bicycle traffic, especially on the weekends. One nifty trick for avoiding some of the congestion and getting to see a truly peaceful Kamakura neighborhood is to take the Dengakuzushi no Michi, which was an important route in days past and is mentioned in many ancient records such as the *Azuma Kagami*. To get to Dengakuzushi no Michi, turn right off Kanazawa-kaido across from the large pea-green buildings belonging to Ganso Pastries. After crossing the small bridge over the carp-brimming Nameri-gawa, turn left. At the crossroads, turn left to get back on Kanazawa-kaido.

Branching off to the right of the path is the road to the Shakado Tunnel, long the most important thoroughfare for moving crosswise from one side of the city to the other. It is flanked by dozens of *yagura* that were used as burial crypts and even as prison cells. The Shakudo has been officially closed because of the danger of falling rocks, but you can still make your way through it to the Omachi area easily enough. It is only ten minutes off the Dengakuzushi, so the best thing to do is to make a detour to it and then come back to the main route.

The Shakado is a sight to see—a towering tunnel dug out of solid rock forty feet high by the order of the Kamakura government. It takes its name from the Shakado ("Buddha Hall") built in 1225 by regent Yasutoki in honor of his father, who had been assassinated the year before. (One begins to wonder if anybody actually died of natural causes in those days.) No one is quite sure where this temple was situated. Incidentally, the four valleys, or *yato*, on this side of the highway were filled with the mansions of Bakufu leaders. The word *yato* is used only in the Kanto region, especially Kamakura, and may well have Ainu origins.

Just to the left of the signals on the other side of the street is the super-steep stone stairway leading up to Sugimoto-dera, founded in 734 by the monk Gyoki as a Tendai temple, making it by far the oldest temple in Kamakura and the first stop for pilgrims setting out to visit Kannon temples in the Kanto region. The pair of guardian deities flanking the gate half-way up are genuinely intimidating; they're the kind of guys you'd like to take with you on a business trip to New York City.

Sugimoto-dera, also known as Okura no Kannon (Goddess of

• MAP 158

Mercy at Okura), is famed for its *mitsumata* flowers that bloom in February and the Eleven-Faced Kannon in the main hall. Leading up to it are steep, moss-covered steps bordered by azaleas; protecting the approach from enemies are two fierce-looking Deva kings. In a fire in 1189, the entire main hall burned to the ground, although the statue miraculously survived. The thatched-roof hall is most unusual in style; take your shoes off and go into the dimly lit interior to observe the Eleven-Faced Kannon (ten smaller statues pop out of the head of the main one), two other Kannon statues, and other treasures such as a *jizo* said to have been carved by Unkei, and statues of Bishamon and Benten. Behind Sugimoto-dera are the remains of Sugimoto Castle and a monument to the sun goddess Amaterasu.

During the Namboku civil war this strategic site overlooking the Kanazawa-kaido was fought over by the Ashikaga and imperial forces. The huge white banners fluttering in front of the main hall (reading Juichimen Sugimoto Kannon—Eleven-Faced Sugimoto Kannon) give the temple precincts something of the air of a medieval encampment.

Another 250 meters farther up and on the same side of the road is the entrance to Jomyo-ji, founded in 1188 by Ashikaga Yoshikane, one of the city's top five Rinzai Zen temples. It used to be a huge complex with thirty-three steeples, but like so many other temples here it was struck by fire on more than one occasion and all that remains now is the main hall constructed during the Edo period and framed beautifully against the mountains to the rear. Jomyo-ji is known for its gorgeous camellias and peonies in springtime, the tomb of Ashikaga Takauji's father, and the statues of Shaka Nyorai and the founding priest, Gyoyu, contained in its storehouse. (Make arrangements ahead of time if you want to see the temple treasures.) The roof of the temple was originally thatched, but now there is a fetching imitation thatch made of copper plates. In the grounds is a very small, very old fox shrine, dedicated to the white fox that supposedly showed Kamatari where to bury his *kama* and thus start Kamakura. Enjoy some tea ceremony–style green tea (*matcha*) and a Japanese cake, while gazing out at the Zen garden.

Across the road from Jomyo-ji is the road leading up 150 meters to Hokoku-ji, the famous "Bamboo Temple," which is also attached to the

• MAP 158

Rinzai sect of Zen. It is nestled in the same narrow valley where writer Hayashi Fusao used to live. On the other side of the road are houses where director Ozu Yasujiro filmed the location shots of some of his classic films like *Tokyo Monogatari*—actress Hara Setsuko also had a house in the neighborhood. Although Hokoku-ji was founded in 1334 by Ashikaga Ietoki, grandfather of Takauji, the garden of thick-stemmed bamboo transplanted from Kyoto is a much later introduction. The buildings have all been built since the Kanto Earthquake. Tombs of early priests of the temple are up above. The mountain behind had the nickname Kinubari-yama, or "Silk Spread Mountain," because at the height of summer Yoritomo liked to have white silk spread over the summit to create the illusion of snow. Writers Kawabata Yasunari and Kume Masao lived here for some time.

Impressive it is, but with all the shutterbugs around not very soul-soothing. A memorial tower dedicated to the repose of the souls of the Hojo and graves of Ashikaga family members are also to be found here. Try the traditional *matcha* tea served on a veranda overlooking the bamboo. If you are lucky, perhaps the brew will induce instant satori.

An interesting "secret" hiking path branches off to the left about a hundred meters behind Hokoku-ji. It's very easy to miss, since it starts between two houses with only a small plaque to indicate its existence. From here it's about a twenty-minute hike to the top of the mountain along what was once a pilgrimage course—you can see cave shrines and Buddhist carvings along the way. Eventually you emerge into the middle of the huge Zushi Highlands housing complex, as close to a California-style yuppie sprawl as you would want to find in Japan. It has a small shopping center and attracts many tourists during the spring because of the hundreds of cherry trees that line its main road.

More and more of the well-heeled are moving to Kamakura, dismaying long-time residents who can remember when most of the town's temples and shrines were dilapidated and the streets were semi-deserted with the exception of New Year's and a few other holidays. Even today you can see many time-warp incongruities: lines of squirrels scampering in Indian file across overhead powerlines, vestmented Buddhist priests speeding along on mopeds, flocks of wild birds and gangs of motorcyclists vying

• MAP 158

to drown each other out with their respective songs. From Zushi Highlands you can take a bus to Zushi or Kamakura stations.

There are two interesting restaurants in this area: Saami, in front of Hokoku-ji, offers *unsui shojin ryori* (Zen-style cooking), and Aoto, up the Kanazawa-kaido on the right, the product of a group of housewives who enjoy cooking, which has Kamakura-style boxed lunches.

Our next stop is the small thatched-roofed Shingon temple Myoo-in, off to the left of the Kanazawa-kaido three or four hundred meters from Hokoku-ji, across from the big cutoff that leads to Zushi Highlands. You can't see it from the highway, but when you see a green sign for the Green Tennis Club, you'll know that it is time to turn.

Founded in 1235 by the fourth shogun, Fujiwara Yoritsune, Myoo-in was one of the largest temples in the city until it fell into decay after the overthrow of the Kamakura shogunate. It was dedicated to Fudo Myoo, the protective deity, and located here because this is the northeast corner of the city—according to Chinese geomancy the direction from which demons and evil influences enter. When the hydrangea are in bloom in June, the small precincts are overrun with flower lovers and photographers. The fall brings beautiful cockscomb and cluster-amaryllis.

For a taste of the bizarre, follow the road to the right (when facing toward the highway) past the tennis club for about five minutes. Suddenly on the right you'll see what looks like a mirage: a whale sitting in the middle of a grass lawn! Closer inspection reveals dogs, horses, and giraffes. All plaster models created by the artist in residence.

A route leading up to the Ten'en Hiking Course begins behind Myoo-in. Not far up is a *jizo* that marks the spot where samurai blew conch shells to call the Hojo warriors to action in a vain attempt to staunch the onslaught of the imperial forces.

From Myoo-in, either exit directly onto Kanazawa-kaido or take the little path to the left that eventually links up with the highway in front of a Jesuit retreat. Cross the road and then turn right just pass the Juniso bus stop. After passing a traditional thatched house, you'll find the entrance to Kosoku-ji, home of the "salt-licking *jizo.*" This temple apparently started out attached to the Shingon sect, but transferred its allegiance to the Jishu Amida sect under the influence of the famous

• MAP 158

"dancing *nembutsu*" priest Ippen Shonin, whose evocative statue is in the garden. To the right of the temple is the "salt-licking *jizo*." As mentioned earlier, the Kanazawa-kaido was important as a transportation route for salt from Mutsuura and points beyond like Chiba. The *jizo*, the guardian deity of children, was originally right next to the highway and salt merchants would make offerings of salt to it. One day an irate merchant, who apparently had had either a bad business trip or a bad night, knocked the statue down and stuffed its mouth with salt. Packages of salt are still placed in front of it as offerings.

Even more famous is the jade-eyed, three-foot-high Hoyake Amida ("Branded-Cheek Amida") stored in the main hall out of view. Its story is illustrated in two scrolls kept at the Kokuhokan repository next to Tsurugaoka Hachiman-gu. An aristocratic lady named Machi no Tsubone had it carved, possibly by Unkei himself, in order to express her reverence for Amida.

A priest much devoted to worship of the statue was falsely accused of theft and then tortured by being branded with a hot iron on his cheek. He called out to Amida in his agony and the torturers found to their dismay that no matter how many times they burned him they could not harm him and no mark was left behind. Later it was discovered that the statue was oozing blood from a burn mark on the cheek. The merciful Amida had taken on the pain of her faithful follower. Even more amazing, no matter how many times efforts were made to correct the burn mark, it always returned. Or so the story goes. (If you call ahead you may be able to see the Amida and other temple treasures, but in principle you need a group of ten or more. ☎ 0467-22-6864)

Fortify yourself for the hike ahead by dropping into Chikuan, just off the road to Zushi Highlands, which serves a mean *tempura*-and-*soba* set at a reasonable price. Return to the main highway and after a few hundred meters you'll see a rather unimposing shrine, Juniso-jinja, on the left on a hill behind a small playground. Although founded in 1278 as an *inari* (fox) shrine within the precincts of Kosoku-ji, it was moved here during the Meiji period when the government was intent on clearly defining the distinction between Buddhism and Shinto. At the lively September harvest festival impressive *kagura* dances are performed here.

• MAP 158

The last part of this walk, through the Asahina Pass, is in many ways the best. A number of trails crisscross the area, including an alternative entrance to the Ten'en Hiking Course. According to legend the pass was carved out in one night by a wonder boy called Asahina Saburo. In fact it took a couple of years to hack it out at the order of Regent Hojo Yasutoki. Reach it by going under the main highway and onto the now disused Old Kanazawa Highway. Halfway through the pass you reach the main cutoff at Kajiwara Tachi Arai-mizu ("Kajiwara Sword-Washing Spring"). Kajiwara Kagetoki was the Kamakura period's Iago. It was Kagetoki who reportedly turned Yoritomo against Yoshitsune, and he himself murdered another Kamakura retainer, Chiba Hirotsune, during a sneak night attack on his mansion; afterwards he came here to wash his sword off.

If you still have any doubts as to whether Kamakura is *inaka* or not, Asahina Pass should settle them once and for all. The tree-canopied path is lit only by filtered sunlight, creating a mood akin to that of the movie *Rashomon*. You are now worlds away from Tokyo. You are also technically out of Kamakura and into Yokohama City. Just before you reach beautiful Kumano Shrine, you'll see a small cave on the right which has a wall carving of a Buddha that looks like it had been lifted directly from the walls of a cave along the Silk Road of Central Asia. Before you finally debouch from the Asahina trail you pass through a very narrow defile cut out of the rock that could have been Kamakura's Thermopylae during the final days of the Hojo. It is clear evidence of the difficulties that invaders faced in attacking the "impregnable" city.

After passing a small factory on the right, you will be back on the Kanazawa-kaido and from here you can catch a bus back to Kamakura or on to Kanazawa Hakkei Station on the Keihin Kyuko Line. From the top of the Asahina Pass it's possible to hike back down to Kosoku-ji, a trek that takes about forty minutes.

Jomyo-ji Teahouse ☎ 0467-22-2818
🕘 10:00–16:00

Saami 左阿彌 ☎ 0467-24-9420
🕘 11:00–16:00; closed Fri.

Aoto 青砥 ☎ 0467-24-9001
🕘 11:30–16:00; closed Weds.

Chikuan ちくあん ☎ 0467-25-3006
🕘 11:30–15:00, 17:00–20:30; closed Weds.

• MAP 158

2

Halls of the Shoguns

○ Kamakura Station 鎌倉駅 (JR Yokosuka Line)—bus from east exit (東口) bound for Daitonomiya (大塔宮) get off at terminus—Kamakura-gu 鎌倉宮 —Zuisen-ji 瑞泉寺 — Kamakura-gu 鎌倉宮 —Kakuon-ji 覚園寺—Egara Tenjin Shrine 荏柄天神—Yoritomo's tomb 頼朝の墓—Tsurugaoka Hachiman-gu 鶴岡八幡宮—Kamakura Station

Although this walk demands a bus ride at its start, it is highly recommended that you follow the order mapped out, especially if you're visiting on a weekend when flowers are in bloom. The tranquil, contemplative effect of Zuisen-ji is ruined if you get there after hordes of other tourists have made their cacophonous entrance. At times so many photographers set up their bulky tripods on its narrow paths that you expect some starlet to appear like an avatar of the goddess of mercy.

Get off at the Daitonomiya terminus; go to the opposite side of the entrance to the Kamakura-gu Shrine, turn left, and follow the road till you pass some tennis courts on the left. Incidentally, these are located on the approximate former site of Yofuku-ji, an extensive temple complex built in 1192 to pray for the repose of the souls of those tens of thousands who died during Yoritomo's expedition against Hiraizumi and burned to the ground in 1405. It should be noted that temples like Yofuku-ji or Hokai-ji were not built because the victors felt sorry for their victims. They were simply terrified that the spirits of the recently dispatched would come back seeking revenge. It is often said that Yoritomo, for example, was a very religious man. But it would be more accurate to say that he was a very superstitious man. At Yofuku-ji Yoritomo also wanted to replicate some of the splendor he had seen at Hiraizumi.

• MAP 170

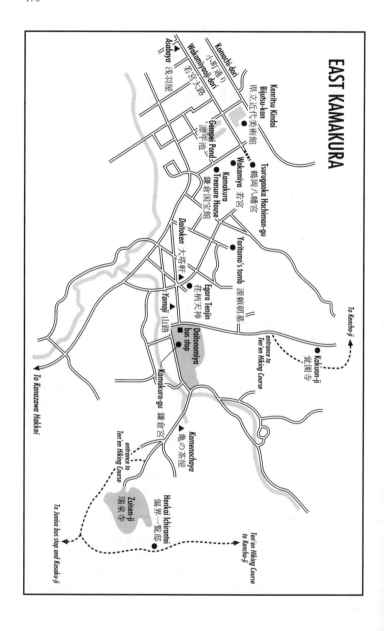

EAST KAMAKURA

Komachi-dori 小町通り

Bijutsu-kan 県立近代美術館
Kenritsu Kindai

Asabaya 浅羽屋

Wakamiyaoji-dori 若宮大路

Gempei Pond 源平池

Wakamiya 若宮

Kamakura Treasure House 鎌倉国宝館

Tsurugoka Hachiman-gu 鶴岡八幡宮

Daitoken 大塔軒

Yoritomo's tomb 源頼朝墓

Egara Tenjin 荏柄天神

Yamaji 山路

Daitonomiya bus stop

entrance to Ten'en Hiking Course

Kakuion-ji 覚園寺

To Kencho-ji

Kamakura-gu 鎌倉宮

Kamenochaya 亀の茶屋

entrance to Ten'en Hiking Course

Zuisen-ji 瑞泉寺

Henkei Ichiromtei 偏界一覧亭

Ten'en Hiking Course to Kencho-ji

To Jumiso bus stop and Kosoku-ji

To Kanazawa Hakkei

At the cutoff, veer to the right past the shop with drink machines out front. You'll pass coffee shops and antique shops before reaching the entrance to Zuisen-ji in a quiet, secluded part of Momijigayatsu (Maple Leaf Valley), about one kilometer from Kamakura-gu. Kamenochaya, a traditional teahouse is irresistible for its homey atmosphere and generous portions of *oshiruko* (おしるこ), or sweet bean soup. The turning for the Ten'en Hiking Course is a bit before the temple entrance on the right.

Zuisen-ji, which belongs to the Rinzai school, was founded in 1327 by Muso Soseki (1275–1351), one of the most distinguished early Zen priests. A 1.2-meter-high image of this remarkable man seated on a chair is enshrined in the Founders Hall. The expression on his face captures the sense of tough love that has filled the hearts of all Zen masters. Unfortunately, you need special permission to view the statue.

The main attraction for most visitors who venture this far off the beaten track is to be found in the adjoining gardens, one a flowering one and the other a rock-and-water Zen masterpiece of austerity laid out by Muso Soseki himself. The designs of the few temple buildings, although interesting in their own right, take a back seat to the gardens in which they sit. The two gardens can be considered as complementary representations of the two sides of reality, seemingly opposed but actually harmonious. They were much praised by poets of old.

The best strategy probably is to take a look at the rock garden behind the main hall first before dealing with the distractions of the real world—namely the photographers. The garden is an evocative medley of stones, sand, water, and evergreen trees. The three-part Angels' Cave in the background is said to be where Muso Soseki sat for hours in *zazen* meditation. However, it and the serpentine Juhachi Mawari staircase leading up to Ten'en Park are now off-limits to closer examination. To make up for this, there is a very fine view of general Kamakura from the Henkai-Ichirantei arbor at the top of the hill behind the temple, another of the founder's brainstorms.

Zen prelates, of course, are fond of contradictions, and no doubt Muso Soseki would savor the irony of the fact that his hermitage of reflection has become a magnet for often noisy sightseers. Zuisen-ji,

• MAP 170

commonly referred to as the flowering garden of Kamakura, is particularly known for its plum blossoms in February and early March, and maple and other autumn leaves in the fall, but its narcissus (late January to mid-February) and wisteria (early May) are equally impressive. And there are also cherry blossoms, peonies, bellflowers, and various other appealing flowers, not to mention a eucalyptus tree transplanted from Australia in 1876, whose trunk is more than three meters around.

Zuisen-ji formerly was ranked second among the top ten Rinzai temples in the Kanto district by imperial order. It was closely identified with the Ashikaga shoguns and much restoration work was done by Ashikaga Motouji, the brother of the second Ashikaga shogun, when he was governor-general of the Kanto area. The temple also suffered at times from its political connections during the civil wars. Another large temple, Eian-ji, once stood nearby, but it was burned down in a civil war among Ashikaga followers in 1439. Later Zuisen-ji slipped into historical obscurity, until the nineteenth century; it came into the limelight again when imperial zealot Yoshida Shoin holed up here and plotted to sneak abroad on an American vessel. His uncle was the head priest at that time. Yoshida was captured and later executed by the Tokugawa authorities, but his ideological heirs won in the civil war that followed.

The next stop on this route, Kakuon-ji Temple, disproves the proposition that all Kamakura temples have forgotten the advantages of quietism. Backtrack to the entrance to Kamakura-gu and then make a right. Go past the bus stop and head straight to the temple entrance, about ten minutes away on foot. Kakuon-ji can also be reached via a very roundabout route by the Ten'en Hiking Course starting from Zuisen-ji.

A resident priest gives a guided tour of main sections of the temple and a detailed explanation of its treasures and religious practices beginning on the hour every hour from 10:00 to 15:00, with a break at noon. The whole thing takes about fifty minutes. Of course, the earlier you arrive the fewer the other enlightenment seekers. Be sure to arrive at least five minutes early for the tour. Note that the temple is closed at the end of the year and during most of August. If you can understand enough Japanese to benefit from the explanations, this is a very educational experience. The gruff demeanor of the priests is also a wonder

• MAP 170

to behold. Absolutely no photography is allowed.

Although Kakuon-ji is now affiliated with the Shingon esoteric sect, in the past it served as an eclectic spiritual training center for priests from four schools. Its origins go back to 1218 when a votive hall was established here by order of Hojo Yoshitoki, the second regent. It was not made a full temple until 1296, but thereafter it was much favored in turn by the Hojo, Emperor Go Daigo, who visited here, and Ashikaga Takauji. At that time it was a sprawling affair with ten subsidiary temples flanking the approach. There are many references to its elegant appearance in the journals of the day. However, it declined in the centuries that followed, becoming at times little more than a ghost-infested wasteland, and after the Meiji Restoration the persecution of Buddhism hit Kakuon-ji particularly hard because of its connection with the tradition of Shugendo ascetic wandering priests and the Hojo and Ashikaga families, whom the modern advocates of imperial rule abhorred as traitors.

The first stop on the tour is the structure outside the gate. Check out the three statues, which include a three-eyed Aizen Myoo and a small experimental Fudo, sculpted by Gangyo, that was the model for a larger version by the same artist for a shrine on the sacred mountain Oyama.

Next is the Buddha Hall, which houses the ancient Yakushi Nyorai (Healing Buddha) statue, whose head, at least, is believed to date back to the early part of the Kamakura period, making it as old as the Great Buddha and therefore one of the city's oldest surviving Buddhas. It is flanked by two attendants, Nikko and Gakko, representing the sun and moon. Compare their feminine features to the obviously masculine beauty of the main piece. The various piles of candles in front of the statues are used in praying for specific wishes, such as protection from accidents and recovery from illness. The Saya Amida in the right recess was a favorite of Kawabata Yasunari, who was much taken with her benevolent smile.

Twelve very individualistic warrior deities line the two sides of the hall. One of them is connected with shogun Sanetomo's assassination, which will be explained later. And if you look hard at the ceiling, you can just about make out a faded painting of a large blue dragon flitting

• MAP 170

among white clouds. Incidentally, one of the advantages of arriving here early is that the natural light shows the statues to their best advantage; there is no artificial light in the hall.

We are next led through the garden to a restored thatched-roof farmhouse that is now used for, among other things, Noh recitals. Here our spiritual guide explains about the traditional divisions of the afterworld and how souls are judged and saved. While explaining about the judges of the netherworld, the priest remarks with a sly smile, "Kindly remember their names for future reference."

Appropriately enough, we next tuck into a *yagura* cave burial chamber before going to see the famous Black Jizo (Kuro Jizo), like the Yakushi Nyorai, an Important Cultural Property. It is said to descend into hell and alleviate the suffering of people there. That is why no matter how many times it is painted, overnight it purportedly returns to its original dark color. Notice the boat-shaped halo that backs the eight-foot-high statue. The Black Jizo is also believed to possess the power to prevent fire, so naturally it is the spiritual protector of firefighters. Traditionally families from Kamakura and the Miura Peninsula visited the Black Jizo at O-bon, the summer festival of dead souls. Today, there is a candlelight ceremony in front of the Black Jizo on August 9 and a major festival that draws thousands the following day. Although you are not free to wander alone around the grounds of Kakuon-ji, you can truly sense its deep feeling of detachment and religious commitment and enjoy the peace and serenity of the Yakushidogayatsu valley.

The *Jizo*

The *jizo* has been described as the quintessential Japanese Buddhist divinity, and of course, you can see *jizo* statues everywhere. For one thing, he is regarded as the guardian of dead, miscarried, or aborted children, so at many temples sorrowing mothers will dress the statues in the clothes of a child no longer of this world. The hope is that the god will reciprocate by reducing the suffering of the tiny ghost who is wandering the dry bed of Sai no Kawara, the River of Souls, a dark land haunted by demons.

The little stones often seen piled around *jizo* statues are symbolic representations of the penances the little one's are made to perform. Other parents leave thanksgiving offerings, such as milk or oranges when a child has recovered from an illness or when a borrowed *jizo*, temporarily taken home, has helped a mother to conceive.

• MAP 170

On the way up to Kakuon-ji, you may have noticed an entrance to the Ten'en Hiking Course on the right side of the road. The trail on the right leads to Zuisen-ji, about an hour's walk away. The opposite direction takes you to Kencho-ji at Kita Kamakura.

In 1869 Emperor Meiji ordered construction of the Kamakura-gu where Toko-ji Temple was formerly located, to honor the memory of Prince Morinaga, the third son of Emperor Go Daigo, who was butchered in 1335 at the age of twenty-seven. It is an example of traditional shrine architecture, epitomized by the Ise and Izumo shrines.

There is no need to linger at Kamakura-gu. History buffs may want to pay the admission fee to go behind the shrine and take a peek from outside at the four-meter-deep cave in which Prince Morinaga lived as a prisoner for nine months. In size it's the equivalent of a ten-mat room. There's also a treasure house with a series of paintings illustrating the main events in the doomed prince's life and paraphernalia related to Emperor Meiji's visit here. About 170 stone steps away on picturesque Richikozan Hill east of the shrine, you'll find the prince's tomb.

Prince Morinaga was involved in the Kemmu Restoration that destroyed the Kamakura shogunate and returned power to Emperor Go Daigo in Kyoto. He opposed the machinations of Ashikaga Takauji and his clan and was slandered by them as a traitor. Ever-gullible Go Daigo believed the calumny and let his son be taken to Kamakura as a prisoner. Just before Hojo Tokiyuki, son of the last regent Takatoki, temporarily regained Kamakura, Takauji's brother Ashikaga Tadayoshi ordered his death. According to tradition, the assassin was so terrified by the expression on the prince's face when he beheaded him after a furious struggle that he threw the precious trophy away.

The pure-hearted loyalty of Prince Morinaga made him a perfect candidate for emulation on the part of the early Meiji government, since it was eager to foster emperor worship and discourage opposition. The annual shrine festival takes place on August 20, the anniversary of Morinaga's death. On September 21–22 hauntingly beautiful Takigi Noh performances take place against a backdrop of burning faggots. This is probably the way these exquisite masks were designed to be seen. Tickets are only available through a postcard lottery. Send a

• MAP 170

return addressed postcard (*ofuku hagaki*), one card per seat, to Kamakura City Tourist Association, 1-9-3 Komachi, Kamakura-shi, Kanagawa-ken, postmarked between September 1 and 8; you cannot choose the date you want to see the performance.

From the main entrance to the shrine head down the shop-lined road. A good noodle shop, Yamaji, is on the left; it uses extra-rich dough to make its *soba* and *udon*. A couple of blocks farther on the right is Daitoken, a very reasonable Chinese restaurant. Turn right on the path near here to the Egara Tenjin Shrine. (Note that it closes at 14:30.)

This is one of the few shrines or temples in Kamakura to predate Yoritomo's arrival. It is dedicated to the righteous ninth-century official Sugawara Michizane, who, although a high official of the utmost rectitude, was unfortunate enough to get on the wrong side of the then all-powerful Fujiwara clan and was exiled to Kyushu in 901. In those days exile from Kyoto was considered the ultimate punishment for aristocrats, and Michizane died two years later, no doubt broken in spirit.

However, strange events followed his demise. Weird natural disasters began to strike the country one after another and they were interpreted as heaven's wrath at the unjustified punishment of this worthy individual. Finally, forty-five years later, Michizane was officially deified as Tenjin, the patron of learning, and enshrined at Kitano Shrine in Kyoto. (This demonstrates the great flexibility of Shinto.)

Egara Tenjin dates back to 1104 when, as the story goes, a scroll featuring Michizane's portrait suddenly appeared out of a stormy sky. Yoritomo made it a tutelary shrine since it was to the northeast, the direction from which danger was supposed to emanate (as viewed from Bakufu headquarters), and built a large complex here.

Enter Egara Tenjin up the long staircase and through the natural *torii* of nettle trees. To the right is a gingko tree that is said to be over nine hundred years old. The main shrine building is red and quite impressive. Hanging up in front are a large number of wooden votive tablets. These are petitions, quite specific in detail, by students trying to pass entrance exams. On the left is the Fudezuka burial mound for

• MAP 170

old *fude*, or writing brushes. A special ceremony is held here every January 25 in which old *fude* and other writing implements are buried. Perhaps this is related to the ancient belief in the sacredness of the written word; in pre-modern days the Chinese used to burn all scraps of paper with writing on them. Notice the *kappa* monument, with its amusing depictions of this mischievous creature by more than 150 manga artists. The calligraphy on the separate *fudezuka* is by Kawabata Yasunari.

Come down the stairs from the shrine, turn right, walk straight, and then turn right again. We're now in the district where the major offices of the Bakufu and the homes of its leaders were once located. There is a staircase leading up the hillside and at the top you'll find two cave graves. The one on the left with the tortoise figure in front belongs to Oe Hiromoto, the scholar from Kyoto who did so much to develop the administrative apparatus that made the Kamakura shogunate operate efficiently for over a century despite frequent internal bloodbaths. He died the same year as Masako, continuing to give advice to the very end. The one on the right is that of Shimazu Tadahisa, an illegitimate son of Yoritomo. His mother got out of town fast when Masako discovered her affair with Yoritomo. The son eventually became governor of Satsuma Province in southernmost Kyushu, and his castle at Shimazu became the name of the clan that continued to rule the area all the way up to the Meiji Restoration, in which it played one of the leading roles.

There is a steep trail leading from these graves to Yoritomo's tomb, but it's easier to go back down the steps, go over one lane further to the right, and then climb the steep flight of steps to the top of the knoll.

For all his faults, there's no doubt that Minamoto Yoritomo was one of the greatest warrior-administrators in Japanese history. No one knows what his original tomb was like, although there is evidence in old chronicles that there was once a Minamoto family shrine here at which Hojo officials regularly paid obeisance. But what survives today is a spectacularly modest monument—an insignificant pile of stones. Overlooking the site where his palace and Choshoju-in, his family temple, once stood is a simple moss-covered grave about 1.6 meters high, surrounded by a stone wall and lanterns, some trees, a snack stand, and a portable potty off to the side. Oh, how the once great are fallen.

• MAP 170

Things seem to have been in even worse shape in days gone by—during the mid-Edo period Shimazu Shigehide put up the wall and present tombstone. This philanthropist's own grave is nearby. Yoritomo seems to have had a rather impressive mausoleum in the early days; in fact Miura forces held out there to the end during their rebellion and it may have been destroyed at that time.

Come back down the stairs, go to the corner, and turn right. At the next corner turn left and follow this wider road down past the school to the corner, where you'll see the wide gravel road leading to the right into the grounds of the Tsurugaoka Hachiman-gu complex.

This is the area where a demonstration of *yabusame* mounted archery is given every September 16 on the last day of the annual three-day shrine festival. Male and female riders charge down the road letting off three arrows in succession at wooden or clay targets. Look Ma, no hands! Shrine maidens signal hits with their fans. The coordination of the riders is a marvel to behold, but get there early to secure a good vantage point.

After about fifty meters turn right. On the right-hand side you will see the Kamakura National Treasure House (Kokuhokan), the repository of many of the finest art objects of the temples and shrines in the Kamakura area. Modeled on Shoso-in, the eighth-century treasure repository in Nara, the concrete structure was built in 1928 in response to the incredible devastation caused by the Great Kanto Earthquake. The museum is home to dozens of works that have been designated as Important Cultural Properties, as well as many other sculptures, paintings, and other objects from the Kamakura and Muromachi periods. The special exhibitions change frequently, so visitors have the opportunity to see something new each time.

On the opposite side of the complex is the three-story Kanagawa Prefectural Museum of Modern Art, which has regularly changing special exhibitions of avant-garde Japanese and foreign artists. In addition, an excellent permanent collection is to be found at the Annex to the museum on the left-hand side of Kamakura-kaido (the main road leading toward Kita Kamakura). These three museums alone can easily occupy a couple of hours for leisurely viewing.

• MAP 170

From the Treasure House, turn right and then curve around to the left through the grounds of the Shirahata-jinja (White Flag Shrine), erected in the memory of Yoritomo and Sanetomo. Much like the street gangs of today, the Minamoto and the Taira sported their own identifying colors when they went into battle. Yoritomo and his boys wore white, while the unfortunate Taira opted for blood red.

We are now in the center of the Tsurugaoka Hachiman-gu grounds. Check out the small red shrine, the Maruyama Inari-jinja, an Important Cultural Property. To the right of the center approach in front of the steps is the small shrine known as the Wakamiya, or Junior Shrine, dedicated to Emperor Nintoku and three deities.

Hachiman, the god of war, was the patron divinity of the Minamoto clan, so the Tsurugaoka Hachiman became the tutelary shrine of the military capital. Actually there was no clear distinction between Shinto and Buddhism at that time, so this area was a vast complex of ornate religious buildings. Most of what remained through centuries of civil strife, natural disaster, and neglect was destroyed in a fire in 1821. Specifically, the shrine is dedicated to the semi-mythical third-century emperor Ojin (who was aposteosized into Hachiman), his mother, Empress Jingu, who allegedly led a military expedition to Korea while he was still in the womb, and a goddess.

The Last Dance of Shizuka Gozen

The Wakamiya Shrine, which dates from 1624, is famous for something that happened centuries before—the last dance of Shizuka Gozen. After her capture, Yoshitsune's mistress Shizuka Gozen was brought with her mother to Kamakura and interrogated as to her lover's whereabouts. The nineteen-year-old beauty was famous in her own right as one of the country's best dancers, and Yoritomo, never one to be too concerned with the sensibilities of others, ordered her to dance for him and his retainers.

She danced all right, but turned her song-and-dance performance into a defiant ode of love for Yoshitsune. Yoritomo was incensed and inclined to eliminate the brave woman, but surprisingly the usually jealous Masako came to the rescue and saved Shizuka Gozen by reminding him that once a woman stood by his side while he was a helpless exile in Izu. Unfortunately, like most Kamakura-period stories, this one does not have a happy ending. Yoritomo found out that the young dancer was bearing Yoshitsune's child but agreed to compromise and promised to spare the baby if it was a girl.

It was a boy. He was duly executed on Yuigahama Beach and, as far as we know, Shizuka Gozen never danced again.

• MAP 170

Several martial articles, such as ancient swords, armor, masks, and robes are preserved in the central shrine buildings clustered around the bright vermilion colonnade on top. (You have to pay to see them.)

The famous gingko tree next to which the young shogun, Sanetomo, lost his head in 1219 is to the left of the steps leading to the main shrine. I leave it to you to judge whether this was the actual tree and whether it can indeed be one thousand years old. One thing is sure: this tree is humongous, some thirty meters high and seven meters in circumference. Nature decorates it with beautiful yellow leaves each November.

The Strange Case of Sanetomo

Why did the sensitive young shogun have to die?

The answer lies in the complicated power struggles that were going on within the shogunate. In 1203 the second shogun, Yoriie, had been removed from office at the instigation of the Hojo and replaced by his younger brother, Sanetomo, who was only twelve. The Hojo, Tokimasa in particular, obviously wanted a pliant puppet at their beck and call.

The commonly accepted story is that Sanetomo was assassinated by his nephew Kugyo, who was then serving as chief priest of the shrine, in revenge for the death of the boy's father, Yoriie. Kugyo supposedly secreted himself inside the trunk of the tree and jumped out when Sanetomo emerged after completing rituals inside. But there are enough loopholes and alternative explanations in this story to satisfy any Kennedy assassination conspiracy theorist.

As he grew older, Sanetomo began showing considerable independence from his handlers which directly threatened their control from the shadows. In fact, the night he was cut down, Sanetomo was returning from a ceremony celebrating his appointment as Minister of the Right, one of the highest ranks among the emperor's courtiers.

Hojo Yoshitoki was bearing the sword of state for the occasion. On the way there, according to legend, they encountered a ghostly dog, which it was later claimed was a messenger from the gods. Yoshitoki then turned home, claiming illness. Tradition has it that the statue of Inugami, one of the twelve guardian statues in Kakuon-ji's Yakushi-do, founded by Yoshitoki, went missing at this time. Just like a Hitchcock movie. What this all adds up to is the common assumption that one or more of the Hojo, maybe even Sanetomo's own grandfather, Tokimasa, had him done in.

There is an alternative theory that Miura Yoshimura convinced Kugyo to kill his uncle, so that in the resulting power vacuum he could eliminate the Hojo and rule through Kugyo. However, Kugyo was executed and the Miura were themselves slaughtered by the Hojo soon after.

It should be remembered, however, that, in addition to being one of the greatest poets in the land, Sanetomo was quite bizarre and certainly manic depressive. Versions of the story agree that, although warned to wear armor the night of his murder, he refused, and in fact wrote a poem before he set out that seemed to refer obliquely to his death.

Could this have been a suicide?

• MAP 170

By the entrance to Tsurugaoka Hachiman-gu is the Gempei (Minamoto and Taira) Pond, the two halves of which are divided by bridges. The former, to the left as you exit, has three islands (*san* can mean three or birth); the other has four (*shi* can mean four or death). The story has it that Hojo Masako had them dug during the final showdown between the two warrior groups. They accurately symbolize the fates of the two rival clans, ironic though it is that a Taira descendant should have thought of the design. In the end the irony was on the Hojo. The *Taiheiki* says that, following his capture of the city, Nitta Yoshisada washed his bloodstained sword in the pond after inspecting the heads of Hojo leaders.

Sit on the benches by the Minamoto pond. In summer pink and white lotuses provide a vision of nirvana on earth. Forget the sweltering heat and the mosquito-like buzz of transiency. Concentrate on the intricate designs of the surfaces of the giant green leaves, the droplets of water sparkling irridiscently cool. Time slips by. It's like the final scenes in Kubrick's *2001: A Space Odyssey*. You're leaving the earth's orbit forever.

Cross the distinctive red Drum Bridge, which in former times could only be used by the elite. It will serve as a good test for your thigh and calf muscles. It is said that if a woman can run over it in one go, she will in the future give birth safely to a boy.

Wakamiyaoji-dori is lined with many shops selling Kamakura-bori, swords, and antiques. Asabaya on the left is a good *unagi* (eel) restaurant, which flies in its wigglies from breeding grounds in Shizuoka. *Jinrikisha* still operate here, in case you want to play the old colonial. A ride for two from Tsurugaoka Hachiman-gu to the station costs about ¥2,000.

Kamakura Treasure House (Kamakura Kokuhokan 鎌倉国宝館) ☎ 0467-22-0753 ⏱ 9:00–16:00; closed Mon. ¥150; special exhibitions ¥300

Kanagawa Museum of Modern Art (Kanagawa Kenritsu Kindai Bijutsukan 神奈川県立近代美術館) ☎ 0467-22-5000 ⏱ 10:00–17:00; closed Mon. ¥250; extra for exhibitions

Kamenochaya 亀の茶屋 ☎ 0467-24-3014 ⏱ 11:30–17:00; no regular hols.

Yamaji 山路 ☎ 0467-25-2249 ⏱ 11:00–17:30; closed Weds.

Daitoken 大塔軒 ☎ 0467-22-5626 ⏱ 11:00–18:00; closed Weds.

Asabaya 浅羽屋 ☎ 0467-22-1222 ⏱ 11:00–20:00; closed Thurs.

• MAP 170

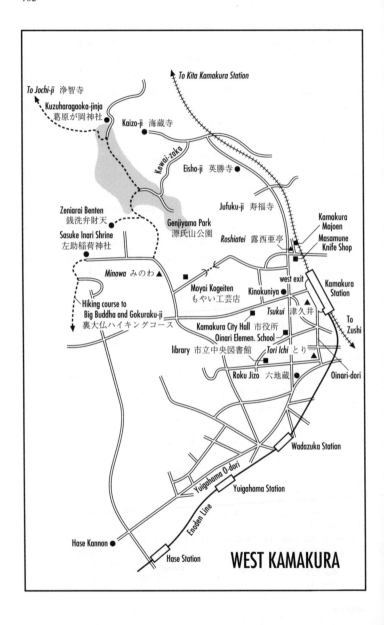

To Kita Kamakura Station

To Jochi-ji 浄智寺

Kuzuharagaoka-jinja
葛原が岡神社

Kaizo-ji 海蔵寺

Kewai-zaka

Eisho-ji 英勝寺

Jufuku-ji 寿福寺

Zeniarai Benten
銭洗弁財天

Sasuke Inari Shrine
左助稲荷神社

Genjiyama Park
源氏山公園

Roshiatei 露西亜亭

Kamakura
Majoen

Masamune
Knife Shop

Minowa みのわ

Moyai Kogeiten
もやい工芸店

Kinokuniya

west exit

Kamakura
Station

Hiking course to
Big Buddha and Gokuraku-ji
裏大仏ハイキングコース

Tsukui 津久井

To Zushi

Kamakura City Hall 市役所
Oinari Elemen. School

library 市立中央図書館

Tori Ichi とり

Roku Jizo 六地蔵

Oinari-dori

Wadazuka Station

Yuigahama O-dori

Yuigahama Station

Enoden Line

Hase Kannon

Hase Station

WEST KAMAKURA

3

Sacred Critters

○ Kamakura Station 鎌倉駅 (JR Yokosuka Line) west exit—Jufuku-ji 寿福寺 —Eisho-ji 英勝寺—Kewai-zaka 化粧坂—Genjiyama Park 源氏山公園—Zeniarai Benten 銭洗弁天—Sasuke Inari Shrine 佐助稲荷神社—Roku Jizo 六地蔵—Kamakura Station

This walk explores some of the old residential neighborhoods to the west of Kamakura Station. It can be taken at a leisurely pace along streets that bask in the serenity of neglect. The west exit is far less crowded than the main exit toward Wakamiyaoji-dori, although many commuters transfer to the Enoden Line here to the immediate left as you come out the west side. There is a little shopping arcade next to the Enoden station that is worth taking a look at.

As you walk straight ahead from the JR station, on the right you'll see a small park with a clock tower—a nice place to take a break. The path that leads around to the right goes under the tracks and emerges on the east side near the entrance to Komachi-dori, Kamakura's most important shopping street.

For this walk go straight ahead down the street that is lined on both sides with restaurants, clothes shops, and other businesses. At the corner you'll be facing the Kinokuniya supermarket and to the left of it across the road is Kamakura City Hall. Turn right and head down the street that is also crowded with restaurants, coffee shops, and pubs—Jimmy on the left past the convenience store is a friendly watering hole. Farther along there are shops selling fresh honey and royal jelly.

Turn right at the crossroads onto the road that crosses the rail

• MAP 182

tracks; on the right is Masamune Kogei Bijutsu Seisakujo, a knife and iron craft shop. In the back of the shop there is a forge. If the swords put you in the mood for cowboys and cossacks, try the reasonable Russian restaurant, Roshiatei, on the other side of the road. To the left up a small street you'll find Kamakura Majoen on the right, a craft shop that also holds regular exhibitions of ceramics, basketware, and other crafts.

Go back to the crossroads, turn right, and go straight. You'll pass two shrines, Tatsumi-jinja on the right and Yasaka-jinja on the left. Our first major stop is Jufuku-ji, on the left on the edge of Ogigayatsu ("Fan Valley"). Originally ranked third among the five *gozan* Zen establishments in Kamakura, it is the oldest Zen temple in Kamakura, and perhaps all of Japan, depending on how you define things. There was a temple here at least as early as 1180, and the spot was closely connected with the Minamoto family, since Yoritomo's father Yoshitomo had built a mansion here. In fact, Yoritomo had intended to establish the shogunate offices here, but he gave up the idea because of the lack of space.

Master Swordsmiths

The owner of the Masamune sword shop is the twenty-fourth-generation descendant of the master swordsmith Masamune. Little is known about the historical Masamune, not even his family name, although it's sometimes listed as Okazaki. Masamune apparently had no children and adopted a successor to carry on the family name and tradition. Even though Masamune is a shadowy figure, there are numerous tall tales and Buddhist instructive tales that concern him. Most of these stories about his folk wisdom originated in the Edo period. He seems to have lived and worked not far from Jufuku-ji farther up the road; a "sword shrine" can still be found nearby.

The present owner, Yamamura Tsunahiro, makes mostly knives and meat cleavers—there just isn't that much demand for head-chopping swords these days. The family prospered especially during the Edo period, when they were the official suppliers of swords for the Tokugawa family and other prominent people. The secrets of swordmaking were passed from generation to generation by word of mouth. Ironically, it was prewar militarists, who considered themselves the spiritual heirs of the samurai, who almost killed off the art. Yamamura's father was drafted and sent to Manchuria, where he was killed in action. Yamamura eventually managed to learn the secrets from an uncle. According to Yamamura it takes about a year and a half to make a sword.

Masamune Kogei Bijutsu Seisakujo
正宗工芸美術製作所 ☎ 0457-22-3962
🕐 8:00–18:00; closed Tues.

• MAP 182

A Zen temple was established here in 1200 at the urging of Masako by the famous priest Eisai, who studied in Song China for four years and brought knowledge of Rinzai-sect doctrines back to Japan with him. Eisai is also known as the great early promoter of the use of tea; his book on the subject is still considered a classic. Beautiful maple, plum, ginkgo, and ancient Chinese juniper trees surround the only existing structure, the reconstructed main hall, whose chief object of worship is a wooden *jizo* statue. Most of the temple went up in flames in 1395. The well-known statue of Eisai that was once here is now at the Kamakura Treasure House (see page 181). The main hall is off-limits, which is a shame because several treasures, including images said to have been traced by the hand of Masako herself, are alleged to be stored here.

Jufuku-ji is best known as the site of Masako's and Sanetomo's tombs, and signs point the way along a splendid path in the *ishi no tatami* (stone tatami) style to their location in the rear graveyard. Actually, there is quite a dispute as to whether the "Nun Shogun" really sleeps here or not. Another temple in Zaimokuza, the Anyo-in, makes the same claim.

The Other Iron Lady

One thing is for sure, when it comes to "iron ladies," Masako makes Margaret Thatcher look like a soggy block of tofu. Arguably she wielded more power than any woman in Japanese history. Daughter of Hojo Tokimasa, Masako married Minamoto Yoritomo during his exile in Izu and was mother of Yoriie, Sanetomo, and two girls. She was frequently referred to as the "Nun Shogun," alluding to the way she often had the final say in the political intrigues of the day despite the fact that she had taken Buddhist vows after Yoritomo's death.

Masako lived to the ripe old age of sixty-nine amidst a bunch of bloodthirsty cutthroats, but it is doubtful whether she left the earth with a peaceful heart. After all, her father was banished into exile by her own hand and her husband (whom she survived by twenty-six years) and her two sons preceded her to the grave due to violence—both her boys apparently dying at the orders of her own kin.

Despite seeing her immediate family decimated by her father and brothers, she never walked out on them. Her attitude too remains enigmatic. She seems to have been especially close to poor Sanetomo, whose brief life was filled with frustration and suffering. Like Masako, his grave is contained in a moss-covered *yagura* at Jufuku-ji, in his case known as the Karakusa Yagura because of the Chinese peony motif of the wall's paintings and carvings. Inside is the five-tiered stone marker indicating the grave of a samurai, and behind, a stone coffin. Very often you'll find flowers placed in front of it.

• MAP 182

Other prominent residents of the graveyard are novelist Osaragi Jiro, haiku poet Takahama Kyoshi, and Meiji-period diplomat Mutsu Munemitsu. Within the grounds of Jufuku-ji there is also a shrine dedicated to Kompira, protector of mariners and those who work at sea.

The huge pair of Nio Deva kings originally belonged to the Tsurugaoka Hachiman-gu Shrine. Prior to the Meiji Restoration, Buddhism and Shinto were so mixed together in what was known as Ryobu Shinto that is was often difficult to distinguish which was which. The Meiji government sought to purify Shinto so as to exploit it for ideological purposes. This in turn led to the outlawing of Buddhism and the destruction of many Buddhist temples and images. Tsurugaoka Hachiman-gu was no exception—anything deemed too Buddhist was got rid of. So that's how the Deva kings ended up here.

The hill behind Jufuku-ji is known to local residents as Ishikiriyama, "Stone-Cutting Mountain," and the large stone on top as Bofuseki, "Husband-Watching Crag." According to legend, when the prominent *bushi* Hatakeyama Shigetada was slain in a battle at Yuigahama, his young wife was watching the battle from this hill. Seeing her beloved cut down, she was petrified with grief—literally.

There is a path to the right of Jufuku-ji's graveyard that leads up through the woods skirting the cemeteries of Jufuku-ji and neighboring Eisho-ji, eventually reaching grassy Genjiyama Park, with its statue of a surly-looking, armor-clad Yoritomo. The steps are easily identifiable by its rabbit posts.

But we are going to take a different route. Next door, to the north of Jufuku-ji, is Eisho-ji, the only active nunnery in Kamakura. The feminine touch is apparent everywhere, especially in its plum and bamboo groves. The plum blossoms of early spring at Eisho-ji are divine and not to be missed. However, the picturesque copper roofs form a pleasant contrast to whatever is in bloom, be it lotuses, camellia, or *hagi* (Japanese bush clover). Most of the grounds are not open to casual visitors, so you must make an appointment ahead of time to look around if you are not satisfied with the little slice that is normally open. The nuns in the convent rightly value their privacy.

Established in 1634 by Lady Eisho, one of Ieyasu's mistresses,

• MAP 182

Eisho-ji belongs to the Jodo sect, so the chief object of worship is the benevolent *jizo*. The temple was built where a mansion of the highly cultured warlord Ota Dokan (1432–86) once stood. Dokan's main claim to fame was that he built the first Edo castle. Despite his well-documented humanism, he was murdered by erstwhile allies, not an uncommon fate in those violent days. Lady Eisho was Dokan's great-great-granddaughter. After Ieyasu's death, she became a nun under the name Eishoin. Her adopted son, Yorifusa, founded the Mito branch of the Tokugawa clan, which provided the last shogun, Yoshinobu. Her granddaughter became the first abbess of Eisho-ji. Eishoin's tomb is in the temple graveyard by the flamboyantly ornamented black and gold building.

Keep continuing along the road that parallels the Yokosuka Line; it curves left into the heart of the Ogigayatsu Valley. The ideal way to get the feel of off-the-beaten-path Kamakura is to wander from *yato* to *yato*. Many end in cul-de-sacs. The Ogigayatsu Valley, surrounded on three sides by mountains, is one of central Kamakura's more secluded areas. It is most beautiful in April when the *yuki yanagi*, a fine white-blossomed shrub, is in flower.

Soon you'll reach Kaizo-ji in a very quiet neighborhood. The origins of the temple remain unclear, but it appears to be a Shingon temple that became a Zen temple. A not uncommon phenomenon. Near the entrance is the Sokonuke bottomless well. A nun is supposed to have achieved enlightenment here when she suddenly saw the moon reflect back at her while gazing down into the well as she drew water.

The temple consists of the quaint thatched-roof living quarters for the priests and the main hall to the left, which has several interesting statues including the seated "Weeping Yakushi Nyorai." One night a priest heard the sound of crying emanating from the graveyard; the next day he dug up the head of a Buddha. The priest then carved a body and placed the head inside the womb. It is believed that this deity brings happiness to children. Ask for permision to visit the Juroku Ido Yagura, or "Sixteen-Well Cave" (十六井戸やぐら), in the hillside south of the temple. The priest will either lend you the key or unlock the door for you himself. Inside are sixteen holes filled with "sacred water," lined up in a four-by-four pattern. Some authorities

• MAP 182

have conjectured that these were burial holes, while others believe they were used in esoteric Shingon rites.

When you've finished your spelunking, head back the way you came till you reach the cutoff to the right. This is Kewai-zaka "Cosmetics Slope," one of Kamakura's seven entry passes, which was the focus of especially savage fighting during Nitta Yoshisada's 1333 invasion of the city. There are two theories on the origin of the unusual name. Most commonly it is said that the heads of dead enemies of the shogunate were washed and made up here before they were formally identified. A more mundane explanation is that this was the site of brothels catering to those coming in and out of the city.

You will pop out in front of Genjiyama Park. This area, which used to belong to Eisho-ji, is a riot of cherry blossoms in the spring and is among the best readily accessible spots in Kamakura for a picnic. It was here that Minamoto Yoshiie raised his white banner and roused the martial ardor of his Kanto warriors before heading off to Oshu in the eleventh century. Next to Genjiyama Park is Kuzuharagaoka Park, notable mainly for the Kuzuharagaoka jinja Shrine. This area was an execution ground during the Kamakura period.

Head back in the direction of Genjiyama Park, following the signs (and crowds) to Zeniarai Benten ("Coin-Washing Benten"). This is one of Kamakura's premier attractions, especially for confirmed materialists like myself. It is believed that if you wash your money in the springs here it will increase in value. Most sources say it will double in value, but others claim its value will multiply ten or a hundred times, and one source even claims it will increase in value ten thousand times over! The sky's the limit! This is better than Las Vegas.

Hard to believe, but the many visitors obviously do believe. These *saifu ga fukuramu*, or "wallet-fattening" waters are said to be especially efficacious on the day of the snake. That brings us to the story about the founding of the shrine.

One fine day in 1185 Yoritomo had a dream in which he was told that the government he was to found would prosper mightily if he had a shrine built at a certain spring in Kamakura. He did so forthwith, and as the day he had the dream was the day of the snake

• MAP 182

according to the Chinese calendar, and the month of the snake to boot, he had an image of Benten enshrined there. Benten, or Benzaiten, the goddess of beauty and good fortune, and also the patron of music and the arts, is frequently associated with snakes.

Also, it should be noted that the deity that appeared in Yoritomo's dream was Uka Fukajin, the deity of grain and fertility. Throughout most of the Orient snakes are a symbol of fecundity and regeneration. Within one of the caves of the shrine is a statue of Uka Fukajin, which sure enough has a cobra-shaped head. Etymologists believe that in ancient Japanese, *uka* might have meant either "hidden cave" or "rice." In any event, there are a number of minature *torii* in the cave, donated by those who feel the goddess has brought them good fortune.

Some time at a later date it was discovered that money that took a dip here gained amazing strength in the process. The trick, however, is to spend the money as soon as possible. For some unknown reason, the regent Hojo Tokiyori encouraged this belief. However, a local resident gave me an alternative version of the foundation of this belief. During the Kamakura period, professional gamblers and robbers, the forerunners of the *yakuza*, congregated in the city to make their fortunes, using this rocky lair and other parts of the Sasuke areas as hideouts. As we have seen, in those days the shogun's city was repeatedly attacked by deadly pestilences, especially smallpox. The thieves believed that if they washed their money before returning to their native districts they would not take the sickness back with them and so would be able to enjoy their ill-gotten gains.

Like those of neighboring Sasuke Shrine, the legends concerning Zeniarai Benten are tied to the stories of *kakurezato*, or mythical lands, that are found throughout Japan. The most famous of these is undoubtedly that of Urashima Taro, of which there are many local variations. In many cases the *kakurezato* is the Palace of the Dragon King at the bottom of the sea. And of course a dragon is really nothing but a big snake.

With all the signs pointing to Zeniarai Benten it is practically impossible to lose your way, unless you have some kind of subliminal pathological aversion to making money. The main entrance is a narrow

• MAP 182

tunnel that has been cut through the rocky hillside. You also pass through a spectacular tunnel of vermilion wooden *torii*, donations from those who found the proverbial pot at the end of the snake's tail. The shrine itself is in a little pocket valley, surrounded by hills.

It goes without saying that Zeniarai Benten Shrine is always crowded, especially on the highly auspicious Mi no Hi (the day of the Snake). This belief in serpentine good luck is also tied in with ancient Chinese zodiacal practices. You will see numerous offerings of eggs and saké, two things guaranteed to get you in the good graces of any snake you might encounter.

Even if you don't take the whole thing too seriously, or you don't need the money, it is fun to walk around Zeniarai Benten, inspecting the various caves, buildings, waterfalls, and pools. You can get a snack at one of the stalls or pick up a talisman to make sure that you survive any recessions unscathed.

Go out the back exit, which also has its share of *torii*. Follow the path going along parallel to the mountainside. In about five to ten minutes you will emerge on a narrow path that leads up to Sasuke Inari-jinja. This is another *kakurezato* wonderland at the end of a *torii* tunnel—this one extraordinarily long. And here too we have a legend connected with yet another dream on Yoritomo's part. (Yoritomo seems to have spent most of his time while in exile in Izu either plotting revenge or dreaming.)

As the story goes, a fox messenger from the god Inari appeared one day in the guise of a white-haired old man while Yoritomo was on his sickbed and told him that he would achieve glory in Kamakura. Shortly after making the area his headquarters, Yoritomo established the Sasuke Shrine. According to one interpretation, *sa* refers to Yoritomo (one of his titles was Sagami no Sukedono) and *suke* is derived from the verb *sukeru*, meaning "to help." All this would be fine, if it weren't for the irksome fact that records indicate the shrine predates Yoritomo's arrival in town.

Another local legend concerns a monk by the name of Kishu, who when walking near the shrine one day saw some children tormenting a baby fox. He made them release it. That evening Kishu had a dream in

• MAP 182

which the white fox of Sasuke Shrine appeared to him and thanked him for saving his fellow fox. As a reward the fox deity promised to give him an herb with which to cure disease. The monk then woke up and found seeds for medicinal plants near his pillow. He planted them and when they grew up used them to make medicine that cured many afflicted people.

After passing through the incredibly long *torii* tunnel, you reach the small hillside shrine dedicated to the fox god. The area is dark under the shadow of towering cryptomerias, and you feel that a fox could pop out at any time and tell you that you are destined to be the king of Roppongi. If you hike up behind the shrine, you will run into the Daibutsu Hiking Course. If you turn left and follow the trail for one kilometer, you'll come out just round the corner from the Great Buddha.

After you've finished looking around the fox shrine, go back down through the *torii* and head straight out to the large road, then turn right. Soon you'll encounter Minowa, a well-known Japanese-style tea shop that incorporates an old private home and garden. You can identify it by the beautiful red umbrellas outside. This is near the site of Renga-ji, another one of Kamakura's many "phantom temples." Keep going straight; off the big road to the left is Moyai Kogeiten, an old wooden house in an overgrown garden housing a ceramics shop featuring works from many different parts of the country. Lots of useful items and very reasonable prices, too.

Get back to the original road and keep going straight to the next major crossroads. If you were to turn left here and go through the tunnel, then just on the other side you would encounter a cute little shrine on your left, Suwa-jinja, and the city hall on your right and straight ahead Kamakura Station.

However, before returning to the station, have an amble through a typical Kamakura neighborhood that has no major tourist attractions. Just keep walking straight ahead for about fifteen minutes, enjoying the atmosphere, until you emerge on Yuigahama-dori. If you still have some time you might want to explore this interesting shopping street (see page 221) by turning right. Otherwise, turn left. You'll soon pass

• MAP 182

the Roku Jizo, six small *jizo* that mark the site of a Kamakura-period execution ground. They certainly seem to have had a lot of execution grounds, but it should be remembered that even during the "peaceful" Edo period over 100,000 people are estimated to have died at just one of Edo's execution grounds! The samurai could teach Clint Eastwood a thing or two about preserving law and order. This site, known as the Kekachi Hatake ("Demon Thirst Field"), was long left unused because of fears of vengeful spirits. It was near here, too, that Shimizu Seiji and his accomplice lay in wait to cut down Major Bird and Captain Baldwin in the Kamakura Incident.

At the corner where the Roku Jizo are, turn left on the fairly wide street and keep going straight. On your left you will see a school that is built on the site where the principal shogunate court used to stand during the days of the Hojo. If you turn in left on the street in front of the school, you'll find the Kamakura Central Library on your left.

The road parallel to the road in front of the school is Oinari-dori which has a couple of enticing restaurants. Opening its doors way back in 1943, Tori Ichi is a famous restaurant that serves chicken *chanko-nabe*, the Mulligan stew that makes sumo wrestlers crow. The stew is made with chickens that are specially reared by the restaurant itself. Tori Ichi also offers various boxed meals and *kaiseki ryori*. If you've had your fill of animals for the time being, drop in for some *okonomiyaki* (Japanese pancake) at Tsukui in a small alley off Oinari-dori near the Enoden station.

Kamakura Majoen 鎌倉まじょえん
☎ 0467-22-6877
🕘 10:00–18:00; open all year

Eisho-ji 英勝寺
☎ 0467-22-3534

Moyai Kogeiten もやい工芸店
☎ 0467-22-1822
🕘 10:00–16:30; closed Tues.

Jimmy ☎ 0467-24-1147
🕘 12:00–02:00; no regular hols.

Roshiatei 露西亜亭 ☎ 0467-24-4457
🕘 11:30–19:00; closed Fri.

Minowa みのわ ☎ 0467-22-0341
🕘 10:00–17:30; closed Mon.

Tori Ichi とり一 ☎ 0467-22-1818
🕘 12:00–14:00, 17:00–21:00; closed Tues.

Tsukui 津久井 ☎ 0467-22-1883
🕘 17:00–21:00; weekends except Aug. 12:00–21:00; closed Tues.

• MAP 182

4

The Nichiren Way

⟳ Kamakura Station 鎌倉駅 (JR Yokosuka Line)—Hongaku-ji 本覚寺—Myohon-ji 妙本寺—Joei-ji 常栄寺—Yagumo-jinja 八雲神社—Anyo-in 安養院—Myoho-ji 妙法寺—Ankokuron-ji 安国論寺—Chosho-ji 長勝寺—Mandarado Remains まんだら堂跡—Hossho-ji 法性寺—Ganden-ji 岩殿寺—Zushi Station 逗子駅 (JR Yokosuka Line)

Nearly all the stops on this route have some connection with the turbulent priest Nichiren, one of the most remarkable men in all Japanese history. You may not like Nichiren, but you certainly have to respect his fortitude. Nichiren was as strong and unbending as a sword made of well-tempered steel. And just as cutting.

Come out of the east exit of Kamakura Station, cross Wakamiyaoji-dori, and then go right. Turn left at the next corner past the post office. On the right, you'll see the side entrance to Hongaku-ji, founded in 1436 by Nisshutsu. For some time the chief priest here was Nichiren's greatest disciple, Nissho. (The names of Nichiren disciples inevitably start with Ni.) Nichiren himself lived in this area for a short time after returning in 1274 from his three-year exile on Sado Island. The temple is said to have a sacred relic in the shape of a bone of the great man. There are monuments to Nichiren and Nissho in the rear. People with eye diseases flock here to let the smoke of the incense waft over them in the hope that they'll be cured.

Masamune, the celebrated swordsmith (see page 184) is buried at Hongaku-ji. According to the tombstone he died on January 11, 1288. A swordmaking demonstration is held annually in the courtyard of the temple.

• MAP 196-97

Cross the Ebisudo-bashi Bridge and head straight up the broad road into the beautiful, deeply forested Hikigayatsu Valley. At the end of the three-hundred-meter approach, along which there are some interesting restaurants and coffee shops (try Umeten's *tempura* course in quiet, rustic surroundings), you'll find Myohon-ji, another Nichiren temple—in fact the largest in Kamakura. The gate is surrounded by stately cryptomeria. This is one of the most beautiful temples in Kamakura and the good news is that it's seldom crowded. Lofty trees, chirping wild songbirds, riotous cicada in summer, and wide-open spaces—what more could you ask for?

The Hikigayatsu Valley derives its name from the fact that Yorito-mo's wet nurse hailed from the Hiki district and she built a home in this area. Yoritomo and Masako visited her frequently, and so close were they that the daughter of her adopted son became the mistress of Yoritomo's oldest son, the second shogun Yoriie. This lady, who was known as Wakasa no Tsubone, gave birth to a son, who was named Ichiman (Chakuryu). He became the indirect cause of one of the first of many tragedies in the early Kamakura period when his family was wiped out by the Hojo.

The Ichiman Tragedy

In 1203, Ichiman's grandfather sought to have Ichiman named as Yoriie's successor, no doubt with the support of the shogun. This constituted a direct challenge to the Hojo, who were already moving to acquire dictatorial powers. To complicate matters, Yoriie himself was planning to attack Hojo Tokimasa, Masako's father. She found out, however, and informed Tokimasa.

Retaliation by the Hojo was swift and thorough. Nearly every member of Ichiman's clan, the Hiki, was hunted down and exterminated. The three-year-old Ichiman died in a massacre at the family mansion. The building was burned to the ground and it was only the next day that a sleeve of the child's kimono was discovered in the ruins. It was buried together with what were assumed to be Ichiman's bones here in the Hikigayatsu Valley.

The killing was not over yet, however. Yoriie gave orders for Tokimasa and the Hojo to be crushed, but shogunate soldiers refused to follow his commands. Instead, Tokimasa had Yoriie arrested and exiled to Shuzenji hot springs on the Izu Peninsula, where he was murdered in his bath. Whether by intent or not, Masako had caused the death of her own son and grandson! Anyway you look at it, Yoritomo's family was not the happiest.

Ichiman's tomb, the Sodezuka ("Sleeve Tomb"), is located next to the walkway leading to the main hall. It is surrounded by stone lanterns. The tombs of other clan members are to the right of the main hall.

• MAP 196-97

A surviving member of Ichiman's family, Dengaku Saburo, built Myohon-ji so that prayers might be made for the repose of the tortured souls of his dead relatives. He was a devout follower of Nichiren and after becoming a priest took the name Nichigaku. Nichiren himself supposedly stayed here for a time in 1274. Slightly to the left and behind the tombs is a beautiful moss-covered staircase that adds to the serenity of the scene. Myohon-ji has several treasures stored out of public view in the Reihoden to the left of the main hall.

Next to the small, deep lake is Jakushi Myojin Shrine, which is dedicated to Wada no Tsubone. Her vengeful spirit is said to have been transformed into a dragon that jealously protects the temple from evil.

Also at Myohon-ji you'll find the grave of Ozu Yasujiro, one of the greatest directors in the history of world cinema. More than any other Japanese director, he was able to catch the essential feeling of the Japanese soul. On his tombstone you will find only one Chinese character, *mu* 無, epitomizing the Buddhist and Taoist concept of "nothingness." No epitaph could be more appropriate.

From the graveyard, come down the driveway past the octagonal kindergarten and turn left at the first small street. You'll soon reach Joei-ji, a small temple on the left-hand side of the road. It is commonly referred to as the Botamochi-dera Temple. This name takes a bit of explaining.

It has to do with Nichiren's near execution in 1271. What was to be his last march from Kamakura has many elements that recall the last passion of Christ and other stories related to that momentous event.

Botamochi is a kind of rice-cake dumpling covered with sweet paste. When Nichiren was being led away to the killing grounds at Tatsu no Kuchi (see page 238), an old nun rushed out and offered him some of these dumplings as a last supper. Her tomb is on the grounds to the left of the main hall. *Botamochi* are offered every September 12, the day that Nichiren was supposed to have been executed.

Continue walking ahead on the same street and soon you'll come to Yagumo-jinja, the tutelary shrine of this commercial district. It is a small, simple edifice that enshrines gods that were transferred here from the Gion-sha Shrine in Kyoto more than nine hundred years ago. Although the Yagumo-jinja is not the oldest Shinto shrine in Kamakura,

• MAP 196-97

it is the oldest exorcism shrine. So if you want to get the devil out of you, head over here. Actually, there seem to be quite a few exorcism shrines and temples in the Omachi and Zaimokuza neighborhoods. Perhaps it's because of the plethora of ghosts who reside in Kamakura. The shrine festival is held sometime between July 7 and 14 each year. The four *mikoshi* "god palanquins" date from the Edo period and are quite interesting in the details of their style. The Gion Hiking Course leading to Harakiri Yagura near Tsurugaoka Hachiman-gu begins behind the shrine.

The road comes out at Route 134. Turn right and you'll find Momozono, a noodle restaurant with a difference—most ingredients are organically grown. The house specialty is Oyster Wheat Noodles (*kakiudon*), available from October to February. Turn left and on the left you'll see a tiny old Jishu temple, the Betsugan-ji, where you can find the tomb of Ashikaga Mochiuji, the well-known Kamakura Kubo, or top official of the Kanto region. In its heyday this temple was greatly favored first by Hojo Tokimune and later by the Ashikaga clan.

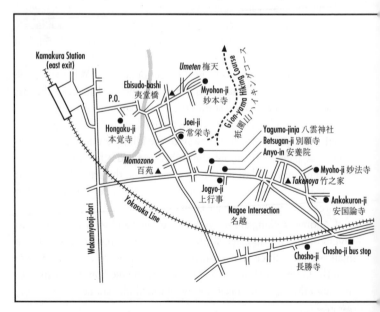

Next door is the Anyo-in, a Jodo temple that was founded by Masako in 1225 to pray for the soul of Yoritomo. It was formerly located in the Sasame Valley near the Great Buddha. The Anyo-in's claims to fame include Masako's grave, exquisite rhododendron, a statue of Amida, and a thousand-armed Kannon that stands 1.58 meters high. According to what is no doubt a tall tale, Masako prayed to this Kannon to win Yoritomo's affection. Her wish came true and thereafter she retained an unshakable faith in the image. Also within the grounds of Anyo-in is a "syphilis-curing" shrine. It is believed that if the afflicted area is rubbed with one of the round stones found in front of the shrine, you will get well again. The pox-bashing deity enshrined here doubles as a goddess of children.

Across the street is Jogyo-ji, which can be easily spotted by the red streamer flying above. It, too, performs exorcisms and ceremonies for aborted fetuses. At the Nagoe intersection, turn to the left and go straight. On the left you'll find Takenoya, a rustic place—try *sanshoku soba*, a sampler of three kinds of soba served on hearty wooden trays.

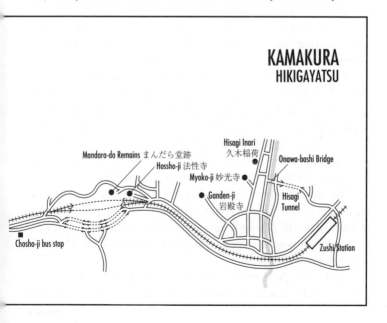

KAMAKURA
HIKIGAYATSU

Mandara-do Remains まんだら堂跡
Hossho-ji 法性寺
Hisagi Inari 久木稲荷
Onawa-bashi Bridge
Myoko-ji 妙光寺
Ganden-ji 岩殿寺
Hisagi Tunnel
Chosho-ji bus stop
Zushi Station

Keep going till you come to the T-junction; turn right, and you'll soon see the entrance to Myoho-ji on the left. The nickname of this temple is Koke-dera, or "Moss Temple," because of its impressive moss-covered stone steps. Leading up from the gate, a donation in the seventeenth century from Ieyasu, to the Hokke-do "Hall of Scriptures," the steps have been renowned for centuries and are especially handsome in May when surrounded by white fringed-irises.

Nichiren had a hut here where he lived for a while after his return from exile in Izu. He liked to meditate in a retreat up at the top of the hill when he wasn't preaching and antagonizing the local residents. The feisty proselytizer was burned out of here on at least one occasion, escaping over a mountain path. Nichiren seemed to have a genius for knowing when it was time to hightail it out of harm's way.

In 1357 a disciple named Nichiei rebuilt the temple, which had been torched yet again, and he became chief priest for a time. This Nichiei was none other than the illegitimate son of Prince Morinaga. He also built a memorial to his murdered father, offering incense there every day. During the Edo period Myoho-ji benefited from the patronage of the Tokugawa shoguns as well as several prominent *daimyo*, including Lord Hosokawa, ancestor of former Prime Minister Hosokawa Morihiro, who greatly renovated it.

The main hall is lavishly ornamented with paintings and flashy Nichiren emblems, and the small piece of bone preserved here is said to be one of Nichiren's own. Among the other temple treasures are statues of Prince Morinaga and his son. There are also two deep caves, one containing a granite representation of Nichiren. The Hokke-do up top has gilt altars and its own statue of Nichiren. The old, green copper bell is an additional attraction of this very beautiful temple.

Although the temple is open from 9:00 to 14:00 in principle, the actual entry times vary and visiting rules are strict. Reportedly owing to a shortage of staff, Myoho-ji has recently only been allowing "pilgrims" (the temple frowns on mere tourists) to enter on weekends. Absolutely no photography is allowed.

Go back to the main road; turn left and on the left at the intersection is one of the most important Nichiren temples, Ankokuron-ji. The

• MAP 196-97

temple is named after *Rissho Ankokuron* (Establish the righteous law and save the country), the treatise Nichiren presented to the shogunate in an attempt to suppress his enemies and force them to adopt his beliefs. Nichiren expressed his view on the matter concisely and to the point: "Unless false religions are banned, the nation will be ruined." A copy of the *Rissho Ankokuron* made by Nissho is preserved here. Nichiren wrote the polemical tract in a cave here that he lived in from 1257 to 1260. The cave is to the right upon entering the gate and there is a statue of him there. The first hermitage he had when he first came to Kamakura in 1253 was also in this scenic area, known as Matsubagayatsu (Valley of Pine Needles). The temple itself was founded in 1274.

Literature about Nichiren frequently portrays him as either a saint or a thug. He was both. Like Martin Luther, the priest from Boso instinctively understood the intimate connection between religion and political power. He indoctrinated his followers in the technique of *shakabuku* (literally "break and subdue"), in which they sought to argue their opponents into the dust. During the early Kamakura period there were many street-corner preachers, and large crowds would gather to hear them talk. Nichiren fanatics would infiltrate the crowds to disturb the proceedings by peppering the speakers with embarassing questions or shouting them down. This was especially true for meetings of believers of the *nembutsu* sects. Both Nichiren and the Amida devotees were competing for the same souls: the rootless, indigent migrants who had poured into the raw new city—people who felt totally at a loss spiritually. Sometimes the conflict between the two groups descended into street fighting like that which occurred between various Red Guard factions during the Cultural Revolution in China.

The savageness of Nichiren's eloquent street-corner harangues and brilliant writings finally became too much for his enemies, and one night in May 1260 they descended on Matsubagayatsu in a force of several hundred, apparently including some samurai, destroying everything in their path. Nichiren escaped over the mountain just in the nick of time, by tradition led by the sleeve over the narrow paths by a white monkey. Several of his followers were less lucky. Naturally, there is a statue of

• MAP 196-97

the magic monkey guiding the indomitable Nichiren to safety.

Ankokuron-ji is famous for its flora, some of which, such as the wild cherry, are said to have been transplanted personally by Nichiren from the Boso Peninsula. The path leading up along the ridge is lined with pines and offers a good view of the more plebeian parts of Kamakura.

Come out of Ankokuron-ji, turn left, and then go straight to the main road; then turn left again and go under the tracks of the Yoko-suka Line. On the opposite side of Route 134 you'll see the entrance to Chosho-ji Temple. It would be hard to miss considering the four-meter-high, four-ton gargantuan bronze statue of Nichiren that stands in the courtyard. This work is by the famous Meiji-period sculptor Takamura Koun, who completed it in 1923. Although I have my doubts about its aesthetic value, Nichiren adherents obviously like it since two copies have been produced elsewhere in the country. We know that Nichiren underwent great spiritual turmoil before finding salvation in the Lotus Sutra, but you would never know that from all the representations of the man—he always seems to be portrayed as dauntless, advancing steadily without a trace of doubt on his face. The statue now stands in front of the Teishaku-do, a new building dedicated to the white monkey deity who helped him on more than one occasion. Around it are clustered four fierce-looking, demon-smashing celestial kings.

Chosho-ji is also well known for its lively festivals, the Ice-Water Festival in particular. Talking of water, notice the Nichiren Koimizu Well, where Nichiren is said to have performed several miracles.

The Chosho-ji Ice-Water Festival

The most famous festival at Chosho-ji is the *Mizu-gori* ice-water ceremony held annually on February 12. Nichiren priests who have just completed a hundred days of extremely rigorous ascetic training on holy Mt. Minobu in Yamanashi Prefecture that includes little eating, little sleeping, but much prayer, come here to show the public that they have learned how to take it. This is the grand climax to their self-imposed ordeal. Clad only in loincloths, these bearded, heavily callused, exhausted-looking men repeat a ritual they have performed seven times a day for the last hundred days—they pour seven buckets of ice-cold water over their bodies.

Chosho-ji 長勝寺 ☎ 0467-25-4300

• MAP 196-97

There is a superb view of Sagami Bay from the graveyard up above, and you can also find a few graves of foreigners here. Come out of Chosho-ji, and head straight along the highway in the direction of the smokestack (it belongs to a crematory) and tunnel in the distance. Get on the left side of the road. This is the area of Nagoe Pass, the principal entry from the Miura Peninsula during the Kamakura period.

On the hills up above is the picturesque site where the Mandarado Temple was supposedly located. Go up the narrow path between houses to the site, which is now filled with flowers—cosmos, irises, camellias, and just about anything else you could name. Then there are the hydrangea that are so famous that the Emperor and Empress reportedly took a secret peek at them in 1992. Look around a bit and you'll also find *yagura*, 104 by one count, and five-tiered samurai tombs. No one seems to know much about the history of the place, but that is to your advantage if you enjoy nature minus the crowds.

Our next stop, Hossho-ji, can be reached either by hiking eight hundred meters along the Sarabatakeyama Okirigishi slope, or by going back down to the highway and through the tunnel. Sarubatake means "Garden of the Monkey" and Hossho-ji rejoices in the sobriquet "Nichiren Monkey Temple." It was established by a Nichiren disciple in 1320 to mark the spot where the heavenly monkey with long white fur brought the master when he was burned out of his hermitage in 1260. His pal later brought Nichiren food until he could beat a strategic retreat. Two white monkeys are carved into the main gate down below.

At first sight, you might well mistake the main hall at Hossho-ji for a traditional farmhouse. At the entrance to the cave where Nichiren lay low is a carving of him and his little friend. An alternative version of the story has three monkeys doing the honors, and here you can also see representations of a simian trio like the famous carving at Nikko.

We are now way off the main tourist route and into the city of Zushi. The next temple, Ganden-ji, is one of the true gems of the Kamakura area and should not be missed. When you come out of Hossho-ji, keep going straight on the same side of the highway for about seven hundred meters until you reach a car agency. Turn left at the next corner and head towards the hills. You'll eventually see signs

• MAP 196-97

pointing the way to the long temple approach road. Hidden away in the hills, Ganden-ji is a stunning mountainside temple belonging to the Soto Zen sect, founded, according to some ancient accounts, way back in the eighth century. It was frequently visited by the first three shoguns and the Hojo family, and the sensitive Sanetomo seems to have been particularly fond of this temple.

During the Meiji period Izumi Kyoka, famous for his frequently macabre, wildly baroque stories, fled here in 1903 with a Tokyo geisha he was having an affair with. He ended up living and writing in Zushi for three years. A memorial tablet can be found inside the front gate to the left. Within the temple precincts there is also the "Kyoka Pond."

The view of the coast from the top of the stone staircase is sublime—the long hike up is well worth the effort. From here the Junreimichi, the Pilgrims' Road used for many centuries, leads across the hills to the Kanazawa-kaido near Sugimoto-dera. According to a local legend, one of the caves here, the Hebi (Snake) Yagura, leads directly to Enoshima Benten several kilometers away. Better pack a picnic.

Go back down the approach road, turn left at the cutoff where the sign for the temple is and follow the road through a residential neighborhood until it emerges on a main road. Turn left here and go straight. On the left you'll see Myoko-ji, a Nichiren temple that dates from the Muromachi period. Enshrined here is a statue of Nichiren that according to tradition was dug out from the ground nearby.

Cross the pedestrian bridge and follow the road to the left of Hisagi Elementary School. Cross the bridge and go through Hisagi Tunnel. Follow the road till it comes out of the mountains onto a wide road. Turn right and not far ahead on the left is the rear entrance to Zushi Station. There is also a nearby crossing into the main part of Zushi.

Mandarado まんだら堂跡
🕐 9:30–15:30; in winter 9:30–15:00; closed when rainy

Umeten 梅天 ☎ 0467-22-5335
🕐 11:30–15:30, 16:30–19:00; weekends 11:30–19:00; closed Tues.
Momozono 百苑 ☎ 0467-22-1922
🕐 11:30–19:30; closed Fri.
Takenoya 竹之家 ☎ 0467-25-3872
🕐 11:00–18:00; closed Mon.

• MAP 196-97

5

The Path to Enlightenment

⊙ Kita-Kamakura Station 北鎌倉駅 (JR Yokosuka Line)—Engaku-ji 円覚寺—Tokei-ji 東慶寺—Jochi-ji 浄智寺—Meigetsu-in 明月院—Kencho-ji 建長寺—Hanzobo 半僧坊—Kamegayatsu-zaka 亀が谷坂—Komachi-dori 小町通—Kamakura Station

This walk might lead one to enlightenment, since it takes in the two largest Zen temples in Kamakura and several of the smaller ones, all of which are clustered in Kita Kamakura. It also takes in a road less traveled and the city's most important shopping street.

Starting at JR Kita Kamakura Station, a four-minute ride from Kamakura Station, our first stop is Engaku-ji, but you don't have to go anywhere to get there. You're already there. No, this is not some kind of Zen riddle. You see, when the government built the railroad, they ran it right through the front part of the temple, in effect snipping off a little part of it, including Byakurochi ("White Heron Pond") and some giant trees that are slowly dying from pollution. I guess that's the price you pay for seeking enlightenment on the seat of your pants. It is admittedly a bit odd, though, to look at the stone memorial marking the formal entrance and then to walk across railroad ties to get to the main gate. But what a glory awaits you beyond.

Engaku-ji, the largest Zen establishment in Kamakura, was founded in 1282 by regent Tokimune for the specific purpose of praying for the souls of those who died in the two Mongol invasions. The first abbot of this Rinzai Zen center was the Zen master Wu-Hsueh Tsu-yuan (1226–86), known in Japanese as Mugaku Sogen. There are many stories about this saintly fellow, who was an exile from Song China. Before

• MAP 204

204

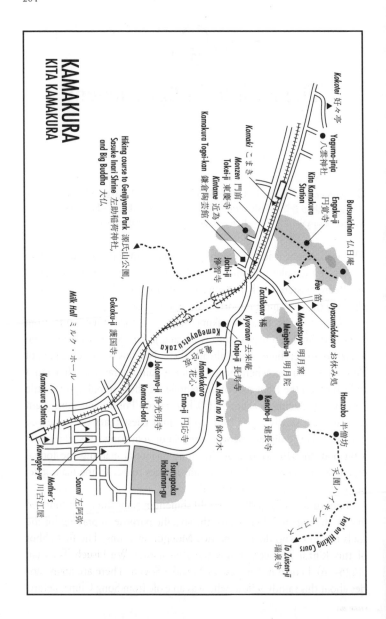

KAMAKURA
KITA KAMAKURA

Kokotei 好々亭

Yagumo-jinja 八雲神社

Komaki こまき

Monzen 門前
Tokei-ji 東慶寺
Kintame 近為
Kamakura Togei-kan 鎌倉陶芸館

Kita Kamakura Station

Engaku-ji 円覚寺

Butsunichian 仏日庵

Jochi-ji 浄智寺

Hiking course to Genjiyama Park,
Sosuke Inari Shrine 左即稲荷神社,
and Big Buddha 大仏

Gokoku-ji 護国寺

Milk Hall ミルク・ホール

Kamakura Station

Kawagoe-ya 川古江屋

Mother's

Saami 左阿弥

Komachi-dori

Jokomyo-ji 浄光明寺

Tachibana 橋

Kyoraian 去来庵

Choju-ji 長寿寺

Meigetsuin 明月院

Meigetsuyo 明月菜

Oyasumidokoro お休み処

Hanamokoro

Enno-ji 円応寺

Hachi no Ki 鉢の木

Kencho-ji 建長寺

Hanzobo 半僧坊

Tsurugaoka
Hachiman-gu

Tenen Hiking Course 天園ハイキングコース

To Zuisen-ji 瑞泉寺

his first visit to Engaku-ji, white herons supposedly heralded his arrival and landed on Byakurochi. Furthermore, once when he was preaching, a herd of white deer gathered and listened entranced to his sermon. At the rear you'll find the White Deer Cave, the spot from which they emerged, and the Hill of Sacred Deer beyond. Mugaku originally intended to return to China, but changed his mind after the Mongol invasion.

You become a bit jaundiced about all the professional murderers in Kamakura history who founded temples for the repose of the souls of their victims. But Tokimune was a truly religious man in addition to being perhaps the most talented of the Hojo regents. He entered the priesthood when he was thirty-four and often went out to the work sites to lend a hand.

Arrive in Kita Kamakura in autumn, and you'll be greeted by the scent of ancient cryptomeria wood and burning leaves. In early summer there's the sweet fragrance of chestnut flowers. A number of beautiful meditation halls lie interspersed with bamboo groves and tranquil Japanese gardens in Engaku-ji's long, gently rising valley, bracketed by green hills punctuated with *yagura* cave mausoleums.

Engaku-ji and Kencho-ji down the road may be compared to the great monasteries of Europe when it comes to the irreplaceable documents and artistic treasures they contain. If at all possible, I recommend a visit during the first week of November when many buildings that are usually out of bounds are opened for *mushi-boshi* "expel the insects" autumn cleaning. The scrolls, calligraphic works, statues, and Buddhist paraphernalia you can see laid out on the *tatami* mats or hung from the walls are simply breathtaking. Half the fun is to be had in bonze-watching. The variety of faces among the Zen priests and acolytes who do guard duty over the temple masterpieces is fascinating. There's also a major airing in August.

Go up the flight of steps. The famous two-story main gate, which dates back to about 1780, does not contain a single nail. This was the edifice referred to in Natsume Soseki's novel *Mon* (The gate), a tale of a man's unsuccessful attempt to achieve spiritual peace through Zen meditation that mirrors Soseki's own experience. He underwent *zazen* training

• MAP 204

at Kigen-in (帰源院) to the right of the gate going towards the belfry, as did Shimazaki Toson, the novelist well known for his Naturalistic style. Like the hero in *Mon*, Natsume Soseki failed to find the answers he sought, and in fact he later wrote satirical poems about the experience.

Steps lead from the right of the gate to the 2.59-meter-high bell, a National Treasure, that was cast in 1301. This bell is now rung only on special occasions such as New Year's Eve. Pity, since the sound is so sweet that on one occasion it is said to have brought a prematurely dead man back from the grave.

If you go straight ahead from the main gate down the tree-lined path, you'll soon reach another flight of steps in front of the Sanmon (山門). Beautiful juniper trees flank the path as it continues on towards a new building, the Butsuden (仏殿 Buddha sanctum). There is a very realistic image of Enma enshrined in the Main Hall. It was carved by Unkei, whose works are so realistic that at times they make your flesh crawl. To the left of the Butsuden you'll pass several small hermitages. Engaku-ji is a very active spiritual training center and many of its buildings are off-limits.

Zazen in Kamakura

Meditation and silence, and strict discipline of mind and body are believed to purify the soul through detachment, reveal the ultimate Buddha nature beyond life and death, and increase chances for attaining Nirvana. There are several opportunities to practice *zazen* in Kamakura. Anyone can join the *zazen* sessions at Engaku-ji and Kencho-ji. Many of them are advanced, so it may be difficult for novices on the road to enlightenment to get into the swing of non-action. Hokoku-ji, the "bamboo temple," and some other temples do have sessions especially designed for beginners, however. The free *zazen* sessions take place on Sunday mornings at Hokoku-ji from 8:00 A.M.

Every Saturday and Sunday from 17:00 to 18:00 there is a regular session of the Kencho-ji Zazenkai, a group which meets to practise *zazen*. Also, every second Saturday and Sunday there is a free overnight session. Engaku-ji has similar free *zazen* sessions at the weekend (April–October 5:30–6:30; November–March 6:00–7:00). In addition, every second and fourth Sunday there are special sermons and in the latter half of July four-day Zen retreats.

Even if you do not achieve satori, *zazen* can be inspiring, since it gets the right kind of brain waves and blood flow going.

Hokoku-ji 報国寺 ☎ 0467-22-0762
Kencho-ji Zazenkai 健長寺座禅会
☎ 0467-22-0981
Engaku-ji Zazenkai 円覚寺座禅会
☎ 0467-22-0478

• MAP 204

Continuing on, you'll pass the Karamon (唐門 China Gate) and a large building that contains the temple library and the abbot's quarters to your right. In front of you will now be the turtle-infested Myokochi (妙香池 Lake of Sacred Fragrance). The path skirts the pond to the Butsunichian (仏日庵) that contains statues of Tokimune and two other Hojo regents. You can also enjoy thick *matcha* tea at the Butsunichian, which was the setting for much of the action in Kawabata Yasunari's novel *Senbazuru* (One thousand cranes).

To the left of Butsunichian is the Shariden (舎利殿 Hall of the Holy Relics), a striking thatched-roof building and the oldest example in Japan of a particular style of Zen-influenced Chinese architecture. The original building was destroyed by fire in 1558, but this is said to be an exact replica. The Shariden claims to possess a tooth of Gautama that was brought from China at Sanetomo's insistence. Many believe that the miraculous powers of the tooth were at least partly possible for the destruction of the Mongol invasion armies. There is also a famous statue of Mugaku here. The only chance to peek inside, however, is during the first three days of the year.

The path to the right of Butsunichian leads further into the valley to Obai-in (黄梅院 Yellow Plum Blossom Temple), that is especially beautiful in March when the white magnolia are in bloom. In the cul-de-sac, there is a small temple with an unusual wooden Kannon that resembles a Polynesian *tiki*.

A small shrine and a temple near Engaku-ji are also worth investigating. Yagumo-jinja to the left of the entrance to Engaku-ji was built in the late 1400s. It enshrines the guardian god for the area, who was brought here from the Yasaka Shrine in Kyoto. He is a manifestation of Susanoo Omikami, the god of storms. The shrine is set among beautiful cherry trees. There is a summer festival here on July 15 in which children carry the oldest portable shrine of its kind in Kamakura.

Keep going on in the direction of Ofuna and after about 100 meters, turn right at the post office; go another 100 meters and you 'll find Kosho-ji, a Jishu temple that is covered with hydrangea in summer and bush clover in fall. The design of the red-lacquered gate is unique. From here head back towards Kita Kamakura Station, unless you

• MAP 204

want to linger at Kokotei, a *kaiseki ryori* joint in a prewar villa.

From Kita Kamakura Station, turn left; about ten minutes down the Kamakura-kaido on the right is Tokei-ji, Kamakura's famous "divorce temple," referred to in Japanese as Enkiri-dera or Kakekomi-dera.

Tokei-ji used to be a nunnery until the Meiji era, but is now a Rinzai temple with only men in residence. The temple has an illustrious history. By tradition, it was first established by Mino no Tsubone. For some reason, it folded, but was re-established in 1285 by Kakusan Shido, Tokimune's widow. The tranquil graveyard contains the mortal remains of many famous people, including Suzuki Daisetsu, the great popularizer of Zen, who lived in Kita Kamakura for decades until his death at ninety-six in 1966, authors Takami Jun and Kobayashi Hideo, Tenshu, a grand-daughter of Hideyoshi, who survived the destruction of the Toyotomi clan by Tokugawa Ieyasu at Osaka Castle, and Tokei-ji's twentieth abbess, Princess Yodo, daughter of Emperor Go Daigo.

The Divorce Temple

By imperial order, Tokei-ji became one of a few nunneries in the country where women fleeing mistreatment from their husbands could find sanctuary. If a woman reached its premises, or, according to some accounts, even managed to toss a shoe over the wall, she could not be extricated or harmed. And if a woman stayed at the convent for three years (later two years), she became entitled to a divorce. This was a pretty radical system for the times, especially considering that women had few legal rights and a common saying was, "The womb is borrowed."

Incidentally, this was not just a passive set-up. During the Edo period, for example, there was a dormitory for women waiting for their marriage walking-papers near the front gate and a special office where an official sought to reconcile couples or otherwise work out a mutually acceptable solution to their marital problems.

Tokei-ji developed a reputation of putting the "happiness of the woman" first. It should be remembered that if a husband agreed to the divorce then that was that; it was only women who were refused a divorce who had to spend the twenty-four to thirty-eight months here. The woman also had to pay for all the expenses.

Well, there are always two sides to a story. According to a 1864 account, Tokei-ji had a reputation as a haven for wanton women. It noted that there were forty-seven residents there at the time and that their ability to pay determined the way that they were treated. The record lamented the fact that if the ladies had money they could be spared any pain for their cuckoldry. An earlier 1717 journal had noted that women who simply disliked their spouses or were afraid of having lewd conduct discovered flocked here.

You be the judge.

• MAP 204

Make sure to visit the Matsugaoka Treasure House (Matsugaoka Hozo 松が岡宝蔵). Among items displayed here are scrolls and sutras written in Tibetan and Sanskrit. The main hall, as well as the Sei Kannon and Suigetsu Kannon statues are Important Cultural Properties.

The grounds of Tokei-ji are especially beautiful when the plum blossoms appear in February and March or when the irises are out in summer.

Nearby is the Kamakura Togei-kan ceramic shop and gallery. The building is well over one hundred years old. It was relocated here from the mountainous Oku Hida region. The cool, dark wood of the pillars is inviting on a hot summer day. On the first floor, where there's an *irori* hearth, works by young potters are exhibited. On the second floor is a coffee shop where pottery of the owner is displayed. In front of the station, and throughout the Kita Kamakura district for that matter, you will find tea houses offering you a chance to imbibe a little atmosphere along with your tea and traditional accompanying sweets. Oyasumi-dokoro near Engaku-ji and Komaki by Kita Kamakura Station are two such teahouses. Check out Kintame, a restaurant using tsukemono, Japanese pickles, to create a new style cuisine. Star attraction here is Ochazuke Bubuzuke, a mixture of Japanese tea and rice.

A little farther on from Tokei-ji is Jochi-ji, founded in 1283 by regent Hojo Morotoki, Tokimune's nephew, but almost totally destroyed during the 1923 earthquake. Although it may not be one of the more splendiferous temples in Kamakura, I love Jochi-ji for its bell tower, a tasty combination of white contrasted against brown—an exotic variation on a Chinese theme. In the Dongeden (曇華殿) you'll find statues of the past, present, and future Buddhas—Amida Nyorai, Shaka Nyorai, and Miroku Nyorai. Notice the huge umbrella pine in front of the hall. The seated wooden *jizo* in the rundown Jizo-do is said to have been sculpted by Unkei. There are tombs and and reliefs in the *yagura*; note, too, the humorous look on the statue of Hotei in the garden.

Like so many Kita Kamakura temples, Jochi-ji comes alive in spring when the thatched library is surrounded by all kinds of different flowers. The sasanqua of late November are also very easy on the eyes. The path that starts on the side of the temple leads to the Kuzuharagaoka Shrine, eventually linking to the hiking course to the Big Buddha.

• MAP 204

One thing that has always puzzled me is how Kamakura could support such a large population in the days of the shoguns considering that it lacks much good water, in spite of being so close to the ocean and on land that was originally underwater. In fact so precious was water that the Ten Clear Wells of Kamakura became major sightseeing points, just like the Seven Passes. The mossy spring here is included in the big ten.

Before we visit our next temple, Meigetsu-in, I should issue one caveat: Avoid it in June when the hydrangea are in bloom. It may be a cliche, but the Japanese do seem to do things all together at the same time in the same place. Half of the population of the Kanto area seems to be gathered at the Meigetsu-in on June weekends. Unless you are a true hydrangea lover, you might want to settle for a gander at the color photos of the famous flowers that are on display.

Meigetsu-in is on the other side of Kamakura-kaido from Jochi-ji and back a few hundred meters. The English rendition of its name, "Temple of the Clear Moon," is simply lovely. It evokes the peaceful atmosphere of the premises when they are not overrun by nature lovers. But there is more to horticulture at Meigetsu-in than hydrangea. There's forsythia, Japanese quince, narcissus, lily of the valley, dogwood, and other flowers. It is a joy to stroll around the green paths surrounding the temple, where the wind caresses the pines and bamboo.

Meigetsu-in, founded in the fourteenth century by Governor General of the Kanto area, Uesugi Norikata, was originally part of a much larger temple, Zenko-ji, abolished during the Meiji period. Meigetsu-in is also famous for the tomb of Tokiyori, the fifth Hojo regent.

Tokiyori, the Philosopher Regent

The Hojo regents were a motley lot. The earliest ones were cunning murderers and the last, Takatoki, degenerate scum. But in between were several very wise rulers, foremost of whom were Tokimune and Tokiyori. By all accounts, Tokiyori was a conscientious administrator and a true philosopher. He wandered through the countryside dressed as a mendicant priest, observing the conditions of the common people and ferreting out wrongdoing. According to tradition he died while seated in the *zazen* position, and so many people imitated him by retiring to a meditative life that laws had to be passed to stop them. He might be regarded as the Marcus Aurelius of Kamakura history. The bust of Tokiyori at Meigetsu-in was supposedly formed from clay mixed with the sage ruler's ashes.

• MAP 204

Meigetsu-in also claims Kamakura's largest *yagura*—three meters in height, where sixteen arhats and other treasures are kept. Behind the temple is the tomb of Ashikaga Takauji, founder of the Ashikaga shogunate. As I noted earlier, it is best not to pay too much attention to the business of tombs in Japan. This one is supposed to contain a hair of the deceased. For many people, including Emperor Go Daigo, that would be a hair from the dog that bit them. The Kame no I (Jug Well) bulges like a ceramic water jug.

A little bit back into the valley behind Meigetsu-in is an off-beat coffee shop. Fue ("Flute") is a laid-back establishment decorated with unusual musical instruments from around the world. Baroque music evenings are sometimes held. You can also try your hand at throwing a few pots at the Meigetsuyo ceramics studio run by a working potter, who holds classes every Sunday from 13:00–16:00. Get a group together and you get a day's course with lunch thrown in. Make reservations in advance. For a taste of Kyoto try the delicious, traditional boxed-lunches at Buan, between Meigetsu-in and Kencho-ji. Another reasonable restaurant is Tachibana, which offers an intriguing mix of Japanese and Western food.

Return to the Kamakura-kaido and turn left. Keep going straight, in about ten minutes you'll see the huge wooden gate of Kencho-ji on the left. This gate is a reconstruction dating from the mid-eighteenth century. *Tanuki* spirits are said to have taken part in its construction, which is why it could survive the 1923 earthquake. There are five hundred arhats on the second floor. This is also where the ghost of Kajiwara Kagetoki, Yoritomo's number one henchman, likes to put in an appearance. A special ceremony to keep it humored is held here on July 15.

Actually, Kencho-ji has a goodly share of strange legends, such as how old Zen priests were likely to be turned into foxes. Founded in 1253, it is generally recognized as the oldest Zen temple in Japan. Although it is still huge, before the earthquake it was even bigger and had more than fifty buildings. In fact, after its heyday in the Kamakura period, Kencho-ji burned down several times, with most of its original buildings perishing in a conflagration in 1415, and suffered tremendous neglect at other times. In the Edo period the Tokugawa family gave it support and the famous Zen prelate Takuan helped it to bounce back.

• MAP 204

However, it took a nosedive again, when the Meiji government started persecuting Buddhism. It benefited, though, in that temples connected with the Tokugawa family were moved here rather than destroyed. So we should be grateful that we still have as many architectural and artistic treasures as we do, even though many of the buildings currently standing here were transplanted from Tokyo.

Like Engaku-ji, the other chief Rinzai Zen center, Kencho-ji "airs" many of its most illustrious treasures every August and November. These include several scrolls showing the newly departed receiving judgment before Enma, king of the dead; a large green bronze lion used as an incense burner, brought from Korea in 1592; relics related to the founder Doryu; and several moving paintings of the death of Buddha (*nehan*).

The valley in which Kencho-ji is located is full of impressive Japanese cedars. It's hard to believe that prior to the temple's establishment, it was an ancient execution ground known as the Valley of Hell. In his desire to make Kamakura the cultural match of Kyoto, Tokiyori invited a famous Chinese priest by the name of Tao Lung, or Doryu in Japanese, to come and teach Zen. He became the first priest to be given the title of *zenji* (master of Zen) in Japan. By tradition his grave is located on a hillside to the right of the bell tower. When Doryu's body was cremated, five *shari* condensed on nearby trees. *Shari* are objects looking like pearls that are sometimes found in the bodies of holy men after their death.

The bell tower is to the right not far from the main gate. The nearly two-meter high bronze bell inside is a National Treasure that was cast in 1255, making it the first or second oldest bell in Kamakura (depending on the source). It is fifteen feet in circumference and many bell connoisseurs consider it the most beautiful in eastern Japan.

The seeds for the wizened Chinese juniper standing in decrepit majesty between the second gate—currently undergoing extensive restoration that won't be completed for years—and the Buddha hall, were supposedly brought from China by Doryu. The main hall, sitting in the midst of more junipers, and the Chinese gate behind it were both moved here in 1646. The walls and ceiling of the hall are decorated with gorgeous paintings. A huge "thunder drum" used by Yoritomo to summon his men while on one of his grand hunts near Fuji-san

• MAP 204

is also here. There is a wooden image of Tokiyori on display that dates from the Kamakura period, and a large, seated *jizo* that is said to have a smaller *jizo* inside it. The story goes that this smaller effigy saved the life of a man named Saita Kingo. He had been brought here to the Valley of Hell to be executed, but twice swords shattered against his neck. The executioners were nonplussed by this extraordinary development and gave the condemned man a body search. In his topknot they discovered this small figure of *jizo* with a sword scar on its back. The larger figure was supposedly donated by Saita's family in gratitude for the miracle.

Temple Cooking in Kita Kamakura

There are several restaurants offering Zen-influenced *shojin ryori* in Kamakura. Monzen near Kita Kamakura Station is a temple-food spot whose name reportedly was thought up by Kawabata Yasunari.

To the right of Kencho-ji is a well-known *shojin ryori* restaurant, Hachi no Ki, "The Potted Tree," that also has a branch near Engaku-ji. The name of the restaurant derives from a story about how Tokimune rewarded an impoverished samurai for burning his most treasured possession, a potted bonsai, to provide the regent warmth when he showed up in the guise of a nondescript traveler one cold winter night. The speciality here is Kenchin-jiru, a stew of vegetables and tofu said to have been taught by the founder of Kencho-ji. According to a *setsuwa* story for religious instruction, an inattentive acolyte dropped a block of tofu meant for the priests' meal. He was going to throw the crumbled pieces away, but thinking it would be a waste, he cooked it up with wild vegetables instead. The potluck meal drew raves, so ever since tofu has been broken up for this dish.

Opposite Kencho-ji is another *shojin ryori* joint, Hanagokoro, "Heart of the Flower"—a very Buddhistic image I should say. Saami on Komachi-dori (another Saami

is near Hokoku-ji) serves reasonably priced Buddhist dishes in very Zen surroundings—even the toilet is Zen style.

The Buddha, of course, condemned the taking of any form of life, but in recent years that commandment has been honored in the breach. In Kamakura you can see priests of Zen and other sects consuming meat and fish with obvious gusto. A priest I asked about this replied, "If we stuck to the traditional diet, we wouldn't be able to get any fresh blood at all into the religious life. Besides, in restaurants it is all but impossible to avoid meat or meat byproducts these days."

Join the priests at Kyoraien, whose beef stew simmers for two weeks! Talk about that good "old time taste."

Monzen 門前 ☎ 0467-25-1121
🕐 11:00–15:00, 17:00–19:30; weekends and hols. 11:00–19:30; open all year

Hachi no Ki 鉢の木 ☎ 0467-23-3723
🕐 11:00–15:30, 17:00–20:00; weekends and hols 11:00–20:00; closed Weds

Hanagokoro 花心 ☎ 0467-22-8848
🕐 11:00–18:00; closed Thurs.

Saami 左阿彌 ☎ 0467-25-0048
🕐 12:00–17:00; closed Thurs.

Kyoraian 去来庵 ☎ 0467-24-9835
🕐 10:30–17:00; closed Fri. and occasionally Thurs.

• MAP 204

Keep going past the huge Hatto (法堂 Hall of Law) meditation building and on to another large structure, the Ryuoden (竜王殿 Hall of the Dragon King). According to tradition, the Japanese garden constructed around a pond in the rear was designed by the famous monk and garden planner Muso Soseki, the founder of Zuisen-ji. A quaint little bridge leads to the island in the pond. Laid out in 1253, this is considered the oldest Zen-style garden in Japan.

Off to the left of the Chinese gate (唐門 Karamon) and main path is the Tengen-in (天源院), where the Kencho-ji abbot resides. Note the old, thatched roof and vine-wreathed gate. Other places of interest at Kencho-ji include several teahouses, the graves of famous priests, and Daigaku Ike (Lake of Enlightenment), which in ancient times was known as Kame no Ike (Tortoise Lake).

Because of the grandeur of scale at Kencho-ji, it's not surprising that its flower should be the cherry blossom. The best place for *sakura* viewing is in the very back of the compound on the road that leads to the Ten'en Hiking course to Zuisen-ji.

After climbing 248 steep steps, you will reach the Hanzobo Temple, a kind of religious grotesquerie inhabited by eleven *tengu* long-nosed goblins. The temple, which only dates back to 1890, is dedicated to Hanzobo Daigongen, the god of the mountain. The fierce-looking *tengu* are no threat to the health, but the hordes of junior high-school and high-school kids who come barreling down the mountain in what sometimes resemble flying horse columns can be. A *tengu* mini-festival is held on the seventeenth and eighteenth of each month.

Across from Kencho-ji is a fascinating "Hades Temple," the Zen-affiliated Enno-ji or Arai no Enma-do. Edgar Allan Poe could have spent several rapturous hours in this hall that was moved here in the mid-Edo period from the seashore at Yuigahama.

A favorite is certain to be the Shozuka no Baba Datsu Eba or "Hag of the Styx," a masterpiece of realistic art. This is the crone who makes little children sent to limbo pile up stones on the banks of the Sai no Kawara river and torments them until merciful *jizo* arrive to save them.

• MAP 204

The statues of Enma and the Ten Kings of Hell (Daio) are mesmerizingly weird. To the devil with Enma, let's continue our saunter. We need to pull a U-turn and head back towards Kita-Kamakura. A couple of hundred meters along, well before the crossing over the Yokosuka Line tracks, there is a road cutting off to the left with a small temple that is usually not open, the Choju-ji, opposite a restaurant that has a model of a giant bowl of shrimp *soba* out front. Choju-ji was built by Ashikaga Takauji's son Motouji for the repose of the soul of his father and became an Ashikaga family temple. Its azalea are well known.

Go up the small tree-lined road. This is Kamegayatsu-zaka, Tortoise Valley Slope, one of the seven "mouths" of Kamakura. Oh, how delightful it is strolling on this road. Most of the tourist crowds do not know about it, and the road gets so narrow that there is no vehicular traffic. Sunlight filters through the trees to light your way to a different age.

All too soon you pop out near the Iwafune Jizo. A stone *jizo* with a ship-shaped stone halo is said to be buried below the wooden *jizo*. You'll now be facing the Yokosuka Line.

The King of the Dead

Enma (Sanskrit Yama) is the King of the Dead, the Prince of the Underworld, the supreme court justice among the eleven brethren who decide how you will be punished for your sins during life and into which of the six levels of existence your soul will be reborn. What makes the Enma statue at Enno-ji so truly terrifying at the subconscious level, are the eyes, eyes which are not only menacing but also all-knowing.

According to a famous story, Unkei created this depiction of Enma, an Important Cultural Property, after returning from the dead. After his premature demise, Unkei went to face Enma, who asked him why no one had ever accurately painted or sculpted his true appearance. "I dunno," Unkei replied. So, he was sent back to take care of the job.

Actually, Unkei supposedly made the "Ten Kings" too, although that seems unlikely, at least in their totality. The fourteenth-century tsunami that wiped out the original temple no doubt damaged everything in it.

In the old days on February 14, the festival of Enma, Japan's equivalent of Hallowe'en, was celebrated. That is supposedly the one day of the year when the old workaholic takes the day off. Normally, Enma is so attentive to his duties and so judgemental, that he is not inclined to listen to prayers from family members of those newly arrived in his kingdom. On this one day, however, he sits back and is open to suggestions (and perhaps a bit of bribery). In certain temples supplicants set up images of Enma and offer propitiatory gifts. Maybe this was the origin of Valentine's Day chocolates...

• MAP 204

Turn left and follow the road by the tracks. Soon you'll reach Jokomyo-ji, a Shingon temple said to have been founded by Hojo Nagatoki. There is an alternative tradition that it was founded by the priest Mongaku at the request of Yoritomo. This is where Ashikaga Takauji is said to have made his fateful decision to topple Emperor Go Daigo and establish a new shogunate. Military rule continued up until the Meiji Restoration. A prison was also established in one of the *yagura* here. The serene atmosphere of the grounds belies this tumultuous history.

The temple owns several notable statues, including a seated Amida Triad, and another with jewels in the crown. Burnished fall foliage, plum, cherry, narcissus, Japanese bush clover—Jokomyo-ji has them all.

The temple's prize possession is to be found in a cathedral-like cave in back of the temple. It is the Amihiki Jizo (Net-Drawn Jizo), covered with a time-induced black patina. The smiling *jizo* was reportedly recovered by fishermen off Yuigahama and so the statue is sprinkled with saltwater when prayers are offered. Near here is the tomb of the famous fourteenth-century poet Reizei. A custom among neighborhood children is to rub themselves with the stones piled up in front of it to keep free of illness.

Keep going down the road next to the tracks. Down a side road to the left you'll notice Gokoku-ji, a somewhat bizarre looking Nichiren temple. At the next big corner turn left. Keep going straight through a residential neighborhood. After about four or five blocks you'll come to a narrow, but crowded thoroughfare. Turn right; you're now on Komachi-dori, the city's biggest shopping street. Often referred to as the "Kamakura Ginza," it has several hundred restaurants, coffee shops, and souvenir and handicraft shops. You could easily spend hours browsing for traditional gifts. Yamago, just before Mother's restaurant on the left, specializes in bamboo products, especially whisks and other tea ceremony paraphernalia. Just after Mother's is Shato, which sells traditional Japanese paper. Ask for the kind of writing paper that Kawabata Yasunari preferred. Further up on the right is Kitotenkundo with 120 varieties of highest quality incense. The shop was founded in 1907 in Sakai, near Osaka. There is also a sniffing club based here.

There are a few quirky restaurants that are worth going out of your

• MAP 204

way for a closer look. Madonnatei is a rather sexist *kaiseki* restaurant on Komachi-dori that only admits women or accompanied men who come as one half of a couple. You have to make reservations at least one week in advance. The owner is a poet who places a *tanka* poem on every meal he serves. The decor is 1920s Japan. Customers can change into old school-girl uniforms with *hakama* skirts. In a similar vein with a pleasant Taisho interior with lots of period pieces is the coffee shop Milk Hall. Kawagoe-ya near the station offers Japanese food in an interior decorated with Buddhist statues and Arita porcelain. For dessert pop up to Kurumi which has the best *shiratama* (sweet dumplings made from sticky rice) in the Kanto area. Finally if you've had enough of Zen for one day it has to be Mother's of Kamakura, a steak and seafood restaurant that features Miura Hayama beef. Only 200 cows are slaughtered in the area each year; the meat is the same grade as world-famous Kobe beef and this is the only place in the country you can eat it. The head chef worked at Rocky Aoki's Benihana chain, so naturally the chefs do a little song and dance with the knives.

Kamakura Togei-kan かまくら陶芸館 ☎ 0467-24-9534 ⊕ 10:00–17:00; closed Mon.

Meigetsuyo 明月窯 ☎ 0467-22-2901 ⊕ 11:00–17:00; closed Fri.

Yamago やまご ☎ 0467-22-1772 ⊕ 10:00–18:00; closed Weds and 3rd Tues.

Shato 社頭 ☎ 0467-22-2601 ⊕ 10:00–18:00; closed 3rd Fri. each month

Kitotenkundo 鬼頭天薫堂 ☎ 0467-22-1081; ⊕ 10:00–18:00; open all year

Kokotei 好々亭 ☎ 0467-46-5467 ⊕ 12:00–21:00; Sun and hols. 11:00–21:00; closed Fri.

Komaki こまき ☎ 0467-22-3316 ⊕ 10:00–17:00; closed Tues.

Oyasumidokoro お休み処 ☎ 0467-25-0411 ⊕ 8:00–17:30; open all year

Fue ☎ 0467-24-9756 ⊕ 10:00–19:00; Fri. 13:00–20:00; closed Weds.

Kintame 近為 ☎ 0467-24-8576 ⊕ 10:00–17:00; closed Mon.

Buan 蕪庵 ☎ 0467-25-1952 ⊕ 11:30–14:30; closed Mon. and Tues.

Tachibana 橘 ☎ 0467-22-0793 ⊕ 12:00–sold out; no regular hols.

Madonnatei 真緻汝亭 ☎ 0467-24-9724 ⊕ 11:00–20:00; closed Fri.

Milk Hall ミルクホール ☎ 0467-22-1179 ⊕ 9:00–23:00; closed Mon.

Kurumi くるみ ☎ 0467-23-1818 ⊕ 11:00–18:00; open all year

Kawagoe-ya 川古江家 ☎ 0467-24-2580 ⊕ 10:00–20:30; closed Thurs.

Mother's ☎ 0467-25-0805 ⊕ 11:30–15:00, 17:00–21:30; closed 3rd Tues. each month

• MAP 204

Time Out: Spelunking in Ofuna

Ofuna is where the Yokosuka Line branches off from the Tokaido Line. Although technically part of Kamakura, its personality is quite different from the refined rusticity of the old city. It is a brash commercial community with a distinctly plebeian feel. A separate trip to Ofuna would not be warranted but for the amazing Taya Caves. Those with a taste for kitsch will enjoy the 25-meter-high Kannon Goddess of Mercy that stares down on the rail traffic from its perch on a hill to the west of the station. The concrete hulk first started taking shape in 1929 (two years before the Manchurian Incident) from the fevered imagination of some of Japan's most ultranationalistic luminaries, who envisaged it rising from the cement mixers "for the sake of world peace." Construction was interrupted by the war, but finally completed in 1960.

Near the entrance to the caves is the ancient Josen-ji Shingon temple that predates the oldest caves, which are roughly of Kamakura era vintage. This is where we begin our spelunking. The caves are in the hill behind the temple. The portion open to the public (less than half a kilometer) is partially lit by electric lamps, although you are provided a candle, as much for psychological reassurance as for assistance in seeing, I should think. The corridors vary in width from 1.5 meters to 4 meters, while the height averages from 2 to 7 meters. Some chambers are the size of a 10-tatami mat room.

Within the three layers of caves are carved staircases, several meditation chambers, hundreds of Buddhist statues from all parts of Japan, flower-decked altars for the worship of Kannon and Benzaiten, and a waterfall whose waters have curative powers (including the ability to make you think clearer), and numerous wall paintings and carvings of fish, birds, turtles, dragons, angels, and famous historical figures. In the wall carvings of one hall, various Sanskrit letters representing the different incarnations of Shakyamuni are portrayed dancing on lotuses. The artists who created these amazing carvings and paintings all remain unknown, but they appear to fall into two categories: Buddhist monks and common people who joined in the fun especially within the last century or so. A local entrepreneur undertook to tap underground springs. His three-decade effort resulted in new tunnels and the inhabitants of the village of Taya took to decorating the walls with primitive, childlike, thoroughly charming depictions of real and mythological creatures.

No one knows for sure when the caves were first excavated. According to one tradition, Ashina Saburo, third son of Wada Yoshimori, installed an image of Benzaiten deep in a cave for private worship. When the Wada clan was annihilated by the Hojo in 1213, it supposedly collapsed, perhaps in sympathetic syncopation. An alternative story has it that the Hojo themselves used the caves as a treasure house and that Hojo remnants concealed themselves here after Nitta Yoshisada captured Kamakura. Later Shingon priests used the caves for esoteric rites and began expanding them. For hundreds of years after the fall of the shogunate, Buddhist monks worked at expanding the labyrinth and decorating it with intricate carvings.

It is quite an experience to wander through this subterranean religious wonderland, with the faint smell of incense in your nostrils and the sound of gentle waterfalls in the distance tinkling in your ears. Contemplate this marvelous monument to faith and patience in the large therapeutic onsen next-door.

Taya Caves (Taya no Dokutsu 田谷の洞窟) ☎ 045-851-2392
🕘 9:00-16:30; open all year. ¥400

⟳ Take a bus from stop #1 (all buses) across from the west side of Ofuna Station; get off at Taya no Dokutsu; alternatively take a bus from stop #2 and get off at Dokutsu-mae.

Big Buddha and the Masked Men

We begin this walk with a short stop in a fashionable museum. Come out of the east exit of Kamakura Station. Slightly to the left across the plaza you'll see a three-story red-brick building with an English sign reading Minami Jewel Museum. Here you can see seventy-seven works by that amazing eccentric Salvador Dali. They include jewel carvings and other trinkets whose bizarre designs reflect the inner dreamworld of the creatively demented Dali and his, oh so Spanish, religious views.

From the museum, go to the corner of Wakamiyaoji-dori, turn right and walk straight, until you get to the Geba Yotsukado intersection, where riders were required to dismount. Turn right, heading up Yuigahama-dori on the left side till the Roku Jizo are on the opposite side of the road from you. Turn left up the big street and walk straight, crossing the Enoden tracks. By Wadazuka Station to your right across the street is the atmosphere-laden Mushinan teahouse. Sit round the open hearth and sample their old-fashioned sweet treats such as *abekawa mochi*, sweet rice cakes, to prepare yourself for the walk back in time.

About a hundred meters the other side of the tracks, you'll see a small park with some monuments. This is the Wadazuka burial mound. During construction on a road here in 1892, a large number of human bones were discovered that bore marks of violence such as furrows left by

• MAP 220

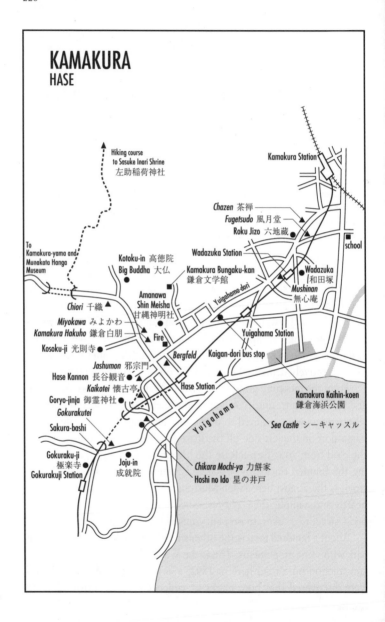

KAMAKURA
HASE

Hiking course
to Sasuke Inari Shrine
左助稲荷神社

Kamakura Station

Chazen 茶禅
Fugetsudo 風月堂
Roku Jizo 六地蔵

To
Kamakura-yama and
Munakata Hanga
Museum

school

Wadazuka Station

Kotoku-in 高徳院
Big Buddha 大仏

Kamakura Bungaku-kan
鎌倉文学館

Wadazuka
和田塚

Mushinan
無心庵

Amanawa
Shin Meisha
甘縄神明社

Yuigahama-dori

Chiori 千織

Miyokawa みよかわ
Kamakura Hakuho 鎌倉白朋
Kosoku-ji 光則寺

Fire

Yuigahama Station

Bergfeld

Kaigan-dori bus stop

Jashumon 邪宗門
Hase Kannon 長谷観音

Hase Station

Kaikotei 懐古亭
Goryo-jinja 御霊神社

Kamakura Kaihin-koen
鎌倉海浜公園

Gokurakutei

Sea Castle シーキャッスル

Sakura-bashi

Yuigahama

Gokuraku-ji
極楽寺
Gokurakuji Station

Joju-in
成就院

Chikara Mochi-ya 力餅家
Hoshi no Ido 星の井戸

swords. They are assumed to belong to members of the Wada clan, who were annihilated by the Hojo in May 1213, although considerable doubt exists on that score today.

Retrace your steps to Yuigahama-dori and turn left. When Kamakura became a fashionable seaside summer resort in the first part of this century, it required some trendy shopping streets. This road became one of the most important of them, and there are still several intriguing old Western-style buildings in the area. It still retains something of that flavor in its art galleries and restaurants. Take the Fugetsudo Coffee Shop, for example. Built in 1932, its Italian stained-glass window evokes a prewar Japan lacking even a whiff of imperialism and insular thinking. At the other end of the scale is Chazen where you can discover the intricacies of Japanese tea in the small tea shop in the Japanese sweet shop, Kawasoen. As for contemporary culture, check out the accessory shop Guild; you can easily spot it by the big, funky painting of the Buddha out front.

The Annihilation of the Wada

Wada Yoshimori, the head of the Wada clan, was one of Yoritomo's most stalwart warriors, equally adept with the sword or bow, becoming one of the supreme council of thirteen that ran the Bakufu. He was also related to the powerful Miura clan. Although he was the grandson of Miura Yoshiaki, he was not accepted into the main clan because he was the son of a courtesan and had to form a subsidiary clan. He was typical of the old style Kamakura warrior; all fight and no finesse.

The Hojo had no use for Wada, however, and determined to destroy him. They accused some of his vassals of treason and punished them, which incensed Wada, as no doubt was the intention. Wada determined to deal with the Hojo in the only way he knew how. He made a mistake, however. He divulged his plans to Miura Yoshimura,

whom he thought was his secret ally. The wily Miura forthwith betrayed his bastard relatives to the Hojo.

During the night of May 2, 1213, Wada attacked the Hojo headquarters with 150 horsemen. Forewarned, the Hojo guards were able to beat off the furious assault although the fighting continued all night and into the next day. As their numbers dwindled, in best Sam Peckinpah style, the Wada samurai fought their last battle with nihilistic determination, slowly retreating down Wakamiyaoji to Yuigahama, where their clan mansion was located. They received scanty reinforcements from some Kamakura Band families, but the Hojo got much larger infusions of fresh blood. On the evening of May 3 Yoshimori and the remaining Wada at last committed *seppuku*. He was sixty-seven.

• MAP 220

If you're a member of Shoppers Anonymous, you can go straight from Wadazuka to the beach and then turn right and continue along the shore all the way to Hase. Kamakura era records refer to hundreds of ships anchored off this stretch of coast; nowadays this area is packed with swimmers and sunbathers during the summer and a big Summer Carnival features live music and fireworks, along with makeshift stalls offering all kinds of food and drink. But be warned, during the warm months Yuigahama beach can get awfully lively and awfully dirty.

When you get down towards the end of the strip of sand you will find the Sea Castle restaurant, which has served sturdy German fare for over three decades. It is run by three German sisters, who make sure you clean your plate with true Prussian efficiency.

Iso Mutsu, an English woman married to a Japanese diplomat, experienced the 1923 Great Kanto Earthquake while talking to a friend in shallow water near here. In her fascinating book *Kamakura: Fact and Legend*, she wrote, "Suddenly, with an ominous roar, the floor of the deep seemed to rush up at us, toppling us over in an instant…the regular hissing throbs of steam of that subterranean explosion clearly audible to our terrifed ears! With thunderous detonation, all the mountains enclosing the plain of Kamakura were riven asunder."

If you want to get some sand in your shoes, that's your prerogative, but for this walk we're going to continue down Yuigahama-dori. Just before the Kaigan-dori bus stop, you'll see the overhead sign for the Kamakura Museum of Literature. Turn right here and follow the road for a couple hundred of meters until you pass through a small tunnel and enter the approach driveway. Suddenly, there before you stands a strikingly beautiful Western-style mansion, with blue-tiled roof, cream-colored walls, stained-glass windows, and decorated terraces. Built in 1936 as a seaside villa for the Kaga Maeda family, which during the Edo period was the richest *daimyo* clan in all Japan, the mansion was a getaway for two prime ministers, Yoshida Shigeru and Sato Eisaku, before finally being converted into the museum in 1985.

The displays concentrate on classic and modern Japanese writers, especially those who have had some kind of Kamakura connection. After the Yokosuka Line opened, not only did the city become a major

• MAP 220

seaside resort, it also became a writer's town, and the expression Kamakura *bunshi*, "Kamakura literary men" came into being. In fact, just about everywhere you look in the city, there are literary associations. Here you can see manuscripts and photos, as well as items owned by such literary luminaries as Kawabata Yasunari, Mishima Yukio, and Natsume Soseki. Kawabata, the first and till now only Japanese to receive the Nobel Prize for literature lived in three places in Kamakura including a spot near here. He committed suicide at his Zushi home on April 16, 1972, at the age of seventy-four. Lectures are held here periodically on literary themes. Take a look at the exquisite rose garden and the *yagura* to the side of the driveway.

Head back to the main street and continue on to the fire station, turn right here and walk straight for about a hundred meters to the Amanawashinmeisha Shrine, which according to tradition is over 1,200 years old, making it probably the oldest Shinto shrine in Kamakura. It is dedicated to the sun goddess Amaterasu Omikami. Although it is of immense historical importance—Yoritomo, Masako, and Sanetomo frequently worshipped here—it has very few visitors except for Hase residents. The view of the ocean is tremendous.

Next stop is the Big Buddha. You may wish to fortify yourself first with some hearty *Küchen* at the German cafe, Bergfeld, on a side street to the left. However, you will have no trouble finding the enormous statue. Follow the signs or the crowds. If you somehow miss both, just remember: when Yuigahama-dori reaches the big intersection, turn right. Up the road on the right is the approach to Kotoku-in, the Jodo temple where the Daibutsu, the pride and glory of Kamakura, sits alfresco. The initial reaction to this artistic and technical masterpiece is a personal interpretation of the same sentiment: Awe.

Perhaps Kipling put it best: "He has been described again and again—his majesty, his aloofness, and every one of his dimensions, the smoky little shrine within him, and the plumed hill that makes the background to his throne. For that reason he remains, as he remained from the beginning, beyond all hope of description—as it might be, a visible god sitting in the garden of a world made new."

The Daibutsu is not only a National Treasure; it is also a world

• MAP 220

treasure. The Goko-san mountain to the rear forms the perfect background for the ageless image of spiritual serenity that is the Daibutsu.

During the Kamakura era, this valley was on the edge of the central part of the city, and became a kind of limbo zone where beggars, lepers, traveling entertainers, and low-class prostitutes gathered. Perhaps they found solace for their respective plights when they woke to the sight of the compassionate face of the Great Buddha.

You approach the Kotoku-in along a gravel path, pay, and step inside the gate guarded by two Deva kings, and there you are standing before the 11.3 meter high statue. At first you are drawn to it like a magnet, but something seems strange, even unsettling. It is only after you examine it from various angles, that you realize the seated effigy is grotesquely malformed, head enormous, and back rounded in a distinctly unhealthy fashion. The artist used the principles of perspective and distortion to create an overwhelming impression if you view the statue from four or five meters directly in front.

The Creation of the Big Buddha

It is not entirely clear how the construction of the Great Buddha came about. The standard story goes like this: when Yoritomo visited Western Japan in 1195 after the establishment of the shogunate, he went to Nara to dedicate the rebuilt Todai-ji Temple, home to the massive Nara Buddha. The structure had been burned down by a Taira army and the statue badly damaged. Yoritomo is said to have been so impressed that he wanted to have something of equivalent grandeur for Eastern Japan.

At first in 1243 a wooden image was created, but it and the temple that enclosed it were leveled by a storm in 1248. The authorities then decided to replace it with the bronze statue that stands today, which dates from 1252 and is the second largest statue of that material in the nation after the Nara Daibutsu. Some art experts have detected Hellenistic influences in the design of the Daibutsu. One thing is for sure, the 121-ton image is a technical feat of the first order. Many things about the Daibutsu are simply mind-boggling. Try these statistics out for size: the length of the face is 2.4 meters, the statue measures 29.4 meters in circumference at the knees, and there are 830 curls in its punch-perm hairstyle.

The Daibutsu seems to prefer to be out in the open. Impressive buildings were repeatedly erected to house it, but they were just as repeatedly wrecked by storms, tsunami, fires, and other disasters. In August 1335 a mammoth typhoon descended upon an army marching out of Kamakura. The commander decided to bivouac inside the wooden temple, but the howling winds collapsed the structure like a pack of cards killing five hundred of his men. Since 1495, the Great Buddha has braved the elements.

• MAP 220

Note the silver boss in the forehead that is supposed to be a source of the light of illumination. The claim in Kamakura era chronicles that the Daibutsu was originally gilded was long doubted. It almost seems that it was meant to be born with the lovely green patina it has today. These doubts persisted until the earthquake of 1923 when the statue was moved forward 50 centimeters and a cheek slightly damaged. During the repair work, experts detected traces of gold foil beneath the surface.

It must have been some sight to see the golden Daibutsu shining in the sun. In my readings I have even run across an incredible reference to the eyes being made of pure gold. I seriously doubt that, since some indigent foreigner would certainly have gotten to them one way or another long before now. Lafcadio Hearn noted that the eyes look calmly at you like those of a child and added, "Its beauty, its dignity, its perfect repose, reflect the higher life of the race that created it."

In a sensuous poem that is reproduced on a plaque in back of the Daibutsu, poetess Yosano Akiko refers to "Shaka," the Daibutsu, as a *bidan*, a "handsome fellow"—or "hunk" if you prefer. She had it wrong on a couple of counts. The image is not of Shakyamuni or Gautama, the historical Buddha. It is rather of Amida Nyorai, a future Buddha. Also, a minor quibble, but aren't Buddhas supposed to have transcended all petty distinctions and distractions like gender?

If you pay extra, you can crawl around inside the statue. An interior staircase allows you to go up to shoulder level. In the late nineteenth century Western missionaries seemed to take a particular pleasure in doing so, perching on various limbs for photographs, or otherwise desecrating the "idol." Even if you lack faith, at least have decency—no matter how strong the temptation to enter the infinite womb, please resist it.

After your spiritual experience at the Daibutsu, you might want to try the tofu specialty restaurant Chiori nearby. Full meals tend to be expensive, but if you settle for a tofu steak or tofu ice cream, you won't bust your budget. There's another tofu restaurant further down toward the Hase intersection on the left on the second floor of the Hakuho building. Less expensive than Chiori, Kamakura Hakuho obtains its tofu from a local tofu maker in the Ogigayatsu valley. A few doors away is the elegant Miyokawa which serves reasonably priced lunch-boxes.

• MAP 220

Try the *hyotan bento* served in a jolly *hyotan* gourd-shaped box.

Note that the two-kilometer hiking course that goes to Sasuke Inari Shrine starts next to the tunnel up the road from the Big Buddha. You can also catch buses from outside Kotoku-in to Kamakurayama.

Kamakurayama

Highly recommended is a side trip to Kamakurayama, where you can easily spend a pleasant couple of hours exploring the neighborhoods. Kamakurayama was only opened up as a residential area in 1930, although it appears to have been sparsely populated before then. It used to be called Koshigoeyama, and as might be guessed from its location, it is justly famed for its cherry blossoms in spring. Actually, there is still a lot of nice nature left around here, and the area is beautiful in any season.

However, the real treasure of the area is the Munakata Hanga Bijutsukan Museum. Munakata Shiko (1903–1975) was a highly individualistic artist from Aomori Prefecture who developed the art of the *hanga*, or modern woodblock print to an extraordinary level. He preferred to call them *banga*, because to him that word had Buddhist connotations. His prints do indeed have a very strong religious element, but they also can be extremely erotic. You might well have run across them as illustrations to novels by Tanizaki Jun'ichiro, such as *The Key* or *Diary of a Mad Old Man*. Munakata's Kannon bodhisattva are both buxom and beatific.

There are also several expensive restaurants up here, including Roast Beef Kamakura, where the basic lunch course goes for ¥6,000. Dinner for two with wine might put you back ¥50,000. A bit pricey for sure, but the landscaped grounds are spectacularly beautiful and the restaurant interior like an English club.

More within the realm of the possible for most of us is Raitei, a restaurant serving delicious Okinawa *soba* buckwheat noodles. But it is far more than that. The *soba* restaurant is located inside an Edo era farmhouse that is only one small section of extensive grounds, which include a beautiful Japanese garden with teahouses and rest areas, and another garden that includes a good portion of a dismantled temple. Many Buddhist statues and other relics are scattered throughout the very beautiful and serene grounds.

To get to Kamakurayama from Kamakura Station take a bus bound for Enoshima going via Kamakurayama, or a bus going to Ofuna.

Munakata Hanga Bijutsukan 棟方版画
美術館 ☎ 0467-31-7642
🕐 10:00–16:00; closed Mon. ¥300. Get off at Asahigaoka bus stop; museum is three minutes away on the right.

Roast Beef no Mise Kamakurayama
ローストビーフの店鎌倉山
☎ 0467-31-5454
🕐 11:30–14:00, 17:00–20:00; closed Tues. Five minutes on foot from Sumiyoshi bus stop (two stops after Asahigaoka bus stop)

Raitei 檑亭 ☎ 0467-32-5656
🕐 11:00–sunset, until 20:30 if reservations have been made; closed the last week in July. By Takasago bus stop (one stop after Asahigaoka bus stop)

From the Big Buddha go back in the direction of Yuigahama. Incidentally, if you're interested in traditional Japanese performing arts, there's a small Noh stage, Kamakura Noh Butai, in the hills to the right, where performances of Noh are staged. To get back to the walk, continue on toward Yuigahama and then take the quiet lane to the right to Kosoku-ji. Along with Zuisen-ji and Tokei-ji, it is counted as one of Kamakura's three "flower temples." The April-blooming aronia are especially renowned, but the plums, peonies, irises, azaleas, ginger, and sasanqua are also magnificent.

Kosoku-ji was built by Yadoya Mitsunori, Nichiren's greatest samurai follower, whose mansion was originally located here. (The characters for Mitsunori can also be read as Kosoku.) After the government exiled Nichiren to Sado, it cracked down on his disciples remaining in Kamakura. Four of the most prominent, including Nichiro—one of the master's favorites—were imprisoned in hillside caves here. A stone next to the mouth of the cave purportedly reproduces the text of a letter of commiseration that Nichiren sent to Nichiro. The stone monuments near the entrance are said to display examples of Nichiren's unique flowing script, a style that was adopted by his followers and can be seen in signs and monuments at most Nichiren temples. After his release from Sado, Nichiren supposedly lived here for a while, and it was here that his flock received a letter from regent Tokimune granting the right to practice their religion freely and rant and roar to their hearts' content.

Head back to the main road, turn right, and then right again up the road lined with traditional shops (check out Jashumon, a retro coffee shop) to Hase-dera, one of the most popular temples in eastern Japan, reputedly founded in 736. It is commonly referred to as the Hase Kannon because of the eleven-headed golden Kannon statue kept here.

The gilded wooden statue has been the object of extraordinary popular devotion for several centuries. It is said to be carved out of one half of the same camphor tree from which the wood for the Kannon statue at the Hase-dera near Nara was taken, and predates the temple itself by fifteen years. Both statues are believed to have been made by the same man, the priest Tokudo. The Hase Kannon stands 9.3 meters tall and is said to be the tallest wooden image in Japan. Kannon, the

• MAP 220

goddess of Mercy, is also the protectress of horses, so farmers whose animals were ill or irascible would present her with *ema* wooden votive offerings. You can see these and images of horses around the temple.

An unusual method of prayer is the octagonal revolving sutra holder. It is believed that one turn of this giant wheel of fortune grants the supplicant the same amount of spiritual merit as a reading of all the sutras within it.

One part of the temple that is sure to capture your attention is the area where thousands of sad little *jizo* are displayed, some wearing red bibs and knitted caps and clutching whirling toy windmills. These are offerings for children lost through miscarriage or abortion. The spirits of these children no doubt are cheered by the crowds that stream through the temple every day. But how lonely they must be at night.

Walk back to the main road, turn right, and cross the Enoden tracks. Follow the narrow lane to the right beside the tracks. Walk five minutes to where the road turns to the right; very soon you'll be at Goryo-jinja.

The Ugly Parade

Goryo-jinja is normally quiet and sleepy. Come September 18, however, and it becomes the site for one of Kamakura's most bizarre festivals, the Menkake Gyoretsu masked parade. This started as a neighborhood festival, but now draws legions of rubber neckers, paparazzi, and other sundry voyeurs. Ten men parade around in ugly masks and other local residents pound drums and chant as they transport *mikoshi* god palanquins through the narrow streets. This is the lineup of the masked men: *Jiji*—the dirty old man; the *oni* goblin; the long-nosed one; *Igyo*—the strange and suspicious-looking one; *Okina*—the wizened one; *Karasu Tengu*—the crow goblin; *Hotei*—a fat and saucy member of the Seven Lucky Gods; *Hyottoko*—the droll, ugly one; *Okame*—the plump-faced ugly woman; and finally the pregnant "woman," who seems to be bearing a whole brood inside of her.

As usual, there is a serious story behind these facetious festivities and it has to do with Yoritomo. It seems that the shogun had constant trouble keeping his kimono closed, much to the consternation of Masako. Not only was he involved with Kame no Mae on a more or less permanent basis, he also formed temporary liaisons with fair damsels whenever he had the opportunity. Yoritomo seems to have been especially frisky whenever Masako was pregnant, which happened on at least four occasions. In any event, Yoritomo became involved with a low-class girl in this area who bore his child. Although Yoritomo couldn't recognize this relationship officially, a *modus operandi* was worked out whereby she and her family all put on masks whenever he visited their neighborhood and it was pretended that they simply did not exist.

• MAP 220

Goryo-jinja is known locally as Gongoro-sama. This name is derived from Gongoro Kagemasa, the most famous member of the Kamakura Bands, whose tomb is supposedly located next to the large 850-year-old tree. Many stories are told about Gongoro, who might be considered the Paul Bunyan of the samurai. Notice the Kagemasa Riki stones that in olden times were hefted by strong boys in contests of strength. The smaller one weighs 60 kilograms and the larger one 115 kilograms. Kagemasa reportedly played ball with the larger one and kept the smaller one tucked up in his kimono sleeve.

The best Gongoro story I know of is supposedly based on an actual historical incident. While fighting for the Minamoto in a battle in Tohoku in 1083, the superhumanly strong samurai was shot in the eye by an enemy arrow. One of his compatriots put his foot on Gongoro's face in his attempt to get the shaft out, whereupon Gongoro drew his short sword and tried to stab his would-be benefactor. He thundered at his friend, "It is a desired fate for a true *bushi* to be killed by an arrow, but under no circumstances can he tolerate having his face stepped on." Somehow or other, Gongoro and his men got the bothersome arrow out, because he fought on and helped turn the tide of battle. He was sixteen at the time.

During the Meiji era, the author Kunikida Doppo, the forerunner of the Naturalist style, lived near Goryo-jinja for a year in the early 1900s, during which time he wrote the novel *Kamakura Fujin* (Kamakura wife). Nearby is Kaikotei, a restaurant that serves excellent Japanese food inside an Edo period farmhouse relocated here from the Hida area. Absolutely no nails or iron clamps were used in its construction; it is held together solely by wood joints and rope. There are antiques galore inside the building.

From Goryo-jinja, cross the Enoden tracks. Down where this street meets the main road, you'll see an old-fashioned building on the right, Chikara Mochi-ya, a purveyor of *chikara mochi*, a type of Japanese sweet rice dumpling. This shop has been here since the late 1600s. Pick up a few of these sweets; the ones shaped like the masks used in the festival, for example, are quite delicious. During the Edo period it became a tradition for pilgrims to Mt. Oyama and tourists to Kamakura to take back

• MAP 220

a batch to Edo. Step back and check out the old wooden sign above the door. Note the characters are read from right to left in prewar fashion.

Turn right here; soon you'll see a covered well, the Hoshi no Ido ("Well of the Stars"). In the old days the waters inside were crystal clear, reflecting the stars even during the daytime. However, one day an inattentive maid dropped a kitchen knife into the well, cutting the ties to the world beyond and letting the stars escape. Go up the stairs to the right to Kokuzo-do. Dedicated to Koku Bosatsu, this temple was established during the Heian period by Gyoki and has a cute *jizo* in a boat.

Across the road is Joju-in, a Shingon temple, connected with Kobo Daishi, since he was supposed to have conducted sacred fire rituals here. The hydrangea here are just as good as those at Meigetsu-in, but without the crowds. There is a realistic statue of Mongaku near the entrance.

After topping the ridge you'll see Gokurakuji Station below. Cross Sakura-bashi, the small vermilion bridge, turn left, and on your right you'll see the entrance to Gokuraku-ji, a Shingon-Ritsu temple.

Ninsho—the Living Saint

The first head priest of Gokuraku-ji was Ninsho, one of the most important religious figures of the Kamakura period. He had close ties to the government and engaged in many public works, including constructing the road through the pass here. But his main claim to fame was the medical facilities Ninsho established within the temple. There was a leprosarium and quarters for the indigent and outcasts. It is recorded that over 50,000 people received treatment from Ninsho or his followers. The pestle and mortar used to grind plants for use in medicinal *okayu* rice gruel is preserved in the courtyard. There were also therapeutic baths and even a hospital for horses within the compound. So famous was Ninsho's reputation as a living saint that even the emperor referred to him as a bodhisattva—one who has attained enlightenment but has decided to remain in the transitory world to help others.

Ninsho was also famed as a rainmaker. On one occasion during a terrible drought he even offered his life for rain. While he was praying for rain, a small white snake came out to listen but soon disappeared. Shortly after a downpour began. Apparently Ninsho's only enemy was Nichiren, who scoffed at his rainmaking efforts. This cannot be considered detached criticism, however, as Nichiren had his own reputation as a first-class rainmaker to uphold. According to the Nichiren version of things, in one instance after Ninsho prayed in vain for a little precipitation, Nichiren went out and did his thing, and quick as a wink the clouds opened.

Ninsho's large tomb in the graveyard to the rear of the temple is considered one of the finest tombs of the era in eastern Japan.

• MAP 220

Gokuraku-ji was established here in 1259 by Hojo Shigetoki, who had a villa built near here in 1261. It was once a huge complex of more than fifty sumptuous buildings, but fire and other natural disasters whittled it down to a vestige of its former self. In fact, most of the temple grounds now belong to two schools and the graveyard is closed to casual visitors. However, the temple still retains sixteen Important Cultural Properties, including the wooden statue of a seated Shakya Nyorai that is the chief object of worship. Unfortunately, they are only displayed once a year, April 7–9. Other important items including fascinating paintings of the death of the Buddha (*nehan*) and a collection of ten emaciated *rakan*, some of the five hundred disciples of the Buddha who attained Nirvana, can be viewed all year round in the tiny Treasure House. During the war these treasures were evacuated to the countryside, and they made their safe return in the back of U.S. Army jeeps.

On the other side of the tracks from the temple is Gokurakutei, a Western-style restaurant, decorated with all kinds of Western antiques.

Minami Jewel Museum (Minami Hoshoku Bijutsukan ミナミ宝飾美術館) ☎ 0467-22-5354
⊕ 10:00–17:30; closed Mon. ¥800

Kamakura Museum of Literature (Kamakura Bungaku-kan 鎌倉文学館) ☎ 0467-23-3911
⊕ 9:00–16:00; closed Mon. and when changing exhibitions. ¥200

Kamakura Noh Butai 鎌倉能舞台 ☎ 0467-22-5557

Guild ☎ 0467-22-0256
⊕ 9:30–19:00; open all year

Fugetsudo 風月堂 ☎ 0467-22-0963
⊕ 9:00–19:00; open all year

Chazen 茶禪 (in Kawasoen 川宗園) ☎ 0467-22-1348 ⊕ 10:00–18:00; closed Fri.

Mushinan 無心庵 ☎ 0467-23-0850
⊕ 11:00–18:00; closed Tues.

Sea Castle ☎ 0467-25-4335
⊕ 12:00–21:00; closed Weds.

Bergfeld ☎ 0467-24-9843
⊕ 11:00–18:30; closed Tues.

Tofu Dokoro Chiori とうふ処千織 ☎ 0467-23-0400 ⊕ 11:00–21:00; Sun. 10:00–21:00; closed Fri.

Kamakura Hakuho 鎌倉白朋 ☎ 0467-25-5760 ⊕ 11:30–15:30; closed Mon.

Miyokawa みよかわ ☎ 0467-25-5556
⊕ 11:00–21:00; open all year

Jashumon 邪宗門 ☎ 0467-25-0533
⊕ 10:00–17:00; closed Weds.

Kaikotei 懐古亭 ☎ 0467-25-4494
⊕ 11:00–15:30, 17:00–21:00; closed Thurs.

Gokurakutei ☎ 0467-22-0322
⊕ 11:00–18:00; closed Fri.

Chikara Mochi-ya 力餅屋 ☎ 0467-22-0513 ⊕ 9:00–18:30; closed Weds., and third Thurs. each month

• MAP 220

232

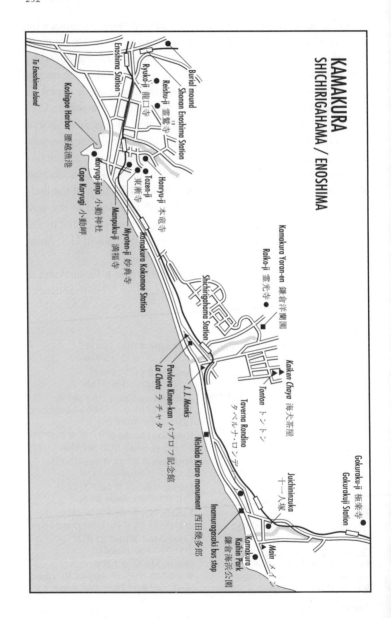

KAMAKURA
SHICHIRIGAHAMA / ENOSHIMA

To Enoshima Island

Enoshima Station

Bunzi mound

Shonan Enoshima Station

Reishu-ji 霊鷲寺

Ryuko-ji 龍口寺

Koshigoe Harbor 腰越漁港

Koryugi-jinja 小動神社
Cape Koryugi 小動岬

Manpuku-ji 満福寺

Myoten-ji 妙典寺

Honryu-ji 本竜寺

Tozen-ji 東漸寺

Komakure Kokomae Station

Raiko-ji 霊光寺

Kamakura Yoran-en 鎌倉洋蘭園

Shichirigahama Station

Pavlova Kinen-kan パブロワ記念館
La Chata ラ・チャタ

J.J. Monks

Nishida Kitaro monument 西田幾多郎

Taverna Rondino タベルナ・ロンディーノ

Tonton トントン

Kaiken Chaya 海尖茶屋

Inamuragasaki bus stop

Juichininzuka 十一人塚

Kamakura Kaihin Park 鎌倉海浜公園

Main メ

Gokuraku-ji 極楽寺
Gokurokuji Station

Surf Bunnies and Mongol Heads

○ Gokurakuji Station 極楽寺駅 (Enoden Line)—Inamuragasaki 稲村が崎 —Cape Koryugi 小動岬—Ryuko-ji 龍口寺—Enoshima Station 江ノ島駅 (Enoden Line)

We start this walk with a ride from Kamakura Station on the Enoden Line (Enoshima Kanko Densha), one of the oldest railways in Japan. If you are arriving by the Yokosuka Line, take the west exit and turn left to find the entrance to the Enoden station. The line was first opened in 1902, although it was not completed until 1910. The cling-clang, ding-dong, cute olive-green and cream cars with their wooden floors are worth a trip in their own right. Actually, an Enoden train might easily be mistaken for a trolley; they average a mere eighteen kilometers per hour, crunch to a halt at traffic lights, run down the middle of the road at some points, and generally maintain an admirable insouciance. You come so close to houses at times that you can check out what the residents are having for breakfast. There are fifteen stations on the ten-kilometer route and it takes approximately thirty-five minutes to go from one terminus to the other. One railroad rule captures the ambiance of the Enoden: surfboards are not allowed aboard during rush hours.

For this walk, we're only going as far as Gokurakuji, the fourth station from Kamakura. Just before you reach it, you zip through a long tunnel between Hase and Gokurakuji. From Gokurakuji Station (opposite is Gokuraku-ji Temple, see page 230), turn right and go down the narrow road. You'll cross a small river, go up a slope, and pass a monument to Nichiren on the right. Inamuragasaki Station is to the right, but keep going straight. On the left is the Juichininzuka (Eleven Heroes Monument),

• MAP 232

which marks the grave of a pro-emperor general and ten of his followers who fought to the end during the battle for the pass near here in 1333.

Next you emerge onto the coast highway. To the left is Inamura-gasaki, the cape forever linked to the legend of how Nitta Yoshisada forced his entrance into Kamakura during the battle and thus was able to wipe out the defending shogunate forces. A park and monuments mark the spot today. Gokurakuji Slope is also where, according to legend, in December 1199 apparitions of Emperor Antoku and several other of Yoritomo's victims appeared to torment the shogun, before he fell from his horse and was carried to what turned out to be his deathbed.

A statue of two young boys commemorates a tragedy that occurred on January 23, 1910, when an excursion boat carrying students from a Zushi junior high school was caught in a heavy storm and twelve were swept out to sea. There is a famous song about the incident, and the memorial here was only erected in 1964, which shows how strong the memory of the incident is in the area. Also here is a large cave that looks like it may have been used for storing ammunition during World War II.

The Lucky Sword

Unlike Kyoto, the shogunate capital was truly a fortress, comparable to those of medieval Europe. All seven passes into Kamakura were formidably fortified with checkpoints, steep embankments, and emplacements for shooting down arrows at the enemy. At first Nitta tried to break through along the Kamakura-kaido, but he was repulsed. So he shifted the main focus of his attack to this area. Although today the cliff drops sheer into the sea, at that time there was apparently a stretch of sand that appeared off the point during low tide, across which the Hojo defenders erected a huge timber barrier. They also had hundreds of small boats offshore with archers in them. During the battle many of the attackers and the Hojo defenders chanted the *nembutsu* as they went to their deaths to ensure their rebirth into the Western Paradise, encouraged by priests who had gathered on the sidelines. However, Nitta's preliminary attacks with twenty thousand horsemen were futile. So the loyalist commander in chief threw a gold sword over the cliff into the ocean while praying to the dragon god of the sea for his assistance. Thereupon, so the story in the *Taiheiki* goes, the sea retreated over a mile and sixty thousand of Nitta's horsemen were able to outflank the shocked Hojo defenders and "fall upon their prey."

Although this story certainly appears apocryphal, it is interesting to note that the earlier *Azuma Kagami*, the official history of the Hojo, reports that in 1216 the tide in the area suddenly receded so far that the island of Enoshima was linked to the mainland by a wide causeway. So maybe, just maybe ...

• MAP 232

Across the highway is Main, a chic European-style restaurant with an attractive black and cream exterior and a sign promising "Outrageously Great Food and Drink." There are several interesting restaurants or drinking spots along this stretch of coast as you head away from Gokurakuji-zaka toward Shichirigahama and Enoshima in the distance. Try Rondino near the Inamuragasaki bus stop if you feel like Italian food.

Inamuragasaki and Shichirigahama ("Seven Ri Coast"), the four-kilometer stretch of coast to Cape Koryugi, are at the heart of surf country. Although even "gremmies" from California or Hawaii might mock the size of the boomers here, you take what you can get in life.

Back in the Kamakura period the coast was known for the high iron content of its sand, which was used in making the steel from which Masamune fashioned his famous swords. Nowadays the name Inamuragasaki conjurs up in young minds images of sun, surf, and sand, music by the Southern All Stars, and the movie *Inamura Jane*. Windsurfers can be observed offshore in all seasons, but in summer the really big crowds come out. When it comes to water sports, this coast has it all— surfing, yachting, motor boating, windsurfing—the works. You'll find several snack bars or coffee shops along the highway, such as J. J. Monks, where you can enjoy a quiet drink above the water.

On the ocean side of the highway you will see an oddly shaped statue that looks like an egg-shaped head, perfectly appropriate in this case since it is in honor of the famous twentieth-century philosopher Nishida Kitaro. Nishida started out specializing in German philosophy before developing his own unique philosophy. He lived in this area for some time. On the other side of the road is a sign for a clothes shop that reads, "Sea Dog for the Beach Bum." Strange juxtapositioning, indeed.

Just about this point, the Enoden pops out next to the highway. At the big intersection turn right and on the left you'll see Shichirigahama Station, where there's a map out front and an eatery with a genuinely X-rated name. Carry on up the road; when you reach the bridge over the river, go to the left, not up the slope. You'll now be in a small valley; a bit farther to the right is Kamakura Yoran-en, a nursery where orchids have been raised since 1963. Potted orchids are for sale, and the proprietors also give hints on how to raise the flowers. Watch out you don't

• MAP 232

get knocked over by the heavenly scent, however. Toward the right is a shopping area with several interesting restaurants, including Sangosho (Coral Reef), a hangout for local surfers known for its tropical drinks and large portions, Kaiken Chaya (Sea Dog Tea House), which serves unusual *donburi* combinations, and Tonton, with monstrous Wiener schnitzel swamped in curry sauce.

Next, you'll see a stone marker and what from this distance is a distinctly unsettling statue of Nichiren up on the hillside. Follow the road up and you'll find Reiko-ji, another Nichiren temple. Nichiren spirited up some rain clouds near here, and some drought-fatigued locals built the temple out of gratitude. Climb up the mountain path and you can see the bronze statue of the rainmaker at work; it is not nearly as intimidating close up as it is from below. The precincts of Reiko-ji are rather interesting, with stones representing wind and sea deities and a "wet" Buddha that can be rubbed down with a scrub brush for good luck.

It is possible to keep going up the road that took you to Reiko-ji into a rather exclusive neighborhood, before swinging back down to the coast near Kamakura Koko-mae Station on the Enoden. However, for this walk we are going to go back to Shichirigahama Station. On the main road not far from the station in the direction toward Enoshima is the Kamakura Pavlova Kinen-kan, the spot where Japanese ballet got its start thanks to the efforts of Eliana Pavlova, a Russian emigrée ballerina of great talent and aristocratic background who became a nationalized Japanese after fleeing the Bolshevik revolution. She died at the age of thirty-nine in China in 1941 from typhoid, her beautiful features reportedly cruelly distorted by the awful disease. Her body was buried at the Foreigners' Cemetery in Yokohama. Her sister, who died at the age of eighty-two in 1982, carried on the mission to spread their art. In the museum are photos, posters, and clothing related to the "mother of Japanese ballet," illustrating what Japanese ballet was like in its early days. Afterwards try out La Chata, the Mexican restaurant and bar next door. Look for the Mexican flag. It also has take-out box lunches.

Continue on the main road and you'll soon approach Cape Koryugi, which sits on one flank of Shonan Harbor. According to local legend there used to be a pine here that gave off sounds like those of a *koto*

• MAP 232

even when there wasn't any wind. The roots of Koryugi-jinja, the protective shrine for this area, are very ancient, but it was supposedly reestablished by Nitta Yoshisada. Among the divinities enshrined here are Susanoo no Mikoto, the troublesome brother of Amaterasu Omikami, the sun goddess. It stages sizable festivals on January 16 and July 7–14. Notice the huge stone shaped like a turtle. To the right of Koryugi-jinja is the small fishing port of Koshigoe, which you enter over a small bridge. You can usually find people fishing off the rocks, and the professional fishermen in the neighborhood are a truly friendly bunch. "Come on out and live around here with us," one of them invited me.

From Koryugi-jinja cross the main road and head straight up the road to Manpuku-ji Temple, easy to identify by its large red sign. The only problem is that the traffic is usually so heavy that it is easier to go to the crosswalk to the right, cross there, and then follow the street up. Manpuku-ji is a very ancient Shingon institution, by tradition founded by Gyoki in 744. But it is most famous for its connection with Yoshitsune.

It was here that the famous warrior and tragic hero was refused entrance into Kamakura in 1185 by his half-brother Yoritomo, when he returned from western Japan after the defeat of the Taira. No doubt he was expecting a handsome welcome. Instead he was met with an order not to enter the city. The temple preserves the draft of Yoshitsune's famous Koshigoe Appeal, a heartbreaking letter to Yoritomo's sage adviser, Oe Hiromoto, pleading complete loyalty, in which Yoshitsune speaks of "weeping crimson tears." It was also to Manpuku-ji that Yoshitsune's head was brought pickled in saké for identification after he was killed in Hiraizumi in northern Japan in 1189. Yoritomo dispatched Wada Yoshimori and other top retainers to identify it, since for whatever reason he preferred not to perform the gruesome task himself.

Although it is small, Manpuku-ji has several things worth seeing, including an intricately carved Kamakura-bori ceiling depicting flowers of the four seasons, twelve paintings to do with Kobo Daishi, the founder of Shingon, and carved wooden sliding doors.

From Manpuku-ji, turn right at the corner and go along the shopping street to the little street that crosses the Enoden tracks just before Koshigoe Station. You'll now be in a residential area with some small,

• MAP 232

attractive Nichiren temples. Take the second right, then turn right to Myoten-ji. Before that, in to the left is Tozen-ji with a gate known as the Yakuimon. In olden days, people who passed through it would pray for long life, and the prayers were believed to be as effective as medicine.

Go back to the intersection, continue to the right, and you'll reach Honryu-ji. Continue on the same road, turn left at the bridge, and cross over the little river to the main street. Turn right here (the road goes to Kamakurayama, see page 226) and get on the other side of the road. Turn in the little road past the Kamei bus stop and then left again at the T-shaped junction. You'll be walking through a quiet residential neighborhood. Keep on this road, passing a street map and the entrance to Reishu-ji temple on the right, until you come out on the main street where the Enoden cuts in to Enoshima Station across the big road.

On your right will be Ryuko-ji ("Temple of the Mouth of the Dragon"), one of the most famous of all the temples connected with Nichiren. The alternative readings for the first two Chinese characters are Tatsu no Kuchi, the name by which the famous execution site that predated the temple was known. This was where Nichiren was supposed to be executed in 1271.

Nichiren's Close Call

Between the entrance to Ryuko-ji and a small shrine to the left is the spot where, as the story goes, the executioner was just about to bring his sword down on the neck of Nichiren, who was fervently chanting sutras, when lightning struck, literally, breaking his weapon, and no doubt prompting Nichiren to say the Japanese equivalent of "I told you so." Well, a rider was immediately dispatched to tell the bosses back in Kamakura what had happened, when, wouldn't you know it, he ran into a messenger from the regent Tokiyori granting Nichiren a reprieve. The spot where the two supposedly met is known as Yukiai-bashi, or the "Bridge of Meeting."

It is hard to accept the story at face value, and of course belief in such miracles ultimately rests on faith. Nevertheless, it is interesting to note that the controversial priest recounted the episode himself in later days and six of his closest disciples built Ryuko-ji to mark the master's deliverance only a few short years later. Add to that the fact that the tale has come to be accepted as part of popular history, regardless of religious affiliation, and it is hard to deny the possibility that something unusual did happen that day at Tatsu no Kuchi. The famous rock on which Nichiren nonchalantly laid his head is displayed each year on September 12 during the Oeshiki festival, when Nichiren believers flock here from all over the country.

• MAP 232

The most beautiful thing about Ryuko-ji is its pleasantly spacious natural setting on a hillside. (For some reason in Kamakura some of the nicest spots seem to have been execution grounds or the scene of atrocities.) Normally there are far more doves than worshippers in the precincts. A day I visited, a blind man was chanting the Nichiren formula *namu myoho rengekyo* in a booming voice, effusively thanking anyone who put a coin into his cup. It reminded me of famous cathedrals in Manila and Mexico City—somehow rendering alms in such a setting seems more real than dropping a few coins into a box in a convenience store.

The architecture of the temple is unusual in several respects. Right off the bat, you'll find a spectacular white gate with green and red dragons on the ceiling. The main temple hall is quite large and ornate—many Nichiren believers make a hundred circuits of the broad gallery around it in order to earn spiritual merit or do penance. Ryuko-ji's intricately carved five-story pagoda, the only such building in the Kamakura area, sits on a small hill and is quite beautiful. The dungeon where Nichiren was imprisoned while waiting for his final end is also to one side of the surrounding hills. One building that is certain to catch your attention is the pure-white Shariden ("Buddha relic hall") that looks like it was just flown in from Thailand. Among the best times to visit Ryuko-ji are late March, when the cherry blossoms are out, and mid- to late-June, when the hydrangea arrive.

There are several small Nichiren temples near Ryuko-ji, including those we visited after leaving Manpuku-ji. The reason is that eight such temples were erected in a protective ring around Ryuko-ji. One of these is Joryu-ji, where there's an interesting burial mound. First the story. In his *Rissho Ankokuron* of 1260, Nichiren lambasted the shogunate for misrule and its relaxed attitude toward "false religions" that he was convinced would lead to civil strife and foreign invasion.

The Mongols led by Genghis Khan and his immediate successors had already conquered most of the known world, including North China, reaching as far as the Danube Valley in 1241. Traders from still-independent Southern Song kept Kamakura posted of developments, so Nichiren's startling prophecy of doom was hardly a blind shot in the dark.

Starting in 1266 emissaries began arriving in Japan from Kublai, the

• MAP 232

Great Khan, demanding that Japan send tribute and acknowledge Mongol suzerainty in return for peace. When the message reached Kamakura in 1268, there was a newly installed Hojo regent, Tokimune, who was a mere eighteen years old. Nevertheless, there was no sign of faltering. Rather there was outrage at the Kublai's insulting tone, and defense preparations were immediately begun in Kyushu and offshore islands.

During the first invasion of 1274 the samurai were clearly getting the worst of it at the hands of the Mongol forces, which employed coordinated mass cavalry tactics and explosive missiles. The evening of the initial landing, however, a huge storm arrived to save the situation, and the Mongol forces returned to Korea.

In 1275 and 1279 new groups of envoys arrived with the Khan's order to "stop all useless resistance." They were beheaded at Tatsu no Kuchi or Katase Beach and their heads pilloried at the water's edge as a warning to the world conquerors. The second invasion in summer 1281 was undoubtedly the largest naval invasion in history prior to modern times, involving close to 150,000 Mongol, Chinese, and Korean invaders. This time, however, the Japanese were better prepared and held their own for nearly two months before another *kamikaze* ("divine wind") arrived to rout the invaders.

To visit the burial mound for the unfortunate Mongol emissaries, continue along the main road in front of Ryuko-ji to the second corner, turn right (on the right is Shonan Enoshima Station on the Shonan Monorail Line, which goes to Ofuna), and continue past the post office. The monument is on the right near the next corner.

Kamakura Pavlova Kinen-kan Museum 鎌倉パブロバ記念館 ☎ no tel. ⏲ 10:00–16:00; open all year. ¥200

Main メイン ☎ 0467-24-0213 ⏲ 11:00–22:00; Sat. 11:00–22:30; open all year
Rondino ロンディーノ ☎ 0467-25-4355 ⏲ 11:30–22:30; 2F 14:00–17:00; open all year

La Chata ラ チャタ ☎ 0467-25-1659 ⏲ 11:30–24:00; open all year
Sangosho 珊瑚礁 ☎ 0467-31-5500 ⏲ 11:30–22:00; closed Mon.
Kaiken Chaya 海犬茶屋 ☎ 0467-31-9052 ⏲ 11:30–22:00; closed Tues.
Tonton トントン ☎ 0467-32-3669 ⏲ 11:00–21:00; closed Tues.

• MAP 232

8

The Magic Island

⟳ Enoshima Station 江ノ島駅 (Enoden Line)—Yacht Harbor 江の島ヨットハーバー—
Hetsunomiya 辺津宮—Nakatsunomiya 中津宮—Okutsunomiya 奥津宮—Enoshima Iwaya
Caves 江の島岩屋—Kugenuma Kaigan Station 鵠沼海岸駅 (Odakyu Line)

Assuming that you're coming from Tokyo or Yokohama stations, the
easiest way to get to the starting point for this walk is to go to Fujisawa
Station on the Tokaido Line and then transfer to the Enoden Line. The
station is across from the south exit. Enoshima Station is the fifth station
en route to Kamakura. If you're coming from western Tokyo, it's easier
to take the Odakyu Line to Katase Enoshima Station; it takes about sev-
enty-five minutes. (Make sure you don't get on the train for Hakone,
Yumoto, or Odawara, or you'll have to buy a different guidebook.)

Katase Enoshima Station, which incidentally is designed to look
like the Dragon King's Palace, is right across from the causeway leading to the readily visible magic island of Enoshima. It is only slightly
more complicated to get there from the Enoden Enoshima Station. A
shop-lined road covers the distance.

The Enoshima experience is fun, especially if it is your first time
and you can avoid the high season. Be warned: the day after the summer swimming season officially begins, the 180,000-square-meter
beautiful wooded island begins to sink visibly from the weight of the
visitors and the garbage they bring.

A six-hundred-meter-long pedestrian bridge, Benten-bashi, takes you
out to the isle of the gods. (Motor vehicles have their own bridge, so you
don't have to worry about becoming shark bait.) Enoshima is really

• MAP 242

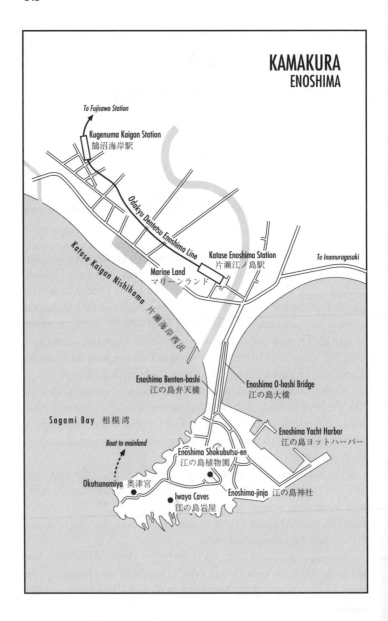

KAMAKURA
ENOSHIMA

To Fujisawa Station

Kugenuma Kaigan Station
鵠沼海岸駅

Odakyu Dentetsu Enoshima Line

Katase Enoshima Station
片瀬江ノ島駅

To Inamuragasaki

Marine Land
マリーンランド

Katase Kaigan Nishihama 片瀬海岸西浜

Enoshima Benten-bashi
江の島弁天橋

Enoshima O-hashi Bridge
江の島大橋

Sagami Bay 相模湾

Enoshima Yacht Harbor
江の島ヨットハーバー

Boat to mainland

Enoshima Shokubutsu-en
江の島植物園

Okutsunomiya 奥津宮

Enoshima-jinja 江の島神社

Iwaya Caves
江の島岩屋

only an island during high tide; at other times a giant sandbar with a thin film of water appears. Perhaps at first it was just another cape, but at some point in prehistory it became a mystic island, floating tantalizingly offshore, clearly a home to gods, fairies, and other supernatural beings.

You reach dry land near a public restroom. The main road to Enoshima Shrine and other delights is straight ahead and is lined with souvenir shops and inns. If you have time to kill, you might first want to explore the third of the island off to the left, an area developed for the 1964 Tokyo Olympics, when the yachting events were held here. It includes the docks of Shonan Harbor, from which ferries regularly depart for Oshima Island—the voyage takes about two and a half hours—Enoshima Yacht Harbor, where you can rent anything from a dinghy to a cruiser, an Olympic memorial fountain, and several souvenir shops selling all manner of geegaws.

Now for the main route. The road going up toward the main shrines is lined with restaurants and shops offering dried seafood treats, as well as places to stay. Marudai Sensui, which has fresh seafood, has been operating here for a century and a half and now has a fourth-generation owner. Because of its direct connection with seafood wholesalers, it gets the best. The storage tanks for the fish are right underneath the restaurant. The restaurant is located near the entrance to the road.

Another renowned local treat, the Enoshima *meoto manju*, a sweet bun, is tied to the story of how the Dragon King and a celestial nymph ended up tying the knot in a plot very similar to that of Beauty and the Beast.

On the left, set off the street about two-thirds of the way up to the first shrine, you'll find a unique musuem, the Enoshima Quilt Bijutsukan, which claims to be the only museum in Japan featuring quilted works. A labor of love on the part of its owner, it opened in June 1992. The quality of the workmanship is amazing.

Accounts by foreigners who visited here not long before the Meiji Restoration confirm that even then this street was packed with worshippers and sightseers. In his journal Francis Hall noted, "It is called the 'island of temples' and is one of the most noted resorts of pilgrims in the empire." At that time apparently there were three Buddhist

• MAP 242

temples and three Shinto shrines, each dedicated to a different female Shinto deity—ancient, unpretentious structures linked by picturesque paths and level outcroppings with fantastic views.

Actually, Enoshima is home to several shrines, many of them tucked away in little corners. Up until the Meiji Restoration Enoshima belonged to the esoteric Shingon sect, and over the years some of Japanese Buddhism's most illustrious leaders are said to have made visits here, including Nichiren and Ippen Shonin. However, the temples were destroyed during the Buddhism-suppression campaign and now it has a distinctly Shinto air to it. Admittedly there always was a Shinto presence here—the shogunate founded Enoshima Myo-jin to pray for rain.

Soon you reach a red *torii* and a steep staircase beyond, the first of many, that leads into the shrine complex. As you trudge upward, your straining tendons and nerves are soothed by the ancient sacred music that floats out from hidden loudspeakers. There are also escalators for those who are not concerned about making a poor spiritual and physical impression before the gods.

A big sign offers exorcism services, especially for men or women who are in their most dangerous years.

The Lucky Stones of Enoshima

Check out the *fukuishi* 福石 good luck stone at Enoshima-jinja. Look carefully round about the stone—according to a local legend, if you find something near here, then you'll be in for a spot of good luck.

Connected with the stone is the story of Sugiyama Kengyo, who developed an innovative system of acupuncture during the Edo period, although the Chinese art had originally been introduced from Korea during the sixth century. With these new techniques he successfully treated the "dog shogun" Tsunayoshi, thereby gaining great fame.

According to the legend, Sugiyama was a blind man who achieved enlightenment of sorts when he came here to pray and fast on Enoshima.

In one version of the story, Sugiyama stumbled into the stone, knocking himself flat but temporarily restoring his sight. There in front of his eyes was a sharp needle pointing at him. Another, more mundane version has him simply being pricked by a pine needle, presumably in the right place, which set him on the road to success.

An interesting wavy rock on the opposite side is known as the Gama-ishi or "toad stone." Supposedly it was named by a famous priest whose meditations were disturbed by its amphibian presence. According to one source it was brought back from China for the shogun Sanetomo.

• MAP 242

The roots of today's shrines go back to 1182, when a temple was built by the famous priest Mongaku at the request of his friend, Yoritomo. The temple was used to pray for the success of the latter's expedition against Fujiwara Hidehira in the far north that confirmed the power of the Minamoto. Two years earlier Mongaku and Yoritomo had come here for three weeks of prayer, fasting, and mystical rites in honor of Benzaiten (Benten), the goddess of beauty, music, and the arts.

The first of the three major shrines is Hetsunomiya, which is on the left at the top of the first flight of stairs. The little red and white Chinese-style treasure hall, the Benten-do, a bit farther up the hill path should not be missed even though there is a small fee. It houses three of the most famous representations of Benzaiten to be found in all Japan.

The second of the big shrines, Nakatsunomiya, located around the bend, has been sanctified over the centuries by countless pilgrims, some of whose requests to the gods were obviously of quite a material sort. The stone lanterns and memorials contributed by Edo brothel keepers, timber wholesalers, and kabuki theater owners are proof positive of this fact. They also contributed to the construction of the huge bronze *torii* at the entrance, originally built in 1747 and reconstructed in 1821.

Benzaiten

According to legend, in 552 the Katase Coast was shaken by a series of major earthquakes, culminating with the emergence of Enoshima from the deep. At the same time Benzaiten descended from the heavens amid radiant clouds to deal with a nasty poisonous dragon that resided in an underwater cavern.

The oldest of the Benten trio in the Benten-do is said to be over 1,400 years old. Next to it is the eight-armed, eighth-century Happi Benten, carved from cypress. Finally, there is the well-known Hadaka ("Naked") Benten, a mere stripling at six hundred years. Incidentally, the statue is said to accurately reproduce exterior female genitalia. You may see kabuki actors praying to the Benten, because she is particularly revered by people connected with the entertainment world.

Benzaiten was not a Japanese deity to begin with. However, after her introduction from India, she became one of the Shichi Fukujin, or Seven Lucky Gods, who have become the object of great popular worship among the Japanese and who are believed to bring a treasure ship of good fortune at New Year. The magnificent seven and the goodies that they are especially equipped to aid people with are: Hotei (happiness), Benzaiten (arts), Jurojin (health), Ebisu (prosperity in business, safety and prosperity for one's family), Bishamonten (wealth, recovery from disease), Fukurokuju (long life), and Daikokuten (success, wealth).

• MAP 242

As you walk along the path from Nakatsunomiya to Okutsu-nomiya—the last of the three major shrines—you will first reach a curve where there are some restaurants with fine views over the yacht harbor, before reaching the Enoshima Botanical Garden, where you can see more than 300 species of tropical plants. There are also 230 varieties of camellia on the island that brighten up the winter scene.

The arboretum was established by Samuel Cocking, a strong-willed Irish merchant who arrived in Japan with his family in 1869. He spent huge sums from 1882 to build hothouses here to grow coconut trees and other kinds of tropical and semi-tropical plant life. Among other things, Cocking was also known for his extensive art collection and his habit of energetically cycling up and down the coast.

For those who find the escalators too demanding (and you would be surprised how many youngsters pay to ride them), there are little go-karts to whisk you around what might well be called Cocking's foliage.

Here, too, is an observation tower-cum-lighthouse. From the top, you get an excellent view of Fuji-san and the smoke-spewing volcano on Oshima Island when the weather gods are cooperating.

A bit further on is Okutsunomiya, whose *torii* is said to have been dedicated by Yoritomo himself in 1882. Another name for the Benten temple here was Kinkisan, or "Hill of the Golden Tortoise." According to legend, a giant turtle inhabited the cave below, known as the "Golden Cave." The point of all this turtle talk is the strange, slightly unsettling image of a turtle painted above the main gate of the shrine in 1803 by Sakai Hoichi. (You have to look carefully to make it out.) The eyes of the turtle appear to be looking in every direction simultaneously.

The big news as far as Enoshima is concerned is that the famous Enoshima Iwaya caves were once again opened to the public in the spring of 1993. For twenty-two years these caves were off limits because of the danger of falling rocks. Erosion by waves cut these natural wonders, which were traditionally believed to be the lair of the dragon god Ryujin, the deity believed responsible for bringing rain.

To get to the caves go down the slope from Okutsunomiya to the Chigogafuchi coast where waves have carved exotic cliffs, some fifty to seventy feet high, and a "stone garden" in the ocean for shellfish

• MAP 242

hunters, fishermen, and other visitors to frolic in. In one spot all is tranquil, while just around the next precipice wild waves boil and surge in a chasm. After clambering over rocky staircases for a few minutes, you'll reach the entrance to Benten Cave, alias Dragon Cave. The nude Benten we ogled earlier at the Benten-do was once kept in a dark recess here, and she must have seemed like an apparition of beauty when viewed by flickering candlelight by the faithful.

The goddess was relocated because of serious landslides and it was predicted that the cave would never be opened again. But it has been opened and in style. What you have is an underground magical mystery tour of the 152-meter-long cavern complete with eerie music and lightning. You stoop and shuffle along the increasingly narrow passages to a shrine in the very tip of the dragon's tail where, according to tradition, a special image of Dainichi Nyorai, the personification of the ultimate reality of the universe, has been stored. The phosphorescent rocks, pure, cold water dripping from crevices and echoing weirdly in the vault, the ancient statues, including those of cobras, the breeze blowing from the tunnel... It all adds up to a pop mystical experience.

Fatal Obsession

Just as mysterious as the atmosphere in the caves is the tragic legend associated with Chigogafuchi, which means "Maiden's Pool." Specifically, it refers to a deep whirlpool nearby, where waves break over sharp rocks and splatter spray and foam in all directions like blue-white dragon's blood. Centuries ago a devout Zen priest by the name of Jikiu came here from the great temple of Kencho-ji in Kamakura for a hundred days of special prayer and austerities in honor of the local goddesses.

However, it was his karma to meet a young acolyte maiden by the name of Shiragiku, or "White Chrysanthemum." He immediately became consumed by hopeless passion and sought to seduce her, but to no avail. The powerful wave of his lust would not subside, however, and the poor girl ran to this pool and threw herself in. The distraught priest continued to pursue her even to the dragon's lair below the waves.

This incident may be the origin of the famous injunction: Under no circumstances take a date to Enoshima or you will be sure to arouse the jealous wrath of the goddesses. In fact, there is a common local saying, "Lovers who go together to Enoshima are certain to separate."

However, the Chinese characters read as "*chigo*" can refer to a page, especially a catamite, so perhaps there is more to this bizarre story than first meets the eye.

• MAP 242

There's another dragon cave a hundred meters to the east, but a visit is not particularly recommended. All you'll find is a hokey electronic dragon that roars and tries to scare you without much effect.

Incidentally, there is a famous legend about a man by the name of Nitan no Shiro, who entered a cave on the west side of Fuji-san and strolled all the way here. Few details are provided, so it's not certain how long his ancient version of the power hike took. No doubt he was ready for a fish fry when he finally emerged into the sunlight.

Back below, where the path from the Okutsunomiya turns toward the dragon caves, there is a cutoff leading to a boat landing where you can catch a launch back to the mainland. Boats leave about every fifteen minutes. One day when I grabbed a ride on one, I got an interesting lesson on the current state of ecological awareness in Japan. As we puttered along, one of the crewmen, whom I assumed was a local fishermen, saw that a customer had left a large soft drink cup on a seat. He nonchalantly tossed it into the sea. For a second I tensed, afraid that one of the subterranean dragons would toss us into the brine in retribution.

After disembarking, straight and to the left across the Katase-gawa River is Katase Enoshima Station. If you're ready to chow down, there are a couple of interesting choices, including a branch of Tony Roma's.

From Benten-bashi, turn left at the main highway and cross the big bridge, Katase-bashi; on your left you'll see Enoshima Marineland. Although over thirty-five years old, this whale museum and dolphin pool is still worth a visit, especially if you have young children. There are six to seven shows a day, depending on the season. The good thing is that you get to see the animals close up. The spunky dolphins do their best to kiss the sky.

On the opposite side of the highway is the two-story Enoshima Aquarium, which has 350 species including giant sea turtles and can be reached by an underground passage from Marineland. The Jellyfish Fantasy Hall is especially interesting. Further down on the Marineland side is the Enoshima Umi no Dobutsuen, or "Sea Zoo." Here you can see sea-lion shows, penguins, pelicans, and sea otters.

Across the main highway is the popular Kugenuma Beach section of the Shonan Coast. This stretch of beach now styles itself rather

• MAP 242

grandly as the "Miami Beach of the Orient." In the old days, the area was famed for its pine trees; recent extensive relandscaping has restored something of its former appearance.

As a matter of fact, even back during the somber Kamakura period, the Katase/Kugenuma area could get rather lively at times. For one thing, it had its own version of today's beachbums, "undesirables" whom the shogunate would not allow into Kamakura. One of these was the famous dancing *nembutsu* priest Ippen Shonin, who came out here for a few weeks of surfside action after being refused entry to the shogun's capital.

Along the highway there are many chain restaurants in various price ranges, including the Enoshima McDonald's with a huge sign reading "5,000 in the World," meaning of course that it was the 5,000th outlet to be opened. Perhaps you will feel like stopping to celebrate. If you're not the type to go with the madding crowd, try Nude Man Steak & Bar.

Ippen Shonin

The "new religion" of the Kamakura period that won the most converts was probably Ippen's peripatetic Jishu sect. Personally he was a fascinating individualist who bears comparison to St. Francis of Assisi. Born the second son of a local magnate in Kyushu in 1239, Ippen lost his mother at the age of ten and shortly thereafter was thrown out of the house by his father. He then began making the rounds of local temples, undergoing ascetic training and studying Jodo and various other teachings.

Ippen came to the radical conclusion that the only way of obtaining salvation was to repeat the *nembutsu* sutra and that it did not matter the least whether the person doing so was pure or not, or believed in Amida Buddha and the formula. He then set out on sixteen years of wandering across the face of Japan from Kyushu to Tohoku, spreading this message. His mass revival "parties" that included ecstatic dancing with people of both sexes attracted thousands of spectators and spawned the expression "dancing *nembutsu*."

When they turned him back at Kobukuro-zaka in 1282, officials told Ippen that the shogun was planning to pass by that way. Ippen refused to move, even after the samurai threatened to beat him, answering that he was prepared to die on the spot. Next, they told him he could go anywhere he liked as long as it wasn't the shogun's city. In reply he staged an all-night *nembutsu* session on the dangerous mountain path. Then he moved the throngs of people down to the beach at Katase for several days of serious dancing and spiritual partying amidst the huts of the beggars who lived down there. Ippen and his followers seem to have been the Hare Krishnas of their day. Then, just as suddenly as they had come, they simply packed up and headed off to the west, perhaps in search of the Western Paradise, no doubt much to the relief of the shogunate.

• MAP 242

After about a thirty-minute walk, you'll reach an estuary where a little river disgorges into the sea. Near an entrance to Shonan Kaigan Park you'll see a memorial to the Chinese playwright and poet Nie Er, composer of China's national anthem, who drowned near here in July 1935.

Cross over to the other side of the highway and head back toward Enoshima. Turn left into the first road; Kugenuma Kaigan Station on the Odakyu Line is five or ten minutes away down a quiet residential road.

🏛

Enoshima Quilt Bijutsukan Museum 江の島キルト美術館 ☎ 0467-24-0260 ⏱ 11:00–16:00; closed weekends, hols. and Aug.

Enoshima Botanical Garden (Enoshima Shokubutsu-en 江の島植物園) ☎ 0466-22-0209 ⏱ 9:00–17:00; open all year. ¥200

Iwaya Caves 江の島岩屋 ☎ 0467-26-3899 ⏱ 9:00–16:00; Jul.–Aug. 9:00–17:00; summer weekends 9:00–18:00; closed in bad weather

Enoshima Aquarium (Enoshima Suizo-kan 江の島水族館) including Enoshima Marineland and Umi no Dobutsu-en ☎ 0466-22-8111 ⏱ 9:00–17:30; Nov.–March 20 9:00–17:00; open all year. ¥1,700 (entrance to all included)

Yugyo-ji Temple 遊行寺
For those with special interest in Ippen Shonin, I recommend a visit to Yugyo-ji, also known as Shojoko-ji ("Temple of Clear Light"), about a kilometer northeast of Fujisawa Station. This is the base for Ippen's Jishu sect. It is sometimes referred to as the "Temple of Wanderers" because from here itinerant priests are sent out all over the country to attend to the physical and spiritual needs of the unfortunate. By tradition they are said to be endowed with special healing powers. In fact, one of the reasons why the authorities looked upon Ippen with a jaundiced eye was that large numbers of lepers and others afflicted with contagious diseases followed in his wake. His followers also dropped like flies from the rigors of the travel. Being a fan of Ippen was no picnic.

Yugyo-ji, originally founded in 1325, has burned down and been rebuilt on several occasions, most recently in 1880. Climb up the forty-eight steps on Iroha Slope to reach the large precincts. The gargantuan gingko tree will undoubtedly be the first thing to catch your attention. Notice the imposing main hall, the belfry, which houses a bell cast way back in 1356, and a stone monument just inside the back gate that was erected in 1418 to commemorate the souls of the people and animals that died in a civil war of 1416–17.

Probably the best time to visit this unusual temple, which has several important cultural assets and buildings, is on the night of November 27, when a fire festival known as the Extinguish the Lamp Festival is staged. It is very lively, and part of a huge *nembutsu* get-together held annually November 21–28. I'm sure Ippen is there in spirit.

◐ Bus from Fujisawa Station (Tokaido, Odakyu, Enoshima lines) or Fujisawa Honmachi Station (Odakyu Line). Treasure House seldom open, but some treasures displayed on Sun. and hols.

Sensui 仙水 ☎ 0466-26-4701 ⏱ 11:00–20:00; closed Tues.

• MAP 242

9

Love—Lost and Stolen

○ Kamakura Station 鎌倉駅 (JR Yokosuka Line)—Enmei-ji 延命寺—Moto Hachiman-gu 元八幡官—Gosho-jinja 五所神社—Kuhon-ji 九品寺—Komyo-ji 光明寺—Zushi Marina 逗子マリーナ—Hiroyama Park 披露山公園—Zushi Station 逗子駅 (JR Yokosuka Line)

This walk offers variety: a downtown commercial district, a beach and Japan's oldest artificial port, one of the largest and most important temples in Kamakura, the site of an old castle, a snazzy marina, a fishing port, a forested mountain, and a stroll through the heart of the neighboring community of Zushi. Try it in summer. That way you can rest your weary parts en route by taking a dip in the ocean.

From the east entrance of Kamakura Station, cross to the opposite side of Wakamiyaoji-dori, and turn right. As you head toward the first *torii*, you'll pass Geba Yotsukado, where riders were required to dismount.

We are going to stop at several small temples. What they lack in size and appeal, they make up for with age. Several were established more than seven hundred years ago. And we all know about age before beauty. However, the first stop, Enmei-ji, to the left across the river, is both old and appealing. The only claim to fame for this unpretentious temple is the fact that it is home to the Hadaka Jizo (Naked Jizo).

According to an ancient chronicle, a nobleman and a lady were playing the board game *sugoroku*. They got a bit bored with the pace of the action and so struck a deal to spice up the proceedings. The loser of the game would have to strip to the buff and climb up on the board. Luck was not a lady that night.

The lovely loser prayed ardently to the merciful *jizo* for emergency

• MAP 252

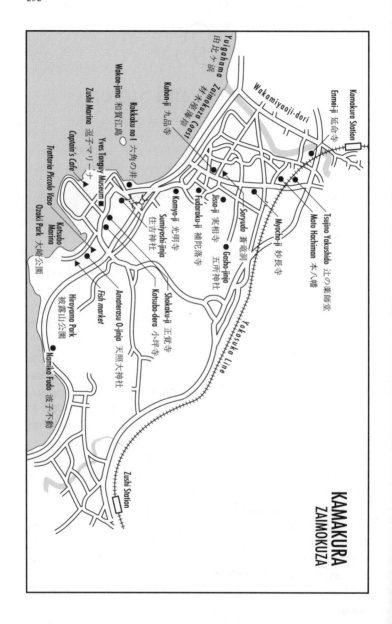

KAMAKURA
ZAIMOKUZA

Zushi Station 逗子駅

Namiko Fudo 波子不動

Ozaki Park 大崎公園

Hiroyama Park 披露山公園

Fish market

Kotsubo Marina

Amaterasu O-jinja 天照大神社

Kotsubo-dera 小坪寺

Shokaku-ji 正覚寺

Sumiyoshi-jinja 住吉神社

Kotsubo-dera

Komyo-ji 光明寺

Gosho-jinja 五所神社

Soryudo 蒼竜洞

Fudaraku-ji 補陀落寺

Jisso-ji 実相寺

Myocho-ji 妙長寺

Moto Hachiman 本八幡

Tsujino Yakushido 辻の薬師堂

Captain's Cafe

Trattoria Piccolo Vaso

Zushi Marina 逗子マリーナ

Yves Tanguy Museum

Rokkaku no I 六角の井

Wakae-jima 和賀江島

Kuhon-ji 九品寺

Zaimokuza Coast 材木座海岸

Emmei-ji 延命寺

Kamakura Station

Yuigahama 由比ヶ浜

Wakamiyaoji-dori

Yokosuka Line

assistance. He came running and helped her keep her side of the bargain by assuming her form and appearing as a vision to the ungentlemanly gambler. It has been suggested that the lady in question may well have been the wife of the regent Hojo Tokiyori, the founder of this temple.

Unfortunately, the statue is seldom shown: normally only on the fourth, fourteenth, and twenty-fourth of each month. If you are looking for something erotically titillating—forget it. The lifesize statue standing on a *sugoroku* board is natural colored and dressed in the robes of a priest. However, the inside scoop is that there is the body of a woman hidden beneath those garments...

Back on the main road, keep walking toward Yuigahama until you get to the next corner in front of the school. Turn left and go straight until you reach a T-shaped intersection. Turn right, take the second left, going to the corner and the Moto Hachiman bus stop. Turn left down the small street and you'll soon reach a small shrine, the Moto Hachiman-gu, that was the forerunner of the huge Tsurugaoka Hachiman-gu.

Although now surrounded by houses, including one on the site where the celebrated author Akutagawa Ryunosuke lived for a couple of years while he was teaching English at a naval college in Yokosuka, the shrine once sat right on the edge of the ocean, and the smell of salt water is still very much in the air. It was founded in August 1063 by Minamoto Yoriyoshi, Yoritomo's father, when he was returning victoriously to Kyoto from Tohoku at the conclusion of the Earlier Nine Years War (1051–62). Come back out to the main street and continue in the same direction until you reach the next big road, then turn left. Walk under the Yokosuka Line tracks to Tsuji no Yakushido; several interesting statues are here: a Heian-period wooden Yakushi Nyorai, a Nikko Bosatsu from the Kamakura period, and twelve guardian deities.

Retrace your steps under the tracks and go straight on what is Zaimokuza's main street. *Zaimoku* means lumber and *za* refers to a system of merchant organizations that were somewhat similar to the guilds of medieval Europe. The *za* specialized in the transport, manufacture, or sale of certain goods such as rice, handicrafts, or, in this case, wood. Such collectives gave the merchants at least a modicum of clout and security in a very unstable age. No doubt there was a

• MAP 252

thriving Chinatown here back in the days when trade with the Song empire was booming. Nichiren temples predominate in Omachi and Zaimokuza: Myocho-ji, for example, founded in 1299 and located past the intersection on the left, was apparently home to Nichiren for a time. A large monument to the fiery bonze has been built there.

At the intersection, turn left and cross to the right side of the road. If you go straight, you'll find Chosho-ji, the big Nichiren temple (see page 200). But we don't want to go that far. At the corner near the coffee shop turn right and head straight. On the left, you will see Raiko-ji. It is easy to spot because, instead of the usual entrance gate, there is a steel arch with a rabbit figure on it. Like so many temples in Kamakura, Raiko-ji started out attached to one sect and ended up with another: in this case the switch was from Shingon to Jishu. Yoritomo built Raiko-ji in 1194 for Miura Yoshiaki, the grandfather of Wada Yoshimori, and others who died for his cause in the grim early days. Yoshiaki's five-tier tomb is here, as is a wooden statue of the old war horse. Can you imagine heading off to battle when you were just about to turn ninety?

In past centuries, this neighborhood used to be full of samurai mansions. At the next corner turn left and head toward Gosho-jinja. This shrine only dates from 1908, when five older shrines on this spot merged into one. A big annual festival is held in June, when three golden *omikoshi* portable shrines, each weighing 750 kilograms, are carried and tossed through the streets and down to the seashore, where they get a rinse in the ocean. The bearers sing special songs as they bounce along on their merry way, including the traditional *kiyari* chants of firemen.

Go back to the crossroads and turn left. On the left is Jisso-ji, a temple connected with the famous story of the revenge of the Soga Brothers. This is where Kudo Suketsune, the villain who took their father's life, had his mansion. At the T-shaped intersection a few blocks farther on, turn right, walk to the main street and turn left. Diagonally across is Kuhon-ji, a Jodo temple founded by Nitta Yoshisada in 1336 for the repose of the souls of those who died in the war. Among the treasures here are three wooden images of Amida and a stone Yakushi Nyorai.

Across from Kuhon-ji is Soryudo, a steak house inside an old Japanese-style house. From Kuhon-ji, cross the street, continue on to

• MAP 252

the next big corner, then turn left. In front of you is the small temple Fudaraku-ji. When founded in 1181, it sprawled on a magnificent scale, but today only a single small building and an adjoining treasure house remain. Yoritomo frequently worshipped here, because its first head priest was his close friend, Mongaku. However, it later fell into decay, perhaps because of a giant waterspout that descended on it, or perhaps because Mongaku was thoroughly discredited after Yoritomo's death. Although tiny, Fudaraku-ji still has several important items in its treasure house, including twenty statues, one portraying Yoritomo in official uniform at the age of forty-two, a Taira banner that by tradition was inscribed by Taira Kiyomori, and a nude statue of Mongaku.

From Fudaraku-ji turn left and then left again at the corner. On the left just after the curve is Komyo-ji (Temple of Shining Light), one of the biggest temples in Kamakura and the only one anywhere near the ocean.

The Two Sides of Mongaku

With his obsession with politics, Mongaku seems to have had a bit of a Cardinal Richelieu complex. Mongaku always had trouble with his strong passions—but before they became political they had been more sensual in nature. Prior to becoming a priest Mongaku was a samurai by the name of Endo Morito, the Morito of Akutagawa Ryunosuke's famous short story *Kesa to Morito* (Kesa and Morito). Mongaku fell madly in love with Kesa, his beautiful cousin, who was married to another samurai. Mongaku pressed her to become his secret lover, but she steadfastly refused until he threatened to kill her mother.

"Murder my husband and I will do anything you desire," Kesa then told him. It seemed she had been possessed by a demon as she told Mongaku exactly where her husband would be sleeping and what he would be wearing. That night Morito crept into the man's quarters and quickly lopped off the head of the sleeping form. Only when he got outside and triumphantly held it up to the moonlight for inspection did he find it was Kesa's.

Morito then went to the husband and told him everything and asked to be killed. The husband refused, and they both withdrew into the religious life. Morito seems to have gained great spiritual insights from this gory incident, but it did not seem to dilute the wild blood coursing through his veins. In 1179, for example, he was banished to Izu for creating a disturbance at the imperial palace in Kyoto when his pride was offended. In Izu he was befriended by a fellow exile, Minamoto Yoritomo. Later, it was Mongaku who first urged Yoritomo to revolt against the imperious Taira. Although his temple was in Zaimokuza, Mongaku lived off the Kanazawa-kaido near Yoritomo's palace and the shogunate offices. He obviously wanted to stay near where the action was. So perhaps his conversion experience was not that deep after all. Mongaku ended his life in exile on desolate Sado Island.

• MAP 252

Komyo-ji is one of the most important Jodo temples in the entire Kanto region. The grounds are as spacious as those of Engaku-ji or Kencho-ji. The temple was officially established by the fourth regent, Hojo Tsunetoki, in 1243. The first head priest was Ryochu (Kishu Zenji), who during his forty years in that position stamped the temple with his personality and laid the foundation for its future success. Later abbots also seem to have had a knack for getting along with power-holders, since Komyo-ji enjoyed considerable support from the imperial family and the Tokugawa shogunate.

The main gate, built in 1533, is claimed as the largest in the Kanto area and is very impressive. The Deva Kings (Gods of the Four Directions) and Shaka Sanzon (Three Saints) here are worth careful examination. Once you pass through the gate, you will see to your right some stone monuments. One of these is dedicated to the souls of dead animals. On one visit I found a cat lounging in front of it, licking his paws. Nearby is a cute Buddha with giant ears. There are two subsidiary temples flanking this main court. Renjo-in on the right may be older than Jomyo-ji itself. Senju-in on the left boasts a Thousand-Armed Kannon.

The mammoth main hall of Komyo-ji contains a golden statue of Amida attributed to Unkei and rated one of his masterpieces. Also kept here is a statue of the artsy goddess Benten, who is believed to hold the key to good fortune. The story goes that a terrible tempest floated the famous Enoshima Benten to the shore near here. It was taken back to its cave, but not long after another storm descended on Kamakura and the same thing happened. The priests finally got the message and had their own Benten statue carved. Apparently the goddess wanted to be in a position to protect both ends of the city's coastline.

There are two famous gardens at Komyo-ji. The garden to the rear of the main building was laid out in the early Edo period by Kobori Enshu, one of the leading masters of landscape gardening and tea ceremony at that time. In July and August it is awash with ruby-red lotuses. The much newer Sanzon Goso no Niwa (Garden of the Three Divinities and Five Founders) on the right of the big hall has a "cold mountain" rock garden, which goes to show that Zen temples do not have a monopoly on this kind of meditation garden. Stored in a large cave to

• MAP 252

the rear is a hoary *jizo* said to have been carved by Kobo Daishi himself.

There are several shrines scattered on the hillside behind the temple. Here you'll also find Tsunetoki's tomb, as well as those of Ryochu and other abbots. The many eulalia (*susuki*) surrounding them add to their elemental beauty. However, what makes a hike up the hill mandatory is the spectacular view. The sharply curved metal roof of the main temple building, painted a peacock hue over many years by the action of the sea breeze, blends in beautifully with the blue of the sea behind.

Komyo-ji is the only temple in Kamakura where you can enjoy *shojin ryori* vegetarian cuisine. The monkish lunch includes treats like sesame tofu (*goma-dofu*), deep-fried vegetables (*shojin age*), and boiled mountain vegetables (*sansai*). You chow down in a fascinating part of the temple normally off-limits to visitors. The meal costs about ¥3,500. Make reservations for two or more people at least a week in advance.

Komyo-ji has also served as a cultural center in many ways. In the postwar period the famous novelist Takami Jun opened a kind of writers' training center here that became known as the Kamakura Academy. However, the big happening of the year at Komyo-ji is the Juya "Ten Nights of Prayer" festival that lasts for four days from October 12. It dates back about five centuries, and traditionally has been regarded as the ultimate plebeian get-together in the Kamakura area. In the old days, families swarmed in by boat. Today, too, you can hardly move for the good-natured crowds. Hundreds of booths selling potted plants, toys, and all kinds of edible goodies pack the temple grounds, and hawkers furiously spout their spiels. You want it, they got it. Fun and games contend with the all-night prayer sessions for attention. Can this really be Buddhism? What about Gautama's teaching that all life is suffering?

Once you come out of Komyo-ji, it only takes a few minutes to walk to the beach, where shellfish gathering has always been a popular activity. The port of Wakae-jima, Japan's first artificial harbor, was located at the eastern end of Zaimokuza Beach. Constructed in the summer of 1232, reportedly in only twenty-six days, the port was dreamed up by a priest called Oamidabutsu, who was concerned with the number of accidents occurring when ships tried to unload off Zaimokuza and Yuigahama. Once the project got going, the shogunate lent its full support.

• MAP 252

Huge rocks were dumped offshore, and a breakwater eight hundred meters long sprang up overnight. This served as the main channel for trade with China until the ports at Nojima and elsewhere were developed and the Asahina Pass opened. Occasionally shards of Chinese pottery and human bones believed to belong to victims of the 1333 fighting are uncovered in the area. When the tide is low, you can wade out to the shoal—all that is left of the once-thriving harbor.

As you maneuver your way around the point, where there used to be little more than sweet-potato fields, you'll find yourself lost in a forest of sailboards. Here and there are eateries with names like Fisherman's Restaurant and the Maui Onion, and in summer music from the Beach Boys blares out from the shops. After about ten minutes you come to an outdoor swimming pool. Take the path up above the tunnel to get to the Rokkaku no I (Six-Sided Well) and the area where Sumiyoshi Castle used to be located. This watering hole is one of the ten famous wells of Kamakura. Legend has it that a famous samurai let loose an arrow from Tensho-yama hill that landed straight into the well. A more farfetched version of the story has him shooting his arrow from distant Hachijo-jima Island, where he had been exiled.

Follow the signs up the path to the right of the pool to a small thatched-roof Jodo temple, Shokaku-ji, which stands on the site of an earlier temple called Goshin-ji that was burned down in 1512 along with neighboring Sumiyoshi Castle, as Hojo Soun's forces waged a scorched-earth campaign against the Miura clan. The remnants that escaped to Arai Castle in the Misaki area were later exterminated. There's not much to be seen in the old castle grounds except for Sumiyoshi Shrine, but be sure to go through the spider-encrusted natural tunnel for the good view from the eagle's-nest perch. Double back past the pool; the road turns as it comes out of the tunnel and leads to the fishing hamlet of Kotsubo. Zushi Marina is on your right, a nautical resort opened in 1971 on reclaimed land. Check out the moderately priced seafood restaurant called Captain's Cafe. On the right as you walk toward Kotsubo is a public library and the Yves Tanguy Museum. Tanguy was a famous surrealist artist, born in Paris in 1900, who incorporated nautical motifs into many of his works. Kotsubo-dera was

• MAP 252

founded in the Meiji period when two Muromachi-era Jodo temples were merged. The small stone Buddhas in front of the main hall are quite appealing. On a clear day you can see as far as the Izu Islands from Amaterasu O-jinja, facing Ozaki Park near the waterfront.

Skirting the local primary school are steps that go up the side of the mountain. At the top you'll find yourself in a Japanese version of Beverly Hills. Turn left and keep veering to the left at each crossroads until you reach the rear entrance to Hiroyama Park. Alternatively, you can follow the pier at Kotsubo to the end and visit Ozaki Park and the nearby shrine to the Dragon King before entering the Hiroyama housing complex and walking up to the park. Hiroyama means "Announcement Hill." The name dates back to the time of Yoritomo, who liked to announce rewards to retainers here. It is a laid-back little park with a nice view of Zushi Marina to the right and the Zushi Coast to the left. Near the parking lot is a monument to Ozaki Yukio (1858–1954), one of the few true liberals in prewar Japan. On the monument is inscribed one of his famous adages: "On life's stage, always be prepared for the future."

The Fishing Hamlet of Kotsubo

The narrow streets of Kotsubo are the kind you would expect to see in a fishing village anywhere from Macao to Portugal. To the left along the hill face are some small temples and shrines worth exploring. They are not famous, but are connected to the simple faith of the fisherfolk who were the only inhabitants around here until the yachtsmen came sailing in two decades ago. During the Kamakura period, the Kotsubo area was known primarily for one thing: scandal. Yoritomo had Kame no Mae, his mistress from his Izu days, ensconced here in a vassal's mansion. Ever-jealous Masako got wind of the arrangement and sent a Hojo subject to burn her out. Once her rival had fled, Masako had the owner of the love nest exiled. Although even the mighty shogun did not have the power to get his confederate released because he was a liegeman of the Hojo, Yoritomo forced the samurai who had done Masako's incendiary bidding to commit *seppuku*. Then he carried on with the young lady just as before. Seems when dragons tussle, only the shrimp suffer.

Kotsubo port specializes in *shirasu*, or young sardines. The fishing boats come in at about 15:00. There is a fish market that is open to the public in the afternoon. You can get superfresh bounty from the deep, but if even that's not fresh enough for you, rent a boat and go fishing for *aji* (horse mackerel) or *saba* (mackerel). Next to the market is an Italian cafe and around the corner a restaurant offering scrumptious *sashimi*. Both are moderately priced.

Trattoria Piccolo Vaso ☎ 0467-24-5858
🕐 11:30–14:00, 17:30–21:00; closed Weds.

• MAP 252

The Namiko Fudo Hiking Course begins near the Ozaki statue, serpentining down a valley filled with evergreens and little brooks. It is dark and cool even on hot summer days. Dragonflies dart in front of you as you work your way down over the slippery rocks. At the bottom you emerge in front of a tumbledown wooden temple painted a flaky red. This is Koyo-ji, famous from time immemorial as an exorcism center and focus of popular worship because of its Fudo statue. Although traditionally known as Namikiri Fudo, it is now usually referred to as Namiko Fudo. This is a case of worship following art.

To understand what I mean, look out into the ocean and you'll see an unusually shaped rock sticking straight out of the water. This has become a memorial to *Hototogisu* (Little cuckoo), a novel by Tokutomi Roka that is one of the most popular love stories in modern Japanese literature. The heroine in this tale of frustrated love set in this area was named Namiko, so the famous statue has come to bear her name. In the story, she and her fiance Takeo visit Koyo-ji. The monument is a popular spot for shell collecting and can be waded out to at low tide.

The one-kilometer Zushi Coast, which lies before you, attracts over one million beachcombers every summer. That represents an awful lot of ice cream. There are cheap but primitive makeshift facilities on the beach where you can shower and beer up or curry down. You'll also stumble upon roadside statues and other relics of the pre-surfing age around here; the old Tokaido highway used to pass nearby.

The Nagisa Brasserie near Zushi Station is a great favorite with locals. To get there, take one of the roads perpendicular to the beach on the other side of the underpass below the coast road.

Yves Tanguy Museum イヴ・タンギー美術館 ☎ 0467-23-2111 (Zushi Marina) ◷ 10:00–16:00; closed Mon.–Weds. ¥1,000

Komyo-ji restaurant 光妙寺 ☎ 0467-22-0603 ◷ Closed Tues., and July, August, and festival days

Captain's Cafe キャプテンズ カフェ ☎ 0467-25-2488 ◷ 10:30–21:30; open all year

Soryudo 蒼竜洞 ☎ 0467-24-2948 ◷ 11:00–14:00, 17:00–23:00; closed Tues.

Nagisa Brasserie ☎ 0468-72-1538 ◷ 11:30–14:00, 17:30–22:00; closed Fri. and 1st Weds. each month

• MAP 252

PART
3
MIURA
PENINSULA

The Miura Peninsula: An Introduction

The Miura Peninsula is a semi-rural wonderland on the doorstep of Tokyo and Yokohama. It has beaches, forests, low mountains criss-crossed by hiking trails, and extensive fields of cabbage, *daikon* radishes, and watermelons, along with groves of tangerine and other trees.

The Miura Peninsula, like Italy, bears a vague resemblance to a boot. Some fascinating comparisons can be made between the two, although it would not do to push the parallels too far. For example, Italy had its Rome, a martial society if ever there was one, and mid-Miura had the samurai lair of the Miura clan. Also, off the southern-most tip of each of the peninsulas lies a fascinating island with scrumptious seafood: Sicily in the case of Italy, and Jogashima in the case of Miura. One big difference, though. On Jogashima you need have no fear of mafioso. The only "sharks" around are real ones—in the water or on your platter.

Getting around the Miura Peninsula is really quite easy. All the walks start either from a station on the JR Yokosuka Line or the private Keihin Kyuko Line, or first require a bus ride from one of these stations. The JR Yokosuka Line originates at Tokyo Station and terminates at Kurihama, about thirty minutes past Kamakura. A majority of the trains do not run directly to Kurihama, however. The Keihin Kyuko Line begins at Shinagawa in Tokyo and terminates at Uraga (about an hour and twenty minutes by express) or Misakiguchi Station. Spur lines go from Kanazawa Hakkei Station to Zushi Kaigan (ten minutes) and from Horinouchi Station in Yokosuka to Miura Kaigan (sixteen minutes).

The southern part of the peninsula, centered around the fishing port of Misaki, is accessed by bus. It takes roughly an hour from Yoko-suka and forty-five minutes from Keihin Kurihama Station.

1

Beyond the Waves

⟳ Zushi Station 逗子駅 (JR Yokosuka Line)—Enmei-ji 延命寺—Rokudai Gozen no Haka 六代御前の墓—Morito Coast 森戸海岸—Hayama Palace 葉山御用邸—Zushi Station

Zushi, the gateway to the Miura Peninsula, has a bit of a split personality. It is home to many writers and artists, but at the same time many of its neighborhoods, especially around the station, have a working-class feel to them. This walk, which should take about four hours in actual slogging time, is perfect for a balmy day, when the hormonal juices are flowing free. Late spring, before the beach bums descend for the summer, would be ideal.

From the main exit of Zushi Station, cross the plaza and go straight down the main street to Yokohama Bank at the second corner. Two streets split off to the left like a wishbone. Take the small one to the left. The big shrine on the one to the right is the Kameoka Hachiman.

Go under the Keihin Kyuko Line and then cross the Tagoshi-gawa River via the Zushi-bashi Bridge. On the left, you'll see a large, modern Shingon temple, Enmei-ji, often referred to as the Zushi Taishi because it is a center for exorcism rituals. The most important deity worshipped is the Zushi Benzaiten; it vaguely resembles a representation of the Virgin Mary or a plastic Jesus. The red miniature shrines are objects of popular worship and lend the whole approach to the temple something of a cheery air, despite the fact that nearby is the grave of Miura Doka, younger brother of Miura Dosun, who was lord of Sumiyoshi Castle at Kotsubo. He committed *seppuku* when his redoubt fell to the onslaught of Hojo Soun. Notice also the Shiva-like multiarmed

• MAP 264

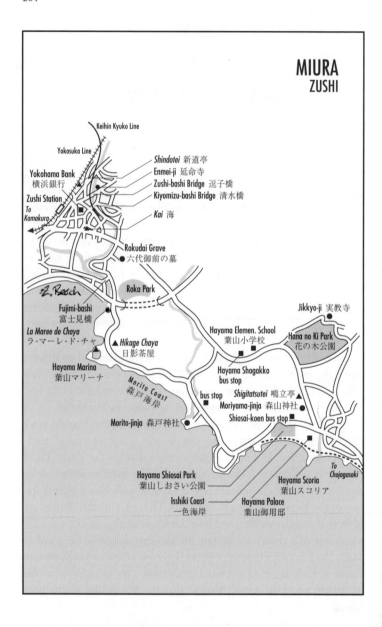

MIURA
ZUSHI

Keihin Kyuko Line

Yokosuka Line

Shindotei 新道亭
Enmei-ji 延命寺
Zushi-bashi Bridge 逗子橋
Kiyomizu-bashi Bridge 清水橋

Yokohama Bank
横浜銀行

Zushi Station
To
Kamakura

Kai 海

Rokudai Grave
六代御前の墓

Roka Park

E. Reach

Jikkyo-ji 実教寺

Fujimi-bashi
富士見橋

Hayama Elemen. School
葉山小学校

Hana no Ki Park
花の木公園

La Maree de Chaya
ラ・マーレ・ド・チ

▲ *Hikage Chaya*
日影茶屋

Hayama Marina
葉山マリーナ

Hayama Shogakko
bus stop

Morito Coast
森戸海岸

bus stop
Shigitatsutei 鴫立亭
Moriyama-jinja 森山神社

Morito-jinja 森戸神社

Shiosai-koen bus stop

To
Chojagasaki

Hayama Shiosai Park
葉山しおさい公園

Hayama Scoria
葉山スコリア

Isshiki Coast
一色海岸

Hayama Palace
葉山御用邸

Kannon and the mama frog with two baby frogs on her back.

On the other side of the tracks from Enmei-ji is Shindotei, a somewhat offbeat restaurant and inn. Bear left from the exit near the Kannon and cross over Shimoda-bashi; Shindotei is on the right. From November to March it offers wild boar cuisine. The boar comes from the Tanzawa district of Kanagawa Prefecture. Napoli-style *kaiseki ryori* is offered throughout the year courtesy of the owner's son, who studied in Italy.

From Enmei-ji, cross the road and turn left in front of a municipal library and gymnasium. Then turn left at Kiyomizu-bashi Bridge just past the police box and big parking structure, so that you remain on the same side of the river. This is a quiet neighborhood, perfect for a stroll.

The road curves as you continue to walk toward the big vermilion bridge. Sodai-ji on the left, another Shingon temple, is dedicated to Daikokuten, one of the Seven Lucky Gods. It has a statue of the clothes-stealing hag from the River Sanzun that dates back to the Edo period. Continue along the river past the traffic lights; a fitness club will be on your left. Just past the bus stop you will see a stone monument on the left marking the spot where the male line of the Taira was extinguished.

The Last of the Taira

Taira Chakuryu was the great-grandson of Kiyomori. He is referred to as Rokudai because he was of the sixth generation of the Kanmu Heike (Taira) family. Rokudai's grave lies on the side of the hill under the shade of a zelkova.

Rokudai was twelve at the time of the Battle of Dannoura, which in those days meant he was practically on the threshold of adulthood. The only thing that saved him from execution was the intervention of the famous priest Mongaku, to whom Yoritomo owed a great personal debt. Rokudai became Mongaku's disciple under the name of Myogaku. He retired to a peaceful life on Mt. Takao, zealously devoting himself to religious studies and developing a reputation as a meditation master.

However, after Yoritomo's death and the feisty Mongaku's banishment to Sado Island for interference in imperial succession politics, Rokudai was left isolated. Many shogunate officials believed that, despite his shaven head, he still remained a samurai at heart. For didn't the savage Kiyomori himself affect the guise of a bonze while alive?

Eventually, Rokudai was arrested for treason, which was no doubt a trumped-up charge. The very final passage of the *Heike Monogatari* describes how he was taken to this riverbank and beheaded at the age of twenty-eight.

The magnificent epic concludes: "Thus did the sons of the Heike vanish forever from the face of the earth."

• MAP 264

On the top of the hill is Roka Park, dedicated to the Meiji-period writer Tokutomi Roka. It is especially beautiful during the cherry blossom season. In the park you'll find a local history and folklore museum, the Kyodo Shiryo-kan. Housed in a former Tokugawa villa built in the 1920s with a spacious sunny veranda, the exhibits concentrate on literature connected with the Zushi area, especially Roka's work.

Continue along on this side of the river past the vermilion bridge. (If you crossed it, you would reach the Zushi Kaigan beach area.) Cherry and willow trees line the riverbanks and carp abound in its waters. There was a major fish unloading spot here during the Edo period and large quantities of seafood were brought in from Izu. Today the water is filled with luxury pleasure boats.

Keep going straight after the big intersection; Nagisa-bashi Bridge will be on your right. Soon you'll reach a small bay with boats for rent. This is the place where yachting began in Japan.

Throughout this area, there are luxury Western and Japanese restaurants and stylish coffee shops. Just past here you'll see a couple: the three-hundred-year-old Hikage Chaya offers reasonable lunches. La Marée de Chaya, in a three-story white-frame building, features the cuisine of southern France. There's also a bar and area for lighter dining.

The backstreet area with the boat-rental shacks is the center of a farmers' and fishermen's market every Sunday morning from 9:00 to 11:00. A little bit farther on is the Hayama Marina complex, with several restaurants. Set courses are available combining a bit of cruising and dining on the boats here. A bit farther along the road is a moderately priced, home-style Italian restaurant, Kikusuitei Antipasto.

The next few kilometers along here are known as the Morito Kaigan, or Morito Coast; it forms a part of the larger entity known as the Isshiki Kaigan, famous for swimming, surfing, and shell collecting. At points the road skirts the beaches and at other times it drifts away a bit; in narrower sections it can be unpleasant to have to put up with the traffic. The invigorating sea breeze at least disperses the fumes from the cars.

Check out Morito-jinja, a basic rural-style Shinto sanctuary overlooking a rocky part of the seacoast, perched on a small promontory. This is home to the protective deities for this whole section of coast.

• MAP 264

The view out to sea from the cliffs toward a little island bobbing there in the offing is eye-soothing. Yoritomo, Sanetomo, and Yoriie all supposedly enjoyed coming here on outings.

When I visited recently, I was surprised to see a gaggle of middle-aged ladies pile out of a bus and in a dither rush excitedly over to a large stone monument, where they started enthusiastically taking photos of each other, amidst shrieks and twittering. After they had departed, I went over to investigate this curious phenomenon.

The monument was erected in July 1989 and is dedicated to the memory of Ishihara Yujiro, the singer and actor who was the younger brother of controversial Dietman Ishihara Shintaro—the Japanese who could say "no." Yujiro became an overnight sensation when he starred in the sexy screen adaptation of his brother's Akutagawa Prize–winning novel *Taiyo no Kisetsu* (Season of the sun), a story of an amoral youth who hung out in the Yokohama and Miura area. Later the smooth-voiced, high-living Yujiro became typecast in movies about tough guys with hearts of gold. Kind of a Humphrey Bogart who could croon.

On the monument is what I take to be an excerpt from the lyrics of one of Yujiro's hits. I paraphrase:

> Let our dreams ride on those distant white sails,
> And disappear, disappear, far out to sea.

As you approach Hayama Palace, the Emperor's summer bunkhouse, you'll see some interesting houses on the hillsides. Before the war this area was a favorite playground for aristocrats. A German physician living in Hayama did much to popularize the benefits of sea, sand, and the clement weather of this area, so that many universities and companies established villas along the Isshiki Coast. On the left you'll see a two-story, white-frame seafood pasta restaurant, Pescatore Hayama.

Hayama was where Emperor Hirohito practiced riding the famous white horses on which he appeared in military reviews. He also did something probably much more to his heart here, namely conduct oceanographic research. The late Emperor was a world-famous expert on shellfish.

Part of the old palace grounds has been converted into a public park, Hayama Shiosai-koen, which includes a Japanese-style garden, a

• MAP 264

hydrangea garden, and Shiosai Museum, with displays of sealife from the area, and local history. The beach area was also returned completely to the public. South of the river is grassy Hayama Park overlooking the ocean.

Hayama Palace was built in 1894 amid natural forest. From the beach, the contrast between the green trees behind the palace and the white sand, and the vermilion bridge and the blue Shimoyama-gawa River is simply exquisite.

A highly unusual scoria rock formation can be seen at low tide near where the Shimoyama-gawa River disgorges into Sagami Bay. The rocks look like dinosaur bones that have been retched up by an angry sea. Scoria formations occur when volcanic eruptions become mixed with sedimentary mud that eventually forms into rock. Then the two are eroded by the ocean to form bizarre deposits like these.

You'll see many special police wandering around the palace perimeter in their combat boots; they will no doubt be watching you with binoculars from watchtowers. Although the Imperial family only spends a few weeks here each year, a palace is of course a palace, and leftist guerrillas would love to have a chance to test their rocket bombs on imperial masonry. You cannot help but feel sorry for these guards, however, when you see them there on a cold winter night guarding someone who is not even there. Pop back to the station by bus from the Shiosai-koen/Isshiki Kaigan bus stop and drink a toast to the guards from more than forty kinds of saké on offer at Kai *yakitori* restaurant.

Zushi Folklore Museum (Kyodo Shiryo-kan 逗子郷土資料館) ☎ 0468-73-1741
🕐 9:00–16:00, closed Mon. ¥100

Shiosai Museum (Shiosai Hakubutsukan しおさい博物館) ☎ 0468-76-1140
🕐 9:00–16:30; closed Mon. ¥300

Shindotei Restaurant 新道亭旅館
☎ 0468-71-2012 🕐 17:30~

Hikage Chaya 日影茶屋 ☎ 0468-75-0014
🕐 12:00–14:30, 17:00–21:30; closed Weds.

La Marée de Chaya ラ マーレ ド チャヤ
☎ 0468-75-6683
🕐 1F 12:00–01:00; 2F, 3F 12:00–14:30, 17:30–21:30; closed Mon.

Kikusuitei Antipasto
菊水亭 アンティパスト
☎ 0468-75-0046 🕐 12:00–16:00, 17:00–21:30; closed Mon.

Pescatore Hayama ☎ 0468-76-1255
🕐 11:00–21:00; closed Tues.

Kai 海 ☎ 0468-73-5957
🕐 17:00–23:00; closed Sun.

• MAP 264

2

Walk it Again, Sam

⟳ Zushi Station 逗子駅 (JR Yokosuka Line)—bus to Hayama (or Hayama Shogakko for Hana no Ki Park 花の木公園)—Hayama Park 葉山公園—Chojagasaki 長者ガ崎—Akiya Coast 秋谷海岸—Joraku-ji 浄楽寺—Rinkai Shizen Kyoiku-en 臨海自然教育園—Sajima Marina 佐島マリーナ—Sajima bus stop for bus to Zushi Station

This walk along the western, Pacific Ocean–side coast of the peninsula is for one of those days when you don't want to worry about absorbing a whole lot of history or high culture, but just walk to get some sun and exercise and have the sea breeze muss up your hair. There's also angling, swimming, sailing, and surfing for the marine crowd.

Take the Yokosuka Line to Zushi Station. Come out the main exit; you'll be facing the bus plaza to your left. Catch one of the buses for Hayama. If you're going to make the optional stop at Hana no Ki Park, make sure that you take one of the buses that stops at Hayama Shogakko (Hayama Primary School). The park is in front of the spanking new municipal offices a few minutes walk away.

Hana no Ki Park is justly famed for its thousands of azaleas and cherry trees and is a riot of color every spring. From late April to early May a great Azalea Festival bash is held outdoors here with tea ceremonies, potted plant sales, and art exhibitions. It is about the closest most of us are going to get to Hideyoshi's famous tea ceremony festival for thousands held at Kitano in Kyoto. Inside the park is a memorial to Hayama's war dead, with the names of all those who died in the Pacific War listed. Somehow it hits you more to see something like this in a small town than in some metropolis like Tokyo where thousands of

• MAP 264

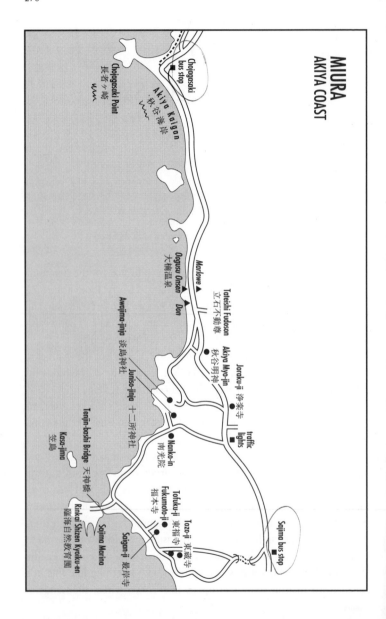

MIURA
AKIYA COAST

Choragasaki
bus stop

Choragosaki Point
長者ヶ崎

Akiya Kaigan
秋谷海岸

Oogusu Onsen
大楠温泉

Marlowe

Don

Tateishi Fudoson
立石不動尊

Akiya Myo-jin
秋谷明神

Joraku-ji 浄楽寺

traffic
lights

Awajima-jinja 淡島神社

Juniso-jinja 十二所神社

Nanko-in
南光院

Tofuku-ji 東福寺

Fukumoto-ji
福本寺

Tozo-ji 東蔵寺

Tenjin-boshi Bridge 天神橋

Rinkai Shizen Kyoiku-en
臨海自然教育園

Sajima Marina

Saigan-ji 最岸寺

Kasa-jima
笠島

Sajima bus stop

names are listed together. One wonders who these men were, how they died, and what their stories were.

Those of you who have an insatiable curiosity about Nichiren will want to visit Jikkyo-ji, a ten-minute walk on the narrow road to the right of the park entrance. I love the back lanes of Miura, because life here is so laid-back and sensible in the old-fashioned sense. Farmers put their produce out on the side of the road and if you want, you take, and in return plop a few coins into the bag provided. The times are a-changing, however. Neighborhoods back from the main roads are plastered with signs opposing large-scale development and the construction of condominiums by outside real estate companies.

Jikkyo-ji is a new temple with a past. That is to say, although the building is new, the temple was founded in 1558 to commemorate something that happened even further back, in 1253. When Nichiren first arrived from Boso that year, he entered Kamakura via this point. Apparently, even Nichiren occasionally got tired, and he rested next to the unusual rock you see in front of the temple hall. This strange slab, like Nichiren, seems to be imbued with some kind of elemental force, the whirls covering its surface almost smelling of the sea and high winds. From here it's possible to head toward the beach via the back roads, or to head back to the main road and continue in the opposite direction from the primary school. At the big intersection turn right and get on the right side of the road, heading in the direction of Hayama Palace. You will pass some interesting restaurants, including a *sushi-ya* in a Western mansion.

You'll soon reach Gyokuzo-in, a temple dedicated to Ebisu, who is closely connected with the sea, and is one of the Seven Lucky Gods. Fishermen often pray to Ebisu for bounty from the deep. To the rear is Moriyama-jinja, whose origins only go back to the late sixteenth century, although much older traditions were transferred here from other shrines. It stages some very unusual *matsuri*, including the Yobakari Shinji water festival on August 21 for good weather and crops and a "Marriage of the Gods" ceremony once every thirty-three years. The roots of this latter festival are said to go back more than 1,200 years.

Farther along on the main road is a super high-class French pastry

• MAP 264

shop, Shigitatsutei, that offers scrumptious goodies inside an old English-style mansion. Don't forget your wallet. The owners are not keen on riffraff who try to squeeze by with just a ¥600 cup of coffee.

Soon you'll come out in front of Hayama Palace (see page 267). Stay on the opposite side of National Highway 134. Above is an old shrine and behind it Manpuku-ji Temple, which you might consider taking a look at. After that stay on the ocean side of the highway. Go down to the beach at Hayama Park and you'll see Chojagasaki ("Millionaire's Point") off in the distance. You can also hike along the beach.

Past Chojagasaki we enter the Akiya Coast. A long promenade continues along the ocean side of the highway with houses or windsurfing shops interspersed here and there, while the opposite side is dotted with restaurants and luxury hotels. Down below are some small beaches. Keep your eyes open for the Shisanseki, an ovary-shaped stone, where the gods of conception and safe births are said to reside.

A kilometer or so along on the right is Enjo-in, a small, rustic temple from whose graveyard you can look down on a miniscule fishing port.

Millionaire's Point

There are a couple of restaurants and shops out in front of Millionaire's Point, which is really a kind of promontory. There's an attempt at a fence and signs warning people to stay away, but no one seems to pay much attention…

On a December visit, I asked one of the shopkeepers whether it was possible to get out there. "If the tide is out, you can get out there easily enough," he said.

After great effort crawling along the crumbling cliffs, I manage to make it out to what amounts to a small island at the tip of the cape. The view was magnificent: a little island off to the left, snowy white yachts in the offing, brightly colored fishing boats chugging back to port. Emboldened by all the romance, I plunge into the jungle on the top of the rise and promptly get lost. I walk around for what seems like an eternity, although from the garbage I know that I have not been the first to come this way.

Eventually, I manage to slide down a jagged cliff to the sand below. Scratched up, exhausted, and chilled, I circle round some rocks and run into this guy walking out of the water toward me in teensy-weensy bikini trunks, as nonchalant as a window shopper in Ginza. Must be a Scandinavian member of a polar bear club, I figure.

"No, I'm from Washington State," he replies. "I jog down here for a swim every day, year round. Do it every day and the water temperature's no problem." Miura's just like California—you get all kinds.

• MAP 264

A shop across the road seems to have mixed motives. Its billboard promises: "Natural foods, saké, and tobacco." If what you're really yearning for is a hard-boiled egg, try Marlowe Restaurant on the left a bit farther along. You can't miss it: it has a huge picture of a Humphrey Bogart–like figure on the roof. This is meant to be Philip Marlowe, the hero (or anti-hero if you prefer) of many of Raymond Chandler's classic private detective stories. Actually, the fifties-style restaurant specializes in seafood. If the walk has been too much for you, you can rest your weary bones at Oogusu Onsen, a hot-springs bath opposite Marlowe.

A hundred meters or so past Marlowe on the left is the entrance to the delightful Tateishi Fudosan Temple. There is a very unusual guardian statue at the gate and a frog spitting out water for worshippers to purify their hands and mouths with. Adding to this charming discovery are a small waterfall and a sparkling river. Across on the ocean side in a small park is the Tateishi (Standing Rock) itself.

Next to the park is the well-known restaurant Don, whose sign says that the first floor is "settle space" and the second floor "placer space." It goes on to make a social statement: "The topic of this house is Humanality (sic) and Performance." While you're contemplating these enigmatic statements, you can enjoy a cake set, beer set, or pizza set. Reminds me of the Pacific Coast Highway/Malibu set in Southern California.

Cross over again to the left side of the road. Soon you'll reach Akiya Myo-jin Shrine, near which is an old Edo-period farm compound belonging to the Kasahara family, with an interesting gate, traditional plaster walls, and tiled roof. Near a bus stop down the road is the entrance to Joraku-ji, a small Jodo temple that houses several precious statues including an Amida Nyorai with attendants on both sides, and a wooden, standing Bishamonten. The Amida statue, like so many other superior works attributed to Unkei, was originally in a Kamakura temple, but was moved here by Masako and Wada Yoshimori after a typhoon. In the rear graveyard is a monument to Maejima Hisoka, the founder of Japan's modern postal system, who sleeps the big sleep here.

Skip back to the ocean side of the road and turn right at the traffic signal; there's a sign pointing to Sajima Marina. You'll pass a small temple, Nanko-in, and come out next to the ocean near a small yacht harbor.

• MAP 270

If you go to the right you'll find Awajima Shrine, a local center of folk belief, where people come from afar to pray for safe births or success in marriage. Things get especially lively during the March 3 Festival of the Bottomless Ladle. Very close by is Juniso-jinja, one of the oldest shrines on the peninsula with a history of over eight centuries.

Go back to the cutoff and this time go straight beside the yacht harbor. You'll pass a seafood factory and a warehouse with a funky mural of a topless mermaid posing in front of an exploding volcano in the distance. Super. Turn right at the signals; cross a small bridge and you'll find several seafood eateries and inns, near the entrance to the Rinkai Shizen Kyoiku-en on Tenjin-jima, which is about a kilometer in circumference. This nature preserve takes up most of the island and neighboring Kasa-jima. The two islands are geologically very unusual combining volcanic ash layers with exotically shaped coral. Black-tailed gulls (the Japanese call them *umineko*, or "sea cats") and other birds breed here. There are also 146 types of sea plants here, several species of which have died out elsewhere. No camping, fishing, or shell gathering are allowed, and the park rangers make sure that the rules are followed. If only there were more such respect for the environment in other popular recreation areas in Japan.

Return to the main road and turn right. There are several interesting fishermen's temples around here—on the hillside are Fukumoto-ji and Saigan-ji, and where the road curves, Tozo-ji and Tofuku-ji. On the way look out for the highly weathered roadside Buddhas, communing in a kind of grotto. Follow the main road (it goes through a tunnel) back to Route 134, or turn left in front of Tozo-ji onto a road that later joins up with the main road. Catch a bus back to Zushi from the Sajima bus stop.

Tenjin-jima Nature Reserve (Rinkai Shizen Kyoiku-en 臨海自然教育園)
🕘 9:00–17:00; closed Mon., Weds. A.M., February 15, New Year. Free

Oogusu Onsen 大楠温泉
☎ 0468-56-8800 🕘 9:00–16:30; ¥1,300 for bath; ¥12,000 for overnight stay

Shigitatsutei 鴫立亭 ☎ 0468-76-1682
🕘 10:00–19:15; open year round

Marlowe ☎ 0468-57-4780
🕘 11:30–22:00; closed Fri.

Don ☎ 0468-57-3436
🕘 11:00–22:00; Sat., Sun. 11:00–24:00; open all year

• MAP 270

3

Anchors Away

○ Anjinzuka Station 安針塚駅 (Keihin Kyuko Line)—Tsukayama Park塚山公園 —
Dobuita-dori どぶ板通—Mikasa Park 三笠公園—Ryuhon-ji 龍本寺—Yokosuka Museum
横須賀市自然人文博物館—Yokosuka Chuo Station 横須賀中央駅 (Keihin Kyuko Line)

This route takes in the scenic port town of Yokosuka, which, deservedly
or not, was long dismissed as a GI jungle. In recent years, however, it
has greatly modernized and shed its dark image. With its cheerful
atmosphere, Yokosuka strikes me as more laid-back than Tokyo.

First, we visit the purported grave of the famous British seaman
Will Adams, known to the Japanese as Anjin-sama, who was the model
for the main character in James Clavell's blockbuster bestseller *Shogun*,
a classic in terms of historical and cultural misrepresentation.

Take the Keihin Kyuko Line to Anjinzuka Station. Come out the
single entrance, turn left, and follow the road that goes under the
tracks and up into the hilly residential neighborhood. Eventually you
will reach a cutoff to the left with a sign for Tsukayama Park. Keep following this steep path until it reaches the crest of the mountain and the
park, about one kilometer from the station or a thirty-minute walk.
The supposed graves of Adams and his wife are immediately to the
right behind a fence. A special memorial service and festival attended
by prominent Japanese and British are held annually on April 14.

According to one tradition, in his will Adams asked to be buried in
a spot where he could see Edo Bay and thus afford spiritual protection
to the capital of the Tokugawa, since he had been granted so many
favors by their first shogun, Ieyasu. However, there is very little or no

• MAP 276

276

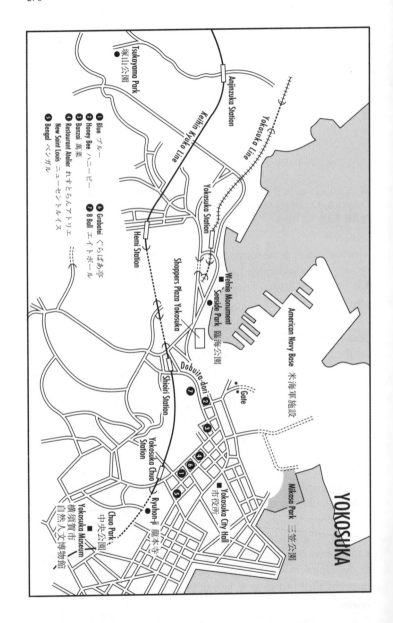

1 Blue ブルー
2 Honey Bee ハニービー
3 Banzai 萬菜
4 Restaurant Atelier おすとらんアトリエ
　　New Saint Louis ニューセントルイス
5 Bengal ベンガル

6 Grabotei ぐらぼあ亭
7 8 Ball エイトボール

Tsukayama Park 塚山公園

Anjinzuka Station

Keihin Kyuko Line

Yokosuka Line

Yokosuka Station

Hemi Station

Shoppers Plaza Yokosuka

Welnie Monument
Senside Park 臨海公園

Dobuita-dori

Shiori Station

Gate

Yokosuka Chuo Station

Ryuhon-ji 龍本寺

Yokosuka City Hall 市役所

Chuo Park 中央公園

Yokosuka Museum 横須賀市自然人文博物館

American Navy Base 米海軍施設

Mikasa Park 三笠公園

YOKOSUKA

possibility that he is actually buried here. Adams died on May 16, 1620, during a visit to the British trading post at Hirado in Kyushu and historians are agreed it is highly unlikely that his remains were transported back here. A year after Adams died, the persecution of the Christians in Japan began in earnest and grave stones at Hirado were ripped out. In 1905 the graves here were exhumed, but absolutely no evidence of anything connected with Adams was turned up. Their occupants remain unidentified. Even so, in the following year a British merchant living in Yokohama had the graves refurbished.

Tsukayama Park is worth exploring, especially when the cherry blossoms are in bloom. Don't forget to take in the panoramic view of Yokosuka Bay far below and Kannon-zaki Point far off to the right. Fuji-san is to the left. Go straight downwards to leave the park; you'll come out on what looks like a large toll-road. Look to the right and you'll see a small mountain path. Follow that until it comes out below near Hemi Station.

The Navigator of Miura

Born in the town of Gillingham, Kent, in 1564, William Adams worked as a shipwright and pilot before starting his own trading company. In 1598 he was commissioned as chief pilot for a fleet of five merchant ships sent by a Dutch trading company to Asia. However, only Adams' ship, *The Charity*, survived the long journey across the Pacific. On April 19, 1600, it arrived off Kyushu.

Ieyasu, who that same summer became hegemon of Japan after his victory at the Battle of Sekigahara, ordered Adams to be brought to him for personal questioning. He was so pleased with Adams' answers that he made the Englishman a personal adviser, especially on matters related to shipbuilding.

Adams was made a vassal by Ieyasu and granted a fief in the Yokosuka area, and given the samurai name Miura Anjin, the Navigator of Miura. One of the ships built by Adams sailed to Mexico in 1610 with a trader from Kyoto

and his party on board. Most likely they were the first Japanese to visit the New World. Apparently, Ieyasu was toying with the idea of turning the Yokosuka area into an international port from which to trade with Mexico and the Philippines.

In 1605 Adams petitioned Ieyasu to let him return to his wife and children in England. He explained the outcome in a 1611 letter to officials at the East India Company's trading post in Indonesia: "With the which request, the emperor was not well pleased, and would not let me goe any more for my countrey, but to byde in his land."

Eventually, Adams was allowed to leave and he made a business trip to Siam, but soon returned to Japan. In the meantime he had married the Japanese woman whose ashes are said to be buried in Tsukayama Park and had two children, Joseph and Susanna.

• MAP 276

Keep going straight till you reach the main highway and Yokosuka Station. Opposite is the Rinkai (Seaside) Park, from where you can watch vessels streaming in and out of the harbor. Follow the path underneath the cliffs to get there. Opened to the public in 1946, this area used to belong to the Japanese Imperial Navy, as did a good part of Yokosuka.

A few years before the Meiji Restoration, there were probably only about 200 households in Yokosuka. By 1907 there were 67,000 people living here and it had become the second-largest city in the prefecture. There were two keys to this rapid growth: industrialization and the development of a huge military port. In the past the ports in this immediate area served as bases for fishing and whale hunting in the Antarctic.

In 1871 the first ship built by the new Meiji government was launched from here. Gradually the Imperial Navy declared this entire district, from north of Kanazawa Hakkei to the entrance to Tokyo Bay at Uraga, a fortified district, and Yokosuka became preeminently a navy town.

The Architects of Yokosuka

The initial scheme to develop Yokosuka was worked out by the progressive shogunal official Oguri Tadamasa (1827–68) and French advisers, who were vigorously attempting to outstrip British influence in Japan. Oguri was one of the most talented men of his time and totally loyal to the shogunate. For this reason he was disliked by the samurai of Satsuma and other anti-Bakufu fiefs. When he was caught by his vindictive opponents in what is now Gunma Prefecture, he was beheaded like a dog. Samurai honor had not improved one whit from the Kamakura period.

Oguri and the French engineer Francois Welnie (1834–1908) worked out a four-year master plan for building a steel plant at Yokosuka, which was duly established in 1864.

The port itself was the brainchild of French minister, Léon Roches, who saw that shogunate finances were in a shambles. He promised to arrange a loan at lower than the market rate in return for Japan promising to ship its silk solely to France, which was at the time the world's largest consumer of the material. At one time there were ninety-eight French engineers at Yokosuka, which shows the scale of the commitment, considering that there were only a couple of hundred foreign experts at most in all Japan. After the Restoration, the Meiji government took over the steelworks and completed the docks begun by Oguri.

In 1869 Welnie built the first Western-style lighthouse at Kannon-zaki (see page 287), but in 1876 he returned to France under a cloud, since the British had already clearly won out in the battle for influence with the new Meiji government. There are busts of the visionary duo, Oguri and Welnie, in Rinkai Park, and they are honored during the annual port festival held every September 27.

• MAP 276

Among other things, Yokosuka was home to naval training, gunnery, and torpedo schools, and the home base for several of the large aircraft carriers that were lost in the decisive Battle of Midway. Along with the navy came cheap saké shops and brothels for common seamen and fancy villas and inns for officers, some of whom were involved in ultra-nationalist plots against the civilian government.

In the postwar era the city developed a three-sided schizophrenic personality: It became a key base for the U.S. Seventh Fleet in the Far East; an industrial area; and a bedtown for office workers who commuted to the Tokyo area. During the height of the antinuclear and anti-war movements during the fifties, sixties, and seventies, it also became the focus of massive anti-American demonstrations, especially when American ships suspected of carrying nuclear weapons arrived in port.

Although not as much in the news as in former days, partly because several facilities have been handed over to the Japanese Self-Defense Forces, Yokosuka is still not controversy-free. The ecological movement that opposes the construction of housing for U.S. military personnel in the nearby Ikego forest area is largely led by former antiwar activists. With Subic Bay in the Philippines now closed, more and more sailors are likely to be arriving in the port for R&R, although they are less and less able to afford Japanese prices than in days past. Increasing friction could well be the result.

Rinkai Park sometimes becomes the scene for impromptu partying by sailors who bring their own bottles of whisky and giant bags of corn chips. The fact that Yokosuka remains preeminently a military port was underlined by an accident in 1989, in which the SDF submarine *Nadashio* rammed a fishing boat, killing or injuring thirty people, and then calmly went on its way in a rather cavalier fashion.

Walk east toward the large buildings in the distance and you'll soon find yourself in front of the main gate of the U.S. base, and Club Alliance, the NCO club. In the days of the Vietnam War the former barnlike structure was the site of so much hell-raising that it should have been preserved as a historical monument. The area around here has changed tremendously during the last two decades. An old salt from those days coming back from the grave would simply not

• MAP 276

recognize the place. That huge shopping center you passed on the right on the way, Shoppers Plaza Yokosuka, was only completed in 1991. It boasts of around 220 shops in close to 50,000 square meters of space. There are three cinemas, a bowling alley, boutiques, a glass-roofed amusement zone, a big supermarket, and many, many restaurants, including a few, like Victoria Station, that are in separate buildings outside. On a weekday, the complex is nearly empty (in Japanese terms), so you can shop till you drop without feeling like you're doing it in a rat maze. Next door is the Yokosuka Prince Hotel, which has a shopping center of its own and a live theater, the Yokosuka Geijutsu Gekijo, which hosts top acts from around the world.

One of the reasons that Yokosuka's population has ballooned to close to 450,000 is that its climate is milder than Tokyo's. It's also easy to get around, since it is built in valleys around an axis: the main road running along the harbor and a crossroad running up past Yokosuka Chuo Station on the Keihin Kyuko Line, along which are located several big department stores. So, theoretically, it is difficult to get lost…

Pig Alley

Across the main road and one street up toward the hills from the main gate of the base, you will find Dobuita-dori, also known as Pig Alley, the scene of many feats of derring-do by American sailors in the last half century. The area featured in the early Imamura Shohei movie *Buta to Gunkan* (Pigs and battleships). These days life along the 700-meter-long road that begins near Keihin Kyuko Shiori Station is rather tame. Little remains of the old base-town look except for the shops catering to GIs. You might want to drop in to the Skin Collection Art Studio for a quick tattoo, or have a drink at one of the bars bearing names like Cotton Club; Popeye; Bar Tennessee; Blue Sky = Cold Beer, Hot Chicks, Cool Music. Filipino restaurants (try the 8 Ball Club) and stores selling silky jackets emblazoned with dragons and other such heraldry add to the U.S. Navy atmosphere.

These days most GIs do their drinking on base or down here on Dobuita-dori. But that is understandable when you realize that the average price of a drink in the rest of town, and we are not talking about a cocktail lounge in the Prince Hotel, is six times what it is at an on-base club.

As a result, more and more local bar owners are switching to a Japanese clientele. In fact, you will see numerous signs with messages like, "No Foreigners Allowed," "Japanese Members Club," or "Good Only for Japanes (sic) Person." The GI bars themselves also tend to be self-segregated along racial lines.

8 Ball Club ☎ 0468-27-4373
🕐 20:00–05:00; closed Mon.

• MAP 276

At nearby Suwa-jinja, founded in 1380 by the Miura clan, there is a large placard reading, "Off Limits to all US Forces Personnnel and Dependants by Order of Commander Fleet Activities, Yokosuka." At first I found this lack of hospitality a bit odd, particularly when a woman eyed me suspiciously as I took a look around.

Later a Korean bar owner explained, "We don't like to have GIs come in because they can't speak the language, and the ones off the boats can get plenty wild." She then pointed outside to a pair of burly Shore Patrol military police, adding, "That's why they have all those SPs around." Note that things get going late in Yokosuka, except when one of the big ships is in. Many bars do not even open until about 20:30.

From the main gate, turn right. Go straight for a couple of blocks, till you reach the Auto Park Mikasa, then turn left. (Note the old copper-fronted building on the right side of the road as you are walking forward. This type of building used to be very common in downtown neighborhoods of Tokyo and Yokohama, but is quite rare now.) At the next corner make another right; you will see a one-third scale model of part of the *Mikasa Maru*. Our next stop is Mikasa Park, where the *Mikasa Maru* is anchored, the famous flagship of Admiral Togo at the Battle of Tsushima Strait, the decisive battle of the Russo-Japanese War of 1904–1905 and one of the most important naval conflicts in modern history. A bit farther on is the entrance to the park where the *Mikasa Maru* was grounded on concrete after being fully restored in May 1961.

Even if you are not a war history buff, a visit to the *Mikasa Maru* is a must, if only to see the differences between the living quarters of the admiral and those of his men. It might even be an exaggeration to call them living quarters, since the men slept in hammocks right next to their duty stations, including the 15-cm and 30-cm guns. Their uniforms are also surprisingly small; they almost look like children's play uniforms.

Before going into action at Tsushima, Togo told his men that the very future of the Japanese empire depended on this single battle. They responded magnificently, and the Russian Baltic Fleet was virtually wiped out; of the 38 ships, 19 were sunk and 12 captured. The only Japanese losses were three torpedo boats. The 15,000-ton *Mikasa Maru* was decommissioned in 1923, in accordance with the limits on tonnage

• MAP 276

agreed on during the Washington Disarmament Conference.

The little island offshore is Saru-jima ("Monkey Island"). Prior to the war it was a secret installation chock-full of gun emplacements. The island was later made into a natural park, boasting more than seventy varieties of subtropical plants and becoming popular with fishermen and campers. Caves in the northern and central parts of the island have also yielded animal bones dating from the Jomon period. However, as of writing, the ferry service to the island (it takes about ten minutes) has been suspended. The park to the left of the *Mikasa Maru* is very much open, however, and a very enchanting park it is, with a colored fountain and artificial waterfall.

From the park, go back to the main road and turn left at the corner to Yokosuka Chuo Station. This is the main shopping road of Yokosuka. The area around the station itself is a maze of little restaurants and other shops. Pay careful attention and turn in at the corner by Kyowa Bank. You'll now be on the Wakamatsu shopping road, which has several interesting, fairly inexpensive restaurants (see page 283).

Farther on the right is Suwa Shrine, which has no connection with the off-limits shrine of the same name visited earlier. Stone steps lead from here to the rear entrance of Ryuhon-ji.

Why Yokosuka Shellfish Are Round

Associated with Ryuhon-ji is another interesting story about Nichiren that features a white monkey. It seems that in 1253 when Nichiren was making his way to Kamakura by boat from his native Boso Peninsula, the ocean suddenly started raging and the bottom of his boat suddenly broke open, revealing a gaping hole. Nichiren chanted with heart and soul and then all of a sudden a giant abalone attached itself to the boat and succeeded in closing off the leak. Then out of the blue a white monkey appeared and guided him to Saru-jima, then known as To-shima.

The next day Nichiren made it to the shore at Yokosuka, but his boat became mired in the shallows and a local man came out to carry him to land. However, just at that moment a giant turbo shell (*sazae*) cut into the man's leg with its tentacles. Nichiren again chanted and the predatory shellfish disappeared.

In gratitude and spiritual awe the man later built a hermitage for Nichiren, which was the forerunner of Ryuhon-ji. The shells of the abalone and turbo in question are said to be preserved here. According to local tradition, thanks to Nichiren's prayers shellfish in the area have been round ever since.

• MAP 276

This Nichiren temple is currently undergoing extensive remodeling that will be completed in 1994. It is a good example of traditional Edo architecture and the roof and ceiling carvings are quite interesting.

Farther up on top of the hill and into the left are the Yokosuka Bunka Kaikan cultural hall and the Yokosuka Shiritsu Hakubutsukan, the metropolitan natural history and local history museum. The latter is highly recommended and apparently rarely crowded. Among the things on display here are specimens of rare marine life and fishing implements traditionally associated with the Miura Peninsula, as well as dioramas depicting life in premodern days up to twenty thousand years ago. During the Tokugawa period this area provided a great deal of Edo's salt and shellfish. Outside are statues of Oguri and Kurimoto Joun, another person involved in the opening of the port, and a somewhat erotic Goddess of Freedom statue. Incidentally, there is an interesting view of Yokosuka port from Chuo Park, where the museum is located. In mid-June the gardenia and hydrangea are quite beautiful. From here head back to Yokosuka Chuo Station.

Mikasa Park 三笠公園 ⏱ April–October 8:00–21:00; Nov. to March 9:00–20:00

Mikasa Maru 三笠丸 ☎ 0468-22-5408 ⏱ April–Sept. 9:00–17:30; March–Oct 9:00–17:00; Nov.–Feb. 9:00–16:30; closed New Year and hols; ¥400

Yokosuka Museum 横須賀市自然人文博物館 ☎ 0468-24-3688 ⏱ 9:00–17:00; closed Mon. Free

Yokosuka offers some very interesting alternatives in the gourmet line. Try these friendly restaurants for a refreshing change from standard Japanese fare.

Graba-tei ぐらばあ帝 ☎ 0468-26-1950 ⏱ 11:00–21:30; open all year
Basement coffee bar offering down-to-earth spaghetti in jumbo portions at tiny prices.

Honey Bee ハニービー
☎ 0468-25-9096 ⏱ 11:50–03:00; closed Weds. Great grungy American diner.

Restaurant Atelier れすとらんアトリエ
☎ 0468-24-4428
⏱ 11:00–22:00; Weds. 11:00–15:00; no reg. hols.
Home-made sausages and hamburgers in pleasant woody interior.

Bengal ☎ 0468-25-8877
⏱ 11:30–21:00; closed Mon.
Curry restaurant.

New Saint Louis ☎ 0468-25-9600
⏱ 10:00–21:00; closed Thurs.
Jazz coffee-shop with real scones and whipped cream, opened in 1930.

Banzai ☎ 0468-27-4423
⏱ 17:00–23:30; Fri., Sat., and night before hols. 17:00–24:00; open all year
Chic restaurant offering a smorgasbord of vegetarian food.

• MAP 276

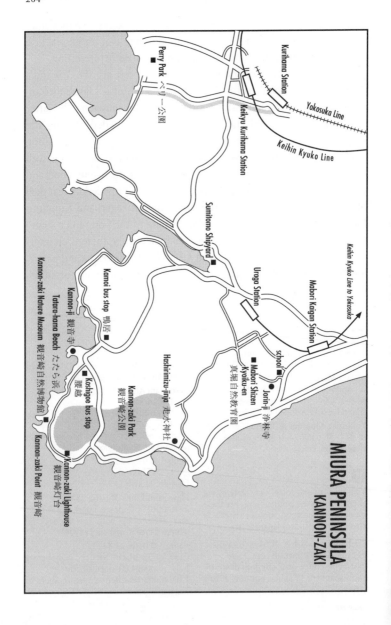

Perry Park ペリー公園

Kurihama Station

Keikyu Kurihama Station

Yokosuka Line

Keihin Kyuko Line

Sumitomo Shipyard

Keihin Kyuko Line to Yokosuka

Uraga Station

Mabori Kaigan Station

Kamoi bus stop 鴨居

school

Jōrin-ji 浄林寺

Mabori Shizen Kyoiku-en
真堀自然教育園

Kannon-ji 観音寺

Tatara-hama Beach たたら浜

Kannon-zaki Nature Museum 観音崎自然博物館

Koshigoe bus stop
腰越

Hashirimizu-jinja 走水神社

Kannon-zaki Park
観音崎公園

Kannon-zaki Lighthouse
観音崎灯台

Kannon-zaki Point 観音崎

MIURA PENINSULA
KANNON-ZAKI

4

Perry's Landfall

○ Mabori Kaigan Station 馬堀海岸駅 (Keihin Kyuko Line)—Mabori Nature Park 馬堀自然教育園—Hashirimizu Shrine 走水神社—Kannon-zaki 観音崎—Koshigoe bus stop 腰越バス停—Uraga Station 浦賀駅 (Keihin Kyuko Line)—Keihin Kurihama Station (Keihin Kyuko Line)—Perry Park ペリー公園—Kurihama Station 久里浜駅 (JR Yokosuka Line)

This walk through the southeast part of Yokosuka takes in areas identified with the ancient legendary hero Yamato-takeru as well as the arrival of Commodore Perry in 1853 and the early days of modernization in the late Edo and early Meiji periods.

Take the Keihin Kyuko Line to Mabori Kaigan Station, which means taking the branch line that goes to Uraga. From the station, turn right on Route 16 and go past the Mabori Junior High School bus stop across from the big housing complex. Turn right at the intersection and continue on the right to the cutoff to the Mabori Nature Park (Jorin-ji Temple will be on your left). An ammunition dump during the war, this area is now a treasure house for encountering the ecology of the Miura area in the flesh. Here you can find about two hundred types of flora, including edible plants like *tsuwabuki* (Japanese silverleaf) and *kikurage* (Judas-ear), as well as numerous kinds of insects and birds.

Retrace your steps back to the main road and keep going on the highway with the apartments on your left. You will soon emerge by the ocean, with a pretty beach to your left where you can stop for a swim. The green grass and leaves of the Japanese sago palms make a pleasant contrast to the blue of the ocean. Just after the road makes a turn near Hatayama Point about twenty minutes along, you'll find the small port

• MAP 284

of Hashirimizu on your left, and on a recessed elevation to your right, the quiet, gingko-girdled Hashirimizu Shrine, dedicated to the legendary culture hero Yamato-takeru no Mikoto and his wife, Ototachibana-hime. There is also a *hochozuka* knife mound where every October a knife-blessing ceremony is held.

Continue on the same road; stop for coffee at Kannon-zaki Beach Hotel and enjoy the superb view of the bay. Behind the hotel is a charming paved road that weaves its way amid rocks and windswept trees to the Kannon-zaki radar and lighthouse. The green, green park out on the point, built on what used to be an Imperial Navy gun emplacement, contains Japanese-style gardens, lawns, and, back in the hills, a monument to seamen who died during World War II. With its magnificent views of the chalk-white lighthouse, the white breakers crashing on the cliffs below, and Futtsu Point and Mt. Nokogiri ("Saw Mountain") on the west side of the Boso Peninsula across the Uraga Straits just over five kilometers away, this spot is perfect for a picnic or just plain beachcombing.

Yamato-takeru and Hashirimizu

While on his famous expedition to pacify the "barbarians" of the Kanto Plain at the order of the emperor, Yamato-takeru incurred the wrath of the sea god of this area and for a time it appeared that the ship carrying him to the Boso Peninsula was going to sink. But when his wife, Ototachibana-hime, jumped into the water after wrapping herself in several layers of leather, silk, and rushes (perhaps to fool the angry deity into thinking that she was her husband), the sea god was indeed mollified and the water seemed to race, thus giving birth to the place name Hashirimizu, or "racing waters." The *Kojiki* goes on to say, "Thereupon the violent waves calmed down and the august ship could proceed."

Seven days later Ototachibana-hime's comb drifted up on the shore, and it was enshrined nearby, perhaps at this shrine. Hashirimizu-jinja was popular with fisherfolk during the Edo period. However, no one seems to be sure of its age, since local records were destroyed during a fire of that era.

The importance of this story is that it is the first real mention of the eastern country in Japan's records. Prior to that time everything concerning Japanese culture had been centered in the Yamato area and other parts of Western Japan.

The story of how the loyal Yamato-takeru died sick and lonely on his way back to the capital after having successfully completed his mission, but was then transformed into a beautiful white swan that flew away, is one of the most famous legends in Japanese history. By tradition, the expedition took place in the first century A.D. and thereafter this area always remained under imperial control. However, it is hard to conceive of the shrine existing for two millennia.

• MAP 284

You can just imagine what it was like during the heyday of Yokohama when tall clippers with billowing white sails graced these waters. Furthermore, the area is a riot of flowers in spring and summer. Be warned, however, that there's no water, so bring your own refreshments.

The fifteen-meter-high octagonal lighthouse has a 140,000-candle-power light, visible thirty-seven kilometers out to sea. The first Western-style lighthouse in Japan, designed by none other than the French engineer Welnie, whom we met in the previous walk, it was built in 1869 but knocked down by the earthquake in 1923. You can get an idea of what the earlier version was like from the photographs inside.

About fifteen minutes on foot south of the Kannon-zaki Lighthouse by Tatara-hama Beach is the Kannon-zaki Nature Museum, which houses over 3,000 specimens of sea life and extensive information on the local fishing industry and folk history. After viewing the ocean dioramas and demonstrations of traditional fishing techniques, you can go compare notes with fishermen at the nearby port of Kamoi. Or visit the huge monument here dedicated to those who went down with their ships during the war. There are also some good hiking trails in this area. From the Koshigoe bus stop near Kannon-ji Temple, catch a bus for Uraga, one stop down the Keihin Kyuko Line from Mabori Kaigan Station.

Today the ports of Uraga and neighboring Kurihama are primarily involved with deep-sea fishing, industrial activities, and support for Self-Defense Force facilities. The commercial and strategic importance of the area has long been appreciated. During the Edo period, Uraga was a vital trade center. Much of the food supply for the capital, especially the all-important staple, rice, was brought in by ship from other parts of the country to Uraga and then shipped by barge from here. In turn, dried sardines were shipped to the Kansai area for use as fertilizer.

At its height Edo was a city of more than one million inhabitants and the Tokugawa shogunate was well aware of its vulnerability from Tokyo Bay. For this reason the government established a magistrate's office at Uraga in 1720 to be responsible for defending the approaches to Edo. Various fiefs were given responsibility for garrisoning the defenses, but local inhabitants of Miura furnished supplies and labor. In 1853 the shogunate established a shipyard at Uraga and later a steel plant.

• MAP 284

Incidentally, the remains of an Edo-period Japanese-style lighthouse, the Tomyodo, are to be found on the opposite side of Uraga Harbor from Kannon-zaki, near the Sumitomo shipyard. The first floor was living space for the lighthouse keepers, while on the second floor was a bronze mirror that burned vegetable oil. It could be seen at a distance of seven kilometers. Close by is a battery built by the shogunate to protect Uraga Harbor.

Foreigners, too, were not unaware of the importance of Uraga—in 1846 American and Dutch ships showed up outside the port, the former commanded by Commodore Biddle, who bore a letter requesting that Japan open up to foreign trade. Not only was the proposal rejected out of hand, a Japanese soldier physically manhandled the commodore. He could not react, however, because he had no authorization to use force. When Perry arrived seven years later, he wasn't going to take no for an answer. When the letter and presents Perry had brought with him were finally turned over to shogunate officials at Kurihama, the ceremony was performed amid absolute silence. Obviously, the Japanese were less than thrilled with their uninvited visitors from afar.

Those interested in Perry should not pass up a visit to Perry Park and Memorial Hall, containing memorabilia concerning Perry and his visit. To get there from Uraga, take a bus or backtrack three stations to Horiuchi Station and then transfer to another Keihin Kyuko train. Get off at Keikyu Kurihama Station and follow the signs to the ferry terminus for boats to the Boso Peninsula (an interesting thirty-five-minute sea cruise away). The park fronts the main street paralleling the harbor.

A memorial stone marks the spot where Perry and his men first landed. A Black Ship Festival is held here on July 14 each year.

🏛

Mabori Nature Park (Mabori Shizen Kyoiku-en 馬堀自然教育園) ☎ 0468-41-5727 ⏱ 9:00–17:00; closed Mon. and last day of month. Free

Kannon-zaki Lighthouse (Kannon-zaki Todai 観音崎灯台) ☎ 0468-41-0311 ⏱ 9:00–16:00; summer 9:00–17:00; open all year. ¥100

Kannon-zaki Nature Museum (Kannon-zaki Shizen Hakubutsukan 観音崎自然博物館) ☎ 0468-41-1533 ⏱ 9:00–17:00, closed Mon. except Jul. and Aug. ¥300

Perry Memorial Hall (Perry Kinen-kan ペリー記念館) ☎ 0468-34-7531 ⏱ 9:00–16:30; closed Mon. Free

• MAP 284

5

Cherry Blossoms of the Samurai

◑ Kinugasa Station 衣笠駅 (JR Yokosuka Line)—Daimyo-ji 大明時—Sogen-ji 曹源寺—Kinugasayama Park衣笠山公園—Daizen-ji 大善寺—Mansho-ji 満昌寺—Seiun-ji 清雲寺—Mangan-ji 満願寺—Bus to Kurihama Station 久里浜駅 (JR Yokosuka, Keihin Kyuko lines)

So, you like your cherry blossoms and making an ass out of yourself under the little pink buds, but you don't like doing it in front of half of Tokyo. Well, this is the springtime jaunt through the hills for you. It wends its way through the original base of the Miuras, the clan that controlled the Miura Peninsula from the late Heian period through the early decades of the Kamakura period. If you avoid the weekends, you can commune with the flowers in semi-solitude.

Take the Yokosuka Line to Kinugasa Station, one station past Yokosuka. From the wicket, turn left and go to the bus stop in front of Miura High School. Turn right and go up to Daimyo-ji, a large Nichiren temple that dates from the Kamakura period but was rebuilt in the Edo period. Located on the hill behind the temple is the grave of Ota Sukeyasu, the son of the famous warlord Ota Dokan. He was married to the daughter of Miura Dosun and died in 1513 fighting with Miura forces against the invading army of Hojo Soun (Go Hojo). Kasamori Inari-jinja, a small shrine in the vicinity, according to the *Miura Kojin-roku*, a local history dating from the Edo period, was a place where many locals, especially seamen, showed up to pray for miraculous cures for their chancres. I wonder if any of Perry's boys joined the line.

Return to the main road and go past the station and big intersection to a small river. At the next road, turn left and go straight up a couple

• MAP 290

MIURA PENINSULA
KINUGASA

To Yokosuka

■ **Miura High School** 三浦高校
● **Daimyo-ji** 大明寺

Kinugasa Station

● **Sogen-ji** 曹源寺

Kinugasa Park 衣笠公園

Castle remains 衣笠城跡 ■

● **Daizen-ji** 大善寺

Yokosuka Line

● **Mansho-ji** 満昌寺

Tozen-ji 東漸寺 ●

Seiun-ji 清雲寺

● **Mangan-ji** 満願寺

To Kurihama Station

■ **bus stop**

To Nobi Station

of hundred meters to Sogen-ji on the mountainside. The origins of this Soto Zen temple are not clear, but by tradition it was founded by the famous priest Gyoki, which would mean that it dates from at least the late Nara period. However, lying as it did close to the original Tokaido highway, Sogen-ji was burned many times over. The principal image is Yakushi Nyorai, the deity of healing, an object of incredible popular devotion during the Edo period because it was believed to cure eye diseases, which were rife because of the lack of hygiene.

Next stop is Kinugasayama Park, home to about three thousand cherry trees, enough to make you dizzy. If Jimi Hendrix were still around, he might well be inspired to write a song called "Pink Haze." To get there, go back to the big intersection and turn left. When you see the sign for the park, about the fifth corner, turn right up the hill. (Don't take the trail behind the shack, which goes behind a golf practice range.) From here there's a spectacular view of most of the peninsula.

About twenty minutes from the park are the remains of Kinugasa Castle, originally established in the eleventh century. Actually, about all that remains now is a stone monument to mark the location of the Battle of Kinugasa in August 1180. When Yoritomo first raised the banner of rebellion against the Taira, the Miura clan was one of the first of the important local families to rally to his cause. Their ancestor, Miura Tamemichi, had originally been rewarded with the area in 1063 for services in war on behalf of Minamoto Yoriyoshi.

Yoshiaki, the eighty-nine-year-old patriarch of the clan, rushed with his troops to join Yoritomo at the decisive battle of Ishibashiyama in the Izu area. However, they were stopped by the flooded Sakawa-gawa River and didn't get there in time. After Yoritomo's rout and flight to the Boso Peninsula by sea, the Taira forces under Hatakeyama Shigetada turned their attention to the Miura. After a sharp setback at Kotsubo, Yoshiaki and his men retreated to their stronghold at Kinugasa.

On August 26, the 400 Miura samurai were surrounded by approximately 6,000 Taira warriors. The Miura spent all their arrows on the same day. Yoshiaki's offspring was ordered to lead the survivors on a dangerous night escape. Thanks to a ruse, they were able to escape to Kurihama and leave by sea from there for the Boso Peninsula, where they

• MAP 290

rejoined with Yoritomo and his local allies. Yoshiaki, however, remained behind and the old lion fought to the death the following morning.

This valiant defense and Yoshiaki's sacrifice were important reasons why Yoritomo later loaded Miura Yoshimura and other members of the clan with honors. The family flourished for four generations despite the constant internecine bloodletting in the early days of the shogunate, including the massacre of Wada Yoshimori, Yoshiaki's illegitimate grandson, and his family. That atrocity took place with the compliance of the new clan leader, Yoshimura, who sought to firm up his high position within the shogunate through intermarriage with the Hojo. However, the Hojo doublecrossed him and launched a sneak attack. As a result, Yoshimura and five hundred of his clansmen committed suicide in Yoritomo's ancestral temple.

Very close to the castle is Daizen-ji, a Zen temple near a forested area also said to have been founded by the famous priest Gyoki. Note the beautiful tiled roof. The famed Fudo Myoo image is known as the Yatori ("Arrow-Grabbing") Fudo. It got that unusual appellation from the fact that it is said to have protected the warrior Miura Tametsugu from enemy arrows during the Sannen no Yaku War (1083–87).

Take the nearby road that leads out of the mountains for about twenty minutes to Mansho-ji on the other side of the big crossroads. Yoritomo built Mansho-ji in 1194 to pray for the repose of the soul of Miura Yoshiaki. This Rinzai temple is famous for a large azalea bush to the left of the main hall, which is said to have been planted by Yoritomo.

Tozen-ji

If you turn right at the big crossroads and walk for a couple of miles, on your right you'll find Tozen-ji, a Jodo temple affiliated with Komyo-ji in Kamakura. The principal deity worshipped here is Amida. However, it is most famous for its Hanka Jizo statue. It only arrived here in the Showa era after making the rounds of various local temples. The fat, if not particularly jolly-looking, gilded *jizo* is seated on a dais with his right leg resting on his left knee. His right hand holds a priest's staff and the left holds a jewel. An inscription says that it was crafted by a Kamakura priest in 1462.

Tozen-ji also contains the grave of Gankai, an ascetic itinerant *nembutsu* priest who was very active throughout the Miura Peninsula during the late Edo period. He was apparently something of a Johnny Appleseed type, but, instead of leaving trees behind, he left *nembutsu* memorial towers with personal inscriptions.

• MAP 290

Gorei-jinja on the hillside to the left of the temple was founded by Wada Yoshimori. It contains a highly realistic statue of Yoshiaki, whose grave is to the rear. It is said to date from the end of the twelfth century.

Across the main road about ten minutes away on an elevated area is Seiun-ji, a Rinzai Zen establishment. At this pretty country temple in the midst of a grove you will find the tombs of several leaders of the Miura clan. Among the temple treasures is the wooden Yauke ("Arrow-Inviting") Bishamonten in the main hall, which, by tradition, protected Wada Yoshimori from the arrows of his enemies. Perhaps it was out to lunch the day the Hojo henchmen went looking for him. It is an impressive work by a sculptor of the Unkei school, dating from the mid-Kamakura period. Another interesting wooden statue, known as the Takimi Kannon, was imported from Song China. The Chinese-style clothing and swirling inscriptions are certainly out of the ordinary.

Our last stop is Mangan-ji, a Rinzai temple with a long history. It is near the Ogawa River about twenty minutes from Seiun-ji. Reach it by turning right past Seiun-ji and going through the housing complex.

Mangan-ji is closely connected with Miura Yoshiaki and Sahara Juro Yoshitsura, a local hero who figured prominently at the Battle of Ichinotani, at which Yoshitsune's spectacular cavalry charge caught the Taira totally by surprise. While everyone was having second thoughts about this lunatic neck-breaking proposal, he reportedly scoffed and said, "Heck, this is nothing but a bump in Miura." Or words to that effect. The five-tiered grave is said to be Sahara's.

There are several things of interest at this usually deserted temple, among them several beautiful statues including ones of Kannon, Bishamonten, and Fudo Myoo. The simple, white-walled style of Mangan-ji against a backdrop of gingko, maple, and other trees gives you a real feel for the aesthetics of the rural *bushi* heroes who hailed from this area. In addition to the main hall, there is also a Kannon Hall and treasure house. To see the statues, make arrangements ahead of time (☎ 0468-48-3138).

The bus stop is five minutes away in the other direction. From here you can catch a bus for Kurihama (Yokosuka, Keihin Kyuko lines) or Nobi (Keihin Kyuko) stations.

• MAP 290

6

The Shattered Miura

○ Misakiguchi Station 三崎口駅 (Keihin Kyuko Line)—bus to Misaki Higashioka 三崎東岡 and Hamamoroiso 浜諸磯—Aburatsubo 油壺—Miura Dosun's Tomb 三浦道寸の墓—Abaratsubo Marine Park 油壺マリーンパーク—Kaizo-ji 海蔵寺—Shirahige-jinja 白髭神社—bus to Misakiguchi Station

This walk takes us to Aburatsubo Bay, a deep-blue body of water seldom disturbed by a single wave that is nestled like a mini-fjord among ever-green hills. In addition to the striking scenery, there is an informative aquarium and several historical sites connected to a little-known story of local samurai that is one of the saddest tales I have run across in a part of Japan that for centuries was regularly washed with blood. What makes Aburatsubo especially nice is that, even in the height of the summer vacation season, the area is seldom crowded.

Take the Keihin Kyuko Line to the last stop—Misakiguchi Station. Although this is currently its southernmost rail terminus, some of the most interesting parts of the Miura Peninsula lie even further south and can only be reached conveniently by bus. Take the bus from the station bound for Misaki Higashioka, about a fifteen-minute ride, and then transfer to a bus to Hamamoroiso. When you get off, the entrance to Hamamoroiso-jinja will be right in front of you.

From the shrine grounds you can enjoy a beautiful view of Hamamoroiso, where we are headed next, and Moroiso Bay to the right. Head back to the bus stop and then turn in to the left. As you walk along the shore, you'll find gorgeous yachts lined up like pretty maids all in a row.

Take a left at the bottom of Moroiso Bay and keep going straight

• MAP 297

toward the yacht harbor of neighboring Aburatsubo Bay. The mini-peninsula that separates the two bays has some trails if you feel like exploring, and you'll also pass a couple of restaurants. Swing around to the left when you reach Aburatsubo Yacht Harbor. Here the view is idyllic, with dozens of yachts posing pertly in the water, their barely perceptible movements the only sign that they are more than elements of a pointillist still-life painting.

Oil Pot

Aburatsubo literally means "oil pot," and there are two explanations for how the bay gained that peculiar but fetching name. One is mundane—the calm water is as tranquil as a vat of virgin oil. The second explanation is far different.

Just before the cutoff where the road curves to the left to the Tokyo University Marine Biology Laboratory are the ruins of Arai Castle. This is where the Miura clan met its end in 1518. As noted earlier, in 1247 the main branch of the Miura clan was annihilated by the Hojo. But the Sahara branch remained a power in the Miura area until the rise of Hojo Soun in the Odawara area in the early sixteenth century. It was one of those true ironies of history that despite the fact that, although Soun had absolutely no familial connection to the Hojo of the Kamakura period, it was he who extinguished the power of the Miura clan once and for all. He chose the name Hojo to signify that he intended to replace the Ashikaga shoguns, who were of Minamoto stock. Solely on the strength of his guile and magnetic personality, this brilliant opportunist had become the pre-eminent power in Sagami Province by the early years of the sixteenth century.

The Miura were the only major independent power left in Sagami and a major stumbling block to Soun's dream of conquering the entire Kanto area and then going on to bigger things. The campaign of extermination began in 1512 and promised to be short, since the allies of the Miura did not come to their aid. Desperate scorched-earth resistance was put up at Sumiyoshi Castle at Kotsubo and other strongholds as the vastly outnumbered forces of Miura Yoshiatsu (Dosun) fell back to Arai Castle. The Miura remnants were surrounded by the ocean on three sides and the Go Hojo forces at the entrance to the peninsula. Yet they held out isolated here for three years! Finally, five and a half years after the invasion began, starvation had taken such a toll that it was clear that the dying time had come at last.

A final banquet was held at which the twenty-year-old heir to the fief, Yoshiaki, danced a slow dance with a fan, upon which was inked a heartbreaking poem he had written. The next morning, July 11, 1518, the gates of the castle were thrown open and the last charge of the Miura commenced.

Soun's men were waiting. So many wound-dripping Miura plunged into the waters of the bay and sank in their heavy armor that the water was dyed an oily darkness—hence the name Aburatsubo. Dosun committed *seppuku* at the age of sixty-nine. According to the *Hojo Godaiki*, before he could be butchered, Yoshiaki chopped off his own head and the horrid trophy went flying to distant Odawara in search of revenge.

• MAP 297

The view from the Aburatsubo Kanko Hotel is especially fine. There is also good angling around here. Follow the road to the left past the Aburatsubo Yotel (yacht hotel) and the turning to the marine research center. The road makes a sharp right and comes out beside Arai-hama beach. To the left is the quay from which a sightseeing water-bus leaves several times a day between 9:30 and 16:30 for Jogashima (see page 301).

Keep walking around the peninsula and you'll reach another beach. At the promontory at the end of it, you'll find Miura Dosun no Haka, the graves of Dosun and his son facing out on the sea of no succor. On Dosun's grave is inscribed his poem: "Destroyers and destroyed alike, when the earthenware is shattered, all that remains is lumps of clay."

Nearby is a botanical garden and Aburatsubo Marine Park, which has more than three thousand specimens of fish and other forms of marine life, including some unusual varieties. Many are contained in an impressive six-hundred-ton donut-shaped tank through which you walk.

Once you feel satiated by your tour of Davy Jones' locker, continue on the road to the second corner. Turn left onto the road signposted to Shibonia Mansion. Turn right and follow the road along the shore until you reach Eisho-ji Temple. A bit farther on is Kaizo-ji, a Zen temple built by Miura Dosun between 1504 and 1520. There are 103 steps leading up to the main hall, where an Eleven-Faced Kannon is preserved. Check out the portraits of Dosun, Arajiro, and other leading members of the Miura family. A votive tablet depicts Arajiro's head hanging from a tree with passersby staring at it.

Five minutes past Kaizo-ji is Shirahige-jinja, "White Beard Shrine." Enshrined here is a statue of Jurojin, one of the Seven Lucky Gods of Miura (Miura Shichi Fukujin). Also here are *kankan ishi* anchor rocks, which when knocked together are said to sound like steel.

Head back to the main road and the nearest bus stop, where you can catch a bus back to Misakiguchi Station, less than fifteen minutes away.

Abaratsubo Marine Park
油壺マリーンパーク ☎ 0468-81-6281
🕓 9:00–17:00; closed end of year

• MAP 297

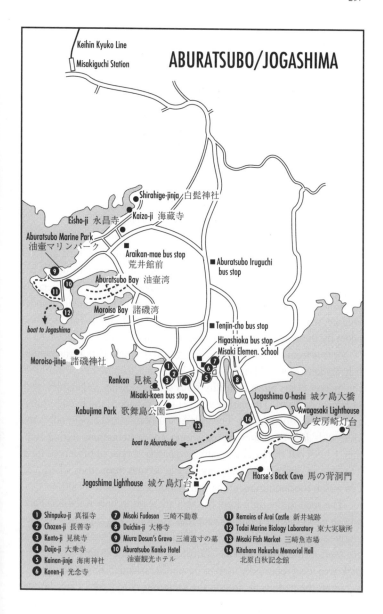

ABURATSUBO/JOGASHIMA

Keihin Kyuko Line
Misakiguchi Station

Shirahige-jinja 白髭神社

Eisho-ji 永昌寺　Kaizo-ji 海蔵寺

Aburatsubo Marine Park
油壷マリンパーク

Araikan-mae bus stop
荒井館前

Aburatsubo Iruguchi
bus stop

Aburatsubo Bay 油壷湾

Moroiso Bay 諸磯湾

boat to Jogashima

Tenjin-cho bus stop

Higashioka bus stop
Misaki Elemen. School

Moroiso-jinja 諸磯神社

Renkon 見桃

Misaki-koen bus stop

Kabujima Park 歌舞島公園

Jogashima O-hashi 城ヶ島大橋

Awagasaki Lighthouse
安房崎灯台

boat to Aburatsubo

Jogashima Lighthouse 城ヶ島灯台

Horse's Back Cave 馬の背洞門

❶ Shinpuku-ji 真福寺
❷ Chozen-ji 長善寺
❸ Kento-ji 見桃寺
❹ Daijo-ji 大乗寺
❺ Kainan-jinja 海南神社
❻ Konen-ji 光念寺
❼ Misaki Fudoson 三崎不動尊
❽ Daichin-ji 大椿寺
❾ Miura Dosun's Grave 三浦道寸の墓
❿ Aburatsubo Kanko Hotel
　 油壷観光ホテル
⓫ Remains of Arai Castle 新井城跡
⓬ Todai Marine Biology Laboratory 東大実験所
⓭ Misaki Fish Market 三崎魚市場
⓮ Kitahara Hakushu Memorial Hall
　 北原白秋記念館

Nature's Bounty at Miura's Boot

○ Misakiguchi Station 三崎口駅 (Keihin Kyuko Line)—bus to Misaki-ko Port 三崎港—Misaki Fish Market 三崎魚市場—Jogashima Lighthouse 城ケ島灯台—Awagasaki Lighthouse 安房崎灯台—bus to Misakiguchi Station from Jogashima

From Misakiguchi Station take a bus for Misaki or Jogashima and get off at Misaki-ko. Misaki is a classic fishing port, where 15,000 boats put in every year. This is a major base for deep-sea fishing, especially for tuna, which accounts for roughly 70 percent of the annual catch by volume, making it the second-largest tuna port in Japan. Total seafood taken by the port is worth more than ¥70 billion a year.

Across from the Misaki-koen bus stop and Misaki Park is the famous fish market (Misaki Uoichiba). Held from six to nine every morning, the market offers more than fifty stalls selling flowers, vegetables, and, of course, seafood. The earlier you get to the market, the livelier things are. The selection is great. The hills of southern Miura are literally covered with *daikon* radishes during winter and watermelons during summer. Check out the local specialty, *magurozuke*, a type of preserved tuna. There is an observation walkway on the second floor from where you can watch the auctioning at the fish market from 7:30 to 11:00.

The road to the right from Misaki Park leads to hilly Kabujima Park, whose name derives from the fact that Yoritomo was supposed to have enjoyed singing and dancing here. *Ka* and *bu* are the same characters as are used in the word "kabuki." Offshore is tiny Kabu-jima Island. The park area itself reportedly used to be another island during high tide.

From the park, walk around the promontory to a rocky area known

• MAP 297

as Renkon or Hachoso, where you can see "wave fossils." These strange marks were made by wave action when the area was under shallow water. Later geological action pushed the rock up above water level. Double back a bit and turn left down the small path where there's a sign showing the way to Kento-ji, a small temple famous for its peach trees. The Hotei enshrined here is one of the Seven Lucky Gods of Miura.

From the rear gate of Kento-ji turn left down a small path surrounded by old houses. Turn left again into Shinpuku-ji, the first of a series of little temples we will be dropping into. Turn right at the next T-junction and head up the slope. On the right is Chozen-ji. At the corner turn left and head down the slope to Daijo-ji. Next, go to the left, coming out on a broad road. Cross the road and at the slope where the elementary school is located, turn right.

Take the small street directly in front and go down the steps. You'll soon find Kainan-jinja, a famous local shrine dedicated to Fujiwara Sukemitsu. This particular Fujiwara is a mystery man. Nothing is known about him except that he was supposed to have subdued pirates who had been preying on the local people when he arrived from Kyushu in the ninth century. The two large gingko trees in the precincts are said to have been planted by Yoritomo himself.

The shrine is known for two festivals. In July the atmosphere here is extremely boisterous, with stalls selling all the essential non-essentials required for a festival. However, the special festival here is Chakkiro, held every January 15, when children dance the *chatsukirako*. It is said that the custom was started by local residents as a form of entertainment for Yoritomo on one of his visits to the area. Wearing Shinto-style costumes, white *tabi* socks, and *eboshi* medieval headgear, neighborhood children sing an odd little ditty to welcome spring.

From Kainan-jinja, turn left and go up the small stairway to Konen-ji. Next door is Honzui-ji, famed for its cherry blossoms. Incidentally, Misaki was one of Yoritomo's favorite play spots and he had peach, cherry, and camellia *gosho* or "palaces" erected for the enjoyment of the buds. Go down to the side of Hojo Bay, turn left, go straight, and you will soon reach Misaki Fudoson. A road curves around to the other side of the bay, where you will find the camellia

• MAP 297

gosho, Daichin-ji. This temple also houses the Kakuon Fukuroju, another of the Seven Lucky Gods of Miura. A boat sometimes runs from near here back to the other side of the bay. Along the Uraga Coast from Miura Kaigan Station on the Keihin Kyuko Line is a five-kilometer-long stretch of beaches. The water is very clear by eastern Japan standards, although the beaches are not likely to strike fear into resort owners in Okinawa or Mexico.

Come back out onto the road facing the bay and turn left, following the road as it curves left and hits the main road running to Jogashima. Turn right here and follow the road to Jogashima O-hashi Bridge leading over to the island.

Jogashima O-hashi, completed in 1960, is 575 meters long and 11 meters wide. You walk well above the water level. Jogashima, four kilometers in circumference, is a glory of rolling green hills, surf-tossed rocky shorelines, and spectacular sunsets. On this course we are going to the more developed western side first before going to the best part of this isle of the blessed.

Sampling Seafood in Misaki

Misaki is a wonderful place to sample fresh seafood at very reasonable prices. Isoyoshi is famous for its *maguro ichimai* tuna steak, but it offers a wide choice from the catch of the day. Hamayu offers good, cheap seafood in a log cabin of all things. The speciality is *saba no sanga* (サバノサンガ), a kind of fish cake. At Minazuki you can sample all kinds of sushi and other seafood, from *maguro no shabu shabu* (マグロのしゃぶしゃぶ) and *tekka-don* (鉄火丼) to reasonably priced courses. Check out the tasty tuna eyeballs (*medama-yaki* 目玉焼) at Tensaki. Baked in foil, these titbits are said to prevent senility. For noodles it has to be Tagoto, which has a great special, *kasane-soba* (重ねそば), three bowls of *soba* with *tempura*, mountain vegetables, and seafood. You can also try seafood the French way at Tasaka Bistro. Finally, if you can get twenty pals together, go for *maguro kabutoyaki* (tuna head) at ¥17,500 apiece at Misaki-kan Honten.

The many reasonably priced *minshuku* inns in this area (see page 311) more than make up for a lack of creature comforts with delicious, fresh seafood.

Isoyoshi 石幾 ☎ 0468-81-2366
⏲ 11:00–14:30, 17:00–21:00; hols. open all afternoon; closed Mon.

Hamayu はまゆ ☎ 0468-81-2299
⏲ 11:00–14:30; closed Mon.

Minazuki 六 ☎ 0468-81-3508
⏲ 11:30–22:00; open all year

Tensaki 天咲 ☎ 0468-82-0970
⏲ 11:00–22:00; closed Weds.

Tagoto 田海 ☎ 0468-81-2653
⏲ 11:00–20:00; closed Thurs.

Tasaka Bistro 田坂ビストロ ☎ 0468-26-3266 ⏲ 11:30–22:30; closed Sun.

Misaki-kan Honten 三崎館本店 ☎ 0468-81-2117 ⏲ 11:30–19:00; closed Tues.

Cross the bridge and take a look at the monument to the poet Kitahara Hakushu on the left, under the bridge. It pays tribute to his 1913 sad poem "*Jogashima no Ame*." In it he speaks of his tears mingling with the rain as he looks out over the water. Anyone familiar with the *enka* tradition of comparing tears to saké should be able to imagine the general drift of the poem. There is a small memorial hall nearby. Although his famous poem is excruciatingly sad, Hakushu loved this area, which he came to in search of spiritual relief. As with so many men who have sensitive souls or overdeveloped passions, he fell in love with someone else's wife. He was formally charged with adultery but was lucky enough to get off with a solatium payment to the aggrieved husband. Much depressed, he came to Misaki, living for a time near Kento-ji. He wrote in his journal, "When I feel lonely I read from [Ueda] Akinari [a gothic writer of the mid-Edo period] or go out and look at the white chrysanthemums."

Turn right and go past the Kankosen Hachakujo bus stop, across from which boats leave regularly for Aburatsubo or a thirty-minute scenic trip round the island that features a running commentary by local fishermen.

The Jogashima Killing Fields

Looking out at the pastoral scenery today, it is hard to believe that Jogashima was frequently the scene of battle between forces of the Go Hojo, who controlled the area, and guerrillas sent by the Satomi clan of Awa Province. Both sides launched hit-and-run raids across the Uraga Straits. Through skillful use of the currents, small boats, with about six samurai per vessel, could get across in three to four hours. If they ran into enemy boats they would board with grappling ropes and hooks for hand-to-hand combat or use *kumate* "bear claws" to drag the enemy in their heavy armor into the ocean to drown. Occasionally there were even full-fledged naval battles in the area.

The Go Hojo were generally on the defensive and even brought in mercenaries from naval-oriented clans in Ise Peninsula to its ports, such as Kotsubo in Zushi. But these forces were very expensive. Naturally, when Satomi pirates were captured, they were executed and their heads staked out on the seashore.

Actually, the Go Hojo always seemed to have naval problems. One reason it took Soun so long to wipe out Miura Dosun at Aburatsubo was that the Miura fleet had control of the sea. Before the castle fell, the ships were shifted to Jogashima, where they were beyond the reach of Soun. Through mediation on the part of the Engaku-ji and Kencho-ji temples in Kamakura, the leaders of the Miura navy became vassals of Soun and remained in the area. Then as now, it would seem, the navy generally had it better than the army.

• MAP 297

At Jogashima bus stop, turn left for Jogashima Lighthouse. There are a number of seafood restaurants in the area. Try the Sazae Shokudo.

The lighthouse looms 29.4 meters above the sea, so its revolving lamp can be seen by seafarers up to thirty kilometers away. The museum inside displays more than three hundred articles related to lighthouse lore, such as Japan's oldest mercurial barometer and a sundial used at a Hokkaido lighthouse. The original lighthouse here was designed by our old friend Welnie (see page 278).

After exploring the lighthouse area, continue on the hiking path that skirts the southern part of the island facing the vast Pacific. Sheer cliffs and pounding waves will make you wild at heart. Another hiking route cuts through the highlands in the center of the island.

Along the way you'll pass Horse's Back Cave, an equine-shaped arch so strong it has withstood the repeated massive earthquakes and tsunami that afflict this part of Japan. You will find many more sea-eaten tunnels farther on at Akabanesaki. This area is also famous among naturalists as a cormorant-viewing spot. From October to April, around two thousand cormorants and other sea birds spawn here. There are several observation platforms from which to observe the birdies on the rocks. Part of this area is within Jogashima Prefectural Park. In early summer it is filled with hydrangea.

After a half hour or so of walking along the coast, you'll come to Cape Awagasaki, where there's an uninhabited lighthouse. You can enjoy rock fishing or picnicking within the grounds of the lighthouse. It derives its name from the fact that from here you can see Awa (the ancient name for the Boso Peninsula) in the distance. Finally, around on the north side of the island is Mizuttare, one of the many areas where Yoritomo enjoyed sipping tea, viewing flowers, and other sublime pastimes when he was not chopping off heads.

Direct buses back to Misakiguchi Station leave from Jogashima.

Misaki Fish Market (Misaki Uoichiba 三崎
魚市場) ☎ 0468-82-1111 ⏰ 8:00–10:00
Jogashima Prefectural Park (Jogashima
Kenritsu Koen 城ヶ島県立公園)
⏰ 8:00–20:00; Oct.–Mar., 9:00–17:00

Sazae Shokudo さざえ食堂
☎ 0468-82-3470
⏰ 9:00–17:00; 8:00–17:00 at weekends;
closed in bad weather and Jul., Aug., and
Sept., when the family operates a beach hut.

• MAP 297

APPENDIX

EVENT CALENDAR: YOKOHAMA

January

Early January: *Dezomeshiki* acrobatic exhibition and firefighting demonstrations by firemen in traditional garb at Minato Mirai 21 and other locations. The firefighters affirm their spiritual roots with the *hikeshi* firemen of the Edo period.

Late January or early February: Chinese New Year Festival. Exact time determined by the lunar calendar. Dragon and lion dances, etc. On the last day of the old year, everybody stays up all night, downing special *gyoza* and rice dishes and letting off fireworks. Ships in the harbor toot their joy. New Year is the biggest event of the Chinese calendar and for days ahead of time the whole area is illuminated, pennants fly, paraders parade, and gongs and drums boom. At least two hundred thousand spectators show up for the parade, so don't count on a leisurely Chinese lunch.

February

Early February: Bean Throwing Festival (*setsubun*) on February 3 or 4 at Soji-ji in Tsurumi-ku and Gumyo-ji Temple in Midori-ku.
Also International Doll Festival at Yokohama Doll Museum.

Mid-February: Plum Festival (*ume matsuri*) at Okurayama Plum Garden in Kohoku-ku.

April

Mid-April: Street performers of all kinds do their thing in the streets of Noge to the delight of over one hundred thousand spectators. They come back in mid-October to do it all over again.

May

2-3: Yokohama Port Festival featuring International Masked Parade; held around Kannai Station.

14-16: Annual festival of Iseyama-jinja; traditional ceremonies and ancient dances.

June

2: Anniversary of the opening up of Yokohama Port.

First week: Yokohama Bazaar commemorating the opening of the port—stalls and shops selling everything from secondhand clothes to houseplants around Yokohama Park and Yokohama Stadium.

First weekend in June: Yokohama Dontaku at various venues from Yokohama Park to Yamashita Park, including a parade of people in Meiji-period costumes, a brass band, local festivals, and a special series of concerts. Bazaars are also held around town from late May to early June.

July

4: Huge fireworks display in Yamashita Park.

8-10: *Shiman rokusen nichi* (46,000 visit) rite at Gumyo-ji temple, Midori-ku.

20: International Fireworks Display at Yamashita Park and out above the water in the early evening; over four thousand fireworks set off, brass band plays before the fireworks.

24: Festival honoring Kantei's birthday at the Chinese temple, Kuan Ti Miao, in Chinatown. Lion dancing and other activities.

27: Yokohama Takigi Noh—Firelit open-air performance of Noh at Yamashita Park with the sea as backdrop; 1,500 people.

August

1: Fireworks at Yamashita Park.

First weeks: *Bon odori* dancing and brass band parade at Yokohama Stadium.

9: Summer Night Festival—sixteen of Yokohama's historical buildings, such as the Prefectural Museum and the Yokohama Archives of History, light up for a special summer extravaganza; also jazz concerts in front of the *aka renga* warehouses, beer garden at Osanbashi, *bon odori* dancing at Yokohama stadium, laser shows, light shows, and outdoor opera at Yamashita Park. National battle of the high school bands takes place at Yokohama Station. During the festival a special night tour aboard a double decker bus is organized.

Third Sunday in August: Fireworks at seaside park near Kanazawa Bunko Station.

Late August: Honmoku Jazz Festival at Honmoku Shimin Koen on last Sunday in August. Take No. 7 bus from JR Negishi Station.

September

Early or mid-September: Osannomiya Autumn Festival—dynamic traditional parade with over sixty *omikoshi* or decorated floats.

23: Yokohama Carnival—traditional parade from Hanmachi Park to west exit of Yokohama Station offering something for all the family, including a parade of Yokohama lantern floats and kiddie shows.

October

1: Chinese Liberation Day—Liberation Day of the Republic of China celebrated in Chinatown with special parades and dragon dances.

10: Double Ten (Taiwan)—coincides with Taiiku no Hi (National Sports Day) so streets are packed with close to a quarter million visitors.

8-10: Yokohama Festival—skateboard contests at *Hikawa Maru*; don't miss the sight of over ninety ships in the cutter race in Yokohama Bay; concerts.

Late October: Honmoku Pumpkin Festival at MyCal Honmoku with costume contests and events of all kinds.

Early to mid-October: Yokohama Autumn Festival with bazaar and concerts in Yamashita Park area.

November

Early November: Basha-michi Festival—rickshaws, horse-drawn carriages, and other period objects are paraded by costumed marchers.

2nd Sunday: Yokohama Marathon with around six thousand runners taking part.
Tori no Ichi (Cock fair) at Otori-jinja in Minami Ward.

December

Mid-December to early January: Winter Illuminations—weekend rock concerts and dragon dances.

New Year's Eve: Ring in the New Year Yokohama-style with foghorns booming from all the ships in the harbor. Whistle away all that bad joss and breathe in deeply for the new year waiting.

EVENT CALENDAR: KAMAKURA—MIURA

January

1-5: New Year's shrine visits made to Tsurugaoka Hachiman-gu and Kamakura-gu. Close to two million visitors come, so if you're the Greta Garbo type, better forget it. Try the Carpentry Ceremony at 13:00 on January 4 or the Bow Ceremony to drive out devils at 10:00 on January 5, both at Tsurugaoka Hachiman-gu.

11: Shio Matsuri festival at Zaimokuza beach; fishermen pray for a year of good, safe fishing. Prayers last from about 10:00 to 13:00.

15: The ancient Chakirakko dance festival in the port area of Miura City. Ten young girls perform a series of folk dances at Kainan-jinja beginning at 10:00. The performance is repeated at a smaller shrine later in the day. The festival name derives from the sound made by the bamboo and bell-sticks the girls carry.

February

3 or 4: Bean-Throwing Festival (*setsubun*) at Tsurugaoka Hachiman-gu, Kamakura-gu, and Kencho-ji Temple, usually from about 13:00.

April

1-10: Cherry Blossom Festival at Tsurugaoka Hachiman-gu Shrine.

4: Tokimune Matsuri festival held in Kamakura to mark the anniversary of the death of the most cultured of the Hojo regents. Tea ceremonies and other events are held.

7-14: Kamakura Festival celebrated throughout the city. The first Sunday there's a morning procession of people in historical costumes (including impersonators of Yoritomo, Yoshitsune, and Benkei) from Yuigahama Beach to Tsurugaoka Hachiman-gu Shrine, followed by the Shizuka-no-mai dance at the shrine to commemorate Shizuka Gozen's defiant dance of love for Yoshitsune. The horseback archery tournament (*yabusame*) is held on the last day of the festival.

2nd Saturday and Sunday: The formerly secret Kanamara Matsuri ("Iron Phallus Festival") at Kanayama-jinja in Kawasaki. At one time the festival was for women who had venereal disease, but now it is a general celebration of the reproductive function. The main ceremony is on Sunday afternoon.

May

22: Yoshitsune Festival at Manpuku-ji Temple.

Last Sunday: Dosun Matsuri near Aburatsubo Marine Park honors the memory of the last lord of the Miura family with a Buddhist funeral and horseback archery demonstration (*yabusame*) in uncrowded circumstances.

July

14: Festival at Yasaka-jinja Shrine in Enoshima celebrating the union of male and female gods.

19: Male and female hemp "lions" in Misaki-ko Port perform an evening lion dance to the accompaniment of chants and songs in order to drive out evil and guarantee prosperity.

Late July: Floating Bon Festival lanterns are sent out to sea after memorial services at Komyo-ji Temple.

Kamakura Beach carnival features construction of huge sand sculptures.

25: Huge fireworks display at Enoshima.

August

7-9: Bonbori Matsuri, or Paper Lantern Festival at Tsurugaoka Hachiman-gu. Elegant, hand-painted paper lanterns decorate the shrine grounds. Ikebana, traditional dance, tea ceremonies, and other demonstrations of traditional arts are staged.

Mid-August: Two thousand fireworks let off at Yuigahama Beach from 19:00.

20: Annual festival of Kamakura-gu.

September

10-13: Oeshiki, annual festival of Ryuko-ji, draws Nichiren adherents from all over Japan. September 12 especially boisterous.

15-16: Annual festival at Tsurugaoka Hachiman-gu. Archery on horseback (*yabusame*) demonstrated on September 16. Get there early.

18: Menkake Gyoretsu, a procession of ten people wearing outrageous masks, from Gongoro Shrine near Hase Station in Kamakura at 11:00.

22: Takigi Noh (torchlit outdoor Noh performance) at Kamakura-gu. Purchase tickets in advance.

October

12-15: Ojuya Festival at Komyo-ji Temple.

November

1-3: Priceless treasures of Engaku-ji and Kencho-ji temples on public view.

1-15: Chrysanthemum Show at Tsurugaoka Hachiman-gu.

December

Last "snake" day of December: Festival at Zeniarai Benten, the money-washing shrine.

31: Ring out the old year at temples in Kamakura and on the Miura Peninsula.

RESOURCE NUMBERS

Yokohama International Tourist Information (Trade Center Bldg.) 横浜市国際観光協会
☎ 045-641-4759

Kamakura Tourist Information (at Kamakura Station) 鎌倉駅前観光総合案内所
☎ 067-22-3350

KAMAKURA RENTAL BICYCLES

Nihon Kotsu Kanko-sha Kamakura Rental Cycles
日本交通観光社鎌倉レンタサイクル
☎ 0467-24-2319
🕘 8:30–17:00; open all year
To the right of Kamakura Station located up a slope is Kamakura Rental Cycles. Cycles can be rented by the hour or for the whole day.

FLOWER CALENDAR

✤ **Plum blossoms** (*ume*): beg. Feb.–beg. March
Zuisen-ji, Engaku-ji, Kotoku-in, Myoo-in, Kakuon-ji, Egara Tenjin, Tokei-ji

✤ **Camellia** (*tsubaki*): mid-Feb.–end March
Hokai-ji, Kakuon-ji, Sugimoto-dera, Hokoku-ji

✤ **Winter peony** (*kan botan*): mid-Feb.
Tsurugaoka Hachiman-gu

✤ **Red magnolia** (*shimokuren*): March–April
Meigetsu-in

✤ **White magnolia** (*hakumokuren*): beg. March–end March
Tokei-ji, Engaku-ji

✤ **Japanese quince** (*boke*): end March–end April
Kencho-ji, Meigetsu-in, Myoo-in, Engaku-ji, Hokoku-ji, Kuhon-ji

✤ **Forsythia** (*rengyo*): end March–beg. April
Hokoku-ji, Meigetsu-in, Engaku-ji

✤ **Cherry blossoms** (*sakura*): end March–end April
Myohon-ji, Kosoku-ji, Komyo-ji, Gokuraku-ji, Genjiyama Park, Kencho-ji

✤ **Azalea** (*tsutsuji*): end April–beg. May
Anyo-in, Komyo-ji, Eisho-ji, Kamakura-gu, Jochi-ji

✤ **Peony** (*botan*): end April–beg. May
Tsurugaoka Hachiman-gu, Jomyo-ji, Tokei-ji, Engaku-ji

✤ **Wisteria** (*fuji*): beg. May–end May
Zuisen-ji

✤ **Iris** (*hanashobu*): beg. June–end June
Kosoku-ji, Tokei-ji

✤ **Hydrangea** (*ajisai*): mid-June
Meigetsu-in, Joju-in, Tokei-ji, Zuisen-ji, Kaizen-ji, Kosho-ji

✤ **Bell flower** (*kikkyo*): early July–late July
Zuisen-ji, Tokei-ji, Jochi-ji

✤ **Lotus** (*hasu*): mid-July–beg. Aug.
Tsurugaoka Hachiman-gu, Komyo-ji

✤ **Bush clover** (*hagi*): beg. Sept.–beg. Oct.
Hokai-ji, Kencho-ji, Eisho-ji, Jokomyo-ji, Kosho-ji

✤ **Late cherry** (*jugatsusakura*): mid-Oct.
Zuisen-ji, Hokoku-ji

✤ **Sasanqua** (variety of camellia): Oct.–Feb.
Jomyo-ji, Ankokuron-ji, Zuisen-ji, Sugimoto-dera

✤ **Daffodils** (*suisen*): mid-Dec.–mid-Feb.
Zuisen-ji, Joei-ji, Tokei-ji

Accommodation

Reasonably priced accommodation is available in family-run *minshuku* and business hotels. Some *minshuku* offer two meals and a *futon* for the night (BD); others charge a flat rate for a room without meals (RC); some offer a room and breakfast (B). The figures state approximate prices—67=¥6,700.

YOKOHAMA

Azuma Ryokan あずま旅館　横浜市西区高島2-10-18
2-10-18 Takashima, Nishi-ku, Yokohama-shi ☎ 045-453-1155 RC 67
2 mins. from Yokohama Station (JR Yokosuka, Tokaido, Negishi, Keihin Kyuko, Yokohama, Sotetsu, and subway lines).

Sakura Ryokan さくら旅館　横浜市神奈川区青木町3-12
3-12 Aoki-cho, Kanagawa-ku, Yokohama-shi ☎ 045-441-3729 RC45 BD65
1 min. from Kanagawa Station (Keihin Kyuko Line), one stop from Yokohama Station.

Kamoya Ryokan 賀茂家旅館　横浜市西区藤棚町2-178
2-178 Fujidana-cho, Nishi-ku, Yokohama-shi ☎ 045-231-0225 RC70~ BD85
Homey ryokan with a fifty-year history; 7 mins. walk from Nishi Yokohama Station (Sotetsu Line).

Echigoya Ryokan 越後屋旅館　横浜市中区石川町1-14
1-14 Ishikawa-cho, Naka-ku, Yokohama-shi ☎ 045-641-4700 RC55—more than 2 people 45
Four-storey building (with a bakery on the first floor) in Chinatown; 2 mins. from Ishikawacho Station (Negishi Line).

Yamashiroya Ryokan 山城屋旅館　横浜市中区日の出町2-159
2-159 Hinode-cho, Naka-ku, Yokohama-shi ☎ 045-231-1146 RC 50—more than 2 people 40
Large rock pool tub, 3 mins. walk from Hinodecho Station (Keihin Kyuko Line).

Daikokuya Ryokan 大黒屋旅館　横浜市西区戸部本町42-1
42-1 Tobehon-cho, Nishi-ku, Yokohama-shi ☎ 045-321-2932 B75
Friendly, helpful ryokan, 10 mins. walk from Yokohama Station.

Business Hotel Sansei ビジネスホテルサンセイ　横浜市中区山下町222
222 Yamashita-cho, Naka-ku, Yokohama-shi ☎ 045 662-0222 RC 68~
Near Yokohama Stadium, 5 mins. walk from south (*minami*) exit of Kannai Station (Negishi Line) or 7 mins. walk from Kannai Subway Station.

San-Ai Yokohama Hotel 三愛横浜ホテル　横浜市花咲町3-95
3-95 Hanasaki-cho, Naka-ku, Yokohama-shi ☎ 045 242-4411 RC73~
Very central but quiet, 5 mins. walk from Sakuragicho Station (JR Negishi, Tokyu Toyoko, and subway lines).

Central Inn Yokohama セントラルイン横浜　横浜市中区伊勢左木町4-117
4-117 Isezaki-cho, Naka-ku, Yokohama-shi ☎ 045 251-1010 RC 79
Central Yokohama, 10 mins. from Kannai Station (JR Negishi) or 8 mins. on foot from Hinode-cho Station (Keihin Kyuko Line) or Subway Isezakicho Station.

Daimaru Hotel 大丸ホテル　横浜市中区吉田町76
76 Yoshida-cho, Naka-ku, Yokohama-shi ☎ 045-261-2333 RC55~
4 mins. walk from Sakuragicho Station (JR Negishi, Tokyu Toyoko, subway lines).

Mer Park Hotel メルパルクホテル、横浜市中区山下町16
16 Yamashita-cho, Naka-ku, Yokohama-shi ☎ 045-662-2221 RC 68
Near the Marine Tower, 12 mins. walk from Ishikawacho Station (JR Negishi Line).

Kanagawa Youth Hostel, 横浜市西区
Nishi-ku, Yokohama-shi ☎ 045 241-6503 RC24 (membership necessary)
7 mins. on foot from Sakuragicho Station (JR Negishi, Tokyu Toyoko lines).

Capsule Inn Yokohama カプセルイン横浜　横浜市西区南幸町2-14-3
Minami Saiwai-cho 2-14-3, Nishi-ku, Yokohama-shi, ☎ 045-314-2251 RC33 (men only)
3 mins. walk from west exit of Yokohama Station.

KAMAKURA

For *minshuku* information and reservations, call Kamakura Tourist Office 0467-22-3350

Minshuku Ai 民宿あい　鎌倉市長谷2-22-31
2-22-31 Hase, Kamakura-shi ☎ 0467 23-0711 B50 (ladies only)
Next door to Kamakura Hotel, 3 mins. south of Hase Station (Enoden Line) near Yuiga-hama beach.

Taisenkaku 対僊閣　鎌倉市長谷3-12-9
3-12-9 Hase, Kamakura-shi ☎ 0467 22-0616 RC60~ DB72
Old-fashioned inn close to entrance of Hase-dera.

Hase Ryokan 長谷旅館　鎌倉市長谷2-17-23
2-17-23 Hase, Kamakura-shi ☎ 0467 22-2916 RC40
Room only; 50m north of Hase Station (Enoden Line).

BB House Inn BBハウス　鎌倉市長谷2-22-31
2-22-31 Hase, Kamakura-shi ☎ 0467 25-5859 B50 (ladies only)
2 mins. on foot from Hase Station (Enoden Line).

Kamakura Kagetsuen YH 花月園　鎌倉市坂ノ下27-9
27-9 Sakanoshita, Kamakura ☎ 0467 25-1238 DB8 (cheaper for YH members)
5 mins. by bus from Kamakura Station then 7 mins. on foot or 8 minutes from Hase Station (Enoden Line).

Suigetsuen 翠月園　鎌倉市扇ヶ谷4-14-2
4-14-2 Ogigayatsu, Kamakura-shi ☎ 0467-24-7906 RC 45
Specially for women, near Kewai-zaka, in hills about 17 mins. from Kamakura Station (JR Yokosuka Line).

Ryokan Komatsu-so 旅館 小松荘　鎌倉市由比ヶ浜2-5-8
2-5-8 Yuigahama, Kamakura-shi ☎ 0467-22-2902 B62
Convenient for the beach (8 mins.); 6 mins. on foot from Kamakura Station (JR Yoko-suka Line).

Komachi-so 小町荘　鎌倉市小町2-8-23
2-8-23 Komachi, Kamakura-shi ☎ 0467-23-2151 RC45
Room only, 5 mins. from Kamakura Station (JR Yokosuka Line).

Akiyama Minshuku 秋山民宿　鎌倉市小町2-8-9
2-8-9 Komachi, Kamakura-shi ☎ 0467-22-3499 RC 29
Budget-price *minshuku*, 5 mins. from Kamakura Station (JR Yokosuka Line).

ENOSHIMA AREA

Rinkai-so 臨海荘　藤沢市片瀬海岸3-21-22
3-21-22 Katase Kaigan, Fujisawa-shi　☎ 0466 25-1190 RC40 B50 D60 BD70
Friendly helpful *minshuku* 8 mins. walk from Odakyu Katase Enoshima Station or Enoden Shonan Kaigan Station.

Watanabe 渡辺　藤沢市江ノ島1-6-30
1-6-30 Enoshima, Fujisawa-shi　☎ 0466 25-6400 RC35 BD58
Small, comfortable *minshuku* located about 12 minutes walk from Odakyu Katase Enoshima Station.

Asae アサエ　藤沢市江ノ島1-5-5
1-5-5 Enoshima, Fujisawa-shi　☎ 0466 23-7705 RC43 BD60
3 mins. from Enoshima Station.

Ogawa-tei 小川亭　藤沢市江ノ島1-5-3
1-5-3 Enoshima, Fujisawa-shi　☎ 0466 22-6782 RC40 BD65
10 mins. walk from Odakyu Katase Enoshima Station.

Kinokuniya Ryokan 紀伊国屋旅館　藤沢市片瀬海岸1-13-16
1-13-16 Katase Kaigan, Fujisawa-shi　☎ 0466-22-4247 RC50~
2 mins. walk from Odakyu Katase Enoshima Station.

ZUSHI

Shindotei Ryokan 新道亭旅館 逗子市逗子2-10-3
2-10-3 Zushi, Zushi-shi, Kanagawa-ken　☎ 0468 71-2012 RC60 B70 BD130
3 mins. from Zushi Station on Yokosuka Line. 5 mins. from Kamakura to Zushi.

Monjiro 紋次郎　逗子市逗子4-15-3
4-15-3 Zushi, Zushi-shi　☎ 0467-25-3795 RC40 BD70
10 mins. by bus from Kamakura Station.

MIURA PENINSULA AREA

For *minshuku* information and reservations, contact Miura Kaigan Minshuku Kumiai 0468-88-5121, or the Miura Minshuku Kumiai ☎ 0468-88-3699

Jogashima Youth Hostel 城ガ島ユウスホステル　三浦市三崎町城ガ島121
Jogashima 121, Misaki-cho, Miura-shi　☎ 0468 81-3893 BD39
Take bus from Misakiguchi Station (Keihin Kyuko Line); get off at Hakushuhi-mae.

Shonan Youth Hostel 湘南ユウスホステル　茅ヶ崎市中海岸3-3-54
3-3-54 Naka-Kaigan, Chigasaki-shi　☎ 0467 82-2401 BD39
15-20 mins. from the south exit of Chigasaki Station (JR Tokaido Line).

Maruhachi Ryokan まるはち旅館　三浦市三崎町小あじろ1421
1421 Koajiro, Misaki-cho, Miura-shi　☎ 0468-82-0808 RC80 BD80
15 mins. by bus bound for Abaratsubo from Misakiguchi Station (Keihin Kyuko Line).
Get off at Araikan-mae bus stop.

Hogetsu Ryokan 豊月旅館　三浦市三崎町小あじろ1152
1152 Koajiro, Misaki-cho, Miura-shi　☎ 0468-81-3301 RC40 B50 BD85
10 mins. by bus from Misakiguchi Station (Keihin Kyuko Line); 1 min. from Abaratsubo Marine Park.

KAWASAKI LODGINGS

Business Hotel Sky Court Kawasaki 神奈川県川崎区南町12-9
12-9 Minami-cho, Kawasaki-ku, Kanagawa-ken ☎ 044-233-4400 RC75~
10 mins. from Kawasaki Station (JR Tokaido Line from Tokyo Station).

Toyoko Inn Ekimae Honmachi 東横イン駅前本町　神奈川県川崎区駅前本町
24-3 Ekimaehon-cho, Kawasaki-ku, Kanagawa-ken ☎ 044-245-2580 RC70
3 mins. walk from Keikyu Kawasaki Station (Keihin Kyuko Line).

Aoki Garden アオキガーデン　神奈川県川崎区小川町18-26
18-26 Ogawa-cho, Kawasaki-ku, Kanagawa-ken ☎ 044-222-2678 RC 30~
Capsule hotel with rock bottom prices—but unfortunately men only.

Business Hotel Fuji ビジネスホテル富士　神奈川県川崎区浜町3-2-10
3-2-10 Hama-cho, Kawasaki-ku, Kanagawa-ken ☎ 044-344-4126 RC41 (W-style) 47 (J-style)
Cheap business hotel; sauna free of charge; 5 mins. by taxi from Kawasaki Station.
Interesting price system—if there's an extra person the room price decreases by ¥200
for each person.

Ryokan Oka 旅館大華　神奈川県川崎区昭和町2-18
2-18 Showa-machi, Kawasaki-ku, Kanagawa-ken ☎ 044-266-9071 RC55 BD70
Near to Kawasaki Daishi Temple; 10 mins. walk from Kawasaki Daishi Station (Daishi
Line from Keikyu Kawasaki Station).

Fukudaya ふくだや　神奈川県多摩区登戸2553
2553 Noborito, Tama-ku, Kanagawa-ken ☎ 044 911-3631 B80
In residential area near the Tama-gawa River, 2 mins. from Noborito Station (Nambu
Line).

Ryokan Shioyu 旅館汐湯　神奈川県川崎区昭和町1-3-23
1-3-23 Showa-machi, Kawasaki-ku, Kanagawa-ken ☎ 044-266-2901 RC48
6 mins. walk from Higashi Monzen Station (Daishi Line from Keikyu Kawasaki Station). Near Kawasaki Daishi Temple.

Takatsu Hotel 高津ホテル　神奈川県高津区溝の口16
16 Mizonokuchi, Takatsu-ku, Kanagawa-ken ☎ 044-833-5511 RC56 BD77
2 mins. walk from Takatsu Station (Den'entoshi Line); hotel famous for its *kaiseki ryori*.

KAMAKURA HIKING COURSES

Ten'en Hiking Course
Zuisen-ji (瑞泉寺)—3.5 km—Kencho-ji (建長寺)

Genjiyama Hiking Course
Jochi-ji (浄智寺)—1.1 km—Zeniarai Benten (銭洗弁財天)—1.9 km—Big Buddha
(大仏)

Asahina Hiking Course
Juniso-jinja (十二所神社)—1.5 km—Asahina Pass (朝比奈切通し)—2 km—Kosoko-ji
(光触寺)

Gion Hiking Course
Yakumo-jinja (八雲神社)—0.9 km—Harakiri Yagura (腹切やぐら)

BOAT INFORMATION

Yokohama Station—MM21—Yamashita Park
Seacom Cruise シーコムクルーズ ☎ 045-212-5431
Catch a water-bus near Yokohama Station for a fifteen-minute trip to Yamashita Park, calling at MM21. The landing is approached by the Kamome pedestrian bridge across from Sogo Department Store at the east exit of Yokohama Station. Boats leave about every twenty minutes from both directions until early evening.

Yokohama Osanbashi Pier 大桟橋—Tokyo Hinode Pier 日の出桟橋
Two boats a day (12:00, 15:20) leaves for the eighty-five-minute trip to Tokyo. ¥2,600

Yokohama Osanbashi Pier 大桟橋—Funabashi Raraport 船橋ららぽーと
One boat per day (18:40) leaves for Funabashi. ¥2,400

Yokohama Osanbashi Pier 大桟橋—Izu Islands 伊豆諸島
Tokai Kisen 東海汽船 ☎ 03-3432-4555
The Tokyo boat for the Izu Islands drops in at Yokohama Osanbashi Pier on Fridays and Saturdays at 23:30 reaching various islands early the next morning. The return boat on Saturdays and Sundays goes via Yokohama, reaching Osanbashi Pier at 18:20.

Yokohama—Vladivostok
Toyo Kyodo Kaiun 東洋共同海運 ☎ 03-3479-2841
Boats leave for Vladivostok three times a month between June and August. The trip takes four days. Prices vary according to class.

Yokohama—Shanghai
Nichu Kokusai Ferry 日中国際フェリー ☎ 03-3294-3351
Boats leave about once a month for Shanghai. The trip takes four days.

Kawasaki 川崎港—Kisarazu 木更津港
Seacom Ferry シーコムフェリー ☎ 044-266-3281
Boats leave frequently for Kisarazu in Chiba. The trip takes eighty minutes.

Kawasaki 川崎港—Hyuga 日向港
Seacom Ferry シーコムフェリー ☎ 044-266-3281
One boat a day (18:00) leaves for Hyuga in Kyushu. The trip costs about ¥18,000

Index

JAPAN UNESCORTED Third Edition
James K. Weatherly

An inexpensive, handy guide to Japan for the independent, budget-minded traveler. Reasonably priced accommodations and restaurants, as well as shopping areas, temples and museums.

Paperback; 214 pp; 128 mm x 182 mm; ISBN 4-7700-1695-6

JAPAN: A Budget Travel Guide
Ian L. McQueen

Provides in-depth information and survival tips for independent travelers on a limited budget. The completely revised and updated edition of what Donald Richie called "the best of all guides."

Paperback; 664 pp; 128 mm x 182 mm; ISBN 4-7700-1645-X

NEW JAPAN SOLO Third Edition
Eiji Kanno and Constance O'Keefe

A must for independent and enjoyable travel, this comprehensive, detailed guide covers all necessities of travel with precise descriptions, maps, and useful "survival" phrases.

Paperback; 512 pp; 128 mm x 188 mm; ISBN 4-7700-1739-1

JAPAN FOR KIDS
Diane Wiltshire Kanagawa and Jeanne Huey

The ultimate guide to entertaining and raising children in Japan. Ideas for rainy days, local travel, health care and education.

Paperback; 320 pp; 110 mm x 182 mm; ISBN 4-7700-1531-3

ANA'S CITY GUIDE: TOKYO
ANA/Kodansha International

This compact guide presents useful information on Tokyo with concise overviews and detailed, bilingual maps.

Paperback; 144 pp; 148 mm x 210 mm; ISBN 4-7700-1527-5

CYCLING JAPAN A Personal Guide to Exploring Japan by Bicycle
Edited by Bryan Harrell

An intimate and fully researched guide for planning and enjoying a bicycle tour. Bilingual maps and concise directions, information on terrain, traffic conditions, and possible route extensions.

Paperback; 272 pp; 128 mm x 182 mm; ISBN 4-7700-1742-1

Bilingual Maps and Atlases
from
KODANSHA INTERNATIONAL

New Tokyo: A Bilingual Atlas
With over 48 bilingual maps, this indexed atlas is the essential survival guide for finding one's way around Tokyo.

Paperback; 154 pp; 150 mm x 212 mm; ISBN 4-06-206590-8

KYOTO-OSAKA: A Bilingual Atlas
The first bilingual reference for the Kansai region. 36 maps of all major metropolitan areas, transportation, and tourist areas.

Paperback; 96 pp; 150 mm x 212 mm; ISBN 4-7700-1610-7

JAPAN: A Bilingual Atlas
The entire country of Japan is covered, from Hokkaido to Okinawa, in more than 50 color maps.

Paperback; 128 pp; 150 mm x 212 mm; ISBN 4-7700-1536-4

TOKYO RAIL AND ROAD ATLAS: A Bilingual Guide
This bilingual atlas for Metropolitan Tokyo provides clear, detailed maps of all major railways, subways, bus lines, expressways, and international airports.

Paperback; 96 pp; 150 mm x 212 mm; ISBN 4-7700-1781-2

TOKYO: A Bilingual Map
A fold-out wall map of central Tokyo, plus detailed maps of major downtown areas.

Folder: 111 mm x 228 mm, Map: 611 mm x 840 mm; ISBN 4-7700-1478-3

TOKYO METROPOLITAN AREA: A Bilingual Map
A fold-out wall map of the Kanto region, plus area maps of cities outside of central Tokyo.

Folder: 111 mm x 228 mm, Map: 606 mm x 856 mm; ISBN 4-7700-1522-4

KYOTO-OSAKA: A Bilingual Map
A fold-out wall map of the Kansai region, including Kobe, Nagoya and Nara.

Folder: 111 mm x 228 mm, Map: 611 mm x 840 mm; ISBN 4-7700-1660-3

JAPAN: A Bilingual Map
A fold-out national map indicating major travel routes, plus detailed maps of seven major metropolitan areas.

Folder: 138 mm x 264 mm, Map: 770 mm x 1058 mm; ISBN 4-7700-1621-2

HISTORY AT A GLANCE

1185   Minamoto clan triumphs over the Taira clan in the Gempei war.

1192   Minamoto Yoritomo named shogun by Emperor. Kamakura becomes de facto capital of Japan.

1199   Yoritomo dies. Succeeded by Yoriie, who is killed by relatives in 1204.

1213   Wada Yoshimori and his clan annihilated by the Hojo.

1219   Shogun Sanetomo assassinated, ending Yoritomo's direct line. Hojo regents become effective leaders of samurai class, operating through puppet shoguns.

1221   Hojo easily crush attempted imperial restoration in Jokyo Disturbance.

1247   Main branch of the Miura clan wiped out by the Hojo.

1252   Completion of the Kamakura Great Buddha.

1253   Kencho-ji established in Kamakura, beginning boom in Zen and Chinese culture. Nichiren begins preaching his revolutionary form of Buddhism.

1275   Kanazawa Bunko built in Kanazawa Hakkei area.

1271   Nichiren miraculously escapes execution at Katase. Exiled to Sado Island.

1274   First Mongol invasion.

1281   Second Mongol invasion.

1282   Ippen Shonin, the dancing *nembutsu* proselytizer, turned away from Kamakura. Retires with followers to Katase for giant revival meeting lasting several weeks.

1333   Nitta Yoshisada and imperial forces capture and sack Kamakura, ending first shogunate.

1516   Hojo Soun captures Arai Castle, killing Dosun and the last of the Miura.

1540   St. Francis Xavier arrives in Japan from Macao.

1603   Tokugawa Ieyasu creates Edo shogunate.

1639   Japanese nationals forbidden to travel abroad or return home from overseas.

1639   Portuguese ships excluded from Japanese ports; only Dutch and Chinese allowed to trade at Nagasaki, effectively cutting off Japan from the outside world.

1667   Reclamation of Yoshida Shinden (present-day Yokohama) completed and village established.

1837   American merchant vessel, the *Morrison*, driven away from Edo Bay.

1842   Opium War comes to an end.

1846   U.S. naval squadron under Commodore Biddle receives cool reception in Edo Bay.

1853   Commodore Perry prises Japan's door open.

1854   Perry and Shogunate officials conclude Treaty of Kanagawa (Japan-U.S. Treaty of Peace and Amity).

1858   Townsend Harris and shogunate officials conclude Commercial Treaty (The Japan-U.S. Treaty of Amity and Commerce)

1859   The port of Yokohama is opened on July 1.

1861   Agreement between Edo wholesalers and Yokohama raw silk dealers prepares Yokohama to become major silk export port.